LEONARD COHEN

UNTOLD STORIES: The Early Years

MICHAEL POSNER

Published by **SIMON & SCHUSTER**

New York London Toronto Sydney New Delhi

SIMON &
SCHUSTER
CANADA

Simon & Schuster Canada
A Division of Simon & Schuster, Inc.
166 King Street East, Suite 300
Toronto, Ontario M5A 1J3

This Simon & Schuster Canada edition October 2020

SIMON & SCHUSTER CANADA and colophon
are trademarks of Simon & Schuster, Inc.

For information about special discounts for bulk purchases,
please contact Simon & Schuster Special Sales at 1-800-268-3216
or CustomerService@simonandschuster.ca.

Manufactured in the United States of America

10 9 8 7 6 5 4 3 2 1

Library and Archives Canada Cataloguing in Publication

Title: Leonard Cohen, untold stories : the early years / Michael Posner.
Names: Posner, Michael, 1947– author.
Description: Simon & Schuster Canada edition.
Identifiers: Canadiana (print) 20200210777 | Canadiana (ebook) 20200210823 |
ISBN 9781982152628 (hardcover) | ISBN 9781982152635 (ebook)
Subjects: LCSH: Cohen, Leonard, 1934–2016. |
CSH: Poets, Canadian (English)—20th century—Biography. |
LCSH: Singers—Canada—Biography. | LCSH: Composers—Canada—Biography. |
LCGFT: Biographies.
Classification: LCC PS8505.O22 Z84 2020 | DDC C811/.54—dc23

ISBN 978-1-9821-5262-8
ISBN 978-1-9821-5263-5 (ebook)

For Lauren, Susan, Sam, Gabriel, Deborah, Joseph, Matan, Max, Nathan, Marianna, and June

Contents

Introduction   ix

CHAPTER ONE   **The House of Cohen**   1

CHAPTER TWO   **Lenny, Prince of Westmount**   23

CHAPTER THREE   **Trace of a Wound, Mantle of an Artist**   59

CHAPTER FOUR   **The Birth of the Magus**   95

CHAPTER FIVE   **All the World Is in Front of You**   143

CHAPTER SIX   **My Freedom Is Fragile**   175

CHAPTER SEVEN   **All the Lonesome Heroes**   211

CHAPTER EIGHT   **Is There Any Fire Left?**   251

CHAPTER NINE   **I Must Be a Singer**   291

CHAPTER TEN   **Never Finished, Only Abandoned**   333

CHAPTER ELEVEN   **Nashville Blues**   391

CHAPTER TWELVE   **A Flake of Your Life**   431

Epilogue   465

Acknowledgements   467

APPENDIX   **Dramatis Personae**   471

Introduction

Somewhere within the vast cybernetic archives of the *Globe and Mail*, my former employer, a brief message is interred. It was sent to me from a much-coveted e-mail address—baldymonk@aol.com—the handle used for many years by Leonard Cohen. I had written to him proposing to organize an oral biography of his extraordinary life, a book based on interviews with his friends, family, bandmates, backup singers, record producers, monks, rabbis, and lovers—a book not unlike the one you now hold, literally or electronically, in your hands.

Cohen, infallibly sympathetic to even the most outlandish journalistic inquiries, responded with alacrity. It was, he allowed, an intriguing idea—I think he might have even used that word. But alas, he was then—this was about 2007—knee-deep in the miasmic swamps of litigation with his former business manager, who stood accused of relieving his bank account of some five million American dollars. It had been enough, he joked in interviews at the time, to put a crimp in his mood.

Therefore, as encouraging as he might have wanted to be, the prospect of his being able to sanction and then cooperate in what he probably would have called my little enterprise, had to be considered remote. Perhaps, he said, we could revisit the proposal when the smoke had cleared, though he would never have resorted to such a prosaic construct. It was as gracious a letdown as one could have hoped for.

Time passed, and Cohen was soon engaged in what would turn out to be the remarkable final chapter of his professional life: a worldwide concert tour that would span the better part of five years and solidify his rightful lease (had it ever been in doubt?) on the penthouse suite in the Tower of Song. Not incidentally, it would also replace the coin allegedly pilfered from the Cohenian coffers. Replace, and then some.

And then, in November 2016, Leonard Norman Cohen passed away, having endured, silently and stoically, the frightful pains and indignities of blood cancer. Not long after, it occurred to me to resurrect the oral biography. Cohen himself was gone, but scores, if not hundreds of people, who had been part of his life were still alive. Their stories were still untold, and they had powerful insights still to share.

And his was a life that deserved to be more closely examined. Not just a poet-novelist, not just a singer-songwriter, he functioned as a kind of seer, a magus. His songs were more than songs—they were hymns and psalms. Often writing in the hip, accessible, ironic vernacular, Cohen had matured into a master cartographer of the human heart and its many mysteries, commingling the sacred and the profane. A friend of his had once cautioned him: "Leonard, you have to decide whether you're a lecher or a priest." Well-intentioned advice, but wrong. He was both—we all are—and our challenge is to come to terms with that reality.

Cohen's body of work, I was further convinced, would stand the test of time. Future generations would continue to read his poetry and novels, to savour his music, and honour his name. Cultural historians would pore over his archives, trying to connect the dots between the life of the man and the works he created. Although several very good biographies of Cohen had already been published, in various languages, I knew there was more to discover, that aspects of the diverse worlds in which he circulated—Jewish and Buddhist, literary and musical, to say nothing of his labyrinthine travels in the realms of romance—were still unexplored and could add significantly to our understanding.

And so I began. Like too much of the rest of my life, my process was largely haphazard and chaotic. But, perhaps inevitably, one interview typically led to two others, and stories, most of them entirely new, began to accumulate. By January 2020, I had completed more than five hundred separate interviews, visited Montreal, New York, Los Angeles, London, Tel Aviv, Austin, and Hydra, and accumulated thousands of hours of tape. By the time I finished transcription, the full manuscript ran north of half a million words, virtually a No Fly Zone for even the most intrepid publisher. It was my incredibly good fortune to find, in Simon & Schuster Canada, a publisher willing to contemplate and ultimately champion not one book but, as currently envisaged, three.

One cautionary note: This is, transparently, a book of recollected memories. But I cannot offer a blanket guarantee of their accuracy. Nor, in many instances, can the interviewees themselves, especially when recalling events that may have occurred decades ago. Moreover, although everyone spoke eagerly and candidly about Cohen, more than occasionally, their recollections and viewpoints were in conflict. I have largely refrained from adjudicating these disputes. That, I submit, is part of the virtue of oral biography; everyone gets to take the stand, and the jurors—readers—decide whose version of the truth they endorse. I cannot think of anyone more likely to embrace the implicit contradictions and ambiguities—this Rashomon version of his life—than Leonard Cohen himself.

And who knows? Perhaps he wasn't simply being kind when he answered my exploratory e-mail thirteen years ago. Perhaps he really did intend, one day, to confer his priestly blessing on my little enterprise. And now, from whatever empyrean realm he inhabits, he has.

—Michael Posner
Toronto
May 2020

CHAPTER ONE

The House of Cohen

I had a very Messianic childhood. I was told I was a descendant of Aaron, the high priest. My parents actually thought we were *Kohenim*—the real thing. I was expected to grow into manhood leading other men.

—Leonard Cohen

The one thing everyone—rich, poor, gentile, Jew, upper, middle, or lower—had in common was, notwithstanding Leonard's success, an extreme anxiety over any sign their children showed that they wanted to emulate him.

—Barrie Wexler

It is appropriate that Leonard Cohen's boyhood home—at 599 Belmont Avenue—was situated along the multiple lines of cultural and ethnic identity that would ultimately shape him. By the standards of Montreal's verdant Westmount, the home was modest, located at the southern terminus of Belmont, the lower end of the neighbourhood's socioeconomic spectrum. But it connected directly to aboriginal, French, British, and Jewish communities.

A brick, semidetached structure, the home backed onto what is formally known as King George Park, renamed for the former British monarch who visited the city in 1939. But in Cohen's youth—and even now—it was popularly known by its original name, Murray Hill Park, in memory of William Murray, the Anglophone industrialist-turned-gentleman-farmer whose family sold it, after his death, to the city in 1920. Barrie Wexler, who grew up in Westmount, was a disciple and friend of Cohen's for thirty years.

BARRIE WEXLER: Murray founded the Beaver Steamship Line. In 1759, he bought a tract of farmland from the Leduc family, which had owned it since 1723. Murray built a Victorian mansion and farmed the surrounding area. He named the house West Mount, which later became the town's name. When the house was demolished, the lands were turned into Murray Hill Park—the green heart of Westmount, a place that still exudes entitlement.

Long before Murray, of course, the area had been settled by immigrants from France, like the Leducs. And for centuries before that, its fourteen acres—and everything for miles around it—had been the ancestral home of Canada's aboriginal peoples, specifically the Iroquois. Indeed, local legend suggests that Iroquois graves still lie beneath the park's grassy slopes.

Belmont Avenue itself may have been named by the French farmers who began arriving in New France in the seventeenth century: *belle mont* or beautiful mountain. But it was more likely named for Father François Vachon de Belmont, a highborn leader of the missionary Society of the Priests of Saint-Sulpice, which played the dominant role in Montreal's development during the late seventeenth and early eighteenth centuries. Belmont, also trained as an architect, built a fortified mission at what is now 2065 Sherbrooke Street West, known as the Fort des Messieurs, or Priests' Farm. It was less than a mile from Cohen's family home.

Two of its original towers still stand. Belmont himself served thirty-one years—1701–1732—as superior of the Sulpicians. There was also a Belmont Street in the downtown core.

Cohen himself once described Westmount as "a collection of large stone houses and lush trees arranged on the top of the mountain, especially to humiliate the underprivileged."

BARRIE WEXLER: You have to understand Westmount in context, especially its upper and middle sectors, which were then made up of affluent WASP and Jewish elites. The rest of Canada always had an uncomfortable relationship with Quebec, and vice versa. And the province has always been extremely wary of Montreal, where the *maudits anglais* lived. And Montreal, in general, always despised Westmount, an enclave of the rich and powerful. At the same time, Westmount's rich and powerful gentiles distrusted the town's emerging rich and powerful Jews, not to mention the fact that the not-so-rich-and-powerful residents of lower Westmount were not huge fans of the ones up the hill. The one thing everyone—rich, poor, gentile, Jew, upper, middle, or lower—had in common was, notwithstanding Leonard's success, an extreme anxiety over any sign their children showed that they wanted to emulate him.

CHARLIE GURD: Westmount was not just a throwback to Victorianism, but to Edwardianism. Westmounters then controlled the economy of Canada. Poetry was about Yeats and the British Lake District Romantic poets.

BARRIE WEXLER: All the kids in upper Westmount and half of those in the middle went to private schools. Everyone I knew, except my family, owned summer homes in the Laurentians or the Eastern Townships. There were cotillion classes in grade school and coming-out debutante balls. Everyone's mother volunteered at a hospital gift shop, and everyone's father belonged to the Mount Royal Club, if they were gentile, or the Montefiore Club, if they weren't.

NORMAN ALEXANDER: You can draw a circle of eight or ten blocks in Westmount and everybody knew everybody. Back then, Westmount had its own police department and school board, very small town, very close. And if the police saw you on the street after six o'clock, they would invariably pull you over and ask why you weren't home.

To enter Westmount was not only to enter a moneyed, privileged enclave, but something of a time warp.

BARRIE WEXLER: Snow was whisked off the streets before the rest of the city had finished cursing. Even French-Canadian taxi drivers obeyed Westmount traffic rules—slowing to twenty miles an hour when approaching intersections. The town maintained all kinds of idiosyncratic regulations. At Westmount's public library, books like J. D. Salinger's *The Catcher in the Rye* and Sylvia Plath's *The Bell Jar* were considered obscene and kept on what they called "a closed shelf"—a locked room. You couldn't skate on the rinks in any of the municipal parks on Sundays. And you couldn't hail a taxi on the street, not even on its main thoroughfare, Sherbrooke. The cabs just wouldn't stop. No one spoke French, of course.

In the 1930s, '40s, and '50s, when Leonard Cohen was growing up, Westmount was only beginning to witness an influx of Jewish families.

BERNIE ROTHMAN: Here's what happened. There were no Jews in Westmount. When my family moved there, there were none. It was rabidly anti-Semitic. I could not get home from school without both fists going. Someone was going to get a bloody nose, me or them. There were no other Jews in my class of thirty people. I knew Morton

[Rosengarten] before Leonard did. I'd been there for two or three years before he arrived, on Upper Belmont. Thank God he did, because then I had someone to fight those nasty gentiles with. They called us "dirty Jew" and "Christ killer." Morton was my first friend—we were very close. If Cohen was in the neighbourhood, I didn't know.

RUTH COHEN: My husband's father, A. Z. Cohen [Leonard's great-uncle], went to McGill in 1905. There were two Jews in the graduating class.

Apart from his family's modified Orthodox practice in the home, Cohen's principal Jewish connection was located a mere ten-minute walk away, at *Shaar Hashomayim* [Gate of the Heaven] Synagogue, at the corner of Kensington Avenue and Côte-Saint-Antoine. The name is taken from a passage in Genesis pertaining to Jacob's dream. From the late nineteenth century, the extended Cohen family had a foundational relationship with the synagogue as donors and volunteer executives.

RUTH COHEN: If there was a Jewish aristocracy, the Cohens were it.

NORMAN ALEXANDER: I don't know if the Cohens were royalty, but they were very prominent, well connected, woven into the entire background of Westmount. Royalty connotes pomp and ceremony and overly due deference. I don't think that was the case.

Canada's second-oldest congregation, Shaar Hashomayim had broken away from the Spanish and Portuguese Synagogue in 1859, in part because its congregants wanted to restore Western European musical traditions to the services. Among members of its 1,300 families are some of the most distinguished Canadians, including more than fifty recipients of the Order of Canada—Leonard Cohen, ultimately, among them. The *shul* even boasted an official coat of arms, presented by Queen Elizabeth II on its 150th anniversary. At Shaar Hashomayim,

Cohen regularly attended Sunday school, holiday observances, and, in 1947, celebrated his bar mitzvah. Of course, synagogue attendance was also a ritual.

LEONARD COHEN: There was no choice in the matter. It wasn't duress and it wasn't choice. It was just something you did. But I never *minded* it. For one thing, I loved the language and I liked the music very much, and I liked my family. We were sitting there in that third row—my uncle Horace, my cousin David, and then me, and then Uncle Lawrence and then the cousins and then Uncle Sidney and the other cousins. There was a whole *string* of Cohens standing up there and singing our hearts out.

GIDEON ZELERMYER: The Cohens sat in row C. The [family prayer] books are there.

In fact, at services, the extended Cohen clan occupied two entire rows.

LEONARD COHEN: Through the long periods in the service when you couldn't really get away with gossiping or talking, there was the prayer book in front of me, and it was fascinating. It was translated on one side. My Hebrew was almost nonexistent *except* for the liturgy. It was right-wing Conservative. I didn't learn so much about this written tradition, but I learned a lot about the responsibility and the love of the tradition—because the people really loved it. These were real events—the Hebrew calendar that was celebrated, Hanukkah. A deep love was being manifested and these were the terms on which we met.

Still, Cohen was conscious of a vacuum at the heart of the observance, one that would evolve into a searing critique of how midcentury Jews practiced their religion.

LEONARD COHEN: What I missed in the tradition was that nobody ever spoke to me about methods, about meditations. I was hungry as a young man—I wanted to go into a system a little more thoroughly. I wanted to be exposed to a different kind of mind.

The Cohens, as the family name implies, were also *Kohens*—descendants of Moses's brother, Aaron, members of Judaism's priestly caste, whose ancestors had presided over the Temple in Jerusalem.

CAROL ZEMEL: Leonard was a *Kohen*, and he consciously lived that life. That was always central to how he thought of himself. He used to, semi-jokingly, refer to the pain in his penis, left by circumcision. Well, more delusions of grandeur. There was a sense of huge wisdom—the wisdom of the *Kohenim*.

LEONARD COHEN: I strongly felt that my family was conscious of representing something important. For example, my name, Cohen, means "rabbi" [it actually means "priest"]. I had the impression that my family took this literally, that they felt that in a way they were rabbis by heredity . . . They were conscious of their own destinies and of their responsibility to the community. They founded synagogues, hospitals, and newspapers. I felt like I had received a heritage that concerned my own destiny in the world.

Jewish observance and identity were effectively coded into Cohen's DNA. His paternal great-great-uncle, Rabbi Zvi Hirsch Cohen (1862–1950)—born in Budwicz, Lithuania, and educated at the Volozhin Yeshiva—arrived in Montreal in 1889 and served as unofficial chief rabbi of both Montreal and Canada. An active Zionist, he was superintendent of the Talmud Torah schools, worked as the Jewish prison chaplain, and presided over efforts to resolve community tensions relating to kosher slaughter. His

1950 funeral attracted one of the largest gatherings of rabbinical and political leaders in Montreal's history.

Zvi Hirsch Cohen's brother, Lazarus (Leonard Cohen's great-grandfather, for whom he was named), emigrated from Lithuania in the late 1860s. He established himself as a merchant and lumberman in Maberly, Ontario, a pioneer Scottish and Irish settlement, about a hundred miles from Ottawa. A few years later, his wife, Frayda Garmaise Cohen, and their three-year-old son, Lyon, followed. Another son, Abraham Zebulon (A.Z.), was born in Canada. In 1883, Lazarus relocated to Montreal, setting up L. Cohen and Sons, coal merchants. In time, his business interests expanded to include W. R. Cuthbert & Co., a brass foundry, in 1895, and in 1900, the Canadian Improvement Co., the first dredging contractor in the country. In fact, the family firm won government contracts to dredge most of the provincial rivers that fed into the St. Lawrence.

Lazarus Cohen, by any measure, was a pillar of the community and of the McGill College Avenue Synagogue (it later became the Shaar Hasho-mayim). He was treasurer of the Baron de Hirsch Institute, on behalf of which he helped establish agricultural settlements for immigrant Jews in western Canada, and was active in B'nai B'rith, the Hebrew Free School.

In 1894, Lazarus Cohen made a journey that few North American Jews in those days undertook—to visit Jewish settlements in Ottoman-ruled Palestine. He even acquired land there, it is said. Although he was sick for many years after 1900, the congregation continued to elect him president. As Rabbi Wilfred Shuchat later wrote, it "had more confidence in an ill Lazarus Cohen than in any other alternative."

Born in 1868, Lazarus's son, Lyon Cohen, was educated at the McGill Model School and the Catholic Commercial Academy, and was a medal-ist and valedictorian at graduation. Arguably even more entrepreneurial than his father, Lyon eventually handed off the coal business to his younger brother, A. Z. Cohen, and focused on the other family businesses: W. R. Cuthbert & Co.; Canadian Improvement Co.; and, in 1906, the Freedman Co., which he bought from Samuel Freedman and turned into one of the country's leading wholesale manufacturers of menswear. It was located in what was then known as the Sommer Building, on what is now De Maisonneuve Boulevard in downtown Montreal.

ALAN GOLDEN: All kinds of nice things were said about Lyon, but I think he was a tough guy in business.

PETER KATOUNDAS: It seems Leonard's grandfather [Lyon] was the entrepreneurial genius who put together this business empire and later passed it on to his sons to manage.

RUTH COHEN: Lyon was a tough guy, bossy. We bought coal from L. Cohen and Sons to heat our apartment. It was a household name. Lyon was the founder of everything and very well respected.

Lyon Cohen, as president of the Clothing Manufacturers' Association of Montreal—and later, president of the Canadian Export Clothiers, Ltd.— was particularly tough on the then-fledgling trade union movement, resisting its efforts to unionize factories. At one point, in 1916, Lyon fired a union rep, claiming his union activity had affected factory production. Despite appeals that he be reinstated, Lyon refused. Soon after, three hundred Freedman employees went on strike. Lyon clandestinely arranged for his suits to be made by another manufacturer, but those workers then struck in solidarity; eventually, more than three thousand labourers from thirteen CMAM-affiliated companies walked out, joined by 1,500 employees from other shops. The strike lasted months, only ending when Lyon Cohen agreed to improve conditions on the factory floor.

In those years, the Montreal textile and clothing business was largely Jewish-owned.

HERSH SEGAL: The Cohens had the Freedman Company. There was Hyde Park Clothes—the Hershorns. The Guttmans had Progress

Brand, the Beutels had Premier Brand, someone else had Empire Brands [Joseph Leibovitch]. My father and uncle had been very successful in that field as well.

BERNIE ROTHMAN: Every Jew was in the clothing business.

Montreal Jews were prominently represented at every level of the industry—as manufacturers, as union organizers, and as workers. As one historical account noted, it was ironic that inside their factories, owners did everything they could to frustrate union power, and to resist wage hikes, and an improvement in working conditions, while simultaneously funding and serving charities aimed at helping these same, largely impoverished workers.

Lyon was a prime example. Like his father, he was extraordinarily active in communal organizations—president of the First Canadian Jewish Congress in 1919; honorary president of the Young Men's Hebrew Benevolent Society, the United Talmud Torahs, and the Montefiore Club; and a member of committees of the Child Welfare Exhibition, the Jewish Rights Committee, which lobbied for equal rights for Jewish children in public schools, B'nai B'rith, the Jewish General Hospital, and Congregation Shaar Hashomayim.

RUTH COHEN: Lyon was president of Shaar Hashomayim forever and ever.

In fact, he presided for twenty consecutive years. Later, the position of honorary president was created so that the synagogue could benefit from his wisdom.

GIDEON ZELERMYER: Among other things, Lyon presided over construction of the current *shul.*

It was Lyon Cohen who actually selected the site for the building, arranged for the down payment, and ultimately laid its cornerstone, in November

1921. He later said he spent more time at the construction site than at his office.

RABBI WILFRED SHUCHAT: Leonard's family, they weren't just presidents. They built this sanctuary. They weren't architects, but they planned it. They had contacts with the chief rabbis in Great Britain and Germany.

In *The Gates of Heaven*, his 2003 history of the synagogue, Shuchat said of Lyon Cohen that "there was no one like him up to the time he appeared and no one like him has appeared after his passing. Where did his uniqueness lie? . . . Lyon Cohen possessed a great vision . . . a vision of what an ideal synagogue should be . . . of what an ideal community should be . . . and of what an ideal Jew should be." Although he was obsessive in his dedication to the building itself, his main concern, Shuchat insisted, was with content, not form, with what happened inside its walls. To that end, despite his myriad obligations, Lyon Cohen not only sat on its various executive committees, but taught post-biblical history in its school.

NOOKIE GELBER: Horace Cohen, Lyon's son, was also president. He was president for two years, then turned it over to his brother-in-law [Moses] Heillig, who was president for about fifteen years. But Shaar Hashomayim was what Leonard Cohen was all about.

In December 1904, during his presidency, Lyon Cohen donated a brass *chanukiyah* (menorah) to the *shul* on the occasion of his son Nathan's bar mitzvah. The forty-by-thirty-two-centimetre candelabra was cast at his own company, W. R. Cuthbert. In addition, Lyon Cohen was honorary president of the New Adath Jeshurun Congregation; honorary vice president of the Zionist Organization of Canada; president of the Associated Jewish War Relief Societies of Canada; president of the Federation of

Jewish Philanthropies; a governor of three Montreal hospitals; and a director of the Civic Improvement League and the Boys' Farm and Training School in Shawbridge, Quebec. Indeed, there is scarcely a single Jewish agency or institution in which Lyon Cohen did not play a leading role, either backstage or up front. When Jewish dignitaries such as Chaim Weizmann, Solomon Schechter, and Rabbi Stephen Wise visited the city, it was in Cohen's Rosemount Avenue home in Westmount that they were typically entertained.

In 1897, with lawyer and future parliamentarian Samuel W. Jacobs and others, Lyon founded the *Jewish Times*, the first English-language Jewish-interest newspaper in Canada. The paper had a clear mandate: to help Canadianize the teeming influx of Yiddish-speaking Jews arriving from Eastern Europe, and to fight what it called the echo of European anti-Semitism expressed in other Canadian journals. Its first issue featured a front-page story on the controversial Dreyfus case in France. The newspaper's name was changed in 1909 to the *Canadian Jewish Times* and, in 1915, merged with the *Canadian Jewish Chronicle.* Essentially, the journal sought to promote the adoption of mainstream, non-Jewish social customs that, religious observance aside, would make Jews indistinguishable from their gentile neighbours.

Like his uncle Zvi Hirsch, Lyon was considered a gifted orator and once wrote and produced a *Purimspiel* that was reviewed favourably in the mainstream press.

LEONARD COHEN: I remember reading speeches of [Lyon's] where he spoke with great pride that the Jewish community of Montreal had absorbed refugees from Kishinev without ever asking the municipality or the government for a single cent. Montreal Jewry was very well organized. And I am proud to say that he was one of the organizers.

Coincidentally, the two brothers, A. Z. Cohen and Lyon Cohen, died within a month of each other in 1937, both in Old Orchard, Maine.

RUTH COHEN: We received an envelope with a fine black border announcing the death of A.Z. He dropped dead in a movie theatre [on July 19]. He died at fifty-seven. A month later—identical black border—Lyon Cohen died, also in Maine.

Lyon Cohen died August 15, 1937. Samuel Bronfman was one of the pallbearers at his funeral.

ANDREW COHEN: My father, Edgar, was twenty-two when his father, A.Z., died. His brother was not a businessman, and his sisters were unable [to run the business]. He ran the L. Cohen and Sons coal delivery company, rebuilt a moribund business, and sold it in 1959.

RUTH COHEN: When A.Z. died, they split the businesses. My husband wanted to be on his own. They tried to take advantage of this young man. He stood his ground. He fought. [When] coal was converted to oil, [it] became a very big business.

Meanwhile, Lyon's marriage to the former Rachel Friedman in February 1891 produced three sons, Nathan, Horace, and Lawrence, and one daughter, Sylvia.

ROZ VAN ZAIG: I met Leonard's grandmother, Nathan's mother. She was a dowager. She reminded me of the queen—very aristocratic, a lovely woman. I imagine that when [the grandchildren] went to visit, they had to be very well behaved. She lived on Sherbrooke Street in a lovely apartment.

NORMAN ALEXANDER: His uncle Horace was a very interesting man. Extremely well dressed, well spoken, a dignified man children had to respect.

GORDON COHEN: Horace wore spats and a monocle.

LEONARD COHEN: [Horace] had a cane. He would go out with his service medals on his tuxedo. A very distinguished, wonderful figure. Very disciplinarian.

Horace and Nathan Cohen ran the clothing business, the Freedman Company. Playing Mr. Inside to Horace's Mr. Outside, Nathan ran the factory, which manufactured suits, topcoats, and dress wear, while his young brother dealt with the retail enterprises that formed its customer base. Another brother, Lawrence, ran W. R. Cuthbert. Handsome and aristocratic, Lawrence was not considered a genius; within the family, it was whispered that he had failed the bar exam nine times.

Leonard's father, Nathan—born December 1, 1891—had an affinity for military discipline. Even before the outbreak of the First World War, Nathan had served as a corporal in the Home Guard. Trained as a dredging engineer, he was drafted into the Canadian army in early 1918, joining the 4th field company of the Canadian engineers, and rising to the rank of lieutenant. His cousin, Herbert Vineberg, also served, as did his younger brother, Horace, who became captain and quartermaster of his battalion. As part of the Canadian Expeditionary Force, Nathan Cohen saw war action later that year, suffering injuries that affected him for the rest of his life. When the brothers returned from the war, they joined the family clothing business.

LEONARD COHEN: He [Nathan] was an army man, a patriarch, an Edwardian kind of gentleman . . . I always loved the army. My father had intended to send me to the Kingston Military Academy, actually. And if he'd have lived, I would probably have been in the Canadian army.

Although Leonard Cohen never joined the army, his life in myriad ways was lived according to what might be considered a military code. He had an iron discipline that extended to his work habits, his diet, and his meticulous dress, which in the 1970s included khaki military fatigues.

He had a fascination with guns and maintained a Spartan decor for his homes. That discipline was also clear in his later monastic observance of Zen custom and ritual, In the early 1970s, he had famously dubbed his touring band the Army, christened a song, and also a later tour, Field Commander Cohen, and, in interviews, often compared life on the road to a kind of military campaign.

BARRIE WEXLER: Now that I think about it, he would often salute when saying good-bye to you as well.

RUTH COHEN: The [family] did not think Nathan was such great shakes as a businessman. They joked about him. But they all had a very good sense of humour. They used to joke about things.

ROBERT COHEN: Nathan was a jolly guy, certainly overweight, roly-poly. He always sat me on his knee. People said he was very dishonest. He had a reputation. My mother used to say, "You can't trust anything he says."

Cohen himself would later refer to his father as "the persecuted brother." And in his novel *The Favourite Game* he would characterize him as "a fat man who laughed easily with everybody but his brothers."

Cohen's father's family also disparaged his mother, Masha, a Russian immigrant who spoke with a distinct accent. But there was significant intellectual achievement on the maternal line as well. Masha Cohen's father, Solomon Klonitzky-Kline—known as "Sar HaDikdook" or "Prince of Grammarians"—authored several scholarly works, including a dictionary of synonyms and homonyms, and the seven-hundred-page *Ozar Taamei Hazal: Thesaurus of Talmudic Interpretations*. The latter, published in 1939, was dedicated to Cohen's father, Nathan, and mentioned his daughter and his then-five-year-old grandson, Leonard, in the introduction.

Believed to have been born in 1868 in Grodo, in what is now Belarus, Rabbi Solomon bar Leib studied under Yitzchak Elchanan Spektor, the chief rabbi of Kovno—among the most respected rabbis in Russia—and later taught at the Isaac Alchonon Institute, a leading centre of Hebrew learning before the First World War. When Reb Solomon Kline died, in 1958, he had been writing a dictionary without using reference books.

LEONARD COHEN: He was a little gone [by then], but nevertheless felt confident enough to sit . . . He was really one of those people who could put the pin through a page and know the letter it touched on the other side. He was one of those minds.

In Jewish lore, it is said that scholars would often challenge each other's knowledge of Talmud by seeing to what depth of a pin's emplacement they could identify the word it struck at the other end.

Fleeing the postwar chaos and anti-Semitism of Russia, Reb Solomon Kline emigrated to the U.S. from France in 1926, settling initially in Atlanta. There, his eldest daughter, Manya (Marian), married Atlanta lawyer Henry Alexander, a grandson of the first Jew of American birth to settle in the city. Alexander worked on the appeal in the notorious case of Leo Frank, a Jew convicted of murdering a thirteen-year-old factory worker, Mary Phagan, and later lynched by an anti-Semitic mob. His younger daughter, Masha, was born in Kovno (Kaunas) in modern-day Lithuania, in 1905—making her fourteen years younger than her future husband—and came to Canada as a nurse.

ROZ VAN ZAIG: I know how Masha met Nathan. She was a nurse with the Red Cross and he was in the war. Nathan had a heart condition.

When Masha Kline's work permit expired, Reb Kline's American son-in-law contacted Lyon Cohen for help in seeking an extension. It was through that connection that Masha and Nathan were ultimately introduced. They were married in 1927. It proved no simple matter for her to find acceptance in the more genteel Cohen family salons.

STEPHEN LACK: Let's cut to the chase. Leonard's mother was fabulous. The rest of the family, Westmount-wise, were snobs. And snobbish towards her. She had an accent and the Westmount crowd, they all had that British affectation. "I say . . . he's a wonderful chap." I even heard Leonard use that language. That's all from the Westmount, anglophile attitude.

SOREL COHEN: They dumped on her; terribly, I thought. She just didn't fit in. She was large, heavy. She had an accent. They would have considered her an outsider. I always felt sorry [for her]. I always thought they weren't generous enough to embrace her.

MUSIA SCHWARTZ: It was a very strong family, very prominent, and to enter it was no easy thing. I remember Leonard saying, "She had no choice. She had to put up with that family."

NORMAN ALEXANDER: Masha was a very interesting woman, very Russian.

BERNIE ROTHMAN: She was so Russian. If she was any more Russian, she couldn't speak [English] at all. Cohen's relationship with her—a respectful one, but not a close one.

STEPHANIE AZRIELI: Masha was quite a lady. A big woman, very handsome and very Russian.

NORMAN ALEXANDER: She had a voice. "Leonard, you must come and do this!" She was always very welcoming, though I don't ever recall having a meal there, which is interesting, because he ate at my place.

ROBERT COHEN: The family was somewhat negative, but I thought she was wonderful and so did my mother, Marjorie, who was much more of a free spirit than the rest of the Cohens. She liked Masha. Masha was unique. I remember coming into their house at two or three in the morning, half-stoned out of my mind, with Leonard, and Masha coming down the stairs with her dressing gown flapping, saying, "Vat do you vant, dear? A leetle steak? Ve have steak, dear." "No, thank you, Masha, we'll just have some tea." But she was always wanting to entertain Leonard and his friends. She was very nice, very, very charitable.

GORDON COHEN: She was a little too unconventional for them, but not bohemian. She was a lovely woman, very kind and very generous, not at all pretentious.

IRVING LAYTON: Here was the traditional Jewish mother and her only son, and she was certainly frustrated. So her eroticism was directed at Leonard, but, on the other hand, she felt she had to nag him, chivy him, reprove him, all those things Jewish mothers are supposed to do, but with more raw peasant energy and with little understanding of his talent and deep sensitivity. Leonard learned to deal with the world, which is essentially rough and philistine, by dealing with his mother. When it comes steamrolling over you, all you can do is utter a prayer. I can still hear Leonard's voice, very patient and wonderfully compassionate, as he tried to explain [something] to his mother who was attacking him savagely, without falling into condescension—and that's the ultimate act of charity.

ROZ VAN ZAIG: Leonard had a good relationship with Masha, but the pressure was on to go into the business.

AVIVA LAYTON: Masha and Leonard? Love and hate. Not hate, but a very complex relationship. He knew that she was totally toxic and yet she was his mother. Masha had a terrible crush on Irving. She would have jumped into bed with Irving. And in fact, neither Leonard nor I is very sure that she didn't. She was closer to his age than I was. But

Leonard, like Irving, had a thing about his mother. All poets do. It's a very visceral, umbilical thing.

RUTH COHEN: I liked Masha a lot. The others weren't so kind to her—they, the in-laws. I felt sorry for her and reached out to her. I had her for a breakfast [at the end of Yom Kippur]. I think she was shy about coming and she told Leonard—she called him "Leenard," like a Russian—and he told her, "Go, Mother. You're family." And she came and had a wonderful time. She was an impressive-looking woman who wore big hats.

LIONEL TIGER: I met his mother. She seemed very eagle-like, and fussy, and brisk.

ROZ VAN ZAIG: She made a wonderful roast beef. But I don't think Masha ever felt she fit in. There was always a distinction. Masha was a very earthy woman, oh God, yes. Sexy. She had her mood swings. I saw a lot of mood disorder. I never understood it then, because I [as the stepdaughter] felt I was being rejected. On the High Holidays, I went to synagogue but I didn't sit with them. I felt like a third-class citizen, actually. She'd get angry at me. I think [Leonard] might have lost his temper with Masha, but I don't remember any of that. I remember Masha with groceries. She phoned the order in and [they] were delivered.

MUSIA SCHWARTZ: He took me home to meet Masha. She spoke Russian well. My impression was that she wasn't much more than a Jewish mother who had to deal with a difficult son, who was not easy. An artist, every inch of him, in his unpredictability, in his certain coolness, because he was cool. There's no doubt in my mind that he loved his mother more than any other woman in his life. Aside from his mother, I don't think Leonard loved any woman. He needed them. Yes, there was friction [with Masha], but friction is not an unusual thing, nor does it affect the depth and strength of the feeling. Sometimes it sharpens it. I didn't need to read *The Favourite Game*. I knew Masha. Was the relationship ambiguous? Yes. Was it ambivalent? Yes. She was not a warm person—that was my impression. Not self-confident.

ERICA POMERANCE: He took me to his mother's house and I met Mom. She was really something, a bit like a hatchet woman, in a way. That's not nice to say. She was a strong, dominant mother. And he was humouring her—"okay, Mother," putting her in her place in an affectionate way. Or raising his eyebrows. But she kept the conversation going all the time, a real stereotypical Jewish mom.

FRANCINE HERSHORN: Leonard took me to meet Masha. She was very nice to me. She was not shy. That house was very antique-y. Years later, the 1960s, nothing had been done to it. The kitchen and the bathroom were old-fashioned, unchanged, but it was nicely furnished.

LENORE SCHWARTZMAN: I adored Masha. She was such a character. She was wonderful. One night, about ten of us were in his room and his mother came up to say hi and she stood in the doorway and started to sing a Russian song. She was just magnificent. It was a real Russian song. It was fabulous. She was very nice to all of Leonard's friends.

PHOEBE WALKER: He told me she had had an incredibly tough life before she came to Canada and, because she was fighting against the fear of that life and the panic of it, there was something that didn't flow. It didn't flow with him and it didn't flow with his sister. He said, "I have created this tragic Greek character, but she actually wasn't."

SELMA EDELSTONE: Masha was a force of nature, a character, very hands-on with Leonard and Esther.

TERESA TUDURY: He was very loved by women as a child—the mother, the sister, a nanny. That's one of the reasons he was successful with women. He was at ease.

BARBARA MAGERMAN: My late husband, Alfie, was in that house in the early 1950s. He came from a [labour] union family, so Westmount was a real eye-opener for him. Leonard's mother was ill at the time, but there was a maid to draw your bath and wash your back with sponges. Leonard was really pampered.

SOFIA HIDALGO: Leonard told me she was very authoritarian. It was her way or the highway. But she overcompensated with him in terms of indulgence or protection or advice and caring: smothering. I have Masha's kosher dessert dishes, six plates and coffee saucers, two or three, all old, seriously old. I asked for them.

VIOLET ROSENGARTEN: He once took me and Morton to his mother's house. He gave me something [of hers] a little, round wicker jewellery box, made of straw. It was obvious that he loved his mother and would never say anything bad about her. He seemed to be always praising her.

CAROL ZEMEL: I never knew him to say anything bad about his mother, which I thought somewhat odd.

RABBI WILFRED SHUCHAT: Masha came all the time to *shul*. She had European stories. If you mentioned the Vilna Gaon [Elijah ben Solomon Zalman, a brilliant leader of eighteenth-century non-Hasidic Jewry], she knew who that was and all the other [great rabbis].

PATRICIA NOLIN: Leonard, he had his shtick. He's Masha's little boy.

IVAN PHILLIPS: She was big and loud, Masha, big and tough.

MARILYN REGENSTRIEF SCHIFF: One time, he invited me for Friday-night dinner—just him and me and his mother. There was [hired] help in the kitchen. He came to pick me up. I knew he had some difficulty at home and I said, "Why are you inviting me?" And he said, "Because my mother wants to meet you." I was surprised, given the inklings I got about his relationship with his mother. Why would she want to meet me? He said, "She's fascinated with the idea that you decided to leave university and become a nurse. Because she was a nurse." So I went for a typical Friday-night dinner, soup, chicken, whatever. I think I was shocked, because Masha was very welcoming, very accepting, very engaged in talking with me about my life, my interest in modern dance. She was much more worldly than I was prepared for. She was articulate. I expected to feel uncomfortable and I did not.

It is into this comfortable, established, and respected milieu that Leonard Cohen was born. He inherited a family name that resonated across the city and the country, evoking status, intellect, and high achievement, commercially and spiritually. And as a Cohen and a Kohen, he would inevitably carry the implicit burden of that distinguished pedigree.

CHAPTER TWO

Lenny, Prince of Westmount

I always thought he would be someone.

—Roz Van Zaig

I always felt that in some way I would address the world. I always felt that.

—Leonard Cohen

On Friday, September 21, 1934, St. Louis Cardinal pitcher Paul Dean threw a no-hitter against the Brooklyn Dodgers, a typhoon struck Honshu Island in Japan, killing four thousand people, and Leonard Norman Cohen was born. In Hebrew, he was named Eliezer (Help of my God) Nechemia (comforter) Ha-Cohen. A future girlfriend, Linda Clark, a professional astrologer, would later read his chart.

LINDA CLARK: He was born at daybreak, about 4:45 a.m. He had late Venus rising, about 28 degrees. He had Venus opposite the moon— the Virgin and the whore. It was a real focal point of his chart.

A much-loved child, he was doted on by his mother, his nanny, and his sister, Esther Frayda Cohen, born four years earlier. By all accounts, Esther was very bright, with a fun-loving personality.

RUTH COHEN: Esther was lively, vivacious, very smart. Esther was a bit flamboyant, dramatic. She liked to dress up.

LENORE SCHWARTZMAN: I really liked her. Esther was fun . . . They all had very high IQs, let's face it—bright and funny and clever. And she was one of them.

ROZ VAN ZAIG: She was very bright, graduated cum laude. She was a librarian.

MEGAN STUART-STUBBS: My mother went to library school at McGill with Esther, [who was] constantly overwrought about what would become of Lenny [as Cohen was often called in his youth]. Lots of wringing of hands. A poet! Not what the family had hoped.

PANDIAS SCARAMANGA: I met his sister—a different person, altogether. We all loved her, but she was totally crazy. She was dressing with loud colours.

GORDON COHEN: Esther wasn't a nice person. She was extremely selfish. It's kind of a trait that runs through our family, though Leonard didn't have it.

ERIC LERNER: Esther was a warm, brassy, bleach-blond Orthodox-temple-going Jew, a wacky creature who loved her brother very much and was beloved by him . . . Esther had a droll wit. You were never quite sure if she was making a joke, or a cutting comment, or just some batty observation, though she wasn't all that batty, usually right on point.

PERLA BETTALA: Esther was not somebody who would express her emotions. She just wanted to have a good time, be social.

BARRIE WEXLER: Esther was always the shortest person in the room, at least a head shorter than Leonard. What she lacked in height—and I'm afraid, looks—she more than made up for in personality. Outgoing, vivacious, joyful. I remember being struck by the huge psychological difference between brother and sister. Her exuberance was fluid and genuine.

KELLEY LYNCH: Esther was like Carol Channing. Cohen's relationship with her was distant. [Later], she was relegated to becoming his ambassador. She's kind of a tragic figure, very sweet. Their relationship was different when [her husband, who had the same last name], Victor Cohen, was alive, because he [Leonard] respected Victor. He didn't want Esther knowing anything about his life, anything about his finances.

Some sense of the comfort and privilege of Leonard Cohen's childhood can be discerned in the family movies that his father loved to shoot. Always impeccably dressed, the young Cohen was attended by a hovering mother, his elder sister, and an Irish nanny. In the early years, there was also a chauffeur, who doubled as a gardener, and a family dog, a black Scottish terrier named Tovarich (comrade), often called Tinkie, because of the sound made by his ID tags. He had been a birthday gift to [Leonard] from his parents.

LEONARD COHEN: He slept under my bed, followed me to school, waited for me. He was my closest friend. He died at age thirteen. He asked to go out one winter night and we never saw him again. It was very distressing. We put ads in the newspaper. We only found him in the springtime, when the snow melted, and the smell came from under the neighbour's porch, where he'd gone to die.

Cohen in later life kept a framed picture of Tinkie on the dresser of his LA home, a gift from his sister, Esther. Other exposures from Cohen's youth also left a mark. His Catholic nanny, Ann Smith, took him frequently to church, and to Christmas celebrations at her home.

MICHEL GARNEAU: He was a Catholic Jew. [Some of] his maids were French-Canadian and believers, and one of them took him to church and transformed his life—a typical French-Canadian church of that period, very theatrical, ornamental. It touched him a whole lot.

LEONARD COHEN: I never saw [the church] as oppressive . . . I didn't have to feel antagonistic towards the church like the young French intellectuals I met. I only saw it as a continuation of the Vicar of Christ. I saw it in its purest form. I thought this was Christianity, the great missionary arm of Judaism. I saw this as absolutely within my tradition, nothing foreign to me. I always loved the church. There was something I always liked about the whole enterprise.

Among Cohen's many childhood friends was Gavin Ross. Writing for the *Westmount Independent* in 2009, Ross recalled that he and Cohen went through the Westmount school system as classmates, from grade one to grade eleven.

GAVIN ROSS: In grade two and three at Roslyn [Elementary School], we were lucky enough to have a very special teacher, Miss Janet Kingsland. She was a real sweetheart and everybody loved her. She looked pretty old to us, but she was about twenty-one.

DAN USHER: I was six months older than Leonard and we were friends all through those years, Roslyn, Westmount, and Hebrew school. There was nothing at the time that I thought of as being extraordinary about him. Nothing I knew of foretold the career he would have. His career was destined to be something else. He was part of the Cohen family that ran the Freedman Company and he had every expectation of becoming an executive of [it]—hence the clothing he wore at his [later] concerts, straight out of the Freedman Company, including the fedora. Right out of the 1950s. I was not aware of his literary ambitions. We designed sets for a class play or skits. He was good at it. But I saw nothing extraordinary. He was just one of the kids. I took him for granted, as he did me.

JOHN FENWICK: I liked him. He was a very nice guy. We were good friends. We used to play together after school. We went through Roslyn together and split up at Westmount; he took Latin and I took science. I knew him well until McGill, when he went into arts and I went into science.

ANTON RAFF: I grew up on Murray Hill Avenue, a three- or four-minute walk from Leonard's house. My brother and I spent much of our growing up time at Murray Park. We played a lot of sports. He was virtually never there—never. We never encountered each other. I read once that he was a hockey player. He never was a [serious] hockey player. But we went through Roslyn and Westmount together. He was a year ahead of me.

DAN USHER: I remember one odd event. To get to Roslyn School from my house, you'd walk through Murray Hill Park. I remember lying in the grass there with him looking at the clouds. In retrospect, it was the first time I'd ever looked at clouds or taken them seriously. And I remember Leonard proposing something to me which I accepted, though I considered it strange: that subsequently, when we grew up, if either of us found ourselves without a job, the other one would supply him with a job. We were very young, perhaps, nine or ten years old.

BYRON WOODMAN: He had a knack to bring people together. He was well liked. I didn't know him as well as others, because I lived in Pointe Claire and took a steam train to Westmount every day, so I didn't have much time for extracurricular activities.

NORMAN ALEXANDER: Our mothers were good friends. His mother called my mother and told her I was a terrible guy because I taught Leonard how to smoke cigarettes. I don't know whether he taught me or I taught him, but I got blamed for it. That was maybe junior high.

Cohen would later cite his mother's love for old Russian and Yiddish folk songs as a musical influence, but his musical tastes growing up were clearly catholic. He also responded to synagogue hymns and melodies, to pop music on the radio, and to the tunes force-fed in elementary school: "Rule, Britannia," "Flow Gently, Sweet Afton," and "The Maple Leaf Forever."

LEONARD COHEN: Those rousing national hymns touched me . . . I was completely hooked on this stuff as a kid—the songs my mother sang, the liturgy, the pop music. There was a certain resonance when something was said in a certain kind of way, it seemed to embrace the cosmos. Not just my heart, but every heart was involved, and loneliness was dissolved, and you felt like you were this aching creature in the midst of the aching cosmos and the ache was okay. Not only was it okay, but it was the way that you embraced the sun and the moon.

BYRON WOODMAN: I was in Leonard Cohen's class. He was a brilliant young man. One thing I remember, we had a math class together and our teacher was a Mr. Smith. We called him Daddy Smith. One year, Leonard wrote a play, based on a Gilbert and Sullivan operetta, and he made Smith a character in the play.

NORMAN ALEXANDER: We also executed Mr. Smith with a guillotine one of the kids made. Leonard was involved with that. His nickname was "Squirt" because he was quite short. One day, somebody brought a soft drink called Squirt to school and left it on his desk. It brought a great deal of laughter to the group. I hung around with Leonard probably two or three nights a week, along with Morty Rosengarten, Harold Pascal, and Malcolm Lefcort. I saw no depression, no moodiness. He was a normal kid; we grew up doing normal things. It was a typical upbringing in our milieu, but he had more poetry, music, an artsy bent.

RONA FELDMAN SCHEFLER: At Westmount Junior High, probably grade seven—it may even have been Roslyn School, grade six—we were the shortest in the class and we were at the tail end of a group on our bicycles on a school trip to the Elmhurst Dairy. We kind of doddled along. We stopped and I remember sitting and talking with him. By the time we got to where the class was, the teachers were a bit frantic because they thought they had lost us. He was pensive, always pensive, always quiet. But he had this very, very appealing half smile, a crooked smile. He had that always, even up to the end. He never showed himself off. He was very close with Nancy Bacal and Mort Rosengarten.

ROZ VAN ZAIG: He always had that sort of smile on his face. Whatever came out of his mouth was brilliant. I said in the very early years, I always thought he would be someone. I never knew to [what] extent.

Cohen met Bacal and Rosengarten in 1944 at Camp Hiawatha, in the Laurentians north of Montreal. They would remain among his closest friends for the rest of his life.

NOOKIE GELBER: Everybody went to Hiawatha. Hiawatha was an institution. Leonard's cousin David Cohen was also there. He was [later] the [head of the] Freedman Company, which collapsed.

NORMAN ALEXANDER: We talked a lot, rode our bikes, listened to a lot of music, folk music specifically. I remember Pete Seeger. The other guys played musical instruments—I didn't. Morton played the trombone—he was his closest friend. I was with them all the time, but in terms of sharing confidences, [they were closer]. Leonard had a good sense of humour. He was a very intelligent guy, a very with-it person, always a good conversationalist, verbal, well liked, prone to entertaining. We had a lot of fun together. He was always well dressed. He could sweet-talk a girl, I'll tell you. He always got their attention. He always had dates. The short guy always got the best-looking girls.

IVAN PHILLIPS: What was he like? I can't remember what I had for dinner last night. But I was never part of his poetry world or his music world or his intellectual world. We were related—some degree of cousin, through the Cohen clan. We drifted apart, frankly.

STEPHANIE AZRIELI: My brother Malcolm Lefcort was good friends with Leonard in high school. Mostly, they hung out at Leonard's house. Leonard was a good guy—skinny, cute, always very pleasant. I knew he played the guitar. My brother played the trumpet. My brother became an engineer, so their paths went different ways. [Romantically], Leonard didn't interest me. I didn't interest him.

NORMAN ALEXANDER: We hung out at each other's houses. We wrote songs together, school stuff. He did most of the work. He was very popular. He played the ukulele and later the guitar. He was over at my house one day and picked up a guitar my brother had bought, and insisted on buying it. I don't know if he had another one. And he did buy it—paid my brother five bucks. That was in high school. I was president of the Menorah Society, the Jewish club, and he was president of the student council, so there was a lot of interaction then.

Cohen's father, Nathan, had never been in robust health. Overweight for most of his adult life, he nursed a heart condition from an early age, and carried the legacy of an injury sustained during World War I. It was the cardiac problem that would ultimately claim his life, in January 1944, at age fifty-two. He seemed to have known it was coming.

BARRIE WEXLER: I'm sure Leonard's lifelong obsession with keeping his weight down was directly related to the obesity that contributed to his father's early death.

ANDREW COHEN: My father, Edgar, was in synagogue one day—it must have been late 1930s or early 1940s—and Leonard's father told him then, "I will not live to see Leonard's bar mitzvah." Once, Leonard began to recite the mourner's Kaddish [normally said only by mourners], but Nathan didn't stop him. He knew his son would be saying it soon enough.

BARBARA DODGE: He saw his father decline, as the first son and the only son. It had an impact on him.

HERSH SEGAL: Leonard was deeply affected by his father's death.

STEPHEN LACK: You know, a lot of Leonard's psychology—he and I never discussed this—is based on the early loss of his father.

Shortly before he died, Nathan Cohen bequeathed to his son an extensive leather-bound poetry library, as well as a book called *The Romance of the King's Army.*

LEONARD COHEN: The quotation in the beginning of the book . . . that . . . really struck me, was "You would be surprised, my son, with how little wisdom the world is governed." The quintessential religious position is that this world, the world that is governed without God, is a world of folly . . . To give that to a kid of eight. It was a very, very strong message.

The aftermath, described in detail in *The Favourite Game*, included an open coffin in the family living room, where the extended family gathered to mourn.

ROBERT COHEN: When Nathan died, I remember standing around with Leonard and Esther and saying, "I'm so sorry. I don't know what to say." And Leonard saying, at nine years old, "Oh, don't worry about it. It's very difficult." He was thinking about *me*, which is kind of interesting.

SOFIA HIDALGO: We were talking about our parents and our family. I said, "How did you feel when you lost your father?" And he said what affected him most was the sorrow other people displayed, the tragedy of this mother left without her young husband, with two young children. It was heartbreaking. He felt for the people.

Among friends, then or later, Cohen seldom mentioned his father.

LEONARD COHEN: I didn't feel a profound sense of loss, maybe because he was very ill throughout my entire childhood.

MARILYN REGENSTRIEF SCHIFF: He did talk to me about it, but not in much detail, just a statement of the fact that his father had died and he was left to the [ministrations] of his mother. He was the first person I knew well who had lost a parent. Years later, when my husband died, and my son, fourteen, was alone with his mother, I thought about Leonard a lot. My friendship with him impacted . . . me and my understanding of losing a father.

BARRIE WEXLER: Leonard rarely talked about his father. Once, after he'd written a poem for my twenty-first birthday with the line "I have green eyes in certain light," I said to him, "I've been looking—you don't have green eyes in *any* light." He laughed and said, "Yeah, I've got my father's eyes, but I'm three and a half inches taller." On another occasion, during a walk in Old Montreal, we passed Bonsecours Market, close to the waterfront. He turned up a street, pointed to a building near the corner, and said, "That's where my father and grandfather lived." I was surprised he knew the building, because it always seemed as though he had walled his father off.

GORDON COHEN: It's probably an oversimplification to say that Leonard was thereafter in search of a father figure: Irving Layton.

On the other hand, to the extent that *The Favourite Game* faithfully renders actual events, Cohen did attend Nathan's funeral and, later, in a fit of anger, shredded pages from his father's books.

GIDEON ZELERMYER: He told me he said Kaddish for his father occasionally, but he wasn't so religious that way. They did come as a family for *Yizkor* [a memorial service].

After his father's death, perhaps as early as the next day, Cohen later said, he wrote a poem or message of some kind.

LEONARD COHEN: I went upstairs and found a bow tie and cut a wing of it and wrote something, some kind of farewell to my father. And I buried it in the backyard. Some attraction to a ritual, a response to an impossible event.

PETER KATOUNDAS: Burying the bow tie with a poem in Montreal in January? I don't think so.

SOFIA HIDALGO: The gesture could have happened when he began missing him in the spring . . . Maybe that was his symbolic burial.

BARRIE WEXLER: He didn't make up the bow-tie story. The only urban legend is that this was the genesis of how he came to be a poet.

Whatever the truth of the bow-tie story, Leonard Cohen, not yet ten years old, effectively became the "man of the house."

CAROL ZEMEL: He cut the roast and sat at the head of the table. The sense of his own place seems to have always been with him, and near the top of whatever he was doing. He was like a prince. He saw himself as a prince.

LINDA CLARK: He literally filled his father's chair after he died? How metaphorical is that? He had to take his father's place. I don't think he ever takes the key out from under his mother's pillow.

In Robert Bly's best-selling book *Iron John,* only by retrieving the key can young men escape maternal bonds and achieve individuation and full actualization.

LINDA CLARK: He is so broken and violated he could never make a full commitment to a woman, because part of his heart still belongs to the mama. Any woman he's with is a betrayal of the mother. It leads to a kind of impotent rage—I don't mean physical—but resentment you can't express, hostility or passive-aggressiveness. It explains Leonard [later] playing tricks on people or trying to get your goat, a devilish prankster, just to fuck with the other person.

GORDON COHEN: After Nathan died, the relationship between Masha and her in-laws was problematic. His mother was a Russian immigrant who spoke with a heavy accent, and the Cohens' shit did not smell, okay?

MEL SOLMAN: When I went to Masha's *shiva* in 1978, I remember hearing how Leonard's aunts hadn't been very pleasant to his mother. They resented her for being the prettiest of the sisters-in-law. There was a falling-out after the father died.

RUTH COHEN: Masha had enough [money], but she did not have a lot. But they supported Masha, because where would she get income?

GORDON COHEN: Her two brothers-in-law were the executors of her late husband's estate. Every time she needed money, she had to go to her brothers-in-law and say, "Lawrence, could you please send me a cheque?" And the kids too. They were not very happy about that. Esther always resented that. Leonard didn't resent it.

BARBARA MAGERMAN: There may have been some bitterness directed at the uncle.

ROBERT COHEN: Horace really had nothing to do with the estate. It was all Lawrence. He took over Leonard's family and he became Leonard's mentor. Horace was anti-Leonard, in fact, until Leonard became famous, at which point Horace turned around and became an incredible supporter.

One summer, Cohen went to Camp Bayview, a Spartan camp on Lake Archambault in Saint-Donat, in the Laurentians.

LENORE SCHWARTZMAN: I met Leonard there. His sister, Esther, was my counsellor, and we became friends, and she invited me to visit her in Westmount. I was talking to her when down the stairs came this young man playing the guitar.

Schwartzman may be confusing the guitar, which Cohen did not begin playing until the age of fifteen, with the ukulele, which he did play earlier.

HELAINE LIVINGSTONE: Later, my sister [Lenore Schwartzman] had dance parties. They'd roll up the rug in the dining room and push the table aside and dance to music. He'd notice me hiding behind doors at my house. He was the first person who ever asked me to dance. I was eight or nine. I'm sure I almost fainted. Nobody else would have paid attention. Leonard was always gracious and kind. As time went by, I realized that he was an exception to the rule. When he'd bump into my mother downtown, he used to bow. Extremely polite.

Beginning in 1946, Cohen spent several summers at Camp Wabikon in northern Ontario. The camp sits on Lake Temagami, about 250 miles north of Toronto. Getting there from Montreal involved a train ride to Toronto, a second one to North Bay, then a bus to Temagami, and finally a boat ride to Temagami Island. On one of those trips, the young Cohen met another Westmounter destined to become a lifelong friend, Bernie Rothman.

BERNIE ROTHMAN: It was the best camp I ever went to. He was eleven. It was a real rugged camp. You couldn't have had a better time. Cohen and I were great friends, immediately. We were there two summers. There is one adjective I'd apply to Cohen more than anybody in the world: he was very interesting. A fascinating man, even then. And he was at Wabikon. There was nobody I'd rather have a conversation with than Leonard Cohen. Our conversations were unbelievable. We were talking about things kids don't talk about. He did read a lot, yes. But it wasn't just that. His perceptions were remarkable. He was a romantic at Wabikon. Its manifestations were talk. Romance is all about talk. Esther was there too. We called her Peppy. She was very peppy.

HERBERT SAMUELS: I remember him as "Lenny." Lenny was the undisputed leader of the cabin. It was not due to his forcing his way into the role. It was rather by the warmth and magnetism of his personality that made you want to follow him. Not athletically inclined, he was physically quite strong. A lot of that strength came from force of will. At a relatively young age, he would swim the length of the pool [twenty-five yards] underwater. Someone read that you could not hold your arms straight out perpendicular to your body more than a certain length of time. He took that as a challenge and proceeded to do it.

ROBERT COHEN: Leonard was not an athlete. He was deceptive. I always was amazed at how he could do things, because he did not do sports like Gordon [Cohen] and I did. How facile he was. How good he was with his hands. How he carried himself. He was deceptive. We did spend a lot of time in Murray Hill Park.

HERBERT SAMUELS: One summer, we became superheroes with towels tied around our neck as capes. Lenny's idea was instead of saying "shazam," like Captain Marvel, we say our names backwards. By his saying "Dranoel Nehoc" or, in my case, "Trebreh Sleumas," we were transformed. He taught me how to comb my hair to achieve the same pompadour he had. Somehow, it didn't attract the girls to me like the way they gravitated to Lenny. He was a magnet to boys as well as girls, but being a chick magnet was something I took note of, especially [since I was] quite the opposite. One summer, my parents visited and brought water pistols for the cabin. [The Samuels family owned a toy company.] We had a short time playing with them before they were confiscated by our counsellors.

ANTON RAFF: We were in the same cabin for a number of years. Again, he was a quiet leader type. He wasn't an athlete, but he was a storyteller, so he would regale us at night, and they were often risqué, especially when we were teens. And he was always a bit of a ladies' man, even at twelve, thirteen, fourteen.

Years later, Samuels ran into Cohen in New York.

HERBERT SAMUELS: We shared a taxi into Manhattan. On the way, Lenny said offhandedly that he often thought of me. Nonplussed, I asked why. He said one of his favourite pastimes, particularly in a new place, was to go into a variety store and leisurely poke around. He often felt he should buy something, and many times, it was a water pistol. I laughed. That was Lenny. Gracious, friendly, down-to-earth, and full of stories. Little would it have occurred to me that my boyhood friend of many summers would become the international superstar. Now that I look back, I'm not at all surprised.

GORDON COHEN: I was close to him as a cousin. We went to Wabikon together. He was charismatic, even as a teenager. Oh, yeah. He was a little guy, very nonathletic, but he had a big smile and he knew how to talk, and he said the right things, and when he smiled and put his arm on your shoulder, it was special. He was a special guy, Leonard. He wasn't an ordinary guy. Anybody who met Leonard Cohen knew that he was special.

BERNIE ROTHMAN: The three of us had the most wonderful time together. We played with guns and we played with girls. Between those two things, that was enough. Rosie is a fabulous man. I always called him Rosie and Leonard always called him Krantz. Robert Hershorn came later. Hershorn was an oddball, but there was a sweetness to him.

HERBERT SAMUELS: He was a storyteller. One night, after lights were out, he spun a tale for what seemed like a half hour. He related how he was waiting for a bus during a heavy Montreal snowstorm. He described the scene, the street name, and bus number in full detail. A passing motorist offered him a ride home, but first had to stop at the driver's first-floor apartment to pick something up. He invited Lenny to come with him out of the cold. His host momentarily left the room and returned holding a knife. He came at Lenny, who evaded him, momentarily, and tried to escape through an open window. We were on tenterhooks. As Lenny was partially out the window, the man "grabbed me by the leg. He started pulling my leg, pulling my leg, just like I'm pulling yours."

BERNIE ROTHMAN: Leonard was very ambitious, you bet. He had the calling at Wabikon. He was already, "do I hear something?" What took him a while was making money.

ANTON RAFF: There was an episode. We pulled a prank, either raiding the girls' camp or stealing one of these big sausages, the kind that hang in a butcher's shop. After that, we were called to task by the owner, a fine man, Irwin Haladner. He called us into his office and gave us a talking-to. We had overstepped. After that, Leonard wrote an abject apology, promising that we'd all do so much better in the future. We'd strive to be ideal campers. He wanted all his cabin mates to sign it. I was the only one who refused—I'm by temperament a rebel. I said it's got to be unanimous. And we ended up having a fight. The fight was no contest. I just pinned him down, slid his head under one of the cots, and waited for him to surrender. There was no animosity. We were friendly after that.

*   *   *

After his twelfth birthday, Cohen started to study with Samuel Lerner for his bar mitzvah. His Torah portion, or *Parshah*, was *B'reisheet*, the first chapter of Genesis.

MARK BERCUVITZ: We started out in Hebrew school together, at seven years old. We were a group. Our Hebrew class was maybe ten guys. I was at his house many times. His family was the standard-bearers for the synagogue. It was a very special Jewish community. You met everybody. I remember when he first got his guitar. I remember him telling me the facts of life.

JACK LAZARE: I knew him then, around the bar mitzvah years. On the rare occasions when I'd go to *shul*, I'd see him with his uncles in their top hats. The Cohens were the establishment. He and Mort Rosengarten eventually divorced themselves from Westmount Jewry. Westmount Jewry did not go to [the plateau]. It was a race to get away from [there].

On October 11, 1947, Cohen celebrated his bar mitzvah at Shaar Hashomayim Synagogue. Rabbi Shuchat officiated. Reportedly, because of his short height, the *shul* set up a footstool so that he would be able to see over the podium. Among the gifts Cohen received that day was a *siddur* (prayer book) from the family of Mr. and Mrs. J. Cohen. Years later, Cohen would loan the book to his friend Steve Sanfield, who, with another friend, Michael Getz, used it to teach Hebrew to Jewish boys in Northern California. Getz still has the *siddur* in his possession.

RABBI WILFRED SHUCHAT: An interesting thing. That bar mitzvah class decided to stay in touch and call each other on [the anniversary of their] bar mitzvahs, including Leonard. In their fifth year, they came to synagogue and had *aliyahs*. In their fiftieth year, they gave a *kiddush* for the whole *shul*. The bar mitzvah was a serious matter for them. In 2017, they celebrated their seventieth year. They didn't realize how ill Leonard was. They were hoping he'd be primary spokesman. But in the intervening years, he'd be called to see if he was interested in being contacted. His answer was always yes. He said, "I travel all the time. I can't really commit. But don't leave me out." Where in the world would you get a group like that?

Years later, after Cohen had achieved fame, Shuchat would invite him to appear or lecture at the *shul*.

RABBI WILFRED SHUCHAT: I wanted him to speak for various purposes. He said, "Look, I'm a pretty good Jew—not the best. But I'm not a spokesman for the Jewish community. Your community knows more about Israel than I do. I can't do what you want me to do. I feel embarrassed to do that." At that point, I stopped inviting him. He was basically asking me not to invite him.

In the same years as his bar mitzvah, 1947, Cohen also served as den master to a Cub Scout troop.

ALAN GOLDEN: He was my den master, he and Danny Usher. I had passed all of my tests for the second star, everything except skipping. I couldn't skip. Leonard said, "Alan, you come to my house and I will teach you how to skip." And for an hour and a half, he taught me how to skip in his basement. I made a lot of noise and his mother was screaming at us, "Boys, let's have a little quiet down there." He was the essence of a good den master. He imposed discipline in a relaxed way. He was very creative in the things we had to do, turned dull things into slightly more interesting things—the perfect model.

BARRIE WEXLER: Leonard loved skipping. He was probably the best skipper in the history of the art. There's a scene in the music video we later shot, *I Am a Hotel*, where he skips while executing a kind of half turn, a move almost as difficult as an extra half rotation in figure skating.

Famously, in his final years on tour, Cohen would skip off the stage at the end of each concert. By his early teens, Cohen had developed another esoteric interest—hypnotism—and had bought books on the subject. In one now-famous story, he managed to hypnotize the family's maid.

ROZ VAN ZAIG: But I remember him telling me he tried. I know he was intimate with one of the maids and it was one of his first experiences. He also tried to hypnotize me and that didn't work. I think he used a pen or something, in the kitchen.

SOFIA HIDALGO: He told me the story. We were sitting on the staircase from the kitchen to the basement, and he shows me this box he got—how to hypnotize, with all the instructions. It was like a time capsule. Everything was saved, perfectly. He opened the box and showed me and there was a drawing of the eyes. He said the nanny had an incredible bosom and he wanted to put his hand on it. One day his mom was out, so he asked her, "Could I try to hypnotize you?" And she said, "Okay, but make sure you bring me back." And he said he hypnotized her. He said at first he thought, "Shit, I did it—how do I undo this? Oh my God." So he woke her up and they did it again, and the second and third time, he completely hypnotized her and she took her shirt off and the whole thing. I said, "Yeah, she pretended to be hypnotized." And he said, "Of course, but I didn't care. I was dying to touch her." I said, "How was it?" And he said she had beautiful nipples, round and big, curved and plump, like when you suck on a bottle. I was laughing hysterically.

MARILYN REGENSTRIEF SCHIFF: He was having issues with his mother and her control, and this was his way of dealing with the subject of control.

In the fall of 1948, Cohen began attending Westmount High. Its motto was *dux vitae ratio*: reason is the guide to life. Soon elected to its student council and later its president, he sat on the school's board of publishers, competed—or claimed to compete—in cycling, cross-country skiing, swimming, sailing, and hockey, chaired the drama club, and published a short skit, written for the Christmas season.

ANTON RAFF: He was always a quiet leader.

GAVIN ROSS: I was on the Westmount High student council and Leonard was president. We were on the school's drama club executive and did a few silly things together. My dog and I delivered his mother's morning paper each day and I'd often walk with him to school. Each year, our high school yearbook, *Vox Ducum*, published a few selected short stories. In the 1950 edition, Leonard had a story, "Kill or Be Killed." It was a good story, and may just be his first published work.

ALAN GOLDEN: I remember once seeing him in the school library. He showed me what he had just written, a composition, something about "the trees quivering tremulously." Later, I saw how [he was so] adamant . . . that it took a long time . . . to craft the words he wanted to appear—I saw that in him in retrospect.

GAVIN ROSS: In 1951, when President Harry Truman fired General Douglas MacArthur, we drove around the schoolyard in the Morris Minor convertible of our classmate David Hogg, with Leonard dressed as MacArthur, complete with corncob pipe, standing in the back yelling, "I shall return, I shall return."

Around this time, Cohen and Bernie Rothman competed for the favours of a young woman, Dundi Weinfeld.

BERNIE ROTHMAN: She went to Westmount High, a very cute Hungarian trollop. I really had a crush on her, as did he. And he got her. But allegedly, she wasn't the first. The Cohen family maid was first.

Both Weinfeld and Lenore Schwartzman make a fleeting appearance in "The Jelly," a poem included in *Death of a Lady's Man*. Dundi is described as "untouchable as the other telephone."

BERNIE ROTHMAN: Cohen got a bad rap as a woman chaser. He was not. Women were Cohen chasers. They never left him alone for a minute, poor darling. He was so poetic and very charming, elegant. But we both loved women. That was a very important part of our lives.

Three, perhaps four, significant events occurred in Cohen's life in 1949–50, the years during which he turned fifteen and then sixteen. The first, although its precise timing is unknown, was his now-well-known encounter with the work of Spanish poet, playwright, and composer Federico García Lorca, murdered during the Spanish Civil War in 1936. Lorca's writings, he said, influenced him more than any other poet. Cohen recounted various versions of his introduction.

LEONARD COHEN: I stumbled on a book of his in a secondhand bookstore . . . and I found something in there that just resonated in my own heart . . . the evocation of a landscape that you really felt at home in . . . It was a universe that I already inhabited, so I claimed him as my brother. Once I knew that there was this landscape that he'd established, I wanted to stay there most of the time.

Cohen reportedly carried the Lorca book with him everywhere, "until the book began to lose its pages."

LEONARD COHEN: I read these lines. "I want to pass through the arches of Elvira, to see your thighs and begin weeping." I began my own search for those arches and those tears. Another line: "the morning threw fistfuls of ants at my face"—this was a universe I understood thoroughly and I began to pursue it . . . follow it . . . live it. What can

I say about a name that . . . changed my way of being and thinking in a radical way? . . . I've never left that world.

DAVID SOLWAY: We had a discussion about Lorca once. I can see the attraction for him. The darker side of Lorca, the *duende* thing—you can hear that in Leonard's last CD, *You Want It Darker*. Lorca had a dark, romantic, doomsday side, and so did Leonard.

Lorca himself, citing Goethe, described *duende* as "a mysterious force that everyone feels and no philosopher has explained." For Cohen, it would become a critical element of his art in song, "not a question of skill," as Lorca wrote, "but of a style that's truly alive." Reading Lorca likely opened the door to the poetry of other foreign writers. Cohen, for example, read Chinese poetry in translation, which also left a deep impression.

LEONARD COHEN: Certainly one of the images I had of myself came from reading Chinese poetry at a very young age. There was a kind of solitary figure in . . . poems by Li Bo and Tu Fu. A monk sitting by a stream. There was a notion of solitude, a notion of deep appreciation for personal relationships, friendships, not just love, not just sensual or erotic or the love of a man or a woman, but a deep longing to experience and to describe friendship and loss and the consequences of distance . . . Thirty years later, I found myself in robes and a shaved head sitting in a meditation hall. It just seemed completely natural.

Almost inevitably, Cohen soon started writing himself.

LEONARD COHEN: I do remember sitting down at a card table on a sun porch one day when I decided to quit a job. I was working in a brass foundry [the family's Cuthbert operation] and one morning I thought, "I just can't take this anymore," and went out to the sun porch and started a poem. I had a marvellous sense of mastery and power, and freedom, and strength, when I was writing this poem.

ROBERT COHEN: Leonard spent a brief time at W. R. Cuthbert, my father's [foundry]. He did a little bit of sales work. He made it sound like he spent a lot of time there, but it was just a couple of weeks, actually.

The second major event of 1949 occurred in February, when Cohen's mother, Masha, remarried Montreal pharmacist Henry Ostrow.

ROZ VAN ZAIG: My father owned a drugstore at Saint-Francis and Saint-Matthew. My mother had a stroke when I was five and died when I was thirteen. She was thirty-eight. My father was a difficult man, though he was wonderful to my mother. But I always felt like I was an albatross. I didn't have the greatest relationship with him, and he didn't communicate. I think he and Masha were introduced by a friend of Masha's. I only sensed what was happening because Masha had slept over and left some lingerie, and I found it. The wedding was a very small ceremony. So we moved in—to 599 Belmont Avenue. I had Leonard's original bedroom, and he moved into a huge book-lined study, next to me. We were the same age. He had a lot of friends. Our housekeeper, Cecile, came to work for Masha, but it didn't last very long. His sister, Esther, was there. Esther was not easy. She did not like my father. There was a lot of tension. She showed disrespect. But my father did not earn respect. He was a difficult man with a terrible temper. She was still at university. She had already met her future husband, Victor Cohen, and he would come from New York to visit. I didn't really get to know him or Esther.

RUTH COHEN: Because Masha married him, we thought we'd use him as our pharmacist. For years, he delivered. The marriage was okay—not a great love affair, not meaningful.

ROZ VAN ZAIG: The chauffeur was gone by 1949. Was the marriage forced on her by her need for income? It's a good question.

KELLEY LYNCH: Leonard thought that's why Masha married him, for his money. Cohen had a mixed relationship with his mother, love/hate, and the stepfather was part of that.

ROZ VAN ZAIG: There was a lot of tension in the house. There was an intellectual gap, a culture gap. It was an intellectual discussion at dinner. They talked about writers. Masha was very bright. There was really a huge lack of respect and I can't totally blame her. I didn't like my father. I was afraid of his temper and I was ashamed of him.

It did not help that Ostrow either came into the marriage with multiple sclerosis or developed it soon after. The sole positive in the house for Van Zaig was Leonard Cohen.

ROZ VAN ZAIG: Leonard was the only one who was really kind and good. He was very sensitive. He wasn't judgemental. We never really had personal conversations, but I never had any issues with him. He always treated me nicely and we were [at] a very difficult age. He'd lost his father. I'd lost my mother, but in those days, we just didn't talk about it. Leonard was fun. He would love to do things. There was a fire once and it was the middle of the night and he asked me, "Do you want to go?" I was thrilled that he asked me. I don't remember how we got there—downtown, somewhere—but I went with him. He had his guitars and he strummed—that's what he did. He had books of music. He was meticulous. He would scrutinize his work. He'd get hungry late at night and make salami and eggs at twelve or one o'clock. And he was a good cook. He was not ostentatious, a class act in so many ways. We were in separate cocoons. We never discussed schoolwork or literature. He was busy with his friends. But Leonard was not vain. With all his intellect, he was always humble.

GORDON COHEN: Leonard was always very gracious. He would never knowingly say anything to hurt anybody or stick it to anybody, or speak disparagingly of anyone. He was just a warm, wonderful guy.

ROZ VAN ZAIG: Leonard was bookish, but Leonard was everything. He read, he wrote, he strummed his guitar, he sang—a lot of Josh White, in those days. It was rare if we did things as a family. We went out to eat, probably at Ruby Foo's, but not often. But living there was not easy. I felt like the stepchild. The marriage was not healthy. I was aware of it. There was a lot of fighting, open fighting, a lot of dissension, a lot of it caused by Esther's dislike of my father, and my father not dealing with that very well.

The third seminal event occurred during the summer of 1950. Cohen got a job as a counsellor at Camp Sunshine, a Jewish community camp for children from poor and working-class families, sponsored by the Baron de Hirsch Foundation. It was located at Sainte-Marguerite-du-Lac-Masson in the Laurentian Mountains, north of Montreal.

MARILYN REGENSTRIEF SCHIFF: Leonard was meeting all kinds of kids that summer, not just the fishbowl of Westmount, where everyone felt the same way. He was meeting people from different backgrounds.

LILI SHATZKY: I met him there. He was fifteen and I was eighteen. We were both counsellors [Cohen may actually have been a counsellor-in-training]. He looked after the younger kids. It's where Leonard really started to sing. He came with his guitar. We used to sit around and sing, usually with the other counsellors.

DAN USHER: Leonard as a kid had studied clarinet. He took up the guitar at camp. As far as I know, he didn't play the guitar at all until he got to camp. He was reasonably proficient. At least more proficient than I was.

MARILYN REGENSTRIEF SCHIFF: My boyfriend that summer was Alfie Magerman, and he and Leonard became extremely close friends. He is the first person I'm aware of that taught Leonard how to play the guitar. Alfie spent a large part of his free time teaching Leonard how to hold the guitar, play chords, fingering, timing. Leonard was a rank beginner when Alfie started teaching him. At that time, Leonard could barely carry a tune. [Alfie] taught him songs from *The People's Songbook*. Songs Pete Seeger sang, the Weavers, Paul Robeson, songs about Negro problems, not Negro spirituals, songs of wrecked lives. I don't know that Leonard led sing-songs, but he certainly participated. He half sung and half spoke. Union songs. "There Once Was a Union Maid." Songs of the Spanish Civil War, which for my generation was like the Vietnam War. Our heroes were people like Norman Bethune, who went to Spain to fight fascism. This exposure for Leonard at age fifteen to the [political] currents was something quite new to him. The camp experience crystallized things for him and became a jumping-off point on many levels.

BARBARA MAGERMAN: Alfie was not an accomplished guitarist and he had a problem keeping a tune. But he loved folk music, particularly songs about social justice, and the Spanish Civil War, the Weavers and Peter Seeger, Josh White. Leonard picked up on all these songs.

DAN USHER: The extraordinary thing about the camp was partly the folk music and partly that [camp director] Irving Morton was a Communist or perhaps a fellow traveller. His glorification of the Soviet

Union was extreme. There were no sermons, but it was somehow there, in the air. We later bought *The People's Songbook* at the People's Bookstore on Mount Royal, near the park.

LILI SHATZKY: I liked him right away. He was mellow, but not depressed. He was always very nice. We had a nice friendship for the whole summer. We took our days off together, took a canoe out, or went into Sainte-Marguerite. We used to go there to buy cigarettes, though we sometimes smoked at camp, though we weren't supposed to.

MARILYN REGENSTRIEF SCHIFF: I taught dancing and there was no actual rec hall where it was possible to do indoor activities on a large scale, so the dancing was done outdoors on a big field. Leonard used to like to watch me teach dancing. Occasionally, he'd dance, but mostly he was a watcher. He hated the beachfront activities because he was very self-conscious, even at that age, about his body. He was short-waisted, and he pointed to his chest and said, "I have a pigeon chest and I don't look wonderful in a bathing suit." So he'd wear T-shirts and avoid waterfront duties as much as he could. He had a wry, impish sense of humour. I'd say to him, "You're so smart, so sharp, you're creative and have such a winning way about you. People aren't looking at whether you are short- or long-waisted." I was a kind of sister figure in his life. Because even then, he was very smart, very intuitive, psychologically. I knew it from how he behaved, reacted to people, his remarks about people. He had a lot of insight into people's behaviours. He was a very tolerant, very forgiving of, accepting of people's behaviours and somehow understood where people were coming from. I felt that about him immediately. In many ways, he was mature beyond his years.

That's precisely the conclusion senior camp officials came to. A formal evaluation of the young Cohen noted that, despite his youth, he was "very mature in many ways. Needs more training and skills. Watch for traces of skepticism. Suggest rehire with training and supervision and winter experience. Had full counsellor responsibility which he took seriously. Conscientious and sincere."

LILI SHATZKY: It was the summer after his mother remarried and we talked about that. All of a sudden he had a stepsister, Roz. He was at a place where he didn't know quite what to do with her. He was not unhappy that his mother had remarried, but having a younger sister affected him. He was someone I could talk to because I was going out with someone who had proposed marriage to me on the first date and my father was quite ill. Leonard was very sweet and a good listener. He was just about to finish high school and really wanted to get out of the house, as did I. I said to him, "You're such a kid," and he said, "This is fine for camp, but when we get back to Montreal, you're certainly not going to want to be seen with me, a young kid."

MARILYN REGENSTRIEF SCHIFF: He was having a rough time with his mother. On one of our days off, he asked me if I was going into Montreal because he wanted to go with me. I said, "No, I'm going to visit my mom and baby sister at my parents' cottage." It was about half an hour away, in Prefontaine. In those days, we hitchhiked. I knew he was not happy about spending an evening at home. Home was not where he wanted to be at that time. So he asked me if he could come along. I said, "Fine, absolutely. But I want to warn you there's no guest bedroom. You may have to sleep on the sofa in the kitchen." He loved that—anything that was strange, out of the norm. He was very open to life and to challenges and new experiences. It was all part of the game. So off we went, hitchhiked to my cottage. Then we arrive and I go in to see my baby sister and she needs her diaper changed and he says, "Can I watch?" So I started changing the diaper, and he says, "Can I do it?" I said, "Lenny, have you ever diapered a baby?"

And he sort of giggled and said no. So I showed him how to hold your hand so you don't stick the baby with the pin, and he ended up diapering the baby. It was a little bit loose, so I fixed it, but he was thrilled that he had diapered the baby. He saw the humour in everything. He had a very quirky sense of humour, and he was genuinely this way—it wasn't put on. Even in tricky situations, he'd find an aspect that was ironic. He had a very strong sense of irony. It came out in his use of language, in how he interpreted various situations. He was not a superficial person. He had a very penetrating mind in terms of what makes people tick. That was part of his charm for me. Other counsellors had very fixed value systems. Leonard was sort of floating. He was open and more responsive.

That summer, Cohen again put his talent for hypnotism to use.

MARILYN REGENSTRIEF SCHIFF: It was announced that the counsellors were getting together because Lenny was going to hypnotize somebody. He created a certain atmosphere—the room was semi-dark, there were candles around, and he instructed this person that when he put her into a trance, he would read something to her and, when he gave her a signal, she would repeat it verbatim. I don't know if it was staged or spontaneous—I never was quite sure—but this is what happened. He picks up a box of shoe polish and starts reading all the directions, on the four sides, including the manufacturer, and he repeats all this to his subject and then he says, "I want you to repeat exactly what I've just said to you." And she did. The whole thing, all the instructions, in the right order. He's all of fifteen years old. That was part of the appeal for him, being in that kind of control of the situation and giving someone directions. He was like a puppeteer. But Lenny was extremely popular. There was something very soft about him.

Cohen had at least one romantic dalliance that summer.

MARILYN REGENSTRIEF SCHIFF: I don't think the person would want it to be publicly known because there were complicating factors. That person was engaged to be married. He did not break up the relationship because she ended up getting married. There was no public phone at camp. If you wanted to speak to family or anyone, [you] had to go into a phone booth in town. So Leonard would be in the phone booth with her and she would sit on his lap with his arms wrapped around her while she called her fiancé. He was quite a Romeo. He also had friendships with a couple of other people—a secretary in the office. I don't know if it was a romance. I know he liked her. Some were quite a bit older.

The guitar Cohen used at camp must have belonged to a friend because Cohen later said he purchased his first guitar that fall, just before his birthday.

LEONARD COHEN: I bought [it] in a pawnshop in Montreal . . . I'd spent a summer at a camp that happened to have a left-wing director, who introduced me to the protest song and, through that, the folk song. The heroes were Paul Robeson, Leadbelly, Pete Seeger, and others like them.

Cohen returned to Camp Sunshine the following summer as a junior counsellor. His follow-up assessment was also positive. "He proved himself very original in many endeavours which his bunk undertook and made ample use of his imagination. His interests were many and varied. He often led the camp in singsong, and made good use of his guitar as an accompanist. A good knowledge of camp crafts was very useful in pioneering and overnight hikes. He also served as assistant to Peter Starke at the waterfront, and directed the Counsellors' show. This impressive list of achievements did not cause him to become swell-headed. He was on excellent terms with the rest of the staff and did much to undermine the efforts of a few members of the staff who tended to exert influence in the wrong direction. Though young in years, Len has shown himself to be quite mature. His interests and activities are not frivolous, but tend to be associated with the finer aspects of our culture. He is an intelligent boy who can fully understand the responsibilities of a bunk counsellor. He was very often entrusted with tasks above the bunk counsellor level, and carried these out in a satisfactory manner."

DAN USHER: The camp influenced us both greatly. It influenced Leonard because it gave him music in a way he never had [it] before. I became interested in politics in a way I never was before.

Cohen stayed in touch with several friends from his camp days, including Marilyn Regenstrief.

MARILYN REGENSTRIEF SCHIFF: I left McGill to go into nursing school and I'd see him occasionally. We'd walk around the hospital or go to a movie. Leonard would come over to my house and have a meal. He enjoyed my family. We were on the same wavelength in terms of politics and religion. My father was an artist by profession and had a creative bent. My parents were very iconoclastic and it was that aspect of me and my family that Leonard was attracted to, that openness to life and to the world.

Their relationship eventually petered out, as their spheres of interest diverged, but not before one other memorable encounter.

MARILYN REGENSTRIEF SCHIFF: We kept in touch for about two and a half years after camp. One Saturday afternoon, he came over to my house and I was talking about our mutual friend Alfie, bemoaning the fact that [Alfie was in Toronto] and 396 miles was a long distance to [conduct] a romance over, and he said something I'll never forget.

He was like a wise old man giving advice. "You are behaving like there is only one person in the whole world you are meant to be with and to love. You know, the world is full of people and who knows? This is how you feel now, but that may not persist. You may meet someone else." He was very clear in his analysis. And I looked at him because this was his close friend too, and I adored Alfie and was very romantically involved and I thought to myself, "Leonard is being so presumptuous that I can even think about someone else at this point." But he was, of course, right and, when I think back, he was a year younger than I was, and hadn't yet had a lot of the life experiences I was having, in terms of responsibility, my life-and-death situations in nursing. But he was absolutely right. His take on people in general, their personality and situations—he could sum them up with a very neat phrase, sometimes sarcastically, sometimes humourously. He could encapsulate a thought quickly, with a word or a phrase.

A fourth pivotal event is thought to have occurred in 1949 as well.

BARRIE WEXLER: Leonard told me that an uncle of his took him to a barbershop in an old downtown hotel. There was a Japanese barber with a shaved head who talked to him about Zen. Leonard liked talking to the guy, and used to go back by himself, timing his visits at off-hours when there weren't other customers so he could engage him in conversation. I recall him saying that the barber would expound on Zen practice for a while, then suddenly break off and say, "Now it's time to cut your hair," and not say another word. Leonard later spent decades involved with Zen Buddhism, but his first encounter with the practice was with a Japanese barber.

According to his high school graduation yearbook, Cohen was also a cheerleader, a member of the Menorah Club, the Art Club, the Current Events Club, and the YMHA. His ambition, he wrote, was "World famous orator." His "Probable Destination: McGill Cheerleader." Cohen listed his prototype as "the little man who is always there." His pastime was "leading sing-songs at the intermissions." Interestingly, his yearbook profile begins with prose by nineteenth-century British writer and poet Walter Savage Landor. The lines published in the yearbook—"We cannot conquer fear, yet we can yield to it in such a manner as to be greater than it"—are actually incorrect. The actual quote reads, "We cannot conquer fate and necessity, yet we can yield to them in such a manner as to be greater than if we could."

But Cohen also found time for girls: on the back of his 1950–51 student-council card are the hastily written names and phone numbers of two female students. By his midteens, likely seeking escape from 599 Belmont, Cohen had already become something of a night owl.

LEONARD COHEN: I used to hang out in Phillips Square and talk to those old men . . . to hang out at Northeastern Lunch that was down on Clark Street, or with the junkies. I was only thirteen or fourteen at the time. I never understood why I was down there except that I felt at home with those people.

These visits were later recalled in "Les Vieux," a poem published in *Let Us Compare Mythologies*.

ANDREW COHEN: This wandering he did in the fifties, a life in the demi-monde. What I'd like to know is, where was Masha in all of this? Why was he, a young teenager, walking in the streets of old Montreal late at night?

Later, Cohen and Rosengarten would walk to St. Joseph's Oratory, a Catholic basilica, and hang out in the cafeteria, smoking and drinking coffee. On other occasions, they'd explore the city's historic port district, looking for girls. It's presumably in high school that Cohen begins to call his friend "Krantz," likely an adaptation of the courtier in *Hamlet*, Rosenkrantz. It's only speculation, but Cohen may well have seen himself as Hamlet—the melancholic prince, given to brooding and introspection, and haunted by the ghost of a dead father.

About that time, Cohen also bonded with his first cousin Robert Cohen, three years older.

ROBERT COHEN: We'd go out drinking or looking for girls. We'd go to really crummy, seedy joints in the east end. They had wonderful rock and roll and I'd drink myself silly—I can't remember if Leonard did— and we'd listen to this loud, loud rock and roll from American blacks.

With Robert, Cohen often stood on the corner of Peel and Sainte-Catherine, singing and strumming.

ROBERT COHEN: We were ignored largely. But Leonard's voice was clear as a bell at that time, not gravelly. He could sing and you could hear his voice for miles. His guitar skills were very elementary, a few chords, and so were mine, though I later studied classical guitar. We sang "Viva la Quince Brigada," "Rumba la Rumba la Rumba-ba-la," and "Los Cuatros Generales, Los Cuatros Generales," "Ay Mañuela, Ay Mañuela"—Spanish Civil War songs—and "Union Maid," "Sticking to the Union"—labour songs—and "Passin' Through," a Christian song. He had quite a repertoire. Pete Seeger was our idol, who Robert Hershorn and I met at a leftist summer camp Hootenanny, in upper New York state. He said, "Boys, strap your guitars on your backs and walk across Canada to learn about the people." Our repertoire came largely from the leftist-leaning *People's Songbook,* volumes 1 and 2, edited and compiled by Alan Lomax. When Leonard would start to sing, Hershorn would chime in, despite a horrible voice. The three of us with our twenty-five-dollar guitars singing these leftist songs. I resented Hershorn ruining the songs. At one point, at an adult summer camp, after much liquor, Hershorn passed out on the floor, as was his wont. I took his guitar over my knee and smashed it. The next morning he confronted me, but I denied doing the deed. I'm sure he knew.

As the young Leonard Cohen prepared to enter McGill University, the foundational aspects of his character were already strongly in evidence; mature beyond his years, sensitive to the problems of others, hungry for culture, prone to ironic observation, romantically very curious. and aware, at some primal, intuitive level, that his life would be marked by a special calling.

CHAPTER THREE

Trace of a Wound, Mantle of an Artist

Leonard was very much the centre of it, without being the centre of it. I can't explain it any better than that. He was a personality from day one. He just had it.

—Lenore Schwartzman

From a very, very early time, I just knew I was going to be a writer. There was never any ambiguity or difficult decision about what I wanted to be.

—Leonard Cohen

The surface life of familial privilege, easy access, and expectation that Leonard Cohen had enjoyed in his boyhood continued as he entered McGill University in the autumn of 1951, just before his seventeenth birthday. If there was any evidence of the depression that would haunt his later years, any hint of an emotional vacuum created by the death of his father, it was carefully masked.

In entering McGill, Cohen would have been conscious of an absurd cultural contradiction. Although a full third of the student population were Jews, the curriculum included not a single reference to Judaism or the Jewish people.

RUTH ROSKIES WISSE: As a result, the undergraduate population tended to devalue our heritage. "Culture" for us meant Matthew Arnold. "Poetry" meant T. S. Eliot and Ezra Pound. Although we were never tempted to deny our Jewishness, it seemed bad form to practice it overtly or to mention it. Cosmopolitan worldliness was our watchword.

Although diligent in his private devotion to poetry—many poems published in his first collection, *Let Us Compare Mythologies*, were written at this time—Cohen pursued a variety of social and intellectual activities. Among these were Zeta Beta Tau, the fraternity; the McGill Debating Union, of which he became president; a Hillel theatrical group that staged *Twelfth Night* in 1952, for which he played musical accompaniment; and the Buckskin Boys, a country-music band he formed with two friends in the fall of 1952. The group took its name from the buckskin jackets that each of them owned—Cohen's had been inherited from his father. Performing at square dances in church basements and high school auditoriums, the group featured Mike Doddman, a Belmont Street neighbour, on harmonica; Terry Davis on the bucket bass—he also "called" the square dances; and Cohen, who did not sing at the time, on acoustic guitar.

SANDRA ANDERSON: Years later, my brother tracked down a story about the band from the Chambly County High School yearbook. It described the February 26, 1954, square dance as "a success in every way possible . . . a bustle of excitement and fun from beginning to end." They forgot to mention that the star of the Buckskin Boys was a Montreal unknown by the name of Leonard Cohen.

Cohen made several new friends at McGill, among them Hersh Segal, whose family was also in the men's clothing business, and Joe Nuss, who also sat on the executive of the Debating Union.

JOE NUSS: We'd see each other at meetings or during debates, usually at Moyse Hall in the arts building—the preferred site—or in the McGill Union building. It was a very active society—debates, public speaking contests, model parliaments—and it involved students from all faculties. In 1953–54, one of the topics was "Resolve that this house deplores the influence of American leadership." Some [topics] were local. "Resolve that the Quebec government was justified in refusing federal grants for education." Or "Resolve that religion is more beneficial to society than law."

Inevitably, as new friendships formed, others faded away.

DAN USHER: Our paths diverged radically when we got to McGill. But it's at that time that Leonard began to be the person we recognize as Leonard Cohen. He became very interested in poetry, began to hang out with Irving Layton. And he began to have followers. He was a charismatic personality, and I did not recognize him as the friend that I knew. He was in the fraternity. I was not. But I was in the debating society with him and we went to a debate in Kingston, at Hillel, at Queen's. He was a very good, very successful debater.

The general portrait that university friends paint of Cohen is remarkably consistent—confident, clearly intelligent, invariably affable, somewhat reserved, always well mannered, quietly charismatic, extremely well spoken, and with a definite interest in young women. And very perceptive.

LIONEL TIGER: I remember sitting in his backyard in Westmount, and I'm a kid from the [lower-class] Plateau. I'm looking around at the vegetation and the houses and he sees what I'm thinking and says, "Yes, Lionel, that's how it is."

RUTH ROSKIES WISSE: The name "Leonard Cohen" was already a draw. Already in college, he bore the trace of a wound, the aura of a lover, the mantle of the artist. [He] was the undisputed star of the artistic Westmount crowd. [He] cultivated the lean and hungry look of someone who feeds on himself but . . . lets you know that he did not take himself all that seriously.

HERSH SEGAL: He had a lot of confidence, Leonard, and a warm, humorous feeling about everything. He would easily burst into a smile.

MARK BERCUVITZ: I just remember his quiet, warm charm—an aura. I get a chill just remembering it. Everyone felt the warmth of his presence. I never heard anybody say a bad word about him.

MORTY SCHIFF: I don't know if the word is "ambitious," but he must have felt he had a calling. But there was nothing about him that suggested that he was a cut above—"I don't have time for you." There was none of that.

VERA FRENKEL: I don't really remember not knowing Leonard. He was just part of the climate.

In February 1952, when Dylan Thomas arrived in Montreal to give a reading, Cohen was among those invited to escort the poet around town.

JOSEPH NUSS: Leonard took him to all of his haunts and there was a lot of drinking. Both of them showed up in high spirits, but they did not suffer for it. It was a marvellous evening [at McGill]. I don't know who was feeding off whom. Probably Leonard was feeding off Thomas.

BARRIE WEXLER: Cohen told me that Irving Layton took Thomas to Ben's [Delicatessen] or Café Andre. Leonard said Thomas had gotten stone drunk, but strangely didn't mention he was with him. Apparently, a few English students went along after the reading, so he may have been one of them.

Layton also took Thomas to his home, but later said, "He was too spifflicated to know where he was." Less than two years later, Thomas was dead, of alcoholism. His last words, allegedly, were, "I've had eighteen straight whiskies. I think that's the record."

When Cohen and others pledged to ZBT, the fraternity, they were required to learn the lyrics of an old folk song, "The Little Turtle Dove."

MARVIN GOLDSMITH: Leonard taught me that tune in the fall of 1951. Leonard was delightful. He used to carry around a dictionary—all the time. Only sixty years later, I bumped into him at Moishes Steak House. He did not remember the song at all, not one word. I had it word for word, and sang it for him.

Written in the eighteenth century, the lyrics have a certain Cohenian sensibility.

> O can't you see yon little turtle dove
> Sitting under the mulberry tree?
> See how that she doth mourn for her true love:
> And I shall mourn for thee, my dear,
> And I shall mourn for thee.

HERB BLUMER: I was the pledge master when Leonard became a member. He was very smart—you could see that. One of the requirements was to learn the Greek [Cyrillic] alphabet.

Scholastically, Cohen's performance was decidedly mixed. Whatever else it might have been, the university lecture hall was not where he wanted to spend too much time. Real life was elsewhere. As his friend Irving Layton once said, "Unlike the scholar or literary historian who writes about life, the poet enjoys it, lives it." At McGill, he might well have thought one essentially studied and therefore lived in the past. Dead languages like Latin, old philosophies, ancient political systems, outmoded forms of English verse, and historic mercantile arrangements all seemed to bear little relationship to modern life. Some echo of the past's relentless grip on life was recorded later in his novel *Beautiful Losers*, "How can I begin anything new with all of yesterday in me?"

Even before he met Layton, Cohen was more focused on the here and now. He did not need professors to provide exegeses of great books. He could do that himself. Cohen did, however, take literature classes with professor and poet Louis Dudek, and befriended the circle of aspiring writers that coalesced around him.

RUTH ROSKIES WISSE: I believe it was Louis who introduced me to Leonard. Certainly it was because of Leonard that I began to call my teacher "Louis." Still an undergraduate, Leonard did not treat his teacher with my kind of deference, but more like a colleague, on equal terms. Louis seemed to prefer it that way.

Another Dudek protégé, Morty Schiff, co-edited *Forge*, the McGill literary journal, with Cohen and Daryl Hine.

MORTY SCHIFF: Leonard was already somehow a presence—at parties, receptions, poetry readings. The *McGill Daily* had a poetry competition. One year, the winning poet was Leonard Cohen and second place was Morty Schiff. From early on, I knew I would never be second to none.

ANNE COLEMAN: That was 1954. He won first prize for "The Sparrows," [which begins] "catching winter in their carved nostrils." I won for the short story. We were both on the front page of the *McGill Daily*.

Decades later, the alumni found themselves side by side once again; the French translation of Anne Coleman's memoir, *I'll Tell You a Secret*, was reviewed on the same newspaper page as a review of the French translation of Cohen's *Book of Longing*.

RUTH ROSKIES WISSE: [Dudek's] Great Writings of European Literature was the only undergraduate course that satisfied my idea of the intellectual life. Dudek . . . drove us through the modern classics like sheep before a storm. October 7: *Candide*; October 12: *Zadig*; October 21: *Rameau's Nephew*; October 26: Rousseau's *Confessions*; November 2: *La Nouvelle Héloïse*.

LIONEL TIGER: The literary community revolved around Dudek, who was remarkably influential in a subversive way, because he was teaching great books that weren't just English literature. I used to write poetry too, and was part of the puffy, self-important literati.

GEORGE ELLENBOGEN: My mentor was Dudek. He was a wonderful teacher, in that he allowed his students to discover themselves.

The class of about fifty met Mondays, Wednesdays, and Fridays, 5 to 6 p.m.

RUTH ROSKIES WISSE: Dudek . . . did not try to convert us to any system of belief. It was enough to pry us loose from the culture of our homes, from bourgeois platitudes, and in particular from religion, which Dudek identified with Catholic dogma, as the root of error. The revolution launched by Rousseau and Voltaire against established authority and the Church was to guide us in the management of our own eventual rebellion. Where we lived, 395 miles north of Greenwich Village, the modern period had barely begun . . . In that suffocating atmosphere, Voltaire's assault on organized religion sounded as seditious as on the day it was written.

Some years later, Dudek told a newspaper reporter how Cohen would sit in his classes, "listening quizzically." One day, after Cohen submitted a poem he'd written, Dudek told him, "Your sex life is no longer a secret, because the poem tells everything about it symbolically." Another, possibly apocryphal, story has Dudek reading new poems by Cohen and, on the spur of the moment, conducting a mock knighting ceremony in a McGill corridor, dubbing his kneeling disciple "Poet" with a rolled-up manuscript.

PETER DALE SCOTT: A poetry group used to meet in my father's house— my father [Frank Scott], Louis Dudek, Irving Layton, Leonard, myself. I lost out, being my father's son. Leonard was obviously going places. It was very inhibiting for me. I was dominated not only by my father, but by someone five years younger than me. The same was true with women. My father would brag to me about his philandering, and Leonard was seeing all these women. Again, I was getting it from both sides. It was embarrassing. I definitely had to get out of there. I joined the Foreign Service.

AVIVA LAYTON: Every Sunday night, Frank would have a soiree. A beautiful house in Westmount. He was the one with position and power. A lovely wife, Marion. And an equally lovely mistress, Phyllis Webb, tall and elegant.

PHYLLIS WEBB: That was kind of awkward, because Peter Scott was quite attracted to me, and when he was trying to seduce me, to put it mildly, I had to tell him—"it's your father," though subconsciously he must have been aware.

AVIVA LAYTON: I was tongue-tied when Irving brought me there. I'd never been in such circumstances. It was very intimidating. Everyone would bring out poems and dissect them. Once, Irving read a poem, and Art [A. J. M.] Smith started sobbing, loudly. *Paroxysms* of tears. He said, "I always cry when I hear great art."

LEONARD COHEN: Scott was an incredible teacher. We used to sit in a group, and he'd be very critical of our work. One time, he read a poem to us, and it really wasn't very good. We attacked him rather viciously, and he started crying. We couldn't believe it. He cried, and admitted that he had been too busy with his law practice, that he hadn't attended to his duty as a poet. It meant a lot to him. He set a wonderful example.

One night, Scott hosted a more intimate gathering that featured Cohen's poetry.

SARAH AVERY KELLY: I was in the same small tutorial group as Leonard for Louis Dudek's class. He came regularly. He was just one of the group. I recall no feeling that he was anybody special. We talked and chatted, to and from class. He was an easy person to talk to, no strain at all. Around November [it might have been 1954] he asked me if I'd go out with him, to an unspecified event. He picked me up at RVC [a McGill dormitory] and we hopped on the bus to Clark Avenue— Frank Scott's house. Marion was there to greet us. Louis Dudek and Hugh MacLennan—I don't remember anybody else. Obviously, it was a night for Lenny, as he was known then, to read his poetry. It was about him. Marion was in and out with soft drinks, tea, and coffee. I was the only other female there. He read his poetry and I could swear he played his guitar. We were there a couple of hours, a very relaxed, positive evening. They held him in very high regard. I felt very much that they were seeing him as the future. They asked him wonderful questions about why he was doing certain things. One of the questions might have been about putting the poetry to music.

It proved to be her first and only date with Cohen.

SARAH AVERY KELLY: It was my one moment of glory. I didn't fulfil his dreams or desires. The potential was there, but we never had to face any issue. I would have said no, no matter what. I probably gave off that vibe. But I would have definitely gone out with him again.

Ironically, Avery ended up marrying into the extended Scott family. Although Peter Scott and Cohen had both attended Westmount High, they had only met at McGill, where Scott, five years older—with a PhD from Oxford—was lecturing in the political science department.

PETER DALE SCOTT: We used to drink at the Café André, which we called the Shrine. I was then engaged to the woman who became my wife, and she was at Radcliffe. Leonard had a friend at the Rhode Island School of Design, Freda Guttman. One fall, 1955, Leonard and I drove down to see them. He had a car and I didn't. He taught me how to drive on that trip. He dropped me in Boston and went on to Providence. Freda was friendly with Yafa Lerner—there was a kind of a set. Freda had trouble with her parents and one night stayed at my house. I presumed Leonard had dated them both.

Cohen contributed poems to *Forge* and to *CIV/n*, a journal edited by Dudek's second wife, Aileen Collins.

JOE NUSS: Every year, a new magazine came out. *CIV/n* was one. But there were others. *Delta*, which had a two-year life-span, and another called *Yes*, taken from the last line of *Ulysses*. You had a very fertile, vibrant literary scene with great figures—A. M. Klein, Dudek, Scott, and of course Layton, who was at Sir George Williams [now Concordia]. Layton was at all the soirees.

GEORGE ELLENBOGEN: Irving was an overbearing presence and a weight many students never managed to shed. Henry Moscovitch was one [under Layton's spell]. Leonard never had that weight over him. He really developed a manner of speaking that was strong enough to overcome any other presence. He was able to admire Layton for the talent Layton had. Layton brought his own idiom to the table. There was no other poet like Layton in the country at that time. There was a brashness about him. He was inimitable.

In addition to Dudek, McGill's English department was then staffed with several remarkable teachers.

MICHAEL GNAROWSKI: Hugh MacLennan had two novels [*Barometer Rising* and *Two Solitudes*] under his belt, and Constance Beresford-Howe . . . had published her first novel at twenty-two. Harold Files, an expatriate American who was a strong believer in creative writing, and Arthur Phelps, author of the pioneer study called *Canadian Writers*. And Frank Scott, not quite English department, but an iconic figure in Canadian modernism in poetry. Thus an environment of influences and mentoring—a powerful stimulus for the writers, poets, and graphic artists who milled about the campus and gathered at drinking spots. In those days, two ten-ounce glasses of beer could be had for a quarter.

Even then, almost everyone seemed to recognize Cohen's talents.

RUTH ROSKIES WISSE: Leonard . . . was clever, shrewd, even a little sly, with a satirist's critical intelligence. [He] gave the impression of being a little unsure about everything—except his talent. Even then, he'd gotten clear of Louis [Dudek], not only because he considered himself the truer poet, but because he was cannier all around, in his handling of people and in his understanding of markets and fame.

GEORGE ELLENBOGEN: You'd have to go back to Ben Jonson writing in the late sixteenth century to find that sensitivity to sound. He had an incredible ear.

VERA FRENKEL: [Leonard was another Westmount Jew] except for his poetry—[and for that] I forgave him everything. It was succinct, personal. I was convinced by it. It did not suffer from an excess of rhetoric. It did seem genuine. He was a very good marketer of pain. It awoke empathy. Poor man. The women lined up to comfort. He did that very well.

MICHAEL GNAROWSKI: Soon after his arrival on campus, Cohen was noticed as someone of unusual imagination and original verbal skills. He read his poems at the McGill Literary Society, had some published in the *McGill Daily* and *Forge*. At Dudek's classes, he appeared, on occasion, with his guitar, which was carefully stood against the wall. Early on, Cohen understood the dramatic potential in something as low-key as the average poetry reading.

It required no small amount of courage, of course, to read one's work before an assembly of equally ambitious poets.

LEONARD COHEN: Our group was quite ferocious. When you read your work it was in your best interest to be ready to defend it. "Why that word? That's shit!" . . . There was a type of aesthetic, never really defined: of confession, of modern language, of strong images, of authority in music. It was not at all academic . . . The academic establishment was still influenced by the Romantic poetry of the nineteenth century—Keats, Shelley, Wordsworth. We were interested in creating a language closer to our rhythms, that spoke to our own towns and our own lives.

Later, citing Dudek, Layton, and Hugh MacLennan as supporters of his work, Cohen would look back on this period as a time of "mutual apprenticeship," one that conferred a sense of belonging. "Training was intense, rigorous, taken very seriously, but the atmosphere was friendly." Occasionally, tears would be shed or rage vented.

LEONARD COHEN: But interest in the art of writing was at the centre of our friendship . . . There were no barriers, no master–student relationships. They liked our girlfriends. These men were so generous that they helped me to become secure with myself. Looking back, their generosity astounds me. But as far as my work goes, I don't think those men influenced me. I was touched by them.

DOUG GIBSON: Hugh MacLennan was very much of his generation. He told me that he and Leonard had frank conversations about the sexual opportunities Leonard was finding opening up. Hugh sat there listening, unimpressed, and finally said, "Leonard, you're just like a girl I knew back in Nova Scotia. We called her Anytime Annie." Leonard liked the story. I don't think in any way it inhibited his behaviour.

MacLennan's love of literature had been almost palpable.

DOUG GIBSON: One day, Leonard told me, Hugh was teaching the modern novel, and became so moved talking about James Joyce, his loneliness in exile, that he collapsed into silence and tears. And the class simply, finally, filed out, to leave him alone. Leonard told it admiringly.

As an aspiring poet, Cohen was already keenly aware of Montreal's literary lineage, particularly its Jewish dimension.

DAVID SOLWAY: Among the Jewish poets, the original prophet was A. M. Klein, and he passed the mantle, like Elijah to Elisha, to Irving Layton. And Irving in later years gave the mantle as a gift to Leonard.

LEWIS FUREY: Leonard said wonderful things about Layton—that he opened the door on writing about your own life. Confessional poetry, which practically all of it was. Irving was as generous with him as Leonard later was with me.

In the early 1950s, after publication of his novel *The Second Scroll*, A. M. Klein began to exhibit symptoms of mental illness—paranoia and feelings of persecution. There were at least two suicide attempts; after one of them, in the summer of 1954, Klein was hospitalized.

SEYMOUR MAYNE: There's an apocryphal story that Klein lost his temper talking to his wife, picked up a kitchen knife, and held it up like Avraham Avinu [our father, Abraham] over the bound Isaac. He was so shocked by his act that he decided to commit himself to the Protestant Hospital that specialized in patients with mental health crises. There, he was subjected to electric shock treatment that clearly unnerved him. He came out, resigned from his law firm and the editorship of the *Canadian Jewish Chronicle*, and began his reclusive public silence.

Klein did speak again, on November 22, 1955, at Moyse Hall, his first public appearance in five years.

LEONARD COHEN: After the reading, I went up and said, "You wrote this review [of my grandfather's book] some years ago." He remembered [my grandfather] and asked after [him].

SEYMOUR MAYNE: Later, Layton took Leonard to visit Klein at his house on Querbes Avenue.

LEONARD COHEN: I visited Klein with Irving several times. I lived the world of Montreal poetry. That was my universe. There were different lines which I thought I inherited: there was a Jewish line; there was Montreal; there was that kind of consecrated expression called poetry; the lines crossed all over the city. And there was the priestly hierarchy, which I took quite seriously. In some part of my young soul, I took that very seriously.

Cohen later acknowledged that his poem "To a Teacher," published in 1961, was about Klein, "a Montreal poet who went over the edge."

LEONARD COHEN: [Klein's] oratorical style was impressive. He was one of the best debaters to ever come out of McGill. I saw Klein as . . . a guy who had a perspective on the country, and on the province. He made a step outside the community. He was no longer protected by it, much less protected than [Mordecai] Richler, for instance. It's not a shtetl that he's talking about. It's not the shtetl sensibility. It's Hebraic, it's biblical. Layton was influenced by Klein's predicament. Layton and I talked about Klein for hours and hours.

MUSIA SCHWARTZ: I met Klein once. He was into his mystical escape. Irving worshipped him. There was no ambivalence there. But then, of course, it helped that [Klein] was dead, intellectually.

If Cohen was interested in anything beyond literature at the time, it was not reflected in his academic performance. He often skipped classes and, according to Hersh Segal, seldom paid attention when he did attend.

HERSH SEGAL: But he always had something smart to say. There was a professor [Michael] Brecher, who taught political science. He always tried to trap Leonard. But Leonard came up with that crooked little smile, and was an excellent speaker and a nice thinker.

MICHAEL BRECHER: Trying to trap a student, even playfully, was never my style in sixty-six years of teaching. My only recollection is that he had no interest in political science and was a very poor student . . . one of the few students among thousands that I encountered who failed to pass my course. His talents clearly lay elsewhere.

A central focus of Cohen's extracurricular activities was the Zeta Beta Tau fraternity house, at 3483 Peel Street. To a man, his frat brothers remember him the way his friend Paul Rosman does—as a "gentle, soft-spoken, very nice person, with an extraordinary winning personality. Everyone liked him."

NOOKIE GELBER: We bought that [fraternity] house around that time. We raised money from parents of members and from graduates. The fraternity was very important, particularly in Montreal, because Herman Abramowitz, who'd been the rabbi at Shaar Hashomayim, had been one of the founders of ZBT. Other fraternities would not accept Jews, so the Jews formed their own.

MARK BERCUVITZ: In first year, Leonard and I won a joint award as outstanding pledges, based on persona. We were different. He was introspective and artistically driven. He used to carry around a dictionary. But he was delightful. He was charming. He was whimsical, wry.

HAROLD ASHENMIL: I was in awe of him because I couldn't believe anybody spoke English like he did. Leonard was one of the boys, but he wasn't that flamboyant. He wouldn't be provocative. He was in some ways retiring.

In his final year at McGill, Cohen was elected president.

HARVEY YAROSKY: It's a rather conventional thing, being a fraternity president, and one would expect the unconventional from Leonard. It's a tribute to him that he could operate on several planes. He was a very popular president.

MARVIN SMITH: Leonard was pretty strict. We took some meals at the frat house and he wanted us to wear shirts and ties for dinner.

DANIEL KRASLAVSKY: Leonard was always special. He had charisma and was the focal point of any gathering, big or small. He was very intuitive. We had a frat brother from New York who seemed reluctant to chase women, but was definitely not gay. Leonard asked him if he had [contracted] a venereal disease from his first sexual exploit [and been] cured physically but not mentally. Leonard got it right.

On one occasion, Cohen, Kraslavsky, and his girlfriend were walking on Stanley Street and came upon a young girl sitting on a collection of household items.

DANIEL KRASLAVSKY: Lenny asked her if she was moving. The girl explained that the stuff belonged to the people in the rental unit above her home. They had not paid their rent, so "we had to throw them out." Leonard went on to talk about how the little girl was being conditioned by her parents to eschew any empathetic instincts she might naturally feel towards the family's tenants. That was exemplary of Leonard—most would not stop to talk, let alone consider the impact an upbringing like hers would have.

BARRIE WEXLER: Leonard not only gave everyone the benefit of the doubt—he went looking for it.

Cohen shared a room with Rosengarten.

MARVIN SMITH: He and Morton—we called him Rosenkrantz—were inseparable.

NOOKIE GELBER: They were always together. They spent a lot of time at Robert Hershorn's home on Westmount Avenue. The three of them got involved with drugs very early. What I remember distinctly is that while all of us went to classes, Leonard was in the fraternity house for hours with his guitar.

HAROLD ASHENMIL: He was always playing guitar, in his room upstairs and in the common room downstairs. The fraternity was our community centre.

LIONEL TIGER: I'd see Leonard at parties. We had the same interest in trying to catch girls with our guitars. He was much more effective. I became painfully aware of his reputation when he'd end up going home with somebody from a party [and I didn't]. He was not rich and famous, but he was kind of famous, and he was thought to be rich, because of the family clothing business.

HARRIET LAZARE: I was dating someone from ZBT, and Leonard was always there in the corner, with his guitar.

MARVIN SMITH: There were several of us living [upstairs]. Paul Rosman— he was studying medicine—used to scream at us because we were making too much noise, clowning around. Leonard on guitar, Morton on banjo. We all pretended we were artistic types, wearing black sweaters, bohemians.

PAUL LOWENSTEIN: He used to lead fraternity meetings with his guitar. On one occasion, the city raised streetcar fares, and the students started to push the streetcars over. Leonard conducted one meeting and made up a song called "Montreal Streetcar," very melodic. My wife still remembers it, though she wasn't even at McGill then.

The streetcar protest—against a fare increase of 2.5 cents (from 10 to 12.5 cents)—occurred on December 9, 1955, and involved 2,500 students. More than one hundred streetcars and buses were damaged. Cohen himself was arrested and charged with obstructing justice, and later appeared in court with his mother, sister, and a lawyer. The charges were suspended.

BARRIE WEXLER: He said he was leaning against a lamppost watching at what he thought was a safe distance, when he was unceremoniously swept up with the protesters by the cops. He described himself as an ambivalent anarchist, which fits in with his later behaviour in Havana [1961] and Aix-en-Provence [1970]. But he was proud of being incarcerated nonetheless.

Many years later, Cohen evoked this event in a poem called "Streetcars," published in *Stranger Music*: *"A lovely riot gathers the citizenry / into its spasms / as the past comes back / In the form of golden streetcars."*
    Cohen wrote at least one other song at the time that is still remembered.

ANTON RAFF: It was a ribald song. "I love my girl, yes I do, yes I do. I love her truly. I love the hole she pisses through. I love her teats, tittely-itz, tittely-itz. And her big brown asshole. I'd eat her goop with a rusty scoop. Indeed I would." It had a melody. He sang it just when we were hanging out.

MARK BERCUVITZ: Leonard had his guitar and we'd sing. I remember singing "Tom Dooley" with him. He was dating Freda Guttman then. At one point, I went out with Nancy Bacal, his friend. Her father was Leonard's pediatrician. But he was already searching, going off on different tangents. I always had the impression that he wasn't really a happy guy. He was always searching for something else. His quest for women was all part of that searching. Many of us, coming from less well-off families, were driven to find financial success. Others, like Leonard, were free spirits.

DANIEL KRASLAVSKY: One basis for our friendship was that I was known to be a wit. I also shared some views with Leonard, especially the issues raised by [George] Orwell in *Homage to Catalonia*. Although I was a lifelong foreigner wherever I was, and Leonard was at home, we seemed to agree about people and events, probably more than he did with his Westmount brethren.

In the fall of 1954, Cohen invited Irving Layton to read from his new book of poetry, *The Long Pea-Shooter*, to frat members. Thus began a friendship that endured for half a century.

MARVIN SMITH: I have that book. It's inscribed, "To Marvin Smith, the biggest pea-shooter of them all."

ZBT's rules allowed women to visit, but barred them—in theory—from sleeping over.

HAROLD ASHENMIL: We had a couple, the cook and the housekeeper— they policed it.

MARVIN SMITH: Possibly, there was some violation of that code of conduct. The group that lived in the house would do things the rest of the brothers or the couple that lived there did not know about. It's possible Freda Guttman spent a night or two in the building.

DANIEL KRASLAVSKY: Leonard's room was nicknamed the UN because he romanced so many foreign women.

At ZBT parties, if women declined his overtures, Cohen resorted to a backup plan.

FRANCES LEFCORT: My dad [Malcolm] and Lenny both lived there. My mother didn't like it, but Lenny would sometimes ask my dad to drive home his dates at the end of the evening.

HAROLD ASHENMIL: Leonard and Rosengarten—they'd have dates and go to dances and be invited to various sororities. But ours was not a drinking fraternity. We were a little subdued.

PAUL LOWENSTEIN: I don't think that's right. I can remember lots of drinking, lots of beer.

MARVIN SMITH: There was beer, which we got for free, donated. There wasn't a lot of it and it was kept somewhat hidden.

It's not clear if Cohen participated in frat house hijinks, but Marvin Smith still vividly remembers the night his brothers "put me in a chair and left me in the street to freeze. I woke up and couldn't believe it."

DANIEL KRASLAVSKY: To supplement my income, I had a job at night as a shill in a Metcalfe Street poker parlour. Leonard kept bugging me—he wanted to play. I tried to dissuade him, but finally took him, gave him strict instructions to sit next to me, and whenever I kicked him, to get out of the pot. Of course, the first time I kicked him, he went all in and lost his stake. He decided he was not going to be a poker player after all.

To develop his literary muscles, in the summer of 1953 Cohen enrolled in a writing program at Harvard University. He later said he spent much of his time in the library listening to its extensive folk and blues music archive. Interestingly, Bob Dylan had done much the same when he first arrived in New York, sampling the folk and blues collection of a Greenwich Village club owner he knew. At Harvard, Cohen made friends with Irwin Fleminger, who became a successful American artist.

ALISON FLEMINGER: When I was in my early twenties, I got into the car with my father [Irwin] and put on one of Cohen's CDs. My father exclaimed, "That's Leonard Cohen! You like his music?" I gushed about my new musical crush. My father began laughing and said, "Oh, he was such a sweet guy. We spent a summer together, at Harvard. We both fell madly in love with the same girl, but she had a boyfriend at home and didn't care for either of us. So we bonded. We had a lot in common—his father made suits and my father made fur coats." I loved this story, because it offered me a precious image of two sensitive, authentic young men just beginning to understand their creative powers.

Fifteen years later, Alison Fleminger was deciding which Cohen biography to buy online and read that he had written a poem about his summer at Harvard—"Friends"—published in *Let Us Compare Mythologies*.

ALISON FLEMINGER: I ordered the book and, when it arrived, tore it open to page 37. I was met with a solid stanza describing a group of young men throwing stones into the Charles River. I remember my father's talent for skipping stones. I could hear him joking about seeing monsters in the water and arguing he was right, just for the sake of feeling truly alive. I didn't need any more proof of his presence, but there it was in the very last line, "And Irwin, who sculptured us all in white marble."

His devotion to writing aside, Cohen was most active in McGill's Debating Union.

JOE NUSS: Leonard was an important personality in that group. He was the quintessence of a courteous, considerate person. He was urbane, and his control of the language was beautiful—his vocabulary. He expressed himself often in poetic terms, even in ordinary speech. I remember when he ran for office in our final year, he was saying why he should be president and said, "I will not wrap myself in a shower curtain of modesty." I've never forgotten that phrase.

The actual line, as reported by the *McGill Daily*, was, "I regret that I can't clothe myself in the political shower curtain of modesty."

DOUG COHEN: I'd been president a year earlier and he became president. After his term, he told me he wanted to disassemble the society. I said, "Leonard, why would you do that? It's been around for eighty years." He said, "That's long enough."

JOE NUSS: I remember one occasion where the chairman was signaling to Leonard that his time was up. Leonard walked over to him and put his hand on the chairman's shoulder as if to say, "Let's you and I be friends and I'll just continue speaking." It was very amusingly done.

MORRIS FISH: Leonard and I weren't close friends, but I was favourably impressed. What was it that favourably impressed me? He was charismatic, even then, manifestly intelligent and articulate. I saw him then, and continued to see him, as a gentle man.

HARVEY YAROSKY: What was wonderful about his debating is that he was a very cultured, literary guy. He'd come up with examples from history and literature. It was a very high-level debating style. He could make references to Greek mythology, for instance, which most people would not be capable of doing.

BERNIE ROTHMAN: Leonard and I won the interfaculty debating championship. The resolution was that horses should be exempted from military service. We argued the positive. I won the debate. I was hilarious. I knew the opposition would say horses are wonderful—why exempt them? But that was my point. Horses had been great soldiers. They should have as much as the rest of us. The judge awarded me best speaker. He was screaming with laughter. I was a good debater. Cohen was a better debater, but not on that occasion.

One year, the tag team of Cohen and Cohen—Leonard and Avrum, no relation—travelled to Norfolk, Massachusetts, to take on inmates from the Norfolk Prison Colony. The inmates, who had an impressive track record in these annual verbal jousts, won the debate. On another occasion, Cohen and Cohen debated a team at the University of Toronto. Cohen stayed with his friend Alfie Magerman.

BARBARA MAGERMAN: Later, my mother-in-law would talk about this little guy wearing a very fancy, beautifully cut suit with a red vest and a watch chain. He was just from another world.

MORRIS FISH: I remember him being cute, in an amusing way. I remember him being elegant, and part of it was the three-piece Cohen suit. He was always formally attired. Leonard was very polished, witty, clear, very quick on his feet. I think he was capable of cutting down an opponent, but wouldn't. If ever he did, it was never obnoxious. I don't remember him ever being offensive.

ROBERT LANDORI-HOFFMAN: That's relatively true. But when you control the language and when you are erudite, you can be scathingly sharp, and he was.

GEORGE ELLENBOGEN: Other debaters won debates through preparation. Leonard won by his extemporaneous speaking skill. He was the type of debater you'd see at Oxford.

AVRUM COHEN: In Toronto, there was a party afterwards with a folk singer, and when he took a little break, Leonard asked him if he could use the man's guitar. And he picked up the guitar and played. I thought he was better than the folk singer.

ROBERT LANDORI-HOFFMAN: I'd run into him in the arts building's basement and at the McGill Union. We were acquaintances, not close friends. I was an immigrant with a very limited circle of buddies. He came from an old Jewish family and was well known. One year, Cambridge University debaters came to Montreal and Leonard debated them. He was very elegant, elegant in expression, very careful how he spoke, always grammatically correct and formal. He spoke—this sounds funny—as he was dressed. He was an immaculate dresser, because he had his daddy's clothes on.

HAROLD ASHENMIL: I was always amazed by his command of the language. Most of his sentences flowed like music. To this day, I've never met anyone who had a command that came even close to Leonard's. I'm not saying his arguments weren't great, but he made them sound so bloody good. The judges were taken in by his eloquence.

In the fall of 1954, Cohen and Landori-Hoffman were matched against undergraduates of Marianopolis College, the first bilingual institution of higher learning for English-speaking Catholic women in Quebec. The topic: Resolve that the world was a better place at the turn of the twentieth century than in 1954. Cohen turned up in a dark grey suit, white shirt, and tie.

ROBERT LANDORI-HOFFMAN: Leonard insisted on addressing me throughout as Mr. Landori-Hoffman. Things started off splendidly and the good sisters were very pleased initially. Then one of our opponents—they were defending the resolution and we were opposing it—postulated that the reason for the world being in better shape than it was [was] because there were fewer condoms available in 1900 than in 1954. This inspired Leonard and [me] to spectacularly humorous, but cynically biting, turns of phrase, which brought the house down. It was enough for Leonard to go ballistic. The girls cried, during the debate, because of our words.

Later, all the debaters assembled at the old Berkeley Hotel, on Peel Street.

ROBERT LANDORI-HOFFMAN: We stayed until closing time, no longer adversaries. We continued debating things that had nothing to do with the topic—including religion. We were having a wonderful time, getting drunker and drunker. The girls drank very moderately. We stayed till 2 a.m., then walked home together, sheltered from the drizzling rain by my very old umbrella. He had further to go, so I lent it to him, and he promised to return it the next day. He never did. I never saw it again. I used to write to him about it, and he'd write back, "next year."

December 1954 found Cohen debating the proposition "Resolve that he who can, does, and he who can't, teaches." Because the debate was being held the same night as the annual McGill prom, Cohen invited all the debate attendees to "come in their tuxedos and flowing white gowns," promising "an hour of exhilarating entertainment featuring a novel twist to verbal encounter." Cohen's appetite for debate extended beyond the formal rostrums of McGill.

LENORE SCHWARTZMAN: One time, we were all at Ben's, the twenty-four-hour delicatessen. It was two or three in the morning. Irving Layton was there with Leonard. All of a sudden they stood up and started shouting at each other, like senators in the Roman forum, arguing back and forth. They weren't being that serious. Then, in the middle, they changed sides and started to argue from the other point of view.

Although Cohen's social circle was wide, by far his two closest friends were Robert Hershorn and Morton Rosengarten. Hershorn was the only son of another prominent Westmount family; his father, Samuel, a Russian immigrant, had built Hyde Park Clothes into what was probably the largest menswear manufacturer in Canada. Over the next fifteen years, Hershorn would come to exercise an enormous influence on Cohen—and vice versa. By all accounts, he was brilliant and intellectually oriented, but was a tortured soul, chafing under the thumb of his strong, autocratic father.

FRANCINE HERSHORN: [My father-in-law] was a man who made it from nothing. He wanted Robert to be a straight little boy in the clothing business. He was a rebel, Robert. He didn't want to fit in.

SELMA HERSHORN: Robert never wanted to become a businessman. But he didn't rebel. He didn't have the strength of character to rebel against my father, which is why he was tortured. He rebelled in small ways. He grew a beard, which my father disliked, and stopped talking to him. Robert studied commerce at McGill and hated it, hated being under the thumb of my father.

Hershorn rebelled in other ways as well. In later years, he dated non-Jewish women, first Alanis Obomsawin, an aboriginal, then an African-Canadian, Joyce Livingston, and finally a French-Canadian, Francine Loyer, who underwent conversion and became his wife and mother of their two children. Among Cohen's friends, Hershorn was a polarizing figure. For Hersh Segal, he was "a terrific guy, a good friend, really bright. He had a sensitivity to life, [but] was not fulfilled." For Leonard's first cousin Robert Cohen, Hershorn was "socially aggressive and awkward, but worshipped Leonard. If someone made a negative comment about Leonard, he'd be upset." For Carol Zemel, he was "repulsive—and there aren't many people I'd say that about. He made my skin crawl. I couldn't see anybody being involved with him, except for his money." Hershorn reminded Ruth Roskies Wisse of Robert Cohn in Hemingway's *The Sun Also Rises*, lacking social scruples and "the more thoroughly dislikable, the longer he tries to hang in with the crowd." Whereas Cohen was infallibly gracious, Hershorn—often drunk or on drugs—could be crude and rude. The character contrast was so stark that Mark Bercuvitz, for one, had trouble understanding their relationship.

BERNIE ROTHMAN: A bit of a drug habit? Bob was an asshole. He was a fool—that's probably a better word. I didn't like being with him. Bright, but socially inept.

HAROLD ASHENMIL: I always found Hershorn aloof, arrogant, not particularly friendly. In later years, he went to see Lenny Bruce, the comedian, and joined that crowd. But not Leonard. In some ways, Hershorn became an outsider because of his drug use.

NOOKIE GELBER: Hershorn later had a relationship with the RCMP, as an informant, and they never bothered him.

GORDON COHEN: A very heavy drinker and drug user, very socially aggressive. Obnoxious. Was he a good friend of Leonard's? Yeah, not an intimate friend. Leonard liked to party and Robert always liked to party.

SOREL COHEN: Robert was always drunk. I thought he was a very close friend of Leonard's. I always thought Robert had father issues.

Cohen's closest friend, of course, remained Rosengarten. Later fictionalized as Krantz in *The Favourite Game*, Rosengarten too came from a prosperous but largely unhappy Westmount family. Like Cohen, he was talented artistically.

LIONEL TIGER: Hershorn was more lordly, a drug addict before it was obvious what a drug addict was. Morton was shorter, always more fox-like and humourous about his life, not as narcissistic as Hershorn was.

VERA FRENKEL: Morton came from an upper-class family and I came from working people, and the difference was marked. Morton slummed a bit.

ALFIE WADE: Morton, he's a beautiful dude. He's the cat for whom the term "laid-back" was invented.

MICHAEL HARRIS: There's a picture of Morton—he was the manager of the school basketball team—and everyone was taller. But Morton always appeared taller than he was, because he had great presence. Morton is a craftsman of the highest order. In his soul, he's a craftsperson. I once watched him install a window—it was textbook. A very precise person, yet voluble and present and always with a smile.

Like Leonard, he had a work ethic. He worked until it was finished. That's a gift.

Rosengarten's family owned a house in the Eastern Townships, which became a gathering spot on weekends.

MARVIN SMITH: Morton was bright, very capable, but more private. I went one weekend with Leonard. We got into trouble. We had some females with us and maybe we didn't get them home on time. I remember Morton's older brother saying he wasn't responsible for us.

Although Cohen would eventually establish a reputation as the consummate ladies' man, it did not happen immediately.

MARILYN BLUMER: He was a terrific guy, always very different—I knew him from Sunday school at synagogue. I don't want to cast any aspersions in terms of his social life. But a friend involved in the fraternity came to me one day and said, "There's a party for the new pledges. Would any of your friends go with [Leonard]?" My friends, all of us, were very fussy, very conventional. I said, "I'm not sure. He's a little bit different." We were all very square. It was the fifties.

JOE NUSS: I was aware of [his reputation]. He was a very attractive person. It was obvious [women] were charmed by him. Generally speaking, he was a very charming person.

MARVIN SMITH: Because of his abilities with poetry and music, he was pretty popular with the females. Something of a ladies' man? Yeah.

TONY ASPLER: His reputation was a legend in the fraternity. At some party, he went up to some woman and took her hair and put it in his wine and sucked the wine off it. My sister, Shirley, was in his French class. He had a terrible crush on her.

DANIEL KRASLAVSKY: In senior year, Leonard got booked for some poetry-reading sessions in various Eastern Township locales. I went along as the presenter. We had entire audiences of bikers. Leonard was flirting with the bike chief's girlfriend and went off with her after the show. Three bikers decided to take it out on me. I was severely beaten. I eventually made my way to my room, but did not see Leonard until I got home to Montreal.

HARVEY YAROSKY: One evening, we were at a party at a friend's house. I remember Leonard trying to get the kid sister of our friend, who was probably in her early teens—to get undressed, so he could look at her beautiful body. Was he successful? No. Or, more accurately, not that I'm aware of. I don't know what happened after the party.

This may be the first reported evidence of Cohen's interest in younger women, which was to become a continuing theme of his sexual life.

Though they were allies on the debating platform, Landori-Hoffman and Cohen were rivals when it came to women.

ROBERT LANDORI-HOFFMAN: We used to compete and I won, hands down. But let's just say he was prolific. And why not? He was a good-looking guy, with the gift of the gab, and charming.

Among the women Cohen dated in the mid-1950s was Judy Greenblatt.

HERSH SEGAL: Judy was sensitive, always searching. So was Leonard, but Leonard, as a *Kohen*, was not hiding his past. He was conscious of it. She was hiding hers. My family had a country house in Dorval on the lake and Leonard would come out there with his guitar and Yafa [Lerner], though he was dating Judy.

By one account, Greenblatt wanted to marry Cohen but, at not yet twenty years old, he declined. She then went to London and, by 1956, had married Vivian Baron Cohen. Cohen apparently saw her one day, pushing a baby carriage. Greenblatt died in 2016. Comedian Sacha Baron Cohen is her grandson. There's a brief reference to her in Cohen's song "Love Calls You by Your Name": "Where are you, Judy, where are you, Anne?" he sings. The latter refers to Anne Sherman, his girlfriend from 1957 to 1958.

BERNIE ROTHMAN: You couldn't keep track of Cohen's women.

AVIVA LAYTON: Leonard was probably the most seductive man I've ever met. Seductive not just to women but to men. What is it that he had? It was magic.

ROBERT COHEN: He'd look at a girl and she'd go to bed with him, right away. All he had to do was look at her. I had a lot of experience with that. I'd be standing there and the girl would go and Leonard would follow, and I'd be left. And it wasn't like I wasn't trying. I was trying like anything.

SELMA HERSHORN: I ran in different circles than Leonard—an empty-headed girl trying to find my way and lick my wounds. But Leonard thought I was pretty. Robert came for dinner one Friday night—I was married by then—and told me he and Leonard had been driving down Sherbrooke Street and I was walking, and Leonard said, "Wow, look at that one." "For God's sake, Leonard," Robert said, "that's Selma!"

In 1955, Leonard Cohen did not graduate in the spring, as was the custom. After taking makeup exams, he graduated with three other arts students on October 6, with an average of 56.4 percent. Asked for a quote to accompany his yearbook photo, he cited Auden's "Atlantis." "You have discovered of course only the ship of fools is making the voyage this year."

JOE NUSS: He just made it. He was a poor student, but I don't think he attended that much.

Graduation, however, only served to crystallize the dilemma that Cohen had been wrestling with for some time—what to do with his life. His ambition was to write, although he knew he would have to do so over the implicit or explicit objections of the wider Cohen family. In some ways, perhaps, the absence of his father allowed Cohen more latitude to test himself as a writer. Still, Cohen doubtless shared his family's scepticism that a poet, even one who had been published at a young age, could earn a decent living through words alone.

JACK LAZARE: I knew nothing of Leonard's literary ambitions. As far as I knew, he was destined for the family business.

JOE NUSS: In our final year, Leonard and I took a European history course from H. N. Fieldhouse. I remember commiserating with him about our final exam, which was difficult. Walking back, I asked him, "What are you going to do [after graduation]—I'm going to law school." He said, "I don't know." He said something about either the family business or maybe going on with literature, but said, "Perhaps I'll do what most people do when they can't make up their minds— go into law school." That was quite usual for people in those days, because you could always do other things with law.

HAROLD ASHENMIL: I encouraged him to go into law school. His poetry was a big thing and Frank Scott was considered a prominent Canadian poet, in addition to being a constitutional law scholar. I said, "C'mon,

Leonard, form some relationship with Scott, and it will be mutually beneficial." Leonard was naive enough to buy my encouragement.

In fact, Cohen was already Scott's friend by that time. Admission to McGill Law School, however, was conditional on passing a university-level course in Latin. Cohen had taken the course and failed.

HERSH SEGAL: Leonard and I both failed Latin, so we took private lessons from an instructor—somewhere on Sherbrooke Street. I mentioned that to a newspaper reporter once and his mother, Masha, phoned me, furious. "My son never failed anything!" She was really a gutsy woman.

PAUL LOWENSTEIN: Many years later, my wife and I got off a cruise ship in Melbourne. Leonard was touring and, lo and behold, he's walking with a couple of chorus girls. We started to reminisce, and I teased him about failing Latin. He really didn't appreciate it. The chorus girls were hysterical. They loved it.

Years later, Cohen did acknowledge taking supplementary examinations to earn his degree. He had done so, he maintained, "to pay off old debts to my family and to my society. I think if there had [then] been the kind of horizontal support for dropping out . . . I would have dropped out." After taking the makeup exam, Cohen attended a four-day gathering (July 28–31, 1955) of writers, editors, critics, and publishers at Queen's University. Later, it became known as the Kingston Conference, though its official title was the Writer, His Media and the Public.

PETER DALE SCOTT: My father was angling to get money from the Rockefeller Foundation to create a Canadian Union of Writers. The conference took place and he invited Leonard and Daryl Hine, but not me.

The assembly featured some of the biggest names in Canadian literary culture, including Cohen's future publisher Jack McClelland, novelists Morley Callaghan and Adele Wiseman, and poets Irving Layton, Dorothy Livesay, Eli Mandel, A. J. M. Smith, and Phyllis Webb. It was out of this conference that, two years later, the federal government created the Canada Council, the country's most important arts funding body. In his opening remarks, A. J. M. Smith maintained that poets essentially wrote for other poets—an argument that the combative Layton fiercely resisted. Insisting that Smith's attitude reflected precisely what was wrong with Canadian poetry, Layton said poets needed to write for the wider public, and be liberated from the dusty classrooms. Cohen would certainly have agreed.

Encouraged by Frank Scott, Cohen enrolled that fall in McGill's School of Law. It wasn't what he particularly wanted to do, but it would, he thought, appease his uncles and offer a fallback position if his writing aspirations were not fulfilled. He lasted a mere three months.

SANDRA DJWA: He did tell me [years later] that he'd taken law because it was a place where Frank [Scott] had prospered—that if he'd taken law and done well as a poet, then Cohen could do the same. He found it was not his cup of tea. Law under [Dean] Maxwell Cohen [no relation] would have been tough, tough, tough.

HAROLD ASHENMIL: Leonard got into law in September, and at the beginning of December, he quit. He found law too disciplined. He was a thinker, a dreamer, and a lover.

JOE NUSS: It wasn't even a semester. He didn't write the midterm exams. My take is that Scott told Cohen there was no way he was going to get through unless he started attending classes. He had to apply himself and do the exams. Cohen's reply was not very encouraging.

HAROLD ASHENMIL: Frank Scott wanted him to stay, but law school—it was so bloody dull. You learn rules and spout them back. That wasn't Leonard Cohen.

JOE NUSS: Scott told him, "You know you can do anything with a law degree—you can write poetry. You don't have to give up your cultural life." Cohen was still resisting. At one point Scott said, "Look, Leonard, you can't leave law to those pin-striped guys on St. James Street. The law needs people like you." Leonard is supposed to have said, "Well, I'll think about it." Whatever the truth, he never came back.

Others think Scott implicitly or explicitly encouraged him to leave.

DON JOHNSTON: There was an oral examination at Christmas, and if you did not pass, you were out. It was vicious. I don't think Leonard took the exam, and I always thought Frank Scott dissuaded him [from taking it], because Scott really liked Leonard Cohen.

AVIVA LAYTON: I remember Leonard said to me, "I can't do this anymore, because this morning I looked into the mirror and saw no reflection." I think he said, "This is what happens to the devil, isn't it?"

It was the late winter of 1955. A law school dropout, Leonard Cohen now faced renewed pressure from his uncles and his mother to join one of the family businesses—a prospect he reviled. He would make no domestic waves, but the choice had been made. Frank Scott, he later said, had given him something far more important than an understanding of law. He had given him "the courage to fail." He was going to be a writer.

CHAPTER FOUR

The Birth of the Magus

You could not own Leonard in any way, shape, or form. At all.
I think he found it difficult to own himself.

—Aviva Layton

Unlike the scholar or literary historian who writes about life,
the poet enjoys it, lives it. Lives it with such intensity that he
is often unable to say coherently or in plain words what the
experience was like.

—Irving Layton

No one who knew Leonard Cohen had been greatly surprised by his decision to abandon law school. As his friend Harvey Yarosky noted, "The
law was too prosaic for Leonard." In support of Cohen's determination
to write, Frank Scott offered him the use of a small cabin he owned on
Lake Massawippi in the Eastern Townships. There, through the late fall
of 1955 and into the winter of 1956, Cohen worked on new poems and
his first novel. Then, needing to earn some money, he reluctantly took a
job at the family-owned Freedman Company.

BARBARA MAGERMAN: His uncle sent him to the shipping room. He hated it.

HERSH SEGAL: Leonard went [there] for a short time. He went over the hill from Westmount to Rosemount [a neighbourhood of Montreal], where their offices were. He told me, "I'm getting to like it," but he wasn't really sold.

LIONEL TIGER: I used to pick him up on Friday after work and we'd go for long walks. He complained bitterly [about the job]. He obviously didn't like what he was doing, but he had some filial sense of ballast and sense of responsibility. He was stuck—he had no income and the family would only give him income if he worked for them. I don't know what he did—shipping, perhaps, the lowest of the Jewish boys' jobs. He said it was making him crazy. I suggested he go to a psychiatrist. I knew one near McGill, a Jewish guy from Halifax. Leonard said, "Well, I'll have to pay him." I said, "Yeah, that's how it works." Then he said, "Well, then I'll have to keep working. That's what's driving me crazy."

BARRIE WEXLER: Just like him. He could see the end of things at their beginning—one step ahead of whoever he was talking to.

LIONEL TIGER: He may have gone for one session. I can't imagine he took it too seriously. Leonard's narcissism was of a very effective kind. He didn't want some guy who came from Halifax telling him how to live. [But] he managed to get me two suits made—wholesale. There were three grades. Three was the lowest. He, as a family member, could only get a Two—and Leonard resented that he couldn't get the best suit from his own family. But I, as a guest, could get One. My mother had once worked for his father.

ANDREW COHEN: Leonard was trapped in a life in which there was an expectation that he would enter the family business. Seriously, Leonard was never going to enter the family business. He was going to escape and his summer at the Freedman Company was not a success. My father, Edgar, a creative soul, [faced] something of Leonard's dilemma, although it was never a dilemma for Leonard.

ROZ VAN ZAIG: There was family pressure to go into the business, I do remember that. And he didn't want to. There were arguments with Masha about that. Leonard stood his ground. I think she respected and understood him.

In his spare time, Cohen continued to work on short stories, and a novel, then called *A Ballet of Lepers*.

KEN NORRIS: *A Ballet for Lepers* is awful, really bad. It had much more in common with *Beautiful Losers* than with *The Favourite Game*. It attempted to be outrageous in the ways that *Losers* is outrageous. He was trying to write a pulp novel, a dime-store novel.

Cohen regularly visited Irving Layton, who had become embroiled in a passionate extramarital relationship with twenty-one-year-old Aviva Cantor. She had arrived from Australia in the fall of 1955, armed with a list of literary contacts, including Layton.

AVIVA LAYTON: I called him up and he brought me to his house. Dudek was there and Louise Scott—Weezie, as we called her—and of course, Irving's wife, Betty [Sutherland]. Leonard wasn't there that night. I thought, "Oh my God, these are my people." Then Irving brought me back home and the rest, as Irving always said, is hysteria. We were together twenty-two years.

In fact, Layton and Cantor did not consummate the relationship for several weeks. After they did, she was never in his house again. Eventually, after a brief affair with a medical intern in Boston, Cantor rented a basement apartment at 3360 Ridgewood Avenue, near the Snowden area, and resumed her relationship with Layton.

AVIVA LAYTON: We had to keep it quiet because the only job he could get was teaching English at the Hebrew school. Had they found out he was living with [someone] or even having an affair, he'd have been fired. The same was true for me, because I [was] teaching English in a private girls' school in Westmount, the Weston School. I had to keep quiet about Irving and pretend I was all by myself.

Eventually, Layton introduced Cantor to his new discovery, Leonard Cohen.

AVIVA LAYTON: Irving said, "I've met somebody and he's the only person I'll trust to meet you. And he's the real thing." Then one afternoon, I open the door and there was a plump Jewish boy called Leonard Cohen. My first impression and my last impression were the same—magic. He was just on another planet altogether. I understood Irving, but Leonard was of a different species. I don't even know what to call that species. I knew it straightaway. I'd see him a lot, at the apartment—never out socially, I was like a hidden woman—and he was the only one I saw.

That same year, Cohen was introduced to Naim Kattan, a young Iraqi Jew who had recently settled in Montreal and was working for the Canadian Jewish Congress.

NAIM KATTAN: Layton invited me to a poetry evening at his house. And there was a young boy who read his poetry—Leonard Cohen. He was twenty-one. I was impressed and told him so. He invited me to another reading he was planning. I went to that and we became friends—not close friends, but he'd send me his books and invite me to readings. I was the only one writing about him in French.

PHYLLIS WEBB: Dudek brought Leonard to Layton's house—that's where we met him. He was Louis's protégé. It's before *Let Us Compare* [*Mythologies*] is published, so 1955, probably. He had a beautiful girlfriend with him. We were all taken with him, because he was very attractive, very sweet. Louis was quite excited about discovering him. We used to gather at Irving's place. I usually went with Frank Scott. Miriam Waddington was occasionally there. Eli Mandel, Al Purdy. Irving would read his—to me at the time—quite difficult poems. He was kind of the star. Because I was involved with [the married] Frank Scott, I had quite a lot of lonely time, so Leonard and I became friends. We went for long drives, down to the harbour.

MAX LAYTON: The parties in my father's house were frequented by actors, sculptors, poets, artists, and bohemians. My mother, Betty Sutherland, was a painter, and Irving, of course, was a poet and teacher. Dudek would have been there—at least until he and my father had a terrible argument and stopped talking to each other. My father got very upset when Louis accepted a full professorship at McGill. He considered it a sellout. Dudek put his penknife on the fireplace mantel and said, "If I ever become an academic, you can use this knife to slit my throat." They had a huge argument and never spoke for, like, thirty years.

MUSIA SCHWARTZ: There was more between them [than an argument over academia]. Louis and Irving—that was not exactly a loving relationship. [Irving's] blanket answer was, "My fame got into his head." It's not an unbelievable statement.

AVIVA LAYTON: They'd been very close in the early days, but Louis disapproved terribly of my relationship with Irving. He wanted Irving to stay with Betty. That was part of [the feud]. Louis was tighter than Irving, much more austere. They had a falling-out and they never had a falling-in. But Leonard would come every week. It was like getting a PhD-plus from Columbia University. They'd take a poem like "The Emperor of Ice Cream," and dissect it, unlock it. Why this word and not that word? And they were total equals, Leonard and Irving. It was never a mentor relationship. It was poet to poet. Irving always called him Leonardo.

MUSIA SCHWARTZ: Irving and Leonard—a very ambivalent relationship. There was admiration—no question—on both sides. Was there jealousy? How can you get this kind of a pair without it? But respect and true appreciation of the achievement, the work. Irving was a prime egoist, but there's no question how much he loved Leonard. If anybody wanted to do something to Leonard's reputation, I think he would run out and kill [them]. But there was Leonard's fame and the age difference. Leonard was entering the arena, when [Irving] was conscious of leaving it. It was Leonard's expression—not Irving's—that he had later sold out.

Max Layton—then about ten years old—remembers watching the party action from a perch on the stairs.

MAX LAYTON: What I remember very clearly is Leonard coming into the living room, where there'd be a lot of very attractive young women, including my cousin, the artist Louise Scott, who was an incredibly beautiful woman, with beautiful eyes and an amazing, radiant smile. And the women would all—you could see it—suddenly start to gravitate towards Leonard. It was like a magnet with a bunch of iron filings. The women would circle around him and he'd go to hug Weezie—that's what we called Louise. But instead of a normal hug, his hand went straight down under the neckline, under her dress. It was the most amazing, astonishing gesture, which I'd never seen any man do before. It was effortless. And it's not like she was unhappy about it.

PHYLLIS WEBB: Yes, we were quite a wild bunch.

MAX LAYTON: I was entranced by his personal magnetism, by his voice and the sound of his guitar. At one point, I asked him if I could hold the guitar. So he let me have it—a beautiful memory, a beautiful nylon-stringed guitar—and showed me E-minor, a chord that takes only two fingers, the easiest chord there is. He let me take the guitar up to my bedroom. My mother later traded a painting of hers in return for Leonard giving me guitar lessons.

In May 1956, Cohen's first book of poetry, *Let Us Compare Mythologies*, was published. Containing forty-four poems written between his fifteenth and twenty-first birthdays, and dedicated to the memory of his father, this inaugural volume of the McGill Poetry Series had a press run of five hundred copies. On the cover was a line drawing by his girlfriend Freda Guttman, depicting a woman either being attacked by or taking shelter under the wings of birds. It was out of print within a year. Today, first editions sell for $14,000 US or more.

RUTH ROSKIES WISSE: Dudek had decided to launch the McGill Poetry Series with a volume of Cohen's verse, to be published while its author was still in college.

Had he remained in law school that year, Cohen would still have been a student.

AVIVA LAYTON: I have a copy of that book. Irving went through it and wrote little notes, like, "Too many prepositions."

HOWARD ASTER: The mystical side of Cohen is written in that first book. That's the key to unlocking Cohen. He spent the rest of his life trying to unlock the mystery he discovered in that book. He tried everything—song, music, women, drugs, Buddhism.

To discuss the project, Cohen, Dudek, and Wisse went to dinner one night to Joe's Steak House on Metcalf Street.

RUTH ROSKIES WISSE: We could not settle on a title, but Leonard's eventual choice, *Let Us Compare Mythologies*, had the Jew playing gracious host to other civilizations, with a touch of formality that was only slightly ironic at his own expense. The title already hinted at his idea of Judaism as but one set of beliefs among many.

AVIVA LAYTON: I think Irving gave him that title.

On a piece of brown cardboard paper, Cohen had listed a dozen other possible titles, including *When I Faced the Ark*, *The Burning Oil*, *The Raven and the Dove*, *Sidewalk Games*, *Saints and Prophets*, and *The Formalities of Passion*.

GEORGE ELLENBOGEN: *Mythologies* is a magnificent book. Clearly he went his way in music and was incredibly successful, and there was something gained. But maybe something lost for the literary world, because I don't think there was a poet in Canada that had the talent Leonard had at the age of sixteen, seventeen, eighteen. He could have been the major North American poet of the last fifty years if he'd just focused on letting *Mythologies* launch him.

Wisse saw the book as a response to T. S. Eliot's *The Waste Land*, which subordinates the insignificance of the present to the grandeur of the past.

RUTH ROSKIES WISSE: If anything, the experience of Jews in our lifetime had dwarfed the agony of all earlier centuries. In our postwar period of mourning, our Montreal orphan poet drew on both the twentieth and past centuries for his psalter of the aching heart . . . In Leonard's presence I always felt alert, as though I had joined a hunter on the trail. No one else I knew took so much license in speaking the truth. One day I saw him standing with Morty Rosengarten on Sherbrooke Street. "Where are you going?" asked I. "We're watching the girls come out for spring," he said. Until he said it, I had not registered that it was already spring, or that one did not have to be King Ahasuerus to arrange for a parade of beauties.

To finance publication, Dudek presold subscriptions to the series, at a dollar a book. An advance sale of five hundred copies would guarantee distribution, as well as a down payment for the printer. Ruth Roskies Wisse appointed herself head of Dudek's sales team.

MORRIS SHOHET: Ruth loved Leonard's poetry and used to flog it all over the university. She was a go-getter, smart and sharp. I bought a copy and still have it.

PAUL ROSMAN: I have a first edition, hardcover, inscribed "To my friend Paul, B'nai B'rith, summer of 1956, Leonard Cohen." I've always treasured that book and keep it well preserved.

RUTH ROSKIES WISSE: Lickety-split, I sold over two hundred advance copies. My work as feature editor at the *McGill Daily* had brought me into contact with so many students and teachers that I was able to sell my quota strictly on campus.

GEORGE ELLENBOGEN: What's interesting about Leonard is that the persona in the poems and song lyrics is an individual who is melancholic, who chooses not to engage with the world. The Leonard I knew at McGill, Leonard the debater, was more Bernard Shaw than the Leonard of the song. Witty—an individual who could reduce a paragraph to a phrase and make that phrase memorable. In the poetry and music, he captures a persona and allows it to speak for him. [William Butler] Yeats talks in "Ego Dominus Tuus" [I Am Your Lord] about the antiself, an unacknowledged voice. Leonard finds it in that persona and he manages it in different genres.

BARRIE WEXLER: Leonard loved Yeats and could quote him. The double self is usually viewed as a dichotomy between the nature of the artist and the persona in his work. Yeats, the poet, may have been happy, but Yeats, the man, was not. In Leonard's case, the persona Ellenbogen describes as melancholic did correspond to Cohen the person. Where Cohen's antiself came into play was whenever he engaged with the world on a social or personal basis, whether debating at McGill or in a Chinese restaurant. That's why you don't find many people who actually saw him in a depressed state.

MICHAEL GNAROWSKI: With [*Mythologies*], Cohen was recognized as an important new voice in Canadian poetry. There was a watershed quality to his appearance. The great modernists had had their say and the way was open for a new generation. Lurking around the corner was the new movement, postmodernism. Cohen was not a true postmodernist, but he was the inheritor of the advances made by that interim generation more closely identified with Jack Kerouac's *On the Road* generation. With its bongo drums, whiffs of cannabis, flashing psychedelic lights—and the angry, raucous warning voice of Allen Ginsberg in the background—Cohen's advantage would be that he was a genuine poet who knew his way around words and ideas, unlike many of his contemporaries, who tried to make songs out of recycled versicles.

MICHAEL HARRIS: Cohen's poetry lies between a purely literary tradition, after E. J. Pratt, and a troubadour tradition, which has melodic influence in terms of line and line breaks and how the stanzas work. It was not musical literarily, but musical troubadourily. "As the mist leaves no scar on the dark green hill"—that's classically literary. But there's a songiness about it that is beyond the usual stanza breaks. He does it perfectly. He's gifted beyond what God should dispense, both in terms of melody and the ability to affix phrases. A. M. Klein is probably the better poet. Leonard is more soul comforting.

Validating his growing reputation, Cohen was invited to recite eight of his poems for the Canadian Broadcasting Corporation, along with Scott, Layton, Klein, Dudek, and Smith. The following year, the tape was turned into a long-playing album, *Six Montreal Poets*, distributed by Folkways Records.

Amid the euphoria that greeted his first book, Cohen spent the summer of 1956 at B'nai B'rith camp in Quyon, Quebec, about fifty kilometres from Ottawa.

PAUL ROSMAN: I was assistant director. I wanted him to be unit head of the senior boys. I convinced him this would be something he'd enjoy. People told me I'd made a big mistake because to be a successful leader of the senior boys you had to be an excellent athlete. That's what they looked up to. I said, "Well, that's not his strength, but he'll do a good job." They believed me, I guess.

BARBARA MAGERMAN: I was unit head for the senior girls, so we had a lot of contact. Leonard was short, quite self-assured, and appeared to be shy. He didn't talk a lot, but he always smiled. You knew he had a brilliant mind. I felt he was observing all the time, taking everything in. Sometimes, I thought there was an arrogance there, because he came from such a different background. He was taking it all in. He didn't miss a thing.

PAUL ROSMAN: The day he came off the bus, the senior boys were standing around and seeing this short person who didn't seem particularly adroit or terrifically well coordinated, and wasn't sure which end of a baseball bat to hold. They almost mocked him, because he was so inappropriate to lead them. Well, it took about one week in which he was playing his guitar after lunches and suppers and leading singsongs, and he absolutely had the whole camp in the palm of his hands—a Pied Piper. They so enjoyed that. It was infectious. That included the senior boys.

SHELDON TAYLOR: I was fourteen. Leonard managed a bunch of really rough and tough counsellors. These guys were athletes—big, lumbering, tough guys. They reported to him and looked up to him. He had complete control of these monster guys, who would sooner take their fists and pound us in the arm—a *zetz*. If you upset their norms, you got nailed. Under Leonard Cohen, nobody got touched. Leonard was charming. They listened to him. He played that guitar—"hey, laddie, laddie." We had to make up verses to that chorus. He got every single kid involved. He was charming, good, unassuming, delightful. He never talked about his poetry. He instituted nightly bonfires, strictly boys. We all had respect for Leonard.

BARBARA MAGERMAN: He came to camp in a little Volkswagen, with Freda Guttman. Having a car was something then.

NOOKIE GELBER: He must have been one of the first guys in Montreal to own a Volkswagen Beetle. We'd sit in that car, talking. Don't ask me [about] what. He was a good talker.

DANIEL KRASLAVSKY: Leonard was certainly the first Jewish customer for the car. I'm not religious, but I was very pro-Jewish and vowed not to buy any German products. Eventually, he prevailed on me to ride in his car, so we could take a thirteen-hour trip to Providence in the snow to see Freda Guttman [then at the Rhode Island School of Design].

LIONEL TIGER: That lovely black Beetle [was] a rebuke to the Nazis. [Later] I bought a VW in London and shipped it home. Both of us were cocking a snoot.

BARBARA MAGERMAN: I don't think the staff were expecting Freda, but she got a job in arts and crafts. She was very artistic, very quiet, very striking. She looked like a real hippie, in handmade outfits, South American style, woven clothing, shiny, long, dark hair in a braid.

EVELYN GREENBERG: Freda was very quiet, slim, lovely figure like a model, but no bling. She didn't wear any lipstick. Pleasant, unobtrusive.

BERNIE ROTHMAN: Freda had been my girlfriend—the first respectable Jewish girl I'd slept with. It was horrendous. Because you didn't sleep with respectable girls. Freda was a free spirit. It was three months. That's all I could handle. It wasn't just her intensity. She was a woman and they're much more mature [than men]. The lucky thing is that Cohen was there, and I gave her to Cohen. They were together for quite a while. Dated is not the right word. If you want to use it, go ahead.

AVIVA LAYTON: Freda was his adolescent love.

PAUL ROSMAN: Leonard was sensational. As camp wore on, he lost a little enthusiasm for the job—he started spending more time with Freda and less with the senior boys.

SHELDON TAYLOR: Leonard was a romantic, a troubadour. We built a tennis court [that summer]. Leonard Cohen was totally removed.

He'd sit on the outside and play his guitar while we worked. It was where his head was at. He was interested in music, the ladies, the playfulness of camp. He was a playful guy.

ABE FEINSTEIN: I was the senior counsellor and worked very closely with him. He had his guitar and we had wonderful singsongs. Obviously, he was adored by all the women—he just had that radiating personality. You couldn't have worked with a more wonderful person. I always wondered how they got him to come, because he was such a great asset.

PHILIP GOSEWICH: Leonard was my unit head, but I don't really remember him much. He must have been self-effacing. He was like a nonpresence. We hardly ever saw him. He was always trying to get laid—that was the rumour why we never saw him. We admired him. If we had a baseball game, he never came. When we put on *tefillen* [or phylacteries, small boxes containing Hebrew texts worn for prayers] in the morning—I don't recall ever seeing Leonard joining us for the *minyan* [a quorum of ten men required for religious services]. We were a rebellious group. We just wanted to stay in our tent and play poker and chess and read comic books. You'd think a unit head would at some point use his authority and order us—he didn't.

SHELDON TAYLOR: That's mostly correct. He had control of the counsellors who were in charge of us. We [weren't] Leonard's responsibility. Leonard was ephemeral. He drifted in and out. He was ghost-like. But he had a magical control over guys who would have sooner punched our lights out. I haven't a clue how he was able to do that. He was elf-like, but he appeared tall. He was unbelievable. He's in my soul.

BERL SCHIFF: I barely slept that summer. He was twenty-one, had just been published, and had a wonderful, attractive girlfriend. I loved her. He was playing his guitar and singing folk songs—an undistinguished singer, but charismatic. But exactly the same guy you see fifty years later accepting the Asturias Prize. The same humility. His words were always carefully chosen, even in speech. He always spoke like a poet. That's how he talked. That's how he smiled. You need some humility to hang out with a seventeen-year-old *shmendrick* like me, who you don't know. He had nothing to gain by being that generous.

DOUGLAS COHEN: There wasn't an ounce of conceit in his nature, not one ounce.

EVELYN GREENBERG: I was in awe. I loved listening to him play the guitar. He was like a wandering minstrel, a lodestone. He wasn't a Robert Redford type, but the girls just wanted to mother him. Women adored him. People ran after him—I was not one. He was quiet and cute, mysterious. He was different. There was just nobody around like him. There was such a charm about him. He'd grown up in a fine household. He had really nothing to prove. He was very easygoing, didn't make waves, a natural star. He had a lot of insecurities, but there was nobody like him. I'm not sure if he spent the whole summer at camp, because coming with a girlfriend was really verboten.

BERL SCHIFF: He was totally present, and you feel he loves you, cares for you. I had that experience. I'm sure many women felt the same. He loved them in that moment and then moved on. He was not a sexaholic. When he made love to them, they felt loved. My guess is the bad press he got from women had to do with that terrible disappointment. But every time I saw him afterward, he was exactly that person. He did not change. What I was not aware of was how turbulent his inner life was.

AVIVA LAYTON: Irving and Leonard were the same. When Irving looked at you, that was the whole thing. But the trouble was, he'd look away and you'd feel totally bereft. The same with Leonard. You could not own Leonard in any way, shape, or form. At all. I think he found it difficult to own himself.

STEPHEN VICTOR: After dinner, two or three times a week, he convened bonfires, but only for the boys aged thirteen and fourteen. He'd take out his guitar and sing songs, folk songs, historic songs, Hebrew and Israeli songs. Everyone enjoyed those, even though we might have wanted mixed socials. Those were unique experiences. You could tell right away he was a very serious guy, very quiet, and at the same time projected very great dynamism and intelligence. He was a quiet force—I could tell that, even though I was fourteen. What came across was he was a really unique guy. He inspired us to look at things a little bit differently.

PHILIP GOSEWICH: I do remember sitting in the mess hall after we ate, when he played "Tzena, Tzena," "Zum Gali, Gali," "Michael, Row [the] Boat Ashore," and "Go Down, Moses."

BARBARA MAGERMAN: He put a microphone inside the guitar for amplification. "The banks are made of marble, with a guard at every door . . . And the vaults are made of silver, that the workers sweated for . . ." Always with a big grin. Different unit heads had to read the day's program each morning on the PA system. When it was Leonard's turn, he always did it to music. He'd play his guitar, often to a calypso beat. Everybody just adored him. He was smiling and laughing—I saw no depression. At night, we'd sit around and talk. He was philosophical, a mind that was searching and looking, taking in information. He liked quiet times, sitting in his tent eating oranges.

STEPHEN VICTOR: I was head boy, and one of my jobs, some mornings, was—reveille was at 7 a.m.—sometime before reveille, go to his tent and wake him up and, if he was sleeping with a girl, to make sure she got out before reveille and went to the girls' side.

SHELDON TAYLOR: Early one morning, probably 6:30 or 6:45, I see this young lady getting out of Leonard's bed. He turns around and goes with one finger—"shhh." That's all he says. There wasn't a word spoken. I nodded my head affirmatively. It might have been Freda. She was zaftig and endowed, curvaceous.

ABE FEINSTEIN: I once discovered him with Freda in his tent at reveille and escorted her through the woods to the other side.

RUSSELL KRONICK: There were a number of evenings when we were awakened to sounds of a carnal nature emanating from his tent.

                            *   *   *

His flirtation with law school over, and his reluctant apprenticeship in the family business at an end, Cohen—in the fall of 1956—enrolled in a graduate English literature program at Columbia University. He resided at International House, on Riverside Drive, but spent many evenings exploring clubs in Greenwich Village, meeting beat writers Allen Ginsberg and Jack Kerouac, among others. His exposure to this counterculture confirmed in Cohen his conviction that the academic world could not sustain him. In a letter to his uncle Lawrence, he confessed that his "long romance with the Academy" was coming to a close. "To expand as a writer, which is really what I want to do, I have to circulate in a different world." While he was away that fall, Cohen's girlfriend, Freda Guttman, had a brief liaison with his cousin Robert Cohen.

ROBERT COHEN: I had an affair with Freda, and he wrote a poem about being cuckolded. Freda was definitely intense—no question. She and

I were competing for being neurotic. I can't be sure if it was only once [that we slept together]. It might have been twice. Leonard knew of it because she told Leonard, absolutely. She would be glad to tell him that because she always taunted him and made herself difficult for him. She was a very complex character. I don't think I would have called Leonard neurotic, because he functioned very well with girls, and I didn't.

Cohen's poem "The Cuckold's Song," published in *The Spice Box of Earth*, contains these lines:

> *I know all about passion and honour*
> *but unfortunately this had really nothing to do with either:*
> *oh there was passion I'm only too sure*
> *and even a little honour*
> *but the important thing was to cuckold Leonard Cohen.*

ROBERT COHEN: I don't think he was too put out about it, especially as the event was great fodder. The poem may have fed into his rich fantasy world. One was never sure with Leonard what was real. I don't think there was any animosity. He might have mentioned it to me later, en passant.

In his novel *The Favourite Game*, the Freda Guttman character is named Tamara. There, Cohen—fictionalized as Lawrence Breavman—writes: "Breavman and Tamara were cruel to each other. They used infidelity as a weapon for pain and an incentive for passion."

STEPHEN LACK: You get trained by your enemies how to behave. What was done to him, he then did to others.

LENORE SCHWARTZMAN: Freda was one of my best friends. She was intense, but a lot of people were. I don't know who broke it off or why. It was one of their first affairs. We were all growing up and learning.

FREDA GUTTMAN: I have no interest in discussing it. Leonard and I were together a very short time; we were very young and we were both messed up.

Some years later, Guttman gave an interview to Montreal archivist Louis Rastelli.

LOUIS RASTELLI: All she had to say was that, even as a McGill student, he was a career-driven opportunist who did not share her concerns about social issues at all. She'd not yet forgiven him for having played a concert for the Israeli army during the Yom Kippur War.

VIVIENNE LEEBOSH: He was completely obsessed with her. But she grew to hate him. Freda was my closest friend, for years. She went through a period—we both did—of starting women's consciousness-raising groups. She felt he was one of the most chauvinistic people she'd ever met. She's pro-Palestinian. They parted company on that issue, but they parted company way before that.

SOREL COHEN: Freda always was presenting me with petitions in favour of the PLO and things like that. I finally said, "We just don't agree. Why don't we drop it?" Apart from that, a very nice person.

BERNIE ROTHMAN: She [wouldn't] talk to Cohen. She had some Communist manifesto he refused to sign. He was disturbed by it [losing her friendship]. He was a very nice man. There's nobody nicer in the world than Leonard Cohen. But Freda was very, very left-wing. An idealist. And a marvellous, lovely woman, a great broad.

In New York, Cohen pursued other amorous opportunities. He briefly dated photographer Susan Brockman and painter Jane Greer, the sister of his brother-in-law, Victor Cohen. Greer later described him as charming, immodest, and irresistible. Returning to Montreal for the Christmas vacation, Cohen and Guttman attended the wedding of his stepsister, Roz Ostrow.

ROZ VAN ZAIG: I told Leonard he had to bring somebody and he brought Freda. She was a character. She lived outside the box and became an artist. But once I left, there was very little connection to Leonard. My father and Masha separated in 1957, just after my wedding.

On New Year's Eve, 1956, Cohen, Robert Hershorn, and others turned up for the engagement party of Ruth Roskies.

RUTH ROSKIES WISSE: Cohen's arrival created a stir. Hershorn quickly got himself drunk. It fell to my father to deal with the ugly scene he seemed intent on creating. This is what I remember: standing beside the makeshift bar in the dining room, my father takes a coin from his pocket and holds it out for Hershorn to see. The bad boy grins. Instead of threatening him with the rules of the house, father challenges his guest to abide by the rules of chance, which were likelier to command his respect: heads or tails—you go on drinking or you stop. Father's sobriety may have determined his win of the toss, allowing the party to continue without incident.

NOOKIE GELBER: It may not have been alcohol. It may have been drugs.

Back in New York, Cohen met and fell deeply in love with a young American woman, Annie Sherman, a lithesome brunette. Born in Albany, she was also studying at Columbia, and worked part-time as a program coordinator at International House. Their relationship is fictionally described in *The Favourite Game*. There, Sherman is called Shell, a name that at once captures her fragility and her strength. The novel suggests that Sherman was unhappily married when they met, but soon left her husband. Cohen then moved into Sherman's apartment.

AVIVA LAYTON: I think she had been married. Irving and I went to visit them one weekend. Annie was a beauty. Her forebears were Daughters of the American Revolution. I think she was a direct relation of General [William Tecumseh] Sherman. American royalty. She was a little bit taller than him, but he was bananas about her. She had very refined sensibilities. She would never, like me, say, "Shut the fuck up." She demands a lot of you, in a marvellous way, a splendid woman. But Annie was ready to commit to a serious relationship and Leonard was not.

To stay close to Sherman, through the fall of 1957 and early 1958, Cohen would drive to New York, sometimes with friends. On one occasion, with Marvin Smith, he drove all night; when they arrived, they went to S. Klein on the Square, a department store on Union Square, and bought dress shirts with white collars and purple bodies. In April 1957, in Toronto, Cohen was feted for *Let Us Compare Mythologies* at a lunch attended by Irving Layton, E. J. Pratt, and Earle Birney.

BRUCE MEYER: They had lunch at Diana's Sweets, and decided to have a picture taken. Irving says, "We can't just have anybody take the picture. This is a momentous occasion." So they hold a beauty pageant on Bloor Street, and judge the women walking by. They choose someone and tell her she's been judged the prettiest girl on Bloor Street. Would you take our picture? It was Tuesday, April 23, 3:45 p.m. It was written on the back by Earle.

In Toronto, Cohen, Layton, and other poets would occasionally read their work at the Greenwich Gallery, run by art dealer Av Isaacs. A future Cohen friend, Don Owen, later recalled that Cohen "always seemed to leave with the most interesting woman there, the one I'd spent all evening trying to get up enough nerve to say hello to."

In early May, Cohen wrote again to his uncle Lawrence, noting that he would soon be $150 over his "intended expenditure." He asked for redemption of his fourth, second-to-last bond, "so I can turn it into gears, brake-lining, food, light, etc." He reported that he had just returned, "sun-burned and incredibly healthy" from a five-day camping trip to the Shenandoah Mountains in Virginia, having borrowed camping gear from his brother-in-law, Victor Cohen. "The mountain wind and rain did my typewriter no good at all." According to Sherman, the couple made two weekend trips, but she recalls the details differently.

ANNIE SHERMAN ORSINI: I remember sleeping in an orchard of apple blossoms in March, then putting up the tent for the rest of the trip in Big Meadows [Virginia]. Cold, but warm during the day. No typewriter. No rain. Another weekend trip, late April, on the [Connecticut], more tented because it did rain the whole time. Camping beside a gypsy caravan. No typewriter. Instead, notebook and pen. No car trouble at that time. Maybe just after we left our neighbours.

Reviewing his academic year, Cohen wrote to his uncle that while he had attended many intolerable lectures, his main accomplishment was completing a book of new poems. "I feel a deep need to support myself," he wrote, "not only because my bonds are running out, but because I crave that sense of personal integrety [sic] and independence. I don't want to ask anyone for money even if it is my money." When he returned home, he would find a job . . . "probably a quite humble job and I hope that none of the family will mind having a chimney sweep or the like for a relative." He didn't know how long the writing disease would persist, but was determined to "let it run its full course, its full fever. Otherwise, I know I'll suffer minor relapses the rest of my little time. And who knows? I might even make a financial success of writing."

That summer, after Cohen returned to Montreal, Sherman came to visit. They drove up to see Layton and Cantor, vacationing at Petit Lac Long, in the Laurentians.

AVIVA LAYTON: They pitched a little tent on a little beach. We'd go there and they'd come to us to eat. We spent weeks and weeks together.

MAX LAYTON: I have a vague recollection of Leonard there with Annie—extremely beautiful and graceful and womanly. That's when my father wrote "Cain": "Taking the air rifle from my son's hand." That was my BB gun and Leonard was there, a little pudgy.

At Lac Prévost, Layton worked on other poems as well. Some of them appeared in his next book, *A Red Carpet for the Sun*. In the foreword, Layton articulates a credo doubtless drilled into Cohen: "Unlike the scholar or literary historian who writes about life, the poet enjoys it, lives it. Lives it with such intensity that he is often unable to say coherently or in plain words what the experience was like . . . For me, a poet is one who explores new areas of sensibility. If he has the true vocation he will take risks; for him there can be no 'dogmatic slumbers.' It will not do to repeat oneself, life is fluid and complex, and become . . . a one-note Johnny. Or having grown respectable, to trot out a sterile moralism or religiosity, that favourite straw of poets with declining powers."

*   *   *

Later that year, Cohen's sister, Esther, married New Yorker Victor Cohen, in a ceremony in Manhattan.

GORDON COHEN: Victor was a textile jobber. He inherited his father's business. They met when Esther was living in New York, a librarian for *Collier's* magazine. Once you acknowledged that Victor was the smartest guy in the world, then he wasn't a bad guy. He was a hundred times more generous than his wife. He was an oddball, but very smart and very religious. I had a closer relationship with Victor than anybody in the family because I used to get him his suits.

By the fall of 1957, Cohen had rented a flat on Stanley Street, the burgeoning centre of Montreal's bohemian culture.

PHYLLIS WEBB: One night he took me to his mother's house, where he introduced me to mangoes. I wrote a poem about that. One line was "I slice the flesh of an old poem I started for you in 1957 called 'Mangoes for Leonard Cohen.'" It ended up being called "Revision." But I don't think we talked about poems and I don't remember him showing me poems or showing him mine. It was a friendly association. We were never lovers—no, no. I was involved with Frank [Scott]. We were very companionable. He was a very charming, attractive person.

Cohen shared the Stanley Street apartments with Don Johnston, a future federal cabinet minister.

DON JOHNSTON: Lenore Schwartzman—we went to high school together—had two rooms, walk-ups. She had sublet half of her apartment to Leonard. He moved in, lock, stock, and barrel. There were two other rooms at the back. I was at the back—a fair-sized room. Then there was the kitchen. The one bathroom was on my side. There was one door into it from my side and one from the hall, which Leonard would use, and a third entrance from another room. You had to put a fire in the stove to have hot water. We became acquainted there and had a great relationship.

DANIEL KRASLAVSKY: Leonard and his cousin Robert Cohen and others would have flamenco guitar sessions in the Stanley Street rooms.

Leonard started to make up his first tunes. Morty Rosengarten usually went to the back room and worked on his sculpture.

DON JOHNSTON: For some reason, we had good chemistry. I actually learned a lot from him—about sensuality. I remember he once came in and said—because I was seeing women too—"You know, Don, I've decided that you're still fucking faces." Because he had a fairly serious relationship with Freda Guttman and she was not a movie star. That was the point he was making to me. He also was friendly with Bunny [Yafa] Lerner, a dancer. About others of whom he was critical, he'd say, "She still believes in the white temple of her body, Don." Like sacred territory. A very unique guy. But I needled him too. On the issue of sexuality, he was a great believer in cunnilingus. One of his poems had a line, "I lost my tongue in that fragrant swamp." [Years later], I'd sneak it into the odd message I sent him.

DOUGLAS COHEN: I remember once he was going to give a poetry reading. He told me he was going to read a poem about fellatio. I said, "Leonard, you're not seriously going to recite that poem, are you?" And he said, "Absolutely," and he did.

Cohen frequently spent weekends at Robert Hershorn's family estate, Sender Lea, near Saint-Hippolyte, in the Laurentians, on Lac Corps Nu (which translates as "naked body").

MANNY VAINISH: I remember Leonard playing his guitar and trying to show Robert Hershorn some chords. He never sang the whole song ["Suzanne"]. It wasn't a song at the time, but the name Suzanne was in the first few lines. He kept playing it over and over. Leonard was like any other twenty-two-year-old. I never would have envisioned him becoming a world-class poet and singer. None of that showed. He was very intent with that guitar.

DON JOHNSTON: I never, ever thought he'd have the career he had, because he was really not a musician and he was not a singer, and his range was narrow. It was extraordinary, what he was able to do, to turn his poetry into music.

In January 1958, at age eighty-nine, Cohen's maternal grandfather, Rabbi Solomon Klonitzky-Kline, passed away. Although he was buried in Atlanta, he'd spent most of his final year living with Masha, his daughter, in Montreal.

LEONARD COHEN: Even though his English was very bad, we were using a Soncino bilingual edition of the Book of Isaiah, so we could read that together. He'd read a passage and kind of explain it in a combination of English and Yiddish. It wasn't really because I was a devoted biblical scholar. It was because I wanted the company of my grandfather. I was interested in Isaiah for the poetry in English more than the poetry in Hebrew. Because he was losing his mind, his finger would slip back to the passage he'd just read, and he'd read it again—with all the freshness of the first reading and begin the explanation over again. Sometimes the whole evening would be spent on one or two lines.

A few months later, Maury Kaye, a jazz pianist, trombonist, and bandleader, opened Dunn's Birdland, in a room above Dunn's Delicatessen on Sainte-Catherine Street.

MICHAEL GNAROWSKI: Birdland was a run-of-the-mill night spot that featured the Sepia Revue, dark-skinned young women who danced in very little clothing to the music of a three-piece band. Louis Dudek received a phone call asking him if he'd be interested in doing a reading, accompanied by this band. In spite of misgivings, Dudek went one evening. His low-key, cerebral poems weren't meant for a nightclub environment. But he bravely suggested someone more at home with poetry reading as performance art. Thus Leonard Cohen stepped onto the stage—one small step for him, but the beginning of a lifetime of spectacularly successful concerts for mankind.

Cohen, of course, was already familiar with the format, having heard Jack Kerouac and other beat poets read to musical accompaniment in Greenwich Village. Cohen talked about his collaboration with Kaye in a 1993 interview with William Ruhlmann.

LEONARD COHEN: I'd come on at midnight, and improvise while [Maury Kaye] played. Sometimes he was playing the piano by himself and sometimes doing . . . arrangements or tunes in a somewhat subdued way, while I took my own riffs. Or sometimes I'd do set pieces, like a poem from *Let Us Compare Mythologies*. We did that off and on for a month.

It was a way, Cohen later said, to distance himself from the cloistered, if not suffocating, world of academe. But even Birdland, he said, seemed "too tame for it, too academic." The reaction of audiences was mixed. Cohen later recalled being "beat up a couple of times for the poems I read."

MARVIN SMITH: I went with him the first night he made an appearance with his guitar. It went over well. There was heckling, but he took a bold approach to the audience.

HARVEY YAROSKY: It was very exciting—first of all, that we knew him, and second, the idea that you should have a "nightclub" where the feature entertainment was poetry.

In one question-and-answer session with the audience, Cohen was asked how a poet, a natural recluse, felt about becoming a nightclub celebrity. Channeling Irving Layton, he said, "What we're really doing is bringing poetry to where it belongs. Not to the people. To the hipsters, to the boozers . . . back to music, and back to an informality and away from the classroom."

MORRIS FISH: He was both reciting poetry and singing. What I went to initially was billed as a poetry recital, or maybe just Leonard Cohen.

ROBERT COHEN: Dunn's was his first professional stint—the first time I heard Leonard play music and poetry together. I remember him singing a Yeats poem—"Down by the Salley Gardens." He wrote music for it.

ARNIE GELBART: I have images of him playing there, very well dressed, in a suit. This was before people were allowed to be bohemians.

The Birdland may not have represented his debut.

CARMEN ROBINSON: I saw him at the Chic N Coop on Sainte-Catherine Street. A room above the restaurant. There was no band—he was on his own. He read poetry and must have played his guitar. It was very casual, but more than anyone else was doing. That was very special then.

DON JOHNSTON: These were late nights. He'd come back with . . . somebody. Judy McDougall [later known as the actress Judy Gault]—he spent a lot of time with. Very attractive. I remember studying for law exams. My best studying was done maybe 2 a.m. to 7 a.m. Imagine—here you are trying to concentrate on the code of civil procedure, and I had to put up with all this activity through the thin walls of our apartment.

That same spring, Cohen received a phone call from a happy Aviva Cantor. There would be no wedding ceremony, but Irving Layton had agreed to buy her a wedding ring so that she could call herself Aviva Layton.

AVIVA LAYTON: I said, "Leonard, you're going to be best man. And we're going to go down to Mountain Street and buy a wedding ring." So we all go down to the store and all of a sudden Irving's buying a silver bracelet—for Betty! Even Leonard was shocked. He said, "Oh, Aviva, I'll buy you a ring." And he bought me a gold ring and put it on my finger and said, "Now you're married." From that moment on, I was Aviva Layton. Then we went to a little restaurant and drank champagne. So I'm the only person Leonard has ever been married to—the only one on whose fourth finger he's put a gold ring.

"Irving was so ambiguous," Cohen later told Layton biographer Elspeth Cameron. "He's very gentle. He never meant to hurt anyone. He probably felt like living with both women. It was the women who demanded a resolution."

That summer, likely to avoid another tedious stretch in the family clothing business, Cohen took a job as a counsellor at Pripstein's Camp Mishmar, in Saint-Adolphe-d'Howard, about ninety minutes north of Montreal.

MOISHE PRIPSTEIN: Leonard was very quiet, clever, and had a great smile. He wasn't one of the leaders, somewhat reticent, not forceful in his interactions, but very present. He didn't distinguish himself in athletics. At that time, he was noted more for his poetry, though he had his guitar and played around with it.

ISAAC SCHIFF: Leonard as a counsellor was just terrific. Everybody loved him and had incredible respect for him. He would be with his guitar, leading the camp in singing. It was really wonderful.

DAVID MAYEROVITCH: Leonard would hold little haiku sessions in the counsellors' lounge. I remember writing something like "The snow drifts / to the ground / and the ground / accepts it."

ISAAC SCHIFF: He spent a fair amount of time with haiku. This was a Jewish camp and some of the children had attitude. Leonard once asked a few kids to do something and they said, "Why should we? What are you going to do for us?" And Leonard said, "I will give you a little bag of honour." The children looked at him as if he had two heads. He said, "You'll get a little bag of honour." For the rest of my professional life, when I sometimes ask people to do something and they say, "Why?" I say, "I'll give you a little bag of honour." Their response is almost the same as the children's.

SHIRLEY PRIPSTEIN BRAVERMAN: Perhaps they did not care for the honour that he would bestow. My father's judgement was very good about people. The sanitized version is that my father thought Leonard was a talented boy, but self-centred. In camp, you need somebody who's willing to stretch a little more.

HOWARD BUCKMAN: Leonard was one of my counsellors. I remember him encouraging us to write conventional poetry—not haiku—and he would read the best ones. There was one talented kid, David Kligman, whose poetry Leonard read and liked. The other thing he taught me was how to throw a knife into a tree, by holding the blade. I don't know how good he was, but I became very good at that.

BARRIE WEXLER: We once tossed a ball around with his son, Adam, and he couldn't even throw that straight. The only thing I ever saw him throw properly were *I Ching* coins.

MOISHE PRIPSTEIN: Of course, the camp experience had an impact because [*The Favourite Game*] had large sections devoted to his experiences in camp. My guess is he didn't have a girlfriend at the camp, but not for lack of trying.

NORMAN SAMUELS: It's hard to believe from today's perspective, but Cohen did not loom as a giant—more the sweet poet, wry humour, serenading the girls. I vaguely recall him playing guitar and singing in small groups. Leonard was a sweet person. He'd sit on his bed across from mine and read me lines from a poem he was working on, and ask how it sounded. Since his poems were songs and often rhymes, I would suggest a word or a line and in they went.

ISAAC SCHIFF: He did seduce one of the counsellors. Do I know who it was? Yes, I do.

ZVI ZEMEL: Faigie Shainblum. Someone identified her from *The Favourite Game*.

ISAAC SCHIFF: Faigie was the arts-and-crafts person. Her father was a well-known teacher at the Jewish People's School, the *folkshul*. She was very pretty.

DAVID MAYEROVITCH: Faigie was a tall, slim, willowy blonde. At the time, she was dating another counsellor—Avi Gistrak.

NORMAN SAMUELS: If there were any relationship between them, "seduction" is not likely to be an apt description. She was a very independent and smart woman who made her own choices.

Shainblum became a multidisciplinary artist based in Chicago, and died in 2016, about seven months before Cohen.

ZVI ZEMEL: Many of Breavman's experiences in the novel are biographical. The book describes in accurate detail the quirky behaviour of a schizophrenic camper [Robert Elkin] interminably rattling off useless statistical data. Later, Cohen ends the camper's life in an accident. Happily, that was only in fiction.

JACK NOVICK: At the flagpole, we'd ask Elkin to recite the names of the top-ten songs. He would, and everyone would cheer.

In the novel, the camper—named Martin Stark—is described as "a holy idiot . . . the rarest creature, a blissful mad-child . . . He's the only free person I've ever met." It is among the first of many sympathetic observations that Cohen would make about more marginal members of society.

ROBERT MAYEROVITCH: I was eleven. I don't remember Leonard Cohen singing. That was not his identity then. He was the nature counsellor and the poet. I recall him sharing his poetry. But he would take us on hikes, go through the forest and look at flowers and, in retrospect, develop a sort of poetic relationship to nature. He might have faked it [his botanical knowledge], but he was just there to exude a sense of connection. At the time, I thought he knew everything to be known. For me, he was marvellously entertaining, an interesting and stimulating guy with slightly exotic taste. It was very much this head-in-the-sky observer of nature, and a teacher of haiku. He was the exotica, the exotic flower who came and went, a slightly bizarre, offbeat guy who made us think about things we otherwise might not have thought about.

Cohen himself seems to have envisaged himself in that role. In *The Favourite Game*, Lawrence Breavman aspires to be "calm and magical . . . to be the gentle hero the folk come to love, the man who talks to animals, the Baal Shem Tov who carried children piggy back." In time, this vision fades. "I," the narrator in Cohen's second novel, *Beautiful Losers*— arguably a stand-in for Cohen himself—becomes a ragged figure, "a freak of the woods."

ELLIE LEVINE: I was the swim instructor that summer. Leonard was friendly, likeable. I remember he had a girlfriend who visited and he took some pictures that [commercial film] developers might not develop. So he took them to David Mayerovitch, who ran the camp's darkroom. All I remember is that she had a one-piece bathing suit, with a *schtickel* material and another tiny piece and a tiny strip connecting the two.

DAVID MAYEROVITCH: I was a junior counsellor. Leonard was already a figure of awe, celebrated as a published poet, and as a ladies' man, somebody pretty special. I had a side assignment as the keeper of the camp dark room. I'd show little groups of campers how to make and take pictures with a pinhole camera, then develop negatives. His girlfriend came up to visit Leonard. I dimly remember her being brunette—that's all. I have a vague notion that she may have been from New York.

ANNIE SHERMAN ORSINI: Yes, I was invited there.

DAVID MAYEROVITCH: After the weekend, Leonard presses a roll of film into my hand and says, "I would not want to take this roll of film to the drugstore. Can you develop it?" I said, "Sure." I developed the negatives and started making prints. So you put the print into the development bath and gradually the image starts to emerge—the image of Leonard's girlfriend who had somehow forgotten to put her clothes on. My eyes popped—I'd never seen a woman with her clothes off.

I was at a stage where even the sight of a woman with her clothes on was mildly exciting. My sexual anatomical education received a great big boost that night. I dried them off, put them in an envelope, and returned them with the negatives to Leonard. He obviously thanked me. But I was either so naive or so honourable that it didn't occur to me to make a second set of prints for myself. But to have these images of his unclad girlfriend coming up there under the lurid darkroom light was a memorable experience. I have no memory of the backdrop. The sight of the body alone blinded me to all other factors.

Cohen was also rumoured that summer to have had a romance with an attractive American woman working as an arts counsellor, Fran Dropkin. His amorous adventures apparently caught the attention of camp owner, Chaim Pripstein.

DAVID MAYEROVITCH: The camp season was eight weeks long. Leonard left after the seventh week. The story I was told was that Chaim found out that Leonard was extending his charms to the local girls in Saint-Adolphe-d'Howard, about a ten-minute drive away. That was grounds for him to ask Leonard to leave. You can imagine—a counsellor at a Jewish camp is known to be tempting and/or debauching the good local Catholic, Francophone girls in 1958. Mr. Pripstein was not eager for that kind of trouble. It was always a mystery to me why Leonard left a week early, and any such explanation would certainly be plausible.

MOISHE PRIPSTEIN: Meyerovitch's story does not ring true to me at all. But after the season, Leonard came back a week later to my camp wedding with a spectacular-looking woman.

When the season ended, Cohen and Jack Novick drove to New York City together.

JACK NOVICK: He was writing "Suzanne" in the car as we were driving. He was working on it as a poem. I didn't see him in the city or afterward. We all had mixed feelings about Leonard—on the one hand, proud that he achieved so much, and on the other, wondering how come he achieved so much? He was a moderately good poet, but a terrible singer and an awful musician. I couldn't quite understand the appeal. There was nothing outstanding about him at that time.

It may have been on this postcamp trip that he finally severed his relationship with Anne Sherman.

AVIVA LAYTON: Obviously very painful, breaking up. She's talked about it and Leonard talked about it. It was his decision. She wanted a very pure relationship, and Leonard couldn't have done that when he was eighty, let alone when he was twenty. He was just beginning. She was very much in love with him and he was very much in love with her. She was one of the great loves of his life.

Back in Montreal, Cohen signed on as a partner to the 1950s version of a start-up. With his friends Morton Rosengarten and Lenore Schwartzman, he launched an art-gallery-cum-bookstore-cum-watering-hole. Staying open until 11 p.m. on weekdays, the gallery organized music and poetry evenings, and sold art, volumes of poetry, and ceramics.

LENORE SCHWARTZMAN: We called it the Four Penny Gallery, taking off on *The Threepenny Opera*. I don't remember who came up with the name. We wanted a place to get together with our friends, and found this space on the second floor of a brownstone on Stanley Street, between Sherbrooke and de Maisonneuve, on the east side. Just below us was the city's first espresso coffee shop. Up the street was the first vegetarian restaurant. Stanley Street became *the* place and continued that way for many years.

DON JOHNSTON: I recall being in the gallery. The coffee shop was the Riviera, a Hungarian place, and there was Pam-Pam and, up the street, Carmen's. There was quite a lot of activity.

CAROL ZEMEL: Montreal was filled with Hungarians who really knew how to run and live café life. They all had side shtick going, shady stuff, because they'd lived in a Communist system and the only way to live was to play the black market. Stanley Street was *the* street. It was called "doing the street."

HELAINE LIVINGSTONE: That studio was really the centre. It was like Greenwich Village. I'd see Leonard there and try to talk to him. I walked into the gallery one day and Don Johnston was the only one there and he tried to seduce me. I suspect he'd been drinking. Another time, I went to the gallery and saw a professor of mine coming out of there with a female student. Assignations took place there.

LENORE SCHWARTZMAN: The Four Penny was something very new. I ran it more, and Mort helped me—I knew Mort much better than I knew Leonard because we went out together and designed sets for shows at McGill and elsewhere, including a play William Shatner was in. But Leonard had the clout even then. I remember Saul Bellow visited and wanted to meet him.

DON JOHNSTON: Marvin Gameroff, a Montrealer who later developed much of Stowe, Vermont, was Bellow's cousin. He brought him to the apartment.

LENORE SCHWARTZMAN: The gallery held poetry readings and served white and red wine. We often spent a night, eight or ten of us, talking and drinking Armagnac, playing chess by the fireside. We were very sophisticated. It was a great time. Leonard was already a ladies' man, but everyone was, in a sense. We were all independent, all very proud of ourselves. There was a huge, fabulous group of poets, artists, sculptors, writers, ceramicists. Leonard was very much the centre of it without being the centre of it—I can't explain it any better than that. He was always an entertainer.

BARRIE WEXLER: I observed something similar whenever we were some-place where nobody knew who he was. It wasn't that people thought they recognized him. It wasn't his gracious manners or charismatic charm. It was more that he naturally embodied a kind of transcenden-tal centre of gravity that drew in others like a black hole. You come into this world with that. It's a blessing and a curse. The magnetic aura he exuded came with an equally powerful negative pole that haunted his interior landscape. It may sound trite, but what he was searching for was the meaning of what he, himself, already embodied—and, you could even say, relief from it.

SOREL COHEN: I always thought the party was wherever Leonard was—just because of his personality. Very unusual. An incredible amount of charm—just amazing. [Later] he had interviewers in the palm of his hand. I couldn't describe what it was exactly.

LENORE SCHWARTZMAN: We were bohemian, even though we all lived at home. Many people came to the gallery and it became well known. We exhibited Betty Layton, Louise Scott, Vera Frenkel, a number of others.

VERA FRENKEL: They might have exhibited me. The Four Penny is a very familiar name. I have no clear memories of it, but a warm feeling.

LENORE SCHWARTZMAN: The rent we managed to cover from sales. It wasn't much. Everything was so intense. We all thought we were really special. But at the same time, we didn't take ourselves too seriously. We'd go out for incredible dinners at French restaurants—six-course meals and wine. Leonard would come with a girlfriend. The group subdivided into different cliques. I dropped out of school after three years. I ended up becoming a commercial artist. Leonard was so involved in writing and I wasn't that involved in art. I remember asking him, "What's the difference [between you and me]?" And he said, "I don't know. I just have to keep doing this." He had no choice. He had to be a poet.

The Four Penny Gallery enjoyed a brief, glorious period of intense popularity, but it did not last. Only a few months after opening, the building housing it was consumed by fire. It was as if a curtain were being drawn across an era.

LENORE SCHWARTZMAN: Right below us was the dry cleaner. That's what started the fire.

MAX LAYTON: The gallery was about to open an exhibit of my mother's art, ten years' worth of work, a solo show, a big deal. The night before the opening, there was a fire. All the paintings except one or two, which were scorched, were destroyed—a lifetime worth of work. I remember her getting the phone call, and the absolute horror of it, the complete wringing out of her life which that represented. I don't believe there was any insurance, so I don't believe she got any money.

LENORE SCHWARTZMAN: I was sleeping—I think at home—and was woken up and ran down to the fire. It was a cold, damp, dark night. We all stood outside and watched. One of the firemen said, "My sister believes in these things [art]," so he put tarps over the paintings. We saved quite a few. Most of Betty's work was destroyed. She [her work] was in the big room and on the wall. The ones saved were in the back room. The fire was the end of it. That was the only really depressing part of my life. I really was depressed. People didn't understand. They were laughing. But it was very sad.

The loss of her art—and a subsequent attack of Bell's palsy—took a severe toll on Irving Layton's marriage to Betty Sutherland. Later that year, she fled with her daughter, Naomi, and poet Avi Boxer to an anarchist commune in California. Young Max stayed behind with Irving.

DANIEL KRASLAVSKY: I was negotiating with Lenore to be a partner in the gallery. My fiancée was a painter and several good friends were artists of quality. It burned down before they got my investment. One night, when we were on the second floor, Leonard said, "Someone is coming up the stairs and he has a voice so beautiful that when he coughs, I put my arms around my woman." Not sure if this in any form made it into his writings, but it should have.

Forced to vacate Stanley Street, Cohen rented a flat in an old house on Mountain Street, north of Sherbrooke, and began to freelance for the CBC. Soon after, he met Madeleine Poulin, president of the student council at Marianopolis College, run by nuns, the Sisters of the Congregation of Notre-Dame.

MADELEINE POULIN: The CBC decided to do a radio show on graduates of 1959, two men, two women, two Francophones, two Anglophones. Leonard had been asked to do the interviews. Somebody phoned me and asked me if I would [be interviewed] and I said yes.

Another interviewee was Tony Aspler, who'd written a speech for a debate at Dartmouth College.

TONY ASPLER: I went to his apartment on Mountain Street and recorded it. He offered me black olives from a brown paper bag. The apartment was pretty small. I was a bit in awe of him, because he'd already published *Let Us Compare Mythologies* and was buddy-buddy with Dudek. Those were really good days.

MADELEINE POULIN: Leonard was recording out of his flat. I was living in residence on Peel Street, a few streets over. He had a huge box-like tape recorder. I think I went twice. The first time there was a technician and then the technician left. We had whisky and apples. I don't know how we did the interview eating apples. And I don't know how I drank the whisky. I really didn't drink. He asked all sorts of questions. Leonard was curious about everything. His curiosity went beyond the subject of the interview. He was looking for something. He would talk about God and faith and asked what it meant to me. He talked about sex and asked what it meant to me, which was not very much at the time. That's what struck me—his interest in God and sex. They were questions that surprised me. He wanted to hear my truth about this. I don't remember if the questions made it into the broadcast. But it all led to a sort of relationship, during which I would visit him in his rooms, in the spring of 1959. I would tell the nuns I was going out for a walk after dinner, and I'd go to Leonard's. He saw me as still in the nunnery, and that interested him. He was extremely respectful of me. He did not sing publicly, but he would sit on a little stool in front of me and sing a song. I was a lady and he was a troubadour—that was our relationship.

One day, Cohen asked Poulin to appear on her balcony at midnight, a bold proposal for a young woman still living with nuns. If she did, he said, he'd bring her something.

DENNIS LEE: Boy, that's really stepping inside his own myth, isn't it?

MADELEINE POULIN: This story sounds improbable, but it's true. My room had a balcony overlooking the street. I told my roommate, Doreen, what Leonard asked me to do and she said, "You can't do that. That's absolutely improper." I agreed and thought I shouldn't, and then thought I [would], but finally I fell asleep. The next day—I don't remember how regularly we saw each other, but it was often, though not every day—he asked me, "Why didn't you come out on the balcony last night?" I said, "My roommate did not think it was proper, so I hesitated and finally fell asleep." And he said, "Because I left a poem for you. On the hedge. Did you find it?" . . . Well, no. I didn't go looking for poems in hedges. So he read it to me—I think. It was called "The Lady and the Pomander." The pomander was a spice box, a latticed metal ball or sac filled originally with dried fruit studded with cloves, but later filled with spices, which ladies in the Middle Ages carried around to avoid foul odours. That's how he saw me and he wasn't quite wrong. I never saw the poem. I went back afterwards to the hedge, but of course there was nothing there. [Years later], I googled it, hoping it might have found its way into one of his books, but it didn't.

PATRICIA NOLIN: This is a *mise-en-scène*, this thing with the balcony. He did that his whole life. It's life as a series of *mise-en-scènes*. And he's the director—an actor, actually. Even when he goes up to the mountain [Mount Baldy] and becomes a [Buddhist] monk. That's a role. You believe in roles when you're an actor. They're real. It's part of the avatars. His most successful avatar was the old man. He became this fantastic old man. But he was extremely mercurial—he's so many things—and would change constantly, like mercury. Is he the real Don Juan who seduces constantly and falls in love, but is never touched himself? But it's not true, because Don Juan is very touched.

Cohen was then still working on poems that would be published two years later under the title *The Spice Box of Earth*. The book ends with a long prose poem, "Lines from My Grandfather's Journal," and concludes with these words:

> *Inscription for the family spice box*
> *Make my body*
> *A pomander for worms*
> *And my soul the fragrance*
> *Of cloves*

MADELEINE POULIN: That wasn't the poem he read to me.

More than five decades after their brief affair, certain moments remain vivid in Poulin's memory.

MADELEINE POULIN: Once, a button on my winter coat was hanging loose, and he said, "You're going to lose that button. Give me your coat." And he sat there and sewed the button back on, because he'd been working in his uncle's clothing factory and had sewn buttons. He had a manuscript on his windowsill. He'd been writing a book [*Beauty at Close Quarters*]. I asked him what it was about and he said, "My obsession with blond goddesses." I wasn't really a blonde and I don't think I ever became one of his goddesses. But he'd been a counsellor at summer camp and told me he'd met a blond goddess there, at least one, maybe two or three.

On another occasion, as she was leaving the apartment, Cohen suddenly said to her, "After everything you did to us."

MADELEINE POULIN: I said, "What do you mean?" And he said, "You know, everything you did to the Jews." I don't think he used the word "Holocaust." It wasn't used at that time, I don't think. I didn't know what he was talking about. We'd heard about concentration camps, but the nuns had told us about the poor priests who'd been held there, and martyred, so it wasn't a Jewish thing for me. And Leonard wasn't for me part of a Jewish community that had been persecuted. The connection wasn't made. I knew Leonard was Jewish, but it did not mean very much to me.

Curiously, Poulin was interested in the Bible and had gone to McGill to learn Hebrew.

MADELEINE POULIN: The reception I got was tepid. I thought, "Why don't they want me to learn Hebrew?" I wasn't encouraged and put it aside.

The Cohen that she encountered was not lighthearted.

MADELEINE POULIN: I was never struck by Leonard's sense of humour, or sharing a joke with him. When you're young, you are deadly serious about things. Leonard was, and I was too, I guess. I didn't have the distance. Things were serious, important, all the decisions in life. It's hard to tell if he grasped my essence, because he was also opaque, dark. I think he was struggling. I was never in love with him and he was never in love with me. He wasn't a man who abandons himself, really. The hyperactive mind or imagination. We were both curious about and interested in each other and he was caring, caring, and I felt that for him. I was touched by him.

One night, Cohen answered the door at his Mountain Street flat to find Aviva Layton sobbing hysterically. She had discovered that Layton had cheated on her.

AVIVA LAYTON: "Never mind, little darling"—that's what he called me—"come sleep in my bed." And he cradled me and we slept in the same single bed for the whole night. I'm probably the only person who's slept in Leonard's bed and not slept with him. He made me breakfast in the morning. Irving fucked everybody and would let me know. It was terrible. But I couldn't leave him.

In April 1959, Cohen was awarded a $3,000 Canada Council grant, designed to finance research for a proposed novel that would take him to Rome, Athens, and Jerusalem. The following month, he submitted a draft of *The Spice Box of Earth*, which had already been accepted in principle by McClelland & Stewart publisher Jack McClelland. Although revisions were requested, he was delighted, proposing that the book be issued as a brightly coloured paperback, to broaden its appeal.

Honouring an old promise, Cohen began to give guitar lessons to Irving Layton's thirteen-year-old son, Max, in return for a painting by his mother, Betty Sutherland. The young Layton had received the guitar as a birthday present.

MAX LAYTON: His flat on Mountain Street, the very last house on the western side, had once been a stately home, but by then had been divided into apartments. Once a week, I made this journey from Côte-Saint-Luc and carried my guitar up the hill. I'd knock on the door, and there'd be this pause, and a scuffling noise, and then the door would be opened by a beautiful woman, not always the same one, but always with a towel wrapped around [her] head, having just had a shower. I understood exactly what was happening. This was part of my admiration for Leonard at that time. A teenage boy's fantasy.

The young Layton was no less in awe of Cohen's teaching ability.

MAX LAYTON: He used songs as a way to teach me chords. His fingering on the guitar was amazingly accurate. There was something very articulate, effortless, about the way his hand would move from one chord to another. He really was a damn good guitar player. It's not like he was a great guitarist, but he was extremely accurate.

In teaching, Cohen was insistent on where the fingers should be placed.

MAX LAYTON: He'd teach me a strum and three chords that went together, and then a new strum, and always teach me a song that went with those chords. He probably taught me nine chords in total, including the relative minors. One song was "Peat Bog Soldiers": "Far and wide as the eye can wander. Heath and bog are everywhere." [A Republican anthem during the Spanish Civil War, it was composed and first performed by prisoners in a Nazi concentration camp.] He also taught me "Go by Brooks," a poem he'd set to music. I'm pretty sure it's the first song he'd done that with. So I may be the only human being who knows the first song Leonard wrote. I sang it once, just after he died, but not before that. It didn't seem the right thing to do.

More accurately, perhaps, it was the first song based on Cohen's own poems. He had written others, including imitations of pop tunes, a few years earlier. In 1992, he told writer Paul Zollo that the first poem he set to music was "The Chant," which contained the lines "Hold me heartlight, soft light hold me, moonlight in your mouth."

MAX LAYTON: After three months, one horrible day, he said, "Max, I've taught you everything you need to know. From now on, you just have to figure it out yourself." No! "Surely there's more you can teach me." So it ended. But he was a really good teacher, very solicitous, patient, never critical. Somehow, he instilled in me a tremendous desire not only to learn, but to please Leonard. If I came back without having got the chords and strum really smooth, I'd have felt absolutely humiliated. So he had that teacher persona already, at only twenty-five. There was a seriousness with which he was approaching this that I understood. And absolutely focused for that hour. We'd do it over and over. And I have to say, since I sat so close to him, how handsome that guy was. His eyes were just amazing. I had no sexual interest in him, but I remember being struck by the sheer beauty of the greenness of his eyes.

It's during this period of the late 1950s that Cohen's friends begin to be aware of his depression.

DOUGLAS COHEN: Leonard would mention occasionally that he was suffering from depression, but he'd never complain about it or dwell on it. And you would never know it.

ROZ VAN ZAIG: I do know he suffered depression, even before he went to Columbia. I saw that—just very sad and drawn.

MADELEINE LERCH: His depression was bad, but Masha's was even worse. She was having electric shock treatments [Masha had been admitted to the Allan Memorial Institute]. She was not well.

AVIVA LAYTON: When Masha was hospitalized, he moved back into Belmont. Irving and I would go for tea. He took us into the kitchen and opened the drawers and there'd be hundreds and hundreds of balls of wound-up string. And corks. Millions of corks. She never threw away a single bit of string.

Madeleine Lerch, a model, had joined the Cohen circle as the girlfriend of filmmaker Derek May, who was also part of Cohen's inner circle.

MADELEINE LERCH: I knew Leonard when he was not famous. He was a lot of fun. We'd go to Morton Rosengarten's apartment and play music. Morton lived across the hall from Derek. Leonard played the guitar. Someone played the washboard. One time, Leonard and I took the bus to visit his sister in New York. We walked around, went to museums. I didn't really consider myself his girlfriend, because I already had Derek.

Cohen had spent much of 1959 working on his novel *Beauty at Close Quarters*. That spring, in conjunction with his Canada Council grant, he signed a first book contract with McClelland & Stewart. His friend Morton Rosengarten had spent time abroad in London, studying art, and doubtless encouraged him to go there. Finally, in December, passport and money in hand, twenty-five-year-old Leonard Norman Cohen embarked by ship for England. It would be as much a voyage of liberation as of discovery—liberation from the past, his mother, the extended Cohen family, the heavy burden of their expectations, and the restrictive norms and conventions with which he had been raised and from which he longed to escape.

CHAPTER FIVE

All the World Is in Front of You

The isles of Greece. No wonder Lord Byron couldn't tear himself away. There the sensual life is fulfilled.

—Harold Norse

It was as if everyone was young and beautiful and full of talent, covered with a kind of gold dust. Everybody had special and unique qualities. This is, of course, the feeling of youth, but in this glorious setting of Hydra, all these qualities were magnified. They sparkled. To me, everyone looked glorious. All our mistakes were important mistakes, all our betrayals were important betrayals, and everything we did was informed by this glittering significance. That's youth.

—Leonard Cohen

Leonard always needed to be saved and lost in the same breath.

—Vera Frenkel

In December 1959, a few months after his twenty-fifth birthday, Leonard Cohen settled in at a three-storey boardinghouse at 19B Hampstead High Street in London. Owned and managed by Jake and Stella Pullman, it conveniently stood at the corner of Gayton Road and Hampstead High Street, adjacent to two pubs, the King of Bohemia and William IV.

LEONARD COHEN: I had a bed in the sitting room and I had some jobs to do, like bringing up the coal to start the fire every morning. [Stella] said to me, "What do you do in life?" and I said, "I'm a writer." She said, "How much do you write?" and I said, "Three pages a day." She said, "I'm going to check at the end of every day. If you haven't written your three pages and you don't bring up the coal, you can't stay here . . ." She did that, Stella Pullman, and it was under her fierce and compassionate surveillance that I wrote my first novel. I owe my discipline to Stella.

BARRIE WEXLER: He once admitted to me it was more like three paragraphs a day. I don't know if he was trying to make me feel better or not.

HARRIET PASCAL FREEDMAN: The boardinghouse was a leasehold, run by Stella Pullman, not Jewish, but married to a Jewish man, Jake, who'd been a pilot in the war. She was a tough old babe, a real taskmaster. Even at ninety years old, she was in charge. She didn't have a lot of money but, through wit and a certain understanding of economy, she managed to acquire a great deal of valuable furniture, jewellery, and silver, all of it stuffed into this living room she cherished. It was as if she'd moved from an eight-bedroom house into a three-bedroom flat and taken everything with her. She was proud of every bit of polished silver. But the rest of the house was very sparse. The bathroom was minimalist.

The manuscript Cohen was labouring over was a novel, *Beauty at Close Quarters*, composed on a green Olivetti Lettera 22 typewriter that he purchased, for forty pounds his first day in London. Soon after, he also purchased a blue Burberry raincoat that he wore frequently and which, a decade later, would be elevated into near myth in his song "Famous Blue Raincoat." The actual raincoat was left behind in a New York apartment in the late 1960s and subsequently stolen.

The Pullman house had become something of a Canadian consulate. Cohen's friend Morton Rosengarten had earlier lived there, while studying art. Two other Montreal friends also resided there, Nancy Bacal and Harold Pascal.

HARRIET PASCAL FREEDMAN: Harold had lived across the street from Leonard, on Belmont. They were the same age. I don't know if they were friends in childhood. My impression is that in university they had more contact because they ended up travelling to London together. The room Harold stayed in was cell-like, in size and simplicity, which might have appealed to Leonard too. The staircase to the upstairs was long and steep, with narrow risers, good for somebody with a size-two shoe. It was near Hampstead Heath, very close to the tube station.

Harold Pascal went originally for a short period and stayed for twelve years, finding a wife and fathering three children, before returning in the early 1970s.

HARRIET PASCAL FREEDMAN: At the beginning, he and Leonard palled around, but afterwards, I think not. They respected each other from afar without falling in love. Harold never went to Hydra. He stayed in London, stoned, screwing everything that moved. He described Leonard as moody and difficult, one of many reasons perhaps why they didn't stay in touch. When he tried to reach out to Leonard, including in later years, he found Leonard to be—unfriendly is too strong—but he didn't want to schmooze about days gone by. Harold did once visit him in his home and came home—what's the word?—disappointed, in the level of communication. But he found Leonard's work exceptional and he was not surprised. Harold took words very seriously and appreciated precision in language and would comment often and graciously about Leonard's ability to compose.

In a playful postcard to Irving and Aviva Layton, Cohen said he had "hidden several English daughters in my velvet *tallis* bag and chortled all the way back to my bed. Golden boy, indeed. You should see me— unshaven, taciturn, and plotting West Indian pogroms against the British and lurking in pubs."

He wasn't entirely joking about pogroms. Through Nancy Bacal, Cohen met her boyfriend, Michael de Freitas, a charismatic half-Portuguese, half- black Jewish Trinidadian, a political activist who, among other unsavoury activities, collected rents for slum landlords in London. In the mid-1960s, de Freitas—increasingly radicalized—founded and led a black power movement, and changed his name to Michael X. Later, converting to Islam, he changed it again—to Abdul Malik. In 1971, fleeing probable long-term imprisonment in England, he returned to Trinidad but, in 1975, was charged, tried, and convicted of murder, and eventually hung. Cohen was among a handful of people, including William Burroughs, Eric Clap- ton, and Marianne Faithfull, who signed a petition attempting to save him from the gallows.

NANCY BACAL: In the early years, it was as though the world had been given to Michael as a party. He was far more Damon Runyon than criminally minded.

MADELEINE LERCH: Michael was a kindhearted crook—very charming, very charismatic. But he always wanted something out of it. I never understood why Nancy was with him. I travelled with him and Nancy to Majorca. They had told me it would not cost me any money. It was spring and I didn't have proper clothes and Nancy said, "Don't worry,

Michael will buy you everything. He'll pay for the trip." Michael got a Jamaican friend to come along. I told him, "I'm not sleeping with you." I'd just been paid for a modelling job in London and this guy, when we got there, demanded money. He was supposed to take the money off me. I said, "I don't travel with the money I make. It's in the bank." We both hated it there and asked Michael if we could go back to London and he said yes, because he didn't get the money. His friend had been robbing all the parking meters in London. I wasn't surprised at all by what happened [later] to Michael. A few months later, Nancy called me and said I owed her money for the trip. I said, "You said Michael would pay for it. I don't owe you anything." That was the last I heard from Nancy.

HERSH SEGAL: I knew Nancy in Montreal. I wanted to go out with her, but she wouldn't have me, though we did go out. I didn't rate with her. Then she moved to London. I looked her up there and she still didn't have anything to do with me.

GORDON COHEN: Nancy was a lovely woman, and beautiful too.

VIVIENNE LEEBOSH: I never got on with Nancy. Very hard to talk to. I found her strange. Very into herself.

Cohen himself later voiced sympathy for Michael X's radical views. "For . . . some men of imagination who are really oppressed, there is absolutely no other way," he told *Zigzag* magazine in 1974. "There's no argument you can have with them. You can't say 'cool it out,' or 'whatever is achieved by this or that except more violence?' [But] Michael . . . was completely against arming the blacks in America—he said it was crazy. They would never be able to resist that machine . . . So you give the blacks a few guns and have them [fight] against armies? His [was] a different kind of subversion. The subversion of real life, to implant black fear. He'd invite me over and serve me a delicious drink. I'd say, 'God, how do you make this?' He'd say, 'You don't expect me to tell you. If you know the secrets of our food, you know the secrets of our race and the secrets of our strength.' It was that kind of vision that he wanted to develop."

In January, Cohen visited the Tate Gallery, and again wrote to the Laytons. "I'm watching a girl of the great blond tradition and wondering why she doesn't know I'm swarming with lyrics." He had produced, he said, forty thousand words of his novel. On another postcard, mailed after a visit to John Keats's house, just off Hampstead Heath, he wrote, "Cohen is flourishing. Keats is dead. Love to you."

One early morning, Cohen arrived at the Hampstead tube station and met his old college friend, poet George Ellenbogen.

GEORGE ELLENBOGEN: I had bumped into Leonard on Sherbrooke Street in Montreal in 1959 and mentioned that I'd be in England. He said he'd be passing through England on his way to Greece, so I said "look me up." When I arrived, I wrote a postcard, "Here's my address," but I inadvertently put the stamp on the wrong side, so the postcard came back. But a few months later, I saw him at the tube station. We came up from underground and sat on the curb and chatted till about three in the morning. We talked about everything. I never saw him again.

Another day, Cohen arranged to visit a noted Pakistani palmist named Mir Bashir.

BARRIE WEXLER: He told Cohen that he'd become world famous. Mir was pretty famous himself and charged a fortune. Leonard took me to see him a decade later. There were various reading levels—the more you paid, the deeper Mir went. As was his nature, Leonard covered me for a full reading. Later, he asked, "Did he say anything earth-shattering?" I said, "He told me I'd live to about seventy-six." Cohen said, "That's what he said to me!"

DESPINA POLITI: The first thing Mir said to me was "You have a scar behind your hairline on your scalp." I said, "No, I don't." He said, "Yes, you do." I told him again that I didn't. He said, "You do, and you know it." And then it came back to me. When I was four, my older brother accidentally pushed me off a swing into a tree. It left a scar which the local hospital had to stitch up. It was not visible. How he knew that I don't know.

MADELEINE LERCH: Bashir told Cohen that he saw him standing before crowds of thousands of people. He told me that he saw me living in a small house that I liked very much and had almost no garden, some rocks around it, in which I would reside for a long, long time. That perfectly describes what happened. It's exactly as he described it.

BARRIE WEXLER: Mir responded to my question about whether I would find success—by predicting I'd spend a long stretch of my life producing other people's work, and would only find success after many years of, as he put it, "advancing other people's words." You can imagine how that went down with a twenty-four-year-old aspiring novelist.

As Bashir predicted, Wexler spent thirty years producing theatrical and television shows in Canada and the United States before returning to Greece in 2012 to write a series of novels. Cohen himself soon had a London girlfriend, aspiring screenwriter Elizabeth Kenrick—she would later write scripts for a two-part series on a history of the British trade union movement.

In the oft-told story of how Leonard Cohen came to Greece, the discovery has been described as entirely serendipitous. It wasn't. In Cohen's account, it always seemed to rain in London and no one had central heating.

LEONARD COHEN: I was going to a dentist, and walked into a Bank of Greece, maybe to cash a traveller's cheque. One of the tellers had a suntan. He was smiling. And I said, "How did you get that expression? Everybody else is white and sad." He said, "I've just come from Greece." I asked, "What's the weather like there?" He said, "It's full spring."

Cohen left for Athens soon after. He invited Kenrick to join him, but she declined. But as his Canada Council grant application had made clear, and as his Montreal conversation with Ellenbogen suggests, he had always intended to go to Greece, as well as Italy and Israel. The only question was when. Ellenbogen wasn't the only one who knew about those plans.

JOSEPH NUSS: In 1959, I got a scholarship to Italy and was preparing to go and bumped into Leonard [in Montreal]. We had lunch or dinner and he told me about his plan to go to Greece. But first he was going to go to London and Paris and then work his way down to Greece by bus or train. So I said, "Come see me in Torino and stay with me." So he said sure—write to him at American Express in Paris, because that's where he'd be in December. So I wrote him and said, "I'm looking forward to seeing you. Here's my detailed address." No answer. Come March, lo and behold, the letter comes back—unclaimed. Later, I bump into him again in Montreal. "Leonard, what happened?" He said, "When I got to London, I stayed longer than I intended and then I saw this ad for a cheap flight to Greece, so I never went to the continent."

Moreover, even before leaving Canada, Cohen had bought insurance for Greece.

ROBERT SILVERMAN: I sold him the insurance policy. He was going to Greece and had won a Canada Council and they required him to have property insurance to cover against robbery or fire. I think the premium was a hundred dollars.

Arriving in Athens, Cohen dropped a quick postcard to the Laytons and Irving's son, Max. "Max, great poem. I've got one just like it which I'll send to you. English knives look too English. I'll send you a Greek knife. More oriental and barbaric as a knife should be." In yet another missive, he tells Max: "You old poet and music man, what are you doing in Canada. Get over here. Having a hard time finding you a decent Greek knife but be patient. Send me poems."

Cohen had toyed with the notion of going to Israel first. An undated postcard from Hydra to the Laytons shortly after he arrived implied as much. "Down with Sinai, Up with Olympus," he wrote. "I've rented a whole house here—14 dollars a month, overlooking olive and almond trees and the sea. Why did we [Jews] ever leave the Mediterranean?"

If Greece was no accident of his itinerary, neither was Hydra. He'd heard about it from Jacob Rothschild, whom he'd met in London.

BARRIE WEXLER: It was Rothschild who first suggested Cohen go there to visit his mother, Barbara Hutchison, who was engaged to a prominent Greek painter, Nikos Hadjikyriakos-Ghikas. Ghikas lived and worked in both London and on Hydra in his ancestral family home, a forty-room mansion high above Kamini. In the forties and fifties, Ghikas hosted parties attended by emerging writers, including Lawrence Durrell, Henry Miller, Patrick Leigh Fermor, George Seferis, Norman Mailer, and Rex Warner—whom Rothschild's mother had previously been married to. Rothschild thought the expatriate artistic community on Hydra would be an interesting experience for a young writer like Cohen.

The steamer Cohen took to Hydra in 1960 was the *Neraida*, likely the only passenger ship then running between Piraeus and the island. A five-hour ride, it included stops at Aegina, Methana, and Poros. It was owned by legendary shipping and banking magnate Yannis Latsis. Neraida is the word Greeks use for "mermaid," but its literal meaning is fairy, which

Latsis thought was a perfect pun for a ferry. Eventually, Cohen made the trek up to Ghikas's grand estate.

BARRIE WEXLER: Leonard turned up, but the staff knew nothing about his impending arrival—Rothschild had said he'd forewarn his mother, but word hadn't reached her—and he was rudely dismissed. [Other accounts suggest Jacob Rothschild's sister turned him away.] Leaving in disgust, he cursed the estate. Four years later, the house burned down—a vicissitude of fate that Marianne attributed to Cohen's curse.

DORIAN MILLER: That's something to chew on—the ability to do that. All the people [on Hydra] were afraid of him after that.

BARRIE WEXLER: Ghikas never returned to Hydra again. To this day, it's a ruin. The British painter John Craxton, staying in the mansion at the time, rescued whatever of Ghikas's work could be saved from the fire.

Despite that frosty reception, Cohen was completely enamoured of Hydra. In a letter to his mother, he wrote that he felt "everywhere else I'd been was culture shock, and this was home."

LEONARD COHEN: Whatever you saw, whatever you felt, whatever you held, was beautiful, and when you picked up a cup you knew by the way that it fitted into your hand that it was the cup that you always had been looking for. And the table that you sat at, that was the table that you wanted to lean on, and the wine, that was ten cents a gallon, was the wine that you wanted to drink, the price you wanted to pay. The people that I bumped into, both the Greek and the foreigner, had the feeling of the people that I was meant to be with. This is the place where I was meant to be.

As beautiful as Hydra was, it had once been even more picturesque. The dense forests that had carpeted its mountains had been effectively clear-cut, in order to build a vast merchant marine fleet. These 150 warships played a critical part in the 1821 war of independence, in which Greece freed itself from three centuries of Ottoman rule. The Turks had essentially ignored Hydra because of its limited water supply. In fact, by the early 1950s, the needs of its growing population forced officials to bring water by boat from Athens every day. The water was poured into pipes, pumped to large tanks up the hill, then fed by gravity to houses.

Other writers and artists had discovered Hydra earlier, among them Craxton, Miller, Durrell, Nobel Prize winner Seferis, Leigh Fermor and his wife, Joan, and George Katsimbalis (the colossus of Maroussi). But the de facto monarchs of the expatriate community—by the time Cohen appeared—were Australian writers George Johnston and Charmian Clift. Arriving in 1955, they reigned over the bohemians that washed up on the island. A favoured watering hole was Douskos Taverna, which dated from 1832. It was familiarly known as Douskos—after the family that had owned it from its inception, but the actual name is Xeri Elia (Dry Olive). ·

The couple saw themselves not only as founders of the artists' colony, but its de facto chieftains; they protected their perceived position by deciding which newcomers would be accepted into the circle. These included Australian writer Alan Moorehead, who actually lived on nearby Spetses; political commentator Mungo MacCallum and his wife; novelist and poet Rodney Hall and his wife, Beth; artist and set designer Cedric Flower, and his wife, Pat; Nancy Dignan, an Australian artist, and her partner Patrick Greer, an Irish writer; Sidney and Cynthia Nolan—he became Australia's best-known contemporary painter and was knighted, while she later killed herself with barbiturates—and writer Gordon Merrick and his partner, Chuck Hulse, a former Broadway dancer.

BARRIE WEXLER: Chuck and Gordon were an elegant, old-school couple who lived in the only house on the island with black shutters and doors. Most of the gay couples had pools. Theirs had a lion's head spewing water at one end. They often held court on the port with the older expatriates. Around '74, they packed up and moved to Bali. Their departure was a kind of declaration that the scene was over.

BRANDON AYRE: Gordon and Chuck—great friends of Leonard's. They were quite flamboyant—island royalty. They helped him a great deal, financially. Gordon would pay his grocery bill at Katsikas. All the expats had accounts there. They helped each other.

BRIAN SIDAWAY: Chuck was very nice, but Gordon had a real mean streak. He was a kind of American aristocrat, and something of a racist.

Cohen's friend, Hispanic-American folk singer Julie Felix, once felt the sting of that animus.

JULIE FELIX: Gordon didn't like me being at the table [in the port]. I felt excluded.

BRANDON AYRE: What Gordon said about Hydra—he had this patrician way of talking—was that it was the second-most-beautiful man-made place in the world. I said, "What's first?" And he said, "Venice." And he was right. Hydra is beautiful. No cars. By some miracle, it was deemed a national monument by the Greek government, so all new buildings had to be in a certain style. And it was cheap, like Paris in the 1940s. Even in the early 1970s, the house we rented was thirty dollars a month. A three-course meal with beer and dessert cost $1.50.

Cohen soon settled into a comfortable routine—rising early to write, then a trip to the beach to "have a drink, look at the girls, talk to the men."

LEONARD COHEN: It was a very free and happy and disciplined life at the same time. There'd be a little table in the port where we were centred around . . . the Johnstons. And there were wonderful conversations, a lot of drinking, a lot of abandon and dancing and drunkenness. Everyone was looking for some kind of amorous opportunity, of course, people paired off and split up and paired off again—that kind of very exciting, sometimes painful activity . . . One felt very free. And foreigners were tolerated, somehow. In fact, we seemed to be their entertainment.

These sentiments were no doubt genuine, though there were times when Cohen confessed he could not bear to hear another Johnston story or more news of their children. The pressure for social engagement ran up against his need for private writing time. Nevertheless, together with the Johnstons, as they were known, and Caroline Gassoumis, then wife of artist Demetri Gassoumis, Cohen signed up for Greek-language classes.

AVIVA LAYTON: Leonard spoke Greek. You know why? Because he went to pre-kindergarten, kindergarten, first grade, second grade, third grade, until he mastered the language. He sat at the little desks with the five-year-olds. He went to kindergarten. That's how he learned Greek.

That account may be somewhat inflated. Actually, the group hired Kirya Pepika, Cohen's former landlady, to give them lessons five days a week for one hour, using children's readers.

ROGER GREEN: He was a bit cagey about how much he knew, but he knew quite a bit more than he let on. It came back to him when we worked together on "Alexandra Leaving" in 1999. He could certainly read the Cyrillic alphabet.

BARRIE WEXLER: Greek is like chess. Unless you really study it, at some point you hit a wall. If he took lessons, he was wasting his money.

His favourite line about that, which he repeated numerous times, was "I've got about twenty words of Greek, which I use in every sentence." I occasionally heard a burst of Greek from him, though, and thought, "Twenty words, my ass."

Once, Demetri Gassoumis was at Cohen's house with a Greek friend from Athens. The other guy jokingly berated Leonard for not speaking much Greek, after having been in the country for so long.

BARRIE WEXLER: Demetri then said something like, "Look, even if you're not a polyglot, there's about six thousand English words that come straight from Greek." Leonard then visibly brightened and exclaimed, "Jesus, I can speak Greek after all!"

Soon after he arrived, Cohen formed a friendship with Redmond Frankton "Bim" Wallis from New Zealand, a writer, and his wife, Robyn. Wallis had come to Hydra because he knew the Johnstons. Initially, they welcomed him and gave him furniture—just as they had earlier given Cohen a single bed, chairs, and his kitchen table. But Wallis eventually parted company with the couple, amid the island's continuing soap opera of marital spats, sexual escapades, pill popping, and alcoholism. The Wallis-Cohen friendship lasted several years during which they sailed, swam, drank, and smoked marijuana together. Wallis would later chronicle the friendship in his unfinished novel, *The Unyielding Memory*, which describes Cohen— fictionalized as Saul Rubens—with startling clarity. "He seemed to be so self-contained, mildly amused by what he saw around him, passionate about work, and deliberately enigmatic. His public utterances were always somewhat non-committal or pregnantly oblique . . . He was, to use a word coming into fashion, cool." Cohen, in Wallis's eyes, was able to engage fully with the Hydriot expatriates and yet remain somewhat aloof. He was also able to discuss literary issues without turning the discussion into a competition.

BARRIE WEXLER: Leonard was competitive with himself, but not with others. He had a very clear notion of his singular gift and the personage he had developed that went with it. He was entirely self-contained. He rarely left the place within himself he operated out of—not when he was manic, not when he was drunk, not even when he was making love. He managed to be there and not there at the same time, his presence somehow intense yet ethereal, completely unto itself. The interior landscape out of which he functioned had an outer skin that enabled his simultaneous interaction with and aloofness from the outside world. It included everything—his typewriter-like hand-writing, his wardrobe, and the standardized formula of words he used for verbal and written salutations. He'd always say, "hello, friend(s)" or "see you later, friend(s)" when coming or going—something he adopted from the Greeks, who say *yasou filos*, hello friend or see you later, friend. All of this served to maintain a certain distance he kept from you, no matter how close the intervening time had brought you. Leonard often referred to things, even feelings, as preferences or choices. In many ways, he made himself up as creatively as the poems and songs he wrote.

Wallis's novel also accurately limned Cohen's political position at the time, "as revolutionary as the songs he sang, but an observer. [He'd] never actively fight fascism. [He'd] look at the results of rebellion, visit Cuba, talk to radicals, observe demonstrations . . . recognize that he was not equipped to man the barricades, but was equipped to stir the emotions, to encourage."

*   *   *

It wasn't until May 1960 that Cohen finally met Marianne Ihlen. As the story goes, she was buying bottled water and milk at Katsikas grocery store when she heard a man's voice asking, "Would you like to join us?

We're sitting outside?" Later, she remembered Cohen wearing khaki trousers, tennis shoes, a shirt with rolled-up sleeves, and a sixpence cap. Cohen had noticed her earlier.

LEONARD COHEN: I remember seeing Marianne several times before she saw me. I saw her with Axel and with the baby, and thinking "What a beautiful holy trinity they are." They were all blond and beautiful and suntanned.

MARIANNE IHLEN: When my eyes met his eyes, I felt it throughout my body. You know what that is. It is utterly incredible. What I didn't know was that he knew everything about what had happened . . . Already when he saw me, he had enormous compassion for me and my child.

HENRY ZEMEL: Hydra, the beach, the whole thing, the blonde, the kid. It's like stepping into a picture postcard. Is a picture postcard real? Take it as you wish.

BARRIE WEXLER: The postcard was real, but only postcards survive travel to and from the island—not the relationships they inspire.

What Cohen knew was that Ihlen's husband, writer Axel Jensen, had fallen in love with an American painter, Patricia Amlin.

PATRICIA AMLIN: We met on a very narrow, dirt goat path on Hydra. I was going to Sunday breakfast. Marianne was nowhere. I didn't know about Marianne.

Ihlen was in Oslo at the time, giving birth to young Axel. Eventually, Jensen and Amlin would leave Hydra for Athens. The relationship proved short-lived, in part because Amlin was involved in a serious car accident that left her hospitalized for several months.

After her first encounter with Cohen, Ihlen returned to her two-room house in Kala Pigadia, "almost a bit intoxicated."

MARIANNE IHLEN: Right away I put on some music, danced around a bit, and thought it all of a sudden was such fun to be with my son and . . . felt it was simple and fine. A lightness had come over me.

*   *   *

In those early years on Hydra, one of Cohen's closest friends was George Lialios, scion of a prominent Greek family. Cohen and Lialios were kindred spirits.

BARBARA LAPCEK: George was a big deal in Leonard's life. Their spiritual selves were matched.

BARRIE WEXLER: Lialios was on his own spiritual trip. He peppered his conversation with things like "Remember, you've got the universe between your toes." One day, talking about Christ, I said, "Jesus was clairvoyant, right?" George nodded. "So he knew what was coming, with Judas, the Romans, and the crucifixion?" He nodded again. "So why didn't he just head for the hills?" And George said, "Because there are some appointments you have to keep."

DAN KLEIN: George was interested in fuzzy spiritual stuff. I didn't know what he was talking about half the time.

Cohen may have adopted Lialios's approach to dress.

BARRIE WEXLER: In summer, Lialios always wore the same thing—a white cotton Indian *kurta* top with drawstring baggy pants. Leonard once said to me that Lialios's costume was perfect because he never had to think about what to put on. Cohen initially wore black, then a blue workman's shirt for a while. That evolved into an all-khaki ensemble—khaki shorts, khaki shirts, and a khaki jacket—for the epauletted colonial field-commander look. I once said to him, "Cohen, where are the medals?" That's all that was missing.

DESPINA POLITI: That military image—Leonard was very sly. He thought that would sell. He was not a dumbhead.

Lialios's money had been inherited.

BARRIE WEXLER: He didn't have to work. His grandfather had bought two very large properties around Syntagma in Athens when there were sheep still grazing in the square. They had many other holdings as well.

AVIVA LAYTON: He came from a very aristocratic family that owned a liberal newspaper. [After the 1967 coup], the junta in Athens arrested him and beat him on his feet, tortured by bastinado. He came off the boat, and both Irving and Leonard had to help him to his house.

In the early sixties, Lialios purchased a large, eighteenth-century stone mansion high up on the colourfully and appropriately named Donkey Shit Lane.

BARRIE WEXLER: There was a run-down grand ballroom on the second floor. He owned a superb sound system in his living room—George's father was a well-known composer. George himself loved classical music and had studied music in Vienna. The living room also had a fireplace in which, George maintained, a ghost resided. Directly across from the house was an abandoned mansion. Word got out among backpackers that you could crash there. George loved it, because there was an endless supply of available girls to whom he could offer more comfortable accommodations, rather than go chasing them in the port.

DON LOWE: A nice man, George. A gentle man. He loved women. We used to have good parties at his place. A lovely house. Leonard would be there.

PANDIAS SCARAMANGA: George was a very nice person but very strange—stingy and generous. Stingy for little things and money—to pay for coffee. But he was a very generous friend. Alexis Bolens once fell off a rock and broke his face, completely destroyed. We thought he was going to die. George went with him to Geneva and paid for the operation and saved his face.

One day, not long after Cohen and Ihlen had met, they headed out on donkeys, with friends, for the all-women monastery of Agia Efpraxia, five hundred meters up the hill from the port.

BARRIE WEXLER: Riding donkeys along the quay is fairly easy. Traversing up and down a long, steep incline is much more difficult. Leonard tried riding every which way—sidesaddle like the Greeks do, and with his legs straddled over both sides of the uncomfortable wooden saddle—and almost slipped off twice. Marianne said by the time they got back to the port, his hands were as white as marble from clasping the swell of the saddle. But he came back with a souvenir—a dark, needlepoint depiction of Christ on the cross, which he hung in the upstairs bedroom.

That first summer, 1960, Cohen also befriended vacationing American poet Ken Koch and his family.

KEN KOCH: We became very good friends. We travelled to Turkey together, to Istanbul. I liked Leonard a lot and so did Janice [Koch's wife]. We saw each other a few times after that. It was nice and intense, but never more than a day.

Koch's daughter, Katherine, then five, had her own memories.

KATHERINE KOCH: Leonard was in love with Marianne . . . [She] was beautiful. I thought Leonard was wonderful, good-looking, looking a little like my father. He had an atmosphere about him, courtly and funny, sharing his good humour. We gave each other nicknames we never forgot: Boodie Leonard and Boodie Katherine. [Boodie meant] silliness and joy.

Another expatriate writer was Don Lowe, a former British merchant mariner and oil rig labourer who had arrived in the late 1950s and lived in a veritable cave. Almost sixty years later, Lowe—having left the island only twice—was still living without electricity or running water. In that time, he produced more than one hundred novels and screenplays, virtually all of them unpublished and unproduced. His primitive lifestyle in part drove two wives to leave him. Only half in jest, Lowe liked to refer to himself as "Robinson, not quite Crucified." When he briefly ran out of money in the early 1960s, Lowe—homeless—caught his own fish by harpooning them in the sea.

DON LOWE: I wasn't initially a big fan of Leonard's, because I lived my own way. I didn't mix with him much. I was the last of his fans. But he is a great poet. We're brothers, in a way. I wrote a book about him—*The Perennial Orgasm*. It's written through the eyes of an Irish poet. Because women used to come here looking for Leonard—these beautiful women. There was one in particular, Oressia, a Polish woman, a displaced person. The book is based on her.

After Cohen met Ihlen, his daily ritual evolved. She and Axel would often accompany him to the beach in the morning, then return to his house for lunch.

MARIANNE IHLEN: Then little Axel would fall asleep, and then Leonard would read poems for me. He reminded me very much of [my] grandma—her energy, her enormous presence. You could really trust in him. It was like . . . is it really possible to be so fond of me? But at that point, I was knocked out.

BARRIE WEXLER: Cohen told me he'd rewrite the poems he read to her, making them simpler so she could understand them, because her English was at the time limited. He credited her with purifying his style. Samuel Beckett originally wrote *Waiting for Godot* in French precisely because his French wasn't that good—the constraints forced him to write as simply as possible. Like Beckett, Cohen's minimalist approach was partially developed by filtering English through the sieve of a foreign language.

LEONARD COHEN: She was an old-fashioned girl, and I come from an old-fashioned background myself, so the things that I took for granted with Marianne, and she perhaps took with me, a certain kind of courtesy and behaviour and ritual . . . There was always a gardenia on my desk where I'd work. There was such a sense of order and generosity that she had.

MARIANNE IHLEN: We lay in the sun . . . we listened to music, we bathed, we played, we drank, we discussed. There was writing and lovemaking and . . . It was absolutely fabulous . . . I was in a state of shock . . . I didn't have a foothold. At the same time, having a child and all—it was really tough . . . If he hadn't been so patient, I

don't know if we would have been together. For when I was dancing Greek dances and drinking retsina, he would sit waiting till I
was finished . . . then we went home together. And it would be so
incredibly peaceful and so harmonious . . . because there was such
tranquility.

BARBARA LAPCEK: He told me Marianne used to bring him tea every
afternoon to his desk—very quietly. He said she never talked to him,
never disturbed him. She was a very, very simple girl. She wasn't in
love with herself, the way Suzanne [Elrod] was.

MARIANNE IHLEN: I didn't believe it when Leonard said, "You're the
most beautiful woman I've ever seen." . . . I think I had too round a
face . . . Skinny. Almost no boobs. To my great regret. [Leonard] was
beautiful. He was marvellous. Neither did he think that he looked
like much. We both had problems. You have no idea. We often stood
in front of the mirror before going out and wondered who we were
today. Oh God, how strange we human beings are.

ROGER GREEN: Marianne used to say that Leonard, before going out,
would stand in front of the mirror and she'd say, "What are you
doing?" And he said, "I'm making myself invisible." Sure enough,
he'd come down to the harbour and he was invisible. I saw it with
my own eyes. I'd see him sitting in the port, and nobody noticed him
or paid any attention to him.

BARRIE WEXLER: It wasn't simply an obsession with body image. It
was more the continuous distillation—in mind and body, spirit and
words—of a continuous distillation of his interior landscape towards
its essence. Like Michelangelo, who just chiseled away everything
that *wasn't* the David, Cohen spent most of his life chiseling away at
everything that wasn't Leonard.

PICO IYER: One of the main things Leonard taught me was how to be invisible. He taught by example. By erasing that person called Leonard Cohen and all the notions many of us bring to him, by being silent and by making you forget you're in the presence of somebody famous and accomplished.

Ihlen, herself, was almost universally adored.

PANDIAS SCARAMANGA: I loved Marianna very much. I admired her. The way she was walking. She was very elegant. I told her one day, "I like the way you carry your head."

BRIAN SIDAWAY: I never saw the fuss about Marianne.

BILL POWNALL: Marianne was charming. I had a memorable evening with her where she played me Leonard songs—Buffy Sainte-Marie had recorded them. The way she spoke about Leonard, I realized she was very, very much in love with him and that this was not going to be an easy trip for him. She knew that as well, by then.

DESPINA POLITI: Marianne was very nice, and very polite. She was older than me and at that stage, it made a difference. She was much more independent, a grown-up woman. She had a very nice body. I remember looking closely and thinking, "Does she have wrinkles? Will I have wrinkles?"

BARBARA LAPCEK: Marianne and I were nurtured by the same magical, mysterious freedom of thought, of art, and of love that those early expats found and cultivated. Leonard was an essential part of it. She was his perfect muse and friend.

LEONARD COHEN: There wasn't a man that wasn't interested in Marianne. It wasn't just that she was a traditional Nordic beauty—that was indisputable—but she was also very kind, and one of the most modest people about her beauty. There was no sense that she was playing her beauty, or maybe she was so brilliant at it that no one saw.

BARRIE WEXLER: Leonard thought she was really beautiful, though she did tell me once she didn't understand what Leonard saw in her physically. I, myself, never saw her that way. But she had an undeniable inner beauty—it was unmistakable—that transcended any man's vision of her.

BRANDON AYRE: I adored Marianne. She had a joy and a purity about her, when she was happy. She'd walk down to the port wearing nothing but a black T-shirt dress, one piece—no underwear, I'm pretty sure—sandals, with a brown wicker basket over her arm, and everyone shouting, *"Yassou, Marianna!"* All the guys would come out [of the shops], like a scene out of a movie.

CAROL ZEMEL: Marianna was a de facto Norwegian aristocrat. She was exquisite. Everything she did, she did with great beauty, grace, and delicacy. And she was understanding to a fault. And she had this magical child, Axel. He was enchanting, adorable.

Still, even from its earliest days, this romantic idyll was tarnished by Leonard's powerful attraction to other women and their attraction to him. A jealous Ihlen wanted to "lock him up, and swallow the key."

MARIANNE IHLEN: He was so incredibly sought after . . . so entertaining and so courteous . . . If he had finished working, he'd go down to the port earlier . . . and I'd wait for the babysitter and [join him] after. And every time he'd be sitting with some fantastic woman . . . It was just good friendship. But it riled me each and every time. It was like being stabbed . . . All the girls were panting for him. You have no idea how hurt I felt. And that destroyed so much. But after all, it was my own insecurity. I should have just held my head high and thought: "But it is me he is living with. It is me he has chosen." And then yes, I would dare go as far as to say that I was on the verge of killing myself due to it. I just wanted to die. There was this fabulous young model from New York, who came to Hydra [Phyllis Major]. They disappeared for an entire day. So I imagined all kinds of things. I curled up like a small fetus . . . People who passed by actually thought I was dead. I refused to communicate with the outside world . . . Oh God, how much pain one can suffer.

PANDIAS SCARAMANGA: Ach . . . On Hydra, everybody was with everybody else. [These infidelities] are details. One winter I came and everything, everyone, had changed [partners]. One was with the wife of the other, the husband of the other. When summer came, they were all back to their old wives and husbands.

In late September 1960, Cohen finally made it to Israel.

RENEE ROTHMAN SIMMONS: I saw him [there] in the autumn. I was there to write my graduate thesis. We travelled around together for a few days. He was a very good friend of my brother, Bernie, and like an older brother to me—what I needed at the time. A good friend. He was a charming person. We were in Jerusalem together, possibly the Negev. He'd already bought his house. I knew about Marianne.

In a letter to Ihlen, written on the beach in Tel Aviv and signed "your friend, Cohen," he confessed to feeling lost in Israel, struggling with his poor command of Hebrew. He briefly contemplated joining an ulpan for three months to learn the language, but decided against it. Although his feelings for Israel would change, Cohen then preferred Greece.

RUTH ROSKIES WISSE: He told me how much more comfortable he felt on Hydra than in Israel, which I took to mean: "Don't expect me to become your Jewish ally." Yet I did assume that anyone as talented and intelligent as he would eventually stop using "Jew" and "war" as metaphors—as he often did in his songs—and begin thinking about them for real. I expected him to shoulder moral authority in a civilization that threatened to unravel.

Cohen spent one night as a house guest of Israeli poet Natan Zach. In his memoirs, Zach recalled meeting Cohen at Café Kassit, in Tel Aviv. Cohen showed him a new anthology of English-language poetry that included one of his poems. "As a funny or sad side remark . . . the same night Cohen asked me to let him sleep in my place, because he couldn't afford a hotel room. And so I did."

On September 27, 1960, six days after his twenty-sixth birthday, Cohen paid $1,500—the asking price—for a three-storey whitewashed home in Greece, with five rooms on several levels, a large terrace, and no electricity, plumbing, or running water. The funds had been bequeathed to him in the will of his grandmother.

HENRY ZEMEL: I understood that he had an annual bequest—two thousand dollars a year. That would have been a lot in those days.

Cohen's friend Demetri Gassoumis acted as adviser on the transaction and witnessed the deed of sale. As per local tradition, a priest later blessed the house by smearing a cross of candle soot by the front door. Cohen hung his blue raincoat on a hook in the entry and placed his green typewriter in his workroom. The street on which the house is located is now called Odos Leonard Cohen.

BARRIE WEXLER: Buying property in Greece is tricky because of the inheritance laws. Long-lost relatives have been known to show up after you purchase a house and claim they owned the kitchen. There was another property that Leonard considered, which, after asking around, Demetri determined was too risky. Neither the seller nor the town hall officials spoke English. More than just acting as an intermediary, Demetri's key contribution was his lineage. His mother's family had lived on the island for as long as anyone could remember. In Greece, who your parents are carries a lot of weight, even more so in a small village. The Gassoumis family name was respected by the locals, and consequently Cohen didn't get taken advantage of. As a foreigner, he otherwise might have.

In a letter to his mother, Cohen described the rooms as "large and cool with deep windows set in thick walls. I suppose it's about 200 years old and many generations of seamen must have lived here. I will do a little work on it every year and in a few years it will be a mansion. Life has been going on here exactly the same for hundreds of years. All through the day you hear the calls of the street vendors and they are really rather musical . . . I get up around 7 generally and work till about noon. Early morning is coolest and therefore best, but I love the heat anyhow, especially when the Aegean Sea is 10 minutes from my door."

Cohen's house, numbered 764, stood on a small side street that could pass for an alley.

BARRIE WEXLER: I once asked Cohen about three corroded brass house numbers that were lying on one of the kitchen shelves. He took me outside and pointed to the barely visible outline of the numbers—764—under the layers of grey paint on the front door. He said, "There must be some numerological interpretation, because there are only three houses on the street."

Some Hydriots maintain the street addresses represented the number of stairs from the house to the port.

BARRIE WEXLER: Perhaps it was once true. But it never made sense to me because when I checked it out, the numbers didn't even vaguely correspond. Leonard's house was no more than three hundred steps from the port.

Sometime after he acquired the house, Cohen learned that neighbours were claiming ownership of a portion of his land, directly below his terrace.

PANDIAS SCARAMANGA: The neighbours claimed the land did not belong to Leonard and he had a lot of trouble, bringing lawyers, going to court. I said to him, "Don't bother. You're going to pay a lot of money to lawyers. These people know they're going to lose in the end, but it will take two, three, five, ten years. Go and tell them how much you're willing to pay to buy it from them and the moment you get it, make a wall and a nice garden, with trees." And he did it. He bought the land and made a beautiful garden. Later, he thanked me and said, "Otherwise, I'd still be in court."

BARRIE WEXLER: An old Greek law that says if someone dumps garbage on your land, or grazes their donkeys on it for twenty years or more, the land is then deemed theirs. That's what Leonard was facing. The stone wall that defined his property was crumbling and the neighbours had been tossing stuff onto it. Leonard had been advised not to repair the wall as, due to the peculiarities of that Greek law, it might prejudice his case. In those days, there wasn't much title registration—the footprint of your property was determined by the perimeter stones. Civil matters in Greece can take ten years or more to be heard by the courts. Leonard and his neighbours were playing a game of let's-see-who-can-outwait-the-other. Over time, the decaying wall gradually spilled towards his neighbours' front gate. After about a decade, they concluded that they were dealing with someone with monk-like patience and settled.

In the first blush of their romance, Ihlen divided her time between her home in Kala Pigadia and Cohen's new house. Occasionally, they took short trips to Athens, strolling the streets, stopping for coffee, collecting mail at the American Express office, and meeting friends for drinks. They usually booked a room in a cheap hotel, the Niki, in the port of Piraeus.

LEONARD COHEN: I remember we had to catch the boat back to Hydra, and we got a taxi, and I've never forgotten this. Nothing happened, just sitting in the back of the taxi with Marianne, I lit a cigarette, a Greek cigarette that had that delicious deep flavour of a Greek cigarette, that has a lot of Turkish tobacco in it, and I'm thinking, I'm an adult. You know. I have a life of my own, I'm with this beautiful woman, we have a little money in our pocket, we're going back to Hydra, we're passing these painted walls. That feeling—I think I've tried to re-create it hundreds of times, unsuccessfully. Just that feeling of being grown up, with somebody beautiful that you're happy to be beside and all the world is in front of you.

MARIANNE IHLEN: If you asked me to describe Leonard in four words, I would say: kindness, creativity, sensitivity, and honesty. I will borrow a phrase that Leonard once wrote on the wall in the Hydra house, "I change, I am the same, I change, I am the same." But my love for Hydra has never changed. Hydra dissolves me and reconstitutes me.

BARRIE WEXLER: He was quoting himself. Those lines are from the prayer in *Beautiful Losers,* which in turn was inspired by the *I Ching.* He scrawled it in gold paint on the downstairs bedroom wall. He said the novel was the only thing he ever wrote—or half wrote—while on acid.

In August, Ihlen had entrusted young Axel to a Scandinavian Airlines crew flying to Oslo and sent him home to her mother. Later, in November, she and Cohen took the ferry to Athens and drove to Norway in Marianne's car, a Volkswagen Karmann Ghia.

MARIANNE IHLEN: That was when I understood this was something more than friendship.

LEONARD COHEN: She liked to drive fast, and I didn't like to drive that fast, but anyway, we got there. That was a wonderful drive, although I remember quarrelling a lot. I don't know whether it was about the driving or not, but I do remember that quarrels arose. But they were healed because we'd stop at some little Italian café and have pasta and a bottle of wine or some cheese and bread, and we'd get over it.

In Oslo, Ihlen was happily reunited with her son and mother. For propriety's sake, Cohen stayed a few nights at the Viking Hotel, then returned to Montreal. Back in his old flat at 3702 Mountain Street, Cohen—in a Christmas Eve letter to Marianne—said they would see each other soon; he didn't enjoy "an ocean between us." He had applied for another government grant—McClelland & Stewart had rejected his novel—and had begun working with Irving Layton on what was envisaged as a series of six television scripts.

MAX LAYTON: I remember being in Leonard's apartment when my dad and Leonard were trying to write plays. They were working on a story of a man climbing on a rooftop and shooting people at random— there had been incidents of this kind already.

This might have been *Lights on the Black Water* or *A Man Was Killed*, two of several screenplays they scripted. Among the other titles: *Up with Nothing*, and *Enough of Fallen Leaves*. The following year, Cohen did sell his own teleplay, *The New Step*, to the CBC. It was eventually produced in 1980 as part of *The Leonard Cohen Show* at the Centaur Theatre in Montreal.

MAX LAYTON: I remember my dad walking up and down and Leonard is the stenographer. His handwriting was absolutely amazing, beautiful, incredibly clear, beautifully shaped. It says something about character. And he wrote this way effortlessly. Occasionally, he would interject. Did you know they also made some money writing letters to each other? Concordia [then Sir George Williams University] was paying twenty-five dollars per letter. So they'd write, "Dear Leonard, blahdeblabbedy blah . . . Dear Irving, blahdeblabbedy blah." We just made fifty bucks. They wrote a whole series of letters that were complete bullshit.

AVIVA LAYTON: That was in the kitchen on Somerled Avenue. My job was to age the letters, so they wouldn't look as if they'd been made up in the last five minutes, which they were. Both Leonard and Irving were laughing their heads off. I was in charge of splashing the letters with ink and crumbling them up, but not too much, so it wouldn't look like a con job. So they were fakes, but authentic fakes. It took me about ten minutes. They did get paid for them and they both needed money at the time.

In his letter to Ihlen, Cohen said he and Layton were writing "like mad." They hoped to turn the television medium into a genuine art form. If their dreams materialized, he'd have enough money to settle in Greece or Spain and "set up a little writing factory." Both were highly motivated—Layton's "revolutionary ideas" had cost him his teaching job, and Cohen needed funds to travel. With three months of intense work, he hoped, he'd earn enough money to last a year, leaving nine months "for pure poetry. It sounds like a good life." He wrote while listening to Mahalia Jackson. "I'm right there with her, flying with you in that glory, pulling away the shrouds from the sun, making music out of everything . . . I give you all my love." The CBC's Robert Weaver later forwarded the plays to various producers. But Weaver was not encouraging, writing to Layton that one script was "terribly wordy . . . ideological and its character two-dimensional." Scrounging for work, Cohen won a commission from *Esquire* magazine to write a profile of pianist Glenn Gould.

LEONARD COHEN: This was before the days of tape recorders. We began to talk. The conversation got heated and I put my pen down. I thought, "I'm going to remember everything he says because it's really fascinating." We talked for a couple of hours and I went back to my apartment and I couldn't remember a thing. *Esquire* phoned me and said, "How did it go?" I said, "I'm working on it." Then they started phoning me every second day. Then every day. Then I stopped answering the phone. I think I had to return the advance.

The Gould debacle might have been a metaphor for Cohen's predicament. He was unhappily home in Montreal, in the dead of winter, separated by an ocean from Marianne, living with his often neurotic mother, and struggling to find paid work. Jealousy gnawed at him. Ihlen, it seemed, had moved on. "I think I know what happened," he wrote to her, "but I want you to tell me."

CHAPTER SIX

My Freedom Is Fragile

Love born on Hydra doesn't travel. Leonard was insightful enough to understand that.

—Barrie Wexler

Hydra was like a theatre, and the port, or as it was known, the agora, was our stage, for it was indeed built like an amphitheatre, and we like so many actors were playing our roles. We would come down to that stage when one of the boats came in with the mail and . . . wait to see who our fellow actors might be that morning. Did we gossip, I wonder, and did we also drink? Of course most people did, for we were all acting out our secret dreams.

—Charlotte Mensforth

I know there will be times when I'll want to go away so I can come back again.

—Leonard Cohen

What Cohen did have in Montreal to elevate his mood was family and friends. His relationship with his late father's brothers, Lawrence and Horace, was cordial but distant. On the other hand, he did warm to an older cousin, Edgar Cohen, son of A. Z. Cohen, brother of Leonard's grandfather Lyon Cohen.

ANDREW COHEN: When other people stood in judgement of him, my father, Edgar, secretly cheered. Because as an aspiring writer himself [Edgar Cohen wrote an unpublished novel and memoir, as well as *Mademoiselle Libertine*, a biography of Ninon de l'Enclos, a seventeenth-century French libertine], he saw in Leonard what he would have wanted to have done for himself. But he just wasn't built that way. Leonard could do that because Leonard could say to hell with everybody. My father also had depression, another point of commonality. My father was in awe of Leonard long before he was singing—that Leonard would follow his muse, choose the life of the writer, the life my father could not choose because he had a family and was more conservative. Leonard led an outsized life, not tethered to convention. My father was well into his eighties when Leonard said to him, "Edgar, let's go find some girls and go into a dark room." But this is key—in my father, Leonard would have seen someone who was not judgemental, who was never going to say, "Leonard, you left the family business." Because my father wanted to leave the family business—L. Cohen & Son, coal and oil, a distributorship. He ran it from 1937 to 1961 and [only then] walked away to write. Leonard once said, "I represent a whole generation of Jewish boys who didn't go into their fathers' businesses."

There was also Layton, of course. In addition to their playwriting sessions, they dissected poetry.

MAX LAYTON: On Somerled Avenue, Leonard was often a visitor. It was more one-on-one—my father sitting in his lovely old armchair, red leather, and Leonard sitting across, probably both smoking. My father would say, "Well, Leonard, let's crack a poem!" And he'd pull down a poem of the great masters and they would dissect it together. They went through one great poem after another. It was not quite a meeting of equals, but my dad was not the teacher. They were doing it together. But my dad loved to talk, and Leonard loved to listen. He'd absorb and make observations, but my dad was leading it.

For a brief time, Cohen's former girlfriend Madeleine Poulin was back in his life. Joining the burgeoning downtown scene of artists and intellectuals, they hung out at the Bistro [Chez Lou Lou] and other clubs.

MADELEINE POULIN: He'd visit me in my room on Simpson Street and take me places. Once, he took me to his house in Westmount. It was a dark house. I remember his mother coming down the stairs in the middle of the afternoon wearing a housecoat, a peignoir, dark red, like velvet. He said to me, slightly bitterly, "Don't mind my mother. My mother's crazy." Or "she's mad." She didn't react to him or me—she just ignored us. He said, "She's crazy. She went through a lot, but she has a beautiful voice. She's a great singer."

Robert Hershorn's apartment on Pine Avenue—in a grand house with a white verandah, overlooking the city—was another prime gathering spot.

DON OWEN: Nearly everyone played an instrument—bongo, harmonica, guitar—and the music would go on till dawn. Leonard occasionally would sing a poem. Some of those moments are captured in spirit on the records, though the mood of 1961 was much gayer. Then Leonard would decide that he had work to do. There'd be a dinner party at the Athens restaurant on Saint-Lawrence with plenty of ouzo and retsina, and then he'd be off to Greece for a few months or a year, and with each successive return would be thinner and more pained looking. Everything else about him would have increased.

MAX LAYTON: I remember a party at the Somerled apartment. Hershorn was there, a very powerful guitar player and singer. He sang a blues song, "St. James Infirmary," with more power than anyone I've ever heard. It was overwhelming. I remember the flecks of spittle at the corners of his mouth. He was probably high as a kite, but I did not know that. His entire soul was in it. I could easily understand why he was a friend of Leonard's. He had a very Jewish face, sensitive, intelligent, strong character. Leonard was there, of course. They knew their stuff and played it with deep passion.

JUDITH GAULT: Hershorn was a junkie, but he was also a charmer, tall, tall, tall, and gorgeous. He and Cohen and Morton Rosengarten— they were the Jewish aristocrats. The way they carried themselves. They were very respectful of women, respectful of everyone. It was in their genes.

DON OWEN: I'd see Leonard come smiling along Sherbrooke Street with either Robert or Morton. They'd be dressed impeccably in dark grey Brooks Brothers suits and button-down oxford-cloth shirts, on their way to the Ritz for a drink and dinner. It was too easy to resent what looked so good and you couldn't be part of.

As he melded into the Cohen circle, Owen's resentment gave way to admiration and respect.

DON OWEN: One of the girls that hung out on Stanley Street became pregnant by a guy who quickly left town. Leonard went around and dug money out of whoever he thought had some, giving the largest amount himself to help her out.

Cohen also threw parties at his mother's Belmont Avenue home.

AVIVA LAYTON: One time, we had a mad party, and Robert vomited in Masha's velvet curtains. He was heavily into drugs. He really led a dissipated life. He was dating Helene Robert, who became [filmmaker] Alanis Obomsawin, a very beautiful Indian princess. She was dyeing hair in those days. She put streaks in my hair, Irving's, and Leonard's. At that time, nobody was smoking dope, but Leonard was. I think he was into heavier things. And that was Robert, because he had the money.

ARNIE GELBART: Hershorn was a really nice guy with a domineering father. He'd have done anything not to be in the clothing business. But he didn't have the talent or the confidence Leonard had. He had inherited this huge business, and he did not hide that he hated it.

Meanwhile, in Norway, Marianne was fending off a marriage proposal from Sam Barclay, the handsome chartered-boat captain who piloted a vessel called *Stormie Seas*; she'd had a brief affair with him a few years previously, during a separation from Axel Jensen. In fact, Barclay was her son's godfather; the boy had been conceived on his boat. Now Barclay wrote to suggest she join him in the Aegean. She declined.

BARRIE WEXLER: Sam took her a lot more seriously than just a one-night stand or, in the framework of Hydra, a one-week stand. She was trying to figure out which way to hop.

Cohen's own feelings for Ihlen were ambivalent and clearly in flux. That winter, he wrote a letter that discouraged her, saying "I do not know what will happen to us. I wish I could say, 'come with me, live with me,' but I can't—or maybe I can. Right now my solitude is necessary. I am lonely for you and I have never been happier than when I was with you." When she confided the letter's contents to Barclay, he wrote back, "Ah,

Marianne! So now at last you have heard from Leonard. I am sorry. You don't have much luck." Later, Cohen called her in Oslo, briefly resurrecting her hopes. But in early April, another Barclay letter said, "I am so sorry, Marianne, that you feel lonely & I am sorry that you feel doubtful." Her doubts were not unjustified. For while Cohen was corresponding with Marianne and keeping the door of possibility open, he was seeing Poulin and other women in Montreal, and still wrestling with his attachment to his old girlfriend, Annie Sherman, even though she had—the previous summer—married prominent New York restaurateur Armando Orsini.

AVIVA LAYTON: We used to joke that if Annie had stayed with Leonard, she'd have been Mrs. Annie Cohen, but she became the Contessa Georgiana Orsini.

In a letter to Sherman that winter, Cohen wrote, "Let's meet in Central Station and kiss shamelessly in front of all the trains. I want to go back to Westmount with you and live on the polished floors of my father's house . . . Be noble, cold, wild. I urge you to join me in my celebrations."

BARRIE WEXLER: Leonard really understood the psychic glue that is Hydra. Call it magic, call it fairy dust—when you step away from it, it dissipates. Love born on Hydra doesn't travel. Leonard was insightful enough to understand that.

Still, Cohen was restless. Not long after he sent that letter, he went to Cuba. He left Montreal March 30, drawn by tales of Fidel Castro's revolutionary fervour, and by his sister Esther's stories of her honeymoon there with Victor Cohen. He was likely aware that one of his literary heroes, García Lorca, had also sojourned there.

BARRIE WEXLER: Apart from their sexual orientation, there are an amazing number of similarities between Cohen and Lorca. Both came from

upper-middle-class families. Both briefly went to graduate school at
Columbia University. Both travelled to Cuba out of curiosity. And
both suffered from clinical depression.

There may have been one additional impetus—Castro himself. Improb-
ably, the charismatic Cuban leader had actually visited Montreal in April
1959, invited by Claude Dupras, then president of the city's Junior Cham-
ber of Commerce. His one-day visit included a press conference covered
by 150 journalists. It's certainly possible that Cohen, then freelancing
for the CBC, was there.

Stopping briefly in Miami, Cohen wrote to ask Layton whether they had
been appointed "commissars of literature. Never mind the gg [Governor
Generals' Award] for literature. Have they made you the gg?" The sun,
he wrote, had made him "quite joyous and wild. I walked the beach all
morning, encouraging the Jews at their waterside calisthenics." His cloak-
and-dagger plan, he disclosed, was that if he intended to say anything
critical about the regime after he reached Havana, he would preface the
comment with a line of poetry and write the opposite of what he meant.

When Cohen arrived, the Cuban revolution was only a few years old and
the situation was still chaotic. Cohen later described himself in a poem as
"the last tourist in Havana." His initial impressions were hugely positive.
On April 5, 1961, writing to Layton, Cohen called it an "exciting and brave
island. It fills me with joy to live in a revolutionary atmosphere. We must
begin one in Canada. Canada si, Yanqui no. American propaganda . . .
is filled with lies about communism. Death to the Invader." In another
letter, to Ihlen, he maintained that all of South America was on the brink
of revolution. "Sometimes I look at my poems and feel quite obsolete
before the forces of history. People must eat. There must be an end to
humiliation."

His youthful idealism was soon tempered. One evening, soon after
arriving at the hotel Miramar at Playa de Varadero, Cohen went out
walking. Wandering about in khakis and carrying a hunting knife, he was

suddenly surrounded by a cadre of soldiers carrying Czech sub-machine guns and arrested; they were convinced he was the first member of America's Bay of Pigs invading force. Cohen offered them the only Spanish phrase he knew that might save him—*Amistad de pueblo*. Friends of the people. It seemed to work. The soldiers ultimately draped him with garlands of shells and bullets. Sometime later, Cohen took a more sober view of his Cuban sojourn.

LEONARD COHEN: I thought maybe this was my Spanish Civil War, but it was a shabby kind of support. It was really mostly curiosity and a sense of adventure . . . They [the Cubans] were under a threat of invasion, so you have to take that into consideration. But just a society that well organized turned me against it. I didn't like the loudspeakers on every corner, and the general sense of gung ho. There were articles in the journals about the bourgeois individualists—artists and that sort of thing. And I found myself characterized very accurately . . . Because, that's really where I am: I am a bourgeois individualist.

BARRIE WEXLER: He told me he wanted to meet Ernest Hemingway. He'd been living outside Havana for about twenty years, but had moved back to the States a few months earlier to be treated for depression. Not long after, he committed suicide.

En route home from Cuba, Cohen stopped in New York City to see Esther and an old friend, Yafa Lerner. On May 4, he attended a Canadian Conference of the Arts at Toronto's O'Keefe Centre, with such literary notables as Mordecai Richler, Anne Hébert, Hugh MacLennan, and Northrop Frye. Cohen read Hébert's poetry in translation and his own.

MADELEINE POULIN: Leonard took me to a bar, and Frank Scott and Irving Layton were there. He introduced me and they started talking about Anne Hébert—I think they wanted to be convivial and I was

French-Canadian. They reminisced about her and how she'd been in a sanatorium. I think it was Frank who raised [the topic]. And Irving knew her. [Cohen had also corresponded with her.] Taking me to meet them was a great gift. It showed he had some respect for me, as well. He had respect when I was still a virgin staying with the nuns, but he still had respect afterward. The sexual relationship did not change anything. I think the basis of our relationship—why did he take me to his house? To see Frank Scott? To his friend's parties?—he felt that I also kept my distances. I was just as reserved as he was. He wasn't afraid of my invading his life. I was safe.

One day, Cohen stopped into the Seven Steps bookshop, at 1430 Stanley, run by a friend, Robert Silverman.

ROBERT SILVERMAN: Cohen bought a lot of books in my store. He read his poetry there and we'd always have polite arguments about art and politics, the Cuban revolution. I was a Trotskyite. He would say art was more important than revolution, and I'd say the revolution was more important than art. He'd say, "If the revolution was more important, Shakespeare would have written fewer poems." His arguments were not unreal. In fact, he was right. He was more upper class than me, a bit snobby, but I didn't have a grudge against him. He wasn't a bad guy. Never mean. Maybe I was jealous of all the girls he got.

Silverman subsequently left Montreal and lived for two years in Cuba. But while his faith in communism eventually wavered, he never entirely abandoned left-wing causes. Some years later, he and Freda Guttman—Cohen's former girlfriend—founded the Jewish Alliance Against the Occupation of Palestine. In the late 1970s, Silverman also created a volleyball league that played in Jeanne Mance Park. Cohen, he says, came once or twice to play. "He wasn't very good, but you didn't have to be."

One evening, shortly after Cohen's return to Montreal that May, Max Layton came home to find a stranger in the family apartment—Alexander Trocchi, a legendary figure in the world of beat literature. Allen Ginsberg once described him as the most brilliant man he'd ever met, while Irvine Welsh dubbed him "the Scottish George Best of the literary world." He was also a complete and unrepentant heroin addict. Charged in the USA with giving drugs to a minor, he faced a potential death penalty if convicted. Trocchi was out on bail when he brazenly demonstrated the use of drugs on American television. Fearing re-arrest, he secured a false passport, borrowed money and clothing from George Plimpton, then editor of the *Paris Review*, and fled by bus to Canada. Cohen met him and took him to Layton.

MAX LAYTON: Trocchi was in hiding in our apartment on Somerled, sitting at the dining room table with Leonard and me, Aviva, and my dad. Trocchi is an amazingly handsome man, half-Italian, half-Scottish, a large, unusual, fantastic physiognomy.

AVIVA LAYTON: I was really impressed with him. He was tall, lean, rangy, a terrific guy, very courtly, charming, with impeccable manners, very romantic but not in a sexual way. The whole story was very romantic. He was on the lam.

MAX LAYTON: Trocchi would be holding forth, and then it was as if a flower had begun to wilt. He would get smaller and smaller and his voice would get weaker and weaker, and he'd say, "Excuse me, I have to use the washroom," and he'd come back a few minutes later and "hello!"—his voice would be powerful again.

AVIVA LAYTON: Part of being an addict is you want people to be voyeurs, so he actually invited us to watch. He said, "I'm going to give myself a fix." I thought he was joking. Who gives themselves a fix on Somerled

Avenue? And he said, "Do you want to see?" Irving did not come in. Irving was very straight.

MAX LAYTON: The four of us crowded into the bathroom while Trocchi put on the rubber band, and Leonard held the thing for him. And we watched him shoot up. Leonard was fascinated by this process. Leonard didn't shoot up—not then.

BARRIE WEXLER: I observed the same thing when Cohen would take a shot of tequila or prepare to toss the *I Ching*. He had a strong sense of the elevating nature of ceremony.

AVIVA LAYTON: We must have been on top of each other. Remember, this is before drugs became a big deal—I hadn't even smoked marijuana, at that point—so the sight of a man shooting heroin into his veins was really something. I watched with a combination of fascination, fear, repulsion, attraction, as he put the tourniquet around his arm and filled the syringe with heroin and started poking around for a vein. He said, "It's lovely. Would you like to try some?" It was like offering me a cup of tea. I said yes at first, but then chickened out. Leonard did look with deep attraction. I remember he also cooked up cocaine in one of my silver spoons. It had a big scorch mark from the flame of a cigarette lighter. I was really annoyed. He gave us a copy of his novel, *Cain's Book*, inscribed, a ragged old paperback, his own personal copy. Oh God, I wish I still had it. I read it in one night. He was a superb writer, absolutely wonderful.

After a night with the Laytons, Trocchi moved in with Cohen. There, Cohen did sample a Trocchi product—what Cohen later described as a mild combination of tap water and opium, heated on his stove. Trocchi invited him to lick the pot, and Cohen did, scraping and consuming "a very large and dangerous amount." The effects were memorable. On their way to a Chinese restaurant, Cohen briefly went blind—"a panicky moment because it was in the midst of traffic." Trocchi dragged him to the curb.

MADELEINE LERCH: I was with them. We went to a club on Peel Street, just south of Sainte-Catherine, a well-known jazz club at the time. And then they went off. Trocchi had an eight-year-old son and he gave him heroin. He told me that. Horrible.

LEONARD COHEN: That was my social introduction to Alexander Trocchi. I did understand that his company had some risks . . . It was only four or five days. In retrospect, it seemed like three or four months or even years, because you couldn't escape the guy.

Yet something in Trocchi's irrepressible spirit clearly spoke to Cohen. A few years later, in *Flowers for Hitler*, he wrote a poem: "Alexander Trocchi, Public Junkie, Prie Pour Nous."

> *Who is purer*
> *more simple than you?*
> . . . .
> *Bonnie Queen Alex Eludes Montreal Hounds*
> *Famous Local Love Scribe Implicated*

AVIVA LAYTON: He needed to get out of Canada too because the feds could have come after him. So they got him a berth on a ship. I think Leonard and Irving paid for it. It was very exciting. We helped him escape.

About this time, Aviva was trying to earn her driver's license.

AVIVA LAYTON: I kept failing the test, like maybe ten times. But one day, I'm driving downtown and I nearly hit a pedestrian—Leonard!

I actually touched his body. I looked in horror and *it was Leonard*. After that, I did not touch the car for decades. I was so frightened. I *nearly killed* Leonard.

Years later, during a drunken night on Hydra, Cohen and Irving Layton revisited the Trocchi affair.

BARRIE WEXLER: It started as a wine-washed debate on the use of drugs in the pursuit of art. Cohen, as you'd expect, made a spirited speech in the affirmative, with Layton delivering an equally energetic rebuttal, each of them trying to one up the other. Suddenly Irving stopped, stared at Cohen, and said, "I don't know how to tell you this, Leonard, but you're starting to look a lot like Trocchi."

MAX LAYTON: I went through periods of not thinking terribly highly of Leonard. Not because of the drug use, though I knew at some level it was happening. But I remember one strange encounter—another visit by Leonard. This time, he is not participating. My dad is doing it all. Leonard is sitting in a strange way, his arm almost wrapped around his head, and the whole time my father is talking, Leonard is licking and kissing his own forearm, like cradling a lover and kissing her—the whole time. I was put off by this, because it was a form of complete narcissism. It may have been a defense mechanism, against my dad, because he was an overwhelming personality, filled not just with ideas but really good lines, a fantastic way of expressing himself. By hugging and kissing yourself while my dad is fulminating, it's a way of preserving yourself. It could easily have been drug-induced. I also found the ladies' man thing, which was happening, somewhat shallow.

Cohen would later insist that his friendship with Layton was not a teacher-disciple relationship, nor one even principally based on poetry.

LEONARD COHEN: I don't like taking advice . . . So if Irving did, in some secret part of his mind, feel that he was giving me instruction, he did it in a most subtle and beautiful way. He did it as a friend. He never made me feel that I was sitting at his feet. There were many people who sat at his feet. I wasn't one of them. We very rarely discussed poetry or art. We discussed other things. In fact, we didn't discuss too much. We used to hang out together.

The suggestion that Cohen and Layton rarely discussed poetry is disingenuous, and contradicted by both Layton's son, Max, and his then wife, Aviva. In fact, for the better part of a decade, from 1954, they spent many hours dissecting poetry. Still, Layton's influence was profound; because of him, Cohen adopted an attitude to life itself, to seize it with both hands hungrily and passionately.

BARRIE WEXLER: It wasn't just Cohen who rejected the mentorship idea. Irving did too. I once made the mistake—not in Leonard's presence—of introducing Layton as Leonard's mentor. He immediately contradicted me, saying something to the effect that Cohen was already who he was when they met. He had just facilitated a few things.

One day that spring, Cohen had a strange encounter with a casual friend, poet and artist Vera Frenkel.

VERA FRENKEL: My memory is that I meet Leonard at the Tokay [a Hungarian restaurant on Stanley Street] and either I'm carrying a piece of luggage he has lost or I'm reporting to him about it. I remember holding a small suitcase. I don't know what was in it. In the back of my mind, there's some railway station. But it was a big thing and he was concerned. And I knew where it was and either assured him or retrieved it somehow. Leonard always needed to be saved and lost in the same breath. I remember the exchange. It's the only time I sat with him, ever. He gazed at me and said, "You must be a healer." No doubt he said that to everybody. I was startled. I was young and impressionable and thought, "Gosh. Okay." I couldn't relate a suitcase to being a healer. We were there the better part of an hour. From whatever depression he was in, he managed to be flattering. But I never wanted to pursue a relationship with him, didn't seek him out. I was probably too self-absorbed.

In late May, McClelland & Stewart issued Cohen's second book of poetry, *The Spice Box of Earth*—eighty-eight poems written between his year at Columbia University and his stay in London. It was launched the same day as Irving Layton's *The Swinging Flesh*. Accompanying the book—dedicated to his paternal grandmother, Mrs. Lyon Cohen, and to his maternal grandfather, Rabbi Solomon Klonitzky-Kline—was a provocative author's statement: "I shouldn't be in Canada at all. Winter is all wrong for me. I belong beside the Mediterranean. My ancestors made a terrible mistake. But I have to keep coming back to Montreal to renew my neurotic affiliations."

SEYMOUR MAYNE: I was still in grade ten, and friends with [poet] Henry Moscovitch. One day he says, "I'm taking you to the Carmen Café. You've got to meet Leonard Cohen." So there's Leonard with two beautiful young ladies, of course, and I'm introduced. It's May 1961—I'm sixteen, he's not yet twenty-seven. There was an aura around him. He was not just the golden kid. He was more than that—the star, the one, of that whole literary circle, a generation younger than Layton and Dudek and F. R. Scott, who obviously had the gift. His first book was a bit of a miscellany, but it still had several wonderful poems and the thing is, he wrote them all before he was twenty. The clincher was the second book, which came out May 29, 1961. His mother, Masha, had a launch party at his house at 599 Belmont. I was invited, along with my friend Kenneth Hertz. We were the youngest in the crowd.

The illuminati, Scott and his wife, Marion, were there, Mort Rosen-garten, Robert Hershorn—seventy to eighty people, crowded. I didn't stay long, because I had a McGill entrance exam to write the next morning, but he did sign my copy of the book and I left with what I thought was my copy. Some days later, I open it up and it says, "For Rose, better than talking, with love, Leonard. May 29, 1961." Now, I don't know if Rose is alive and I don't even know her last name. Of course, it could have been one of his mother's friends, or a name he called one of his girlfriends, like [painter Louise] Weezie Scott. He had a harem at that time.

The next month, in another letter to Ihlen, Cohen restated his funda-mental position. "My freedom is very fragile," he wrote. "I can buy it for very little, but I would hate myself if I left you and the child to preserve it, and I would hate you if I didn't leave and lost it . . . I can't seem to make commitments . . . I'm so lonely for you, and yet I know there will be times when I'll want to go away so I can come back again."

BARRIE WEXLER: That letter is the best articulation of the threshold issue. Infidelity is often a *casus belli* in relationships, but I don't think it played that big a role in their breakup. In the main—I know this directly from her—it was Leonard's unwillingness to commit.

A few days later, walking along the docks in Montreal, Cohen spotted a Yugoslav freighter soon bound for Genoa. The captain offered him low-cost passage across the Atlantic. He left that night, with only three hun-dred dollars. On Hydra that summer, Cohen forged a new and important friendship—with Steve Sanfield, another spiritually hungry Jew. Originally from Massachusetts, he was three years older than Cohen.

SARAH SPARKS: Steven had decided to write the great American novel in Greece, and that's when he met Leonard. Someone introduced him to *The Tibetan Book of the Dead* and he decided to go to Tibet and teach English to young monks, in exchange for spiritual guidance. They were taking a lot of drugs, and that feeling of enlightenment hit him pretty hard. Then Steve decided to become a holy man.

ROGER GREEN: That's where it began, with Leonard, Steve, and George Lialios taking the LSD they'd gotten from the drug company Sandoz, in Switzerland, and reading Walter Evans-Wentz's translation of *Tibetan Book of the Dead.*

The LSD came courtesy of author Aldous Huxley's niece, who lived on the island and had met Sanfield. She arranged for Sandoz to ship a parcel of liquid LSD to Hydra. It came with a request to take the drug and report the results. Evans-Wentz was an American anthropologist best known for his 1927 translation of the Tibetan Buddhism classic.

JACQUIE BELLON: Steve never got to Dharamsala. He went back to L.A. to get rid of his stuff and ended up in Gardenia [a suburb of Los Angeles], studying with Roshi [Zen teacher Joshu Sasaki Roshi].

SARAH SPARKS: He met Roshi—this is 1962 or '63—and he really caught him. So he decided to stay in L.A. It was Steve who later introduced Leonard to Roshi.

Despite periods of friction and jealousy surrounding women, the Sanfield-Cohen friendship successfully spanned almost fifty-five years, until Sanfield's death, in 2015.

One night that summer, Cohen attended his friend Alexis Bolens's annual summer party.

ALEXIS BOLENS: I was standing close to him on the terrace when somebody said they'd dropped a tablet of LSD on the floor. Leonard immediately went down on his hands and knees, poking under the legs of tables and the other guests, trying to find the acid. It went on for quite a while. You'd have thought someone had lost a diamond earring.

Cohen used other drugs as well, including hashish and opium, but complained in a letter to Ihlen, who was in Norway, that they made him as "tired as alcohol. I keep wanting to blur myself even though I am happiest when I am most sober."

JULIE FELIX: I think she was probably having an abortion.

If she was having an abortion, Cohen could not have been responsible; they'd been apart for seven months. More likely, it was simply the first of many separations. Cohen alluded to it in the same letter saying, "We gave each other such comfort. Do you think it will ever work again?" In another missive, addressing Ihlen as "my dearest Mu," he insists that "all that I want to tell you is you are important to me . . . I look out the window and everything is connected with you."

That summer, Cohen befriended Zina Rachevsky, the beautiful American daughter of wealthy Jews, then living in the fast lane in Athens. Her maternal grandfather was Simon Straus, who amassed a banking fortune. The paternal side was also Jewish, but Russian. Either Sanfield or Allen Ginsberg, who also visited Cohen on Hydra that summer, introduced him. It's not clear if they became lovers, but Cohen was clearly smitten.

BARRIE WEXLER: Cohen met her in Kolonaki, an upscale neighbourhood of Athens, where she was living. He said he fell head over heels for her. She eventually went from being a socialite and party girl to a practitioner of Tibetan Buddhism. She moved to Tibet, shaved her head, was one of the first foreigners to study with the lamas, and became the abbess of a monastery. In the summer of 1973, Leonard got word that Zina had died in Nepal from accidentally eating poisonous mushrooms, though he later said she had contracted cholera.

Another arrival that summer was artist Barbara Lapcek, from New York City.

BARBARA LAPCEK: I was looking for directions to my pension. Leonard and some friends were sitting at a table. My first impression? He was like the people I was looking for. I always loved the guy—who he was and what he represented. Our relationship was very nice, very solid. He only hit on me once, and that felt like a brotherly gesture, to tell you the truth. It was such a normal thing. He was a womanizer, but not in a crude sense. He was such an honest man, lighthearted. He didn't take himself too seriously. He seemed to have respect for everyone. I never saw him be anything but gracious—I never saw depression. He likely kept that hidden.

On September 12, 1961, Cohen wrote to the Laytons, saying he'd been sick "with several humiliating diseases," one of which made him feel like he was "peeing red hot fishing hooks. And you must pee every five minutes, plus fever and hallucinations. Ha, ha." He planned to go to Athens to have a "clever doctor soak him in penicillin." Cohen said his novel was beating him up pretty thoroughly but he hoped to finish "by Chanukah and good riddance." His friend, Madeleine Lerch came to visit, "nursed me, fed me, cleaned the house, sewed bed covers, napkins, convinced me I was thin (I always wanted to be thin), even caught a disease or two for company's sake. And her name will be blessed evermore . . . She tells me the Italian papers were full of photos of Anne [Sherman] and Orsini . . . doesn't anything retire?"

BARRIE WEXLER: The most revealing line is "I always wanted to be thin." It's an off-the-cuff vision statement. Leonard didn't start out with a thin physique. That he maintained one throughout his life speaks to his enormous discipline. In a way, he also wanted the body of his work to look like his own, trying to say what he wanted to say with as few words as possible.

MADELEINE LERCH: I went twice to Hydra that summer. I was working as a model in Paris. I don't remember getting sick. I don't remember Anne. I came with a friend from Italy and we both stayed at his house. There was a French journalist there too, and he and the Italian girlfriend hooked up. My friend had to go back to Italy and I went back with her, then returned to Hydra and stayed longer. I don't know if he and Marianne had broken up, but there were tons of other women in his life.

Although Cohen's romance with Marianne Ihlen was little more than a year old and he was enjoying the company of Lerch and others, Annie Sherman continued to remain on his mind. In a notebook entry dated September 1961, there's a poem—"To Anne."

> *I'd no sooner forget you*
> *than pretty houses or legends*
> *or success*

BRIAN SIDAWAY: Marianne told me this—that she was convinced Leonard never really got over Annie Sherman.

Indeed, years later, Ihlen told her biographer, Kari Hesthamar, that she thought his song "So Long, Marianne" was inhabited by Sherman's ghost. At the same time, he was writing letters to Ihlen, pleading with her to come to Hydra. "Come, even for a little while, no promises, no commitments, except the commitment to talk honestly. I want to see you. It's very simple. I can't read the future. I'm probably being very selfish asking you to come but how else can we know anything?"

JULIE FELIX: I was there that autumn. I actually had a small part in *Phaedra*, as an extra, the Jules Dassin film. I remember they had us jumping around in the sea and it was cold. They kept filling us with ouzo to keep us warm.

MADELEINE LERCH: They were shooting *Phaedra*, and I'd go down and watch. Leonard was very easygoing, easy to talk to and make conversation with, not complicated. But he was melancholy all the time. So was I, so we had something in common. On Hydra, I swam, hung out at the port in the evenings, drinking. I met Allen Ginsberg there—he didn't stay with Leonard, when I was there. He was interesting. They hung out a lot.

Later, there were rumours that George Johnston, his wife, Charmian Clift, actress Melina Mercouri, and actor Anthony Perkins had been seen carrying on in the back room of Katsikas grocery.

JULIE FELIX: I met Leonard very soon after I arrived, through Chuck Hulse, who was living there with Gordon Merrick. They found me a room to rent. I thought I'd be invited to stay with them but I wasn't because, as homosexuals, they were living very secret lives. They were good friends with Leonard and with George and Charmian Johnston. Every night, they'd get together at the agora—Leonard and George. I was very young and impressionable. I didn't know very much about the literary world. I remember thinking they were all intellectual. Leonard was quite quiet compared to the others. George was the one who held court. Leonard was always very kind, gentle and quiet. Marianne was not there, but he spoke of her. I did meet Madeleine

Lerch. She was tall. I said to him once, "You always fall in love with tall women," and he wrote back, "I'm shrinking, so they're all tall now." Madeleine really impressed me, because she picked herbs from nature and knew what to do with them.

One night, Felix lost the key to her room. Everyone else had returned home.

JULIE FELIX: I knew where Leonard lived, so I went to his house and said, "I can't get in [to my place]," so he said, "You can stay here." He had this little tiny house, with a great big, metal double bed. He was on his own. I was kind of worried, so I left on all my clothes, and hugged the side of the bed. He was very respectful. We weren't lovers then, not at all. The next morning, the window was open and he was writing, typing, his first book, *Beauty at Close Quarters*, and this big gust of wind blew through the window and blew all his pages out into the street. So we ran out, chasing all these typed pages blowing all over the place. I would have been really upset, my life's work blown out the window, but Leonard was laughing. We went running up and down the street. I think we got most of the pages back.

Felix, already a folk singer, was travelling with her father's Mexican guitar.

JULIE FELIX: Leonard and I would trade songs. Neither of us was writing songs at the time. I was singing Woody Guthrie and Mexican songs my father had taught me. "Michael, Row the Boat Ashore." He sang mainly union songs. That influenced me, because I wasn't that politically aware.

Cohen remained on Hydra through December. Irving Layton had sent him his poem "A Tall Man Executes a Jig." In a December 8 letter to Layton,

Cohen said it was "the poem you've always wanted to write and includes everything you knew up to the day you wrote it . . . It's a masterpiece, that's simple to see, and there's no point even congratulating the author, regardless of the polishing, because poems like that are handed down." Cohen told Layton he had finished his novel. "It's a miserable mess, but I can't help feeling it's an important mess. I've told very few lies in it, which is something for that many pages." He had also begun another novel—a thriller, just for recreation. "Before I'd written 30 pages it began to get serious on me. A few years ago, I began to write horror stories as a lark, but all my prose now and most of my poetry are horror stories. Do you suppose that's my real world?"

Cohen's need for change was apparent. "Hydra is . . . the most beautiful place I have ever seen," he wrote, "but I am hungry for the city and all-night movies and the polemics they inspire. I'm out of my head to leave this sun for a northern city." His destination was Oslo—and Ihlen. "I've got to confront her mystery in the snow," he wrote. They had not seen each other in a year. The day before leaving—and starting a week-long train trip across Europe—he wrote to her, "my little ghost," saying the trip would determine if their relationship could resume. Acknowledging his jealousy and his uncertainties, Cohen said, "I cannot forget you. I must see what will happen to us when we are together. Perhaps it will be nothing, perhaps everything."

*   *   *

In Montreal, his friend Robert Hershorn had begun publication of *Exchange*, a new magazine of politics and culture. Against the advice of his father, clothing magnate Sam Hershorn, he used his own financial resources to get it launched.

SELMA HERSHORN: *Exchange* was extraordinary—Norman Mailer, Pierre Berton, Hugh MacLennan, Leonard Cohen, Irving Layton, Robert

Fulford, Malcolm Lowry all wrote for it. There were only three issues, two at the end of 1961 and the last one, their swan song, in early 1962.

Hershorn originally approached Cohen to edit it, but he demurred, instead recommending Hungarian émigré Stephen Vizinczey.

STEPHEN VIZINCZEY: Leonard said that Stephen knows more about literature—that's how I came to edit *Exchange* from my apartment. Leonard was a good friend. [Earlier] we lived next to each other on Mountain Street and used to talk about literature late into the night. Leonard was fired up by what I had told him about existentialism and Camus and Sartre. I advised him to read *The Idiot*, which he loved. I didn't think he knew much about European literature. Dostoevsky was news to him, but he was a very bright intellectual, and a wonderful poet.

VIVIENNE LEEBOSH: I was seeing another friend of Leonard's—Dave Tenser [now deceased]. We used to have dinner at La Tour Eiffel, on Stanley Street. Hershorn was always there. He was living with Alanis Obomsawin—fighting and living. I don't know how much they lived together. They had huge fights. I was invited to their house one night. Vizinczey was there. Vittorio Fiorucci—he was a close friend. It was just gorgeous, on Pine Avenue, big rooms. Everyone was smoking marijuana. Leonard was there and they asked him to play the guitar. He sang and played—I don't remember what. I thought he was incredible, but there were a lot of folk singers around then—Pete Seeger, Leadbelly. That's when I met him. Let's put it this way. Between Leonard and Hershorn, Derek May—I later named my son after Derek—and a few other people, that was the group I wanted to be part of.

ARNIE GELBART: Robert hired Vittorio as his art director. I was friends with Vittorio [now deceased] and became associate art director of

Exchange. Vittorio was a big personality, very smart and very talented. He's one of the great poster artists of the world. He created brands before brands existed, finding the image that encapsulated something. Leonard contributed a few poems.

STEPHEN VIZINCZEY: I fought with Hershorn to pay for poems. I had huge shouting arguments with him, threatening to quit unless he paid contributors well. That was one of the chief reasons for the magazine's success. Layton told me he had never got as much money for a poem as I paid him. But every time poor Bob wrote a cheque, he aged years. Incidentally, he had nothing to do with the magazine, apart from financing it. I did not tolerate any interference with the content, and we had many fights, as he wanted a safer, less controversial magazine. Once he brought his rich friends from the Montreal clothing dynasties—[but] they were afraid even to subscribe.

MANNY VAINISH: I was the accountant for Robert. He wasn't fond of the clothing industry or the business. He was always looking for some kind of more exciting life.

In the magazine's first issue, November 1961, Vizinczey reviewed Cohen's *The Spice Box of Earth*, praising the collection as "rich in universal relevance and beauty—with us, yet ahead of us." Referencing the inwardly directed sarcasm of "The Cuckold's Song"—"The important thing was to cuckold Leonard Cohen. I like that line because it's got my name in it"—Vizinczey notes that with his ability to accept "the paradox of the sad and the ridiculous, of joy and pain, [Cohen] rises above them, achieving both personal and poetic victories." However, he objected to the more specifically Jewish poems, saying they showed Cohen "susceptible to a ghetto complex, given to brooding over the special purpose and special cross of being a Jew."

STEPHEN VIZINCZEY: We were so controversial that after three issues, Robert's father said he'd disinherit him if he continued to support it.

MANNY VAINISH: I can't say I ever heard that. But it wouldn't surprise me—not a bit. I would believe that in a flash.

STEPHEN VIZINCZEY: Poor Bob went back to selling clothes, which he hated. After Bob died [in 1972], Vittorio—a genius of an art director—met his father on the street and asked him, "Now, are you glad that your son no longer publishes a magazine?"

HENRY ZEMEL: Leonard thought Robert should never have given up. He thought he should have spent every last penny to save it.

In January 1962, Scope, a McGill University cultural organization, brought in American novelist Norman Mailer to speak. Hershorn hosted a party on January 19 in his honour.

ROBERT COHEN: I remember sitting around a table in Robert's house with Mailer, Saul Bellow, Louis Dudek, Irving Layton.

ISRAEL CHARNEY: I was Robert's assistant on the magazine. A warm and wonderful character, and very funny. I liked him a lot. He introduced me to Lenny Bruce. He introduced me to pot. We laughed hysterically for a couple of years. It was all very fun and very creative. But eventually it turned weird. There were a lot of parties at his place, with interesting people. Who could ask for more, growing up? The landlord was the Greek consul.

ARNIE GELBART: I remember the party. Mailer got quite drunk and said to Alanis, "You know, the problem with you Indians is that you're stupid." Meaning, you've allowed yourself to be taken advantage of.

That's what he meant. But she took it the wrong way and it ended up in a huge fight. She went after him and tried to pull his eyes out or something.

ISRAEL CHARNEY: She slapped him across the face. I'd been thumb-wrestling with Norman. But this story didn't stop at the slap. They really hit it off, Mailer and Alanis. There was passion in the slap, definitely. And Mailer had his way with words. I'm sure the story did not end there. Leonard—I don't even know if he was there. Leonard was in and out. He wasn't around a lot. In fact, most of the time, Leonard was mostly not there. He was always peripheral to what was going on.

Irving and Aviva Layton were also there.

AVIVA LAYTON: Irving and Mailer were both pugilistic. They both exuded this fierce, creative energy, which was catnip for women. Norman came up to Irving and said, "We're the only two lions in this room." Then he drew back his right arm and punched Irving in the gut and winded him. I was standing right there. Then he disappeared. Irving [later] wrote a poem about it ["The Dazed Steer"], and Leonard, in the persona of Irving, wrote a poem about it in *The Energy of Slaves*, threatening to kill him and his entire family.

CARMEN ROBINSON: Hershorn had his own apartment, which was very unusual at the time. His girlfriend was aboriginal, which was really unusual. I went to a couple parties [there]. They were seriously into drugs, heavy-duty stuff. Leonard was into drugs then. He was attractive, he was appealing, he was smart—he wasn't the conventional, doing-the-right-thing, staying-on-the-straight-line. They were a whole alternative group—more interesting, doing things people weren't doing.

If the party wasn't at Hershorn's, it was on Phillips Square, where Morton Rosengarten had a studio.

ISRAEL CHARNEY: At Morton's, they played jazz music and we danced. His family owned the building next door, the former stock exchange. His work space was the trading floor. Every Friday night, he'd have parties. All the visual artists came—Armand [Vaillancourt], Vittorio [Fiorucci], Derek [May]. I was ten years younger than these guys. It was a treat. I knew Morton. I knew the poets too, but they were very competitive, very ambitious. They were to be avoided, as far as I was concerned.

AVIVA LAYTON: Morton did a bust of my head in that studio. I was sitting there in an old dental chair, which I helped him find at [the] Salvation Army. When he was sculpting, Leonard came in and took up a chisel and started pretending to sculpt my face, literally on my face, pretending to knock things off, while Morton was sculpting. I kept the head on Somerled for ages, but Morton asked for it back to put it on a proper base. That was sixty years ago. Leonard and I used to call him up every year and say, "Where's the head, Morton? Where is the head of Saint John the Baptist?"

One afternoon, Cohen bumped into his old college friend Ruth Roskies Wisse at Hershorn's flat.

RUTH ROSKIES WISSE: [It was] the first time I remember feeling disappointed in Leonard . . . On the otherwise bare coffee table lay a book I'd never heard of, the *I Ching* . . . Leonard explained to me that this was actually a way of life, or rather a way of determining life.

Cohen took some Canadian dimes from his pocket, demonstrating how, by flipping the coins and consulting them in tandem with the writings of the *I Ching*, one could alter otherwise ego-driven behaviour.

RUTH ROSKIES WISSE: It seemed such utter nonsense that I was sure it must be a game, perhaps an Asian form of Monopoly. The more eloquently he described the subtleties of the method, the more ridiculous I thought he was being. When I realized that Leonard took all of this seriously, and when he realized that I did not, the conversation ended . . . I was shocked that anyone whose ancestors had written the Talmud could profess enthusiasm for this stuff. In the years that followed, Leonard's interest in the *I Ching* gave way to a series of enthusiasms: for Immanuel Velikovsky's theory of creation; for cabalistic mysticism; for Indian meditation. Almost every time I saw him, he seemed under the impression of some new idea or new way of experiencing the world.

At least with the *I Ching*, Cohen did not lose his fascination.

BARRIE WEXLER: I saw him throw *I Ching* coins until the mid-1980s. He had a copy of the book on Hydra. He had a little red box of old Chinese coins that he bought in Chinatown and gave away to people. He was quite ceremonious when he tossed, shaking the coins in his hand for a long time before letting them spill onto the kitchen table. He liked the ritual as much as anything. I never heard him ask a question, but he was always clearly concentrating. Once, I did it with him and got something like, "The wise man has his yes and he has his no." I said, "Cohen, what the hell is that supposed to mean?" But he thought it was a brilliant answer—you know how he loved the orchestration of opposites. On the other hand, he was also fond of fortune cookies.

On another occasion, after throwing the *I Ching* on Hydra, Wexler asked Cohen if he thought the advice he got was helpful. He said it was second rate, "but it was the best he could do on the island because there were no Chinese restaurants."

With his growing reputation, other aspiring writers began to visit Cohen and pay homage.

DAVID SOLWAY: I was among a group of younger poets who regarded him as some kind of idol. I'd visit from time to time, and I was really quite poor. And I didn't know that Leonard had come from an upper-middle-class family and never had any real financial concerns. But I was worried about him, and so the joke was that one day I bought a box of groceries for him and spent forty dollars—my last forty dollars, actually. I recall walking up to his apartment carrying the box on my shoulders and offering it to him so that he'd have something to eat. He had a bemused expression on his face when he thanked me for my largesse.

By March 1962, Cohen had returned to London, unpacking his bag in the now familiar confines of Stella Pullman's Hampstead boardinghouse. His immediate mission was to revise his novel—now titled *The Favourite Game*—for his British publisher, Secker & Warburg. Hearing that the novel had found a publisher, Irving Layton had told Cohen's mother that 1962 would be a great year. "Now," Cohen asked, in a letter saluting Layton's fiftieth birthday, "is this a great new year or merely a continuation of the great year you promised last year? If it's a new one, you might as well know that the last one wasn't very great at all." That month, Marianne Ihlen came for a short visit. In a letter to her soon after, he expressed loneliness for her, for Montreal, and for "brown bodies that speak to one another in a language we don't want to understand."

Among the friends Cohen saw in London was Lionel Tiger, then completing a postgraduate degree at the London School of Economics.

LIONEL TIGER: I said, "What are you doing?" He said, "I'm on the Leonard Cohen seventy-day plan to success." What the hell is that? He says, "A thousand words a day." We'd walk on the [Hampstead] Heath, four or five hours.

Tiger was then married to Marquita Crevier, an aspiring poet from Montreal.

BARRY MCKINNON: She was a small, wispy woman, with flowing dark hair, fine features—delicate—a worldly forties-movie-star look. She was mysterious and seemed haunted, to say the least. She was a friend of Layton's, and a onetime lover of Leonard Cohen.

SEYMOUR MAYNE: I met her later, in 1970. I even went on a date with her once or twice. She told me she had been one of Leonard's lovers in London. She was proud of the fact. I didn't want to be involved with someone who was part of Leonard's army of lovers. She was definitely in the crowded constellation around Leonard's varied solar adventures, but she was a minor moon—or even just a fast-moving comet that swung into his orbit for a short trajectory.

LIONEL TIGER: There was some circumstantial occasion which may have led to her relationship with Leonard, which I did not know about, though she had mentioned him. She was beautiful, eccentric, extraordinarily imaginative about her life. She claimed she had been a ballerina with the Royal Winnipeg Ballet and left for health reasons. On her mother's side, she claimed her family were Scottish aristocrats who owned coal mines, which she did not want to inherit. She was always elegantly dressed and had good posture.

HENRY ZEMEL: Marquita was very much a poser. She was always posing. She was very attractive and she wanted to be attractive. She was always working at it.

At one point, Crevier had a book of poetry accepted by Faber and Faber in England but, because of a psychological breakdown and lack of interest in being published, had rejected the deal.

LIONEL TIGER: This would be par for the course for her, something that would occupy her for a couple of years. Should I sign, not sign?

In 1967, Crevier was hospitalized for a recurring emotional disorder. Her book, *Marquita Crevier: Selected Poems*, was published in 1976 by a small Montreal press. Crevier eventually had a brain aneurysm, suffered a debilitating stroke, was paralyzed, and took her own life.

Cohen had hoped to return to Canada, but, as he wrote to Layton, "won't for a while, owing to penury and love and spite at not winning the Governor General's Award. I want to tear at everything that nourishes me." Instead, he resolved to follow Ihlen to Oslo. "It's so easy and Marianne is so ordinary. Can I help it if she's a priestess whose nature is to make everything difficult and prosaic? . . . I've been working on my novel with a scalpel. I won't be able to save it, but it's one of most interesting corpses I've ever seen." Later, in another postcard to Layton, Cohen said he was writing a thousand words a day and "very little else. I walk all over the place and can't face my typewriter for pleasure. I've written 30,000 words of a 70,000-word novel and I'm closer to peace than I've ever been. Chekhov was right—work is salvation."

On the freighter to Norway, Cohen met a young Canadian geologist, Leslie Kaye.

NAOMI STANLEY: My dad [Kaye] was very artistic. He saw Len scribbling in a notebook, writing poetry, and they struck up conversation. They just clicked. He saw straightaway that Leonard was extremely talented. Apparently, they had relatives who came from the same parts of Poland and Russia—this also impacted their first meeting. My father had fought for Israel in 1948; prior to that he smuggled weaponry from Canada to British Mandate Palestine. Len was very impressed by my father's tales. They bonded as Jews and thought they were probably related. Later, my father was disappointed in his records, saying they were "depressing" musically and that he should have stuck to poetry. He was wrong there, eh? They met several times over the years.

On the freighter, Cohen contracted lice and later spent considerable time trying to rid himself of the pests. According to Ihlen's memoir, the couple saw an Ibsen play at the National Theatre, dined on boiled, dried cod, and visited friends and family. In a letter to Layton from Oslo, Cohen said, "I've been working on my new book but today feel like giving up writing. The air is too sweet for all this working of the mind, the herrings are too tasty. When I am not watching blonde girls, I am eating herring and sometimes I do both."

While abroad, Cohen received a long letter from Layton. It testified to Cohen's wanderlust ("O little boy blue, where are you? . . . He's here, he's there, he's gone!"), and to the esteem in which the older poet held him, calling him "golden boy" and "wunderkind." The letter reported that a Montreal theatre director wanted to stage the plays they had written, touring them across the country, but nothing came of this.

By June, Cohen and Ihlen were back on Hydra. Having sung the sun-drenched virtues of Mediterranean life, he began to regret his advocacy. In a letter to his sister, Esther, he insisted, "I don't intend to open my gates to everybody whose only excuse for bothering me is that they can afford the fare and know my name . . . My commitment here is serious and they are on holiday . . . This is a workshop." Filmmaker Jules Dassin, he complained, had shot a movie on "the very spot where I happen to swim." That was the previous summer. And he was expecting a visit from his cousin Alan Golden, "whom I had never spoken to except over my shoulder at *shul*." Golden and his friend Morris Fish did not arrive on Hydra until the following spring.

Work on the novel *The Favourite Game* was frequently delayed; it would only get worse. That summer, [Cohen's] mother, Masha, descended. To avoid offending her sense of propriety, Marianne temporarily moved out. She quickly returned, at Leonard's request, becoming an important buffer during the visit. Masha was temperamental, complaining one day about heat and the next about cold. Once, resolved to leave, she packed her suitcases, only to change her mind. Cohen subsequently told Marianne he would have killed his mother had it not been for her.

BARRIE WEXLER: Masha packing and unpacking happened several times. Cohen had Anthony Kingsmill and me in hysterics when he told the story. Apparently, with each successive episode, he managed to move the suitcases ever closer to the front door, but never quite through it.

Still, he was working. In an August letter to his publisher, Cohen said that he had "eliminated a kind of self-conscious melancholy that is fine for a 'first-novel.' . . . The new book is tough. The author isn't sticking his personal pain at you in every chapter; that's why the new version hurts more. Mostly it's a question of cutting away the blubber and letting the architecture of bone show through." By October, he was finished.

To Layton, he wrote that he was not entirely satisfied, but "anyone with an ear will know I've torn apart orchestras to arrive at my straight, melodic line . . . In a way that means more to me than the achievement itself. I walk lighter and carry a big scalpel. Everything I've read in the past week is too long . . . I don't know anything about people—that's why I have this terrible and irresistible temptation to be a novelist."

In the fall, Cohen met Canadian documentary filmmaker Harry Rasky, who had stopped on Hydra after a trip to Egypt. They forged a modest friendship that led to occasional meetings. In New York, the following year, Cohen told Rasky he had once applied for a job at *Time* magazine. Almost two decades later, Rasky would make *The Song of Leonard Cohen*, a documentary. Soon after, Cohen and Ihlen left Hydra. They parted in Vienna. There, he told her it would not be long before they'd be together again, but he could guarantee nothing, and she knew it.

BARRIE WEXLER: Marianne said he was always up front. She knew he was ambivalent at best about committing himself. But it's not what she wanted to hear at the time.

Heading home to Canada, Cohen stopped in Paris—invited by CBC Radio to moderate a panel discussion with Malcolm Muggeridge, Mary McCarthy, and Romain Gary on the topic Is There a Crisis in Western Culture? It was recorded at the Hotel Napoleon. Cohen spent two days before the taping in the Hotel Cluny Square reading the work of his guests. In Paris, Cohen saw both Madeleine Lerch and Julie Felix.

JULIE FELIX: Leonard was on his way back to Canada. I'd run out of money and was going to go back to Ibiza and Madeleine said, "I have a car. Let's go together." So we did. She drove a hundred miles an hour.

In 1969, the *Partisan Review* published Cohen's short story "Luggage Fire Sale," which chronicled his Paris experience, including a brief dalliance with a blond medical student he met early one morning in a Boulevard Saint-Michel café and took back to his room. Under a shelf on the wall of the room, with a fountain pen, Cohen composed "a very perishable aphorism in small italic script: 'change is the only aphrodisiac.'"

The CBC must have liked what Cohen did. Soon after, it commissioned broadcaster Nona Macdonald to moderate a discussion between him and his friend, anthropologist Lionel Tiger.

LIONEL TIGER: Harry Boyle, who was running radio, took a shine to us and said, "Why don't you do a conversation?" We must have spent eight or ten hours talking about the future of Canada. We were both garrulous and proud of how we spoke. Then Harry went off to television and lost interest.

Decades later, Cohen would reflect on that turbulent period and his insecure relationship with Marianne Ihlen.

LEONARD COHEN: She'd go back to Norway, I to Canada to try to make some money. We were young, and both of us interested in all kinds of experience, so there was something fragile about the relationship. I was hungry for experience as any young writer is. I wanted many women, many kinds of experiences, many countries, many climates, many love affairs.

BARBARA LAPCEK: They both played around. My son, Jeff, as a young kid didn't like Marianne because she played around, and he thought she was hurting Axel, who was his friend. Leonard played around less visibly.

LEONARD COHEN: It was natural for me then to see life as some kind of buffet where there was a lot of different tastes. I'd get tired of something and then move on . . . never terribly happy doing it, leaving one thing for the next because the thing I had didn't work, whether it was the woman or the poem or the city. Until I understood that nothing works . . . and to accept that. I have a sense that I was privileged. The sunlight, the woman, the child, the table, the work, the gardenia, the order, the mutual respect and honour that we gave to each other. That's what really matters. I know there were all kinds of problems. We were kids, and we lived in a period during which the old forms were overthrown. We wanted to overthrow [those] forms, but at the same time maintain things that seemed to be nourishing. Those relationships on Hydra were all doomed. We didn't know it at the time, but they couldn't withstand what life imposed on us. Those relationships that were formed idealistically or sexually or romantically couldn't survive the challenges that ordinary lives would confront them with.

CHAPTER SEVEN

All the Lonesome Heroes

Leonard, he was always doing his own thing.

—Alfie Wade

This island is full of writers. They all come here and drive themselves crazy. This one can't write, that one can't stop. They all go nuts in the end. Everyone on this island is hiding something.

—Margarita Karapanou

Leonard Cohen spent the early winter of 1963 in New York City. His U.S. literary agent was trying to interest American publishers in *The Favourite Game*. His financial situation was desperate—down to his last seventy dollars. Yet, as he wrote to Marianne Ihlen, he was "happy in a wild sort of way, optimistic, ready for anything." His uncle Lawrence had suggested setting up a revenue stream from Cohen's father's estate. Even before that, however, Cohen had sublet a Greenwich Village apartment and expressed hope that Ihlen would join him there. She didn't. Their relationship continued to be riven by its fundamental fault line—her need for a commitment, if not marriage, that he could not and would not deliver; and his anger and jealousy when, in search of more secure, romantic possibilities, she partnered with other men. It's hard not to be struck by Cohen's double standard, since he was pursuing every pretty girl he saw.

BARRIE WEXLER: Nothing brought out Cohen's anxiousness more than his suspicion of a woman's infidelity. The go-to response of a cuckolded man is to say that lying about it bothers him more than the betrayal itself—and that was definitely true of Leonard. There was only one standard when it came to cheating—his. It didn't take long for things to come unglued with Marianne. Leonard used to talk about poetry being the ash of experience but, with Marianne, it was the embers—he was creating poems and songs out of their lives *while* they were living them. The bottom line is that she didn't want to live in a song, and he didn't want to live in a marriage.

In March, Cohen returned to Greece.

BRIAN SIDAWAY: I ran into him as we boarded the ferry to Hydra. He was going to nap, but we went upstairs for coffee and cognac and had a three-hour conversation about women. He told me, "Don't ever change yourself for a woman."

That month, Cohen purchased four old chairs, retained a workman to repair them, and hired a housekeeper, Kyria Sophia. All that was missing was Ihlen and, after further entreaties, she appeared. Then guests arrived—his cousin Alan Golden, and his former McGill Debating Union partner, Morris Fish. Both lawyers, they had just concluded a scholarship year in Paris.

ALAN GOLDEN: We didn't tell Leonard we were coming, though I may have written him the year before saying maybe we'd visit. I went to the hardware store and wrote out the name "Leandros Cohen" on a business card, and made gestures indicating I was looking for Leandros Cohen.

MORRIS FISH: We no sooner asked than he appeared.

BARRIE WEXLER: The Greeks actually called him "Leonardo."

ALAN GOLDEN: About an hour later, someone tapped me on the back and handed me the card—Leonard. We hiked up the hill at least twice to Leonard's place.

MORRIS FISH: He found us a bed-and-breakfast place. We went for a day and stayed two and three. He was living with Marianne and Axel. Marianne was beautiful, lovely, gracious, and considerate. Soft-spoken is how I remember her.

ALAN GOLDEN: Marianne was a stunning woman, very nice, and a good cook. She made us a meal of a Greek variety. I was struck by how well integrated [she and Leonard] were—shopping for food, etc. As we were leaving Hydra, he came to me urgently and said, "I have a message for the people at the Freedman Company [the family-owned business], when you get back. Tell them I'm not coming back." That was Leonard's sense of humour.

In an April letter to Layton, Cohen reported that his mother was in a Montreal hospital recovering from idiopathic thrombocytopenic purpura, a disease characterized by low platelet counts. "Marianne is perfect, even the way she demands masterpiece from me is soft and funny and much more subtle than she understands. I miss you both terribly and can't help using everything we've done together as a standard that turns so much into shit."

By May, he had finished correcting galleys for the British edition of *The Favourite Game*. "The book is nothing to be ashamed of," he wrote.

"It reads like a huge, disciplined, unimportant poem. The only thing that keeps me from despair is the certainty that nobody living could have done it half as well."

BARBARA LAPCEK: He told me I was the first person to read the novel. I loved it.

It's instructive to read the bravado in Cohen's words in light of the tone routinely adopted in later interviews—a modesty about, even a disparagement of, his talents. There was, in the youthful Cohen, a confidence that at times bordered on arrogance. Part of this was mere persona, derived from Layton himself, who seldom stopped declaiming his own genius, but Layton wasn't the only influence.

BARRIE WEXLER: The bravado displayed by F. Scott Fitzgerald in his letters to Maxwell Perkins played a role. Cohen had a book of their correspondence in his Montreal bathroom, and *The Crack-Up* on Hydra.

FRANCIS MUS: Younger people have the image of the old wise sage on the stage. The humble man. He hasn't been humble his whole career. He was really arrogant. You see it in the poetry and the novels. *The Favourite Game* has some horrifying scenes. The poem "A Kite Is a Victim"—it shows the will to be in charge. It's about power. The kite is a victim. You can tame it and put it in your drawer. It's very sadistic.

Scraping together funds to return to Montreal in June, he stayed with his friend filmmaker Claude Jutra, at his Mackay Street apartment. But he had to borrow fifty dollars from Layton to pay the rent, and was again woefully short of cash. In a letter to Ihlen, he complained that "something in me is gone . . . I'm sick of being a brilliant young success. It was such a lie . . . It's curious to see all the battles I'd won at such a high cost begin to reverse themselves." The letter again cited friction in the relationship. "We have not been very good to one another, and I'd like to find out who began the failure of courtesy and kindness."

By August, Cohen was back on Hydra. Awaiting publication of the novel, he worked on new poetry—some of it later appeared in *Flowers for Hitler.* That summer, Cohen met visiting American beat poet Harold Norse. Recalling their encounter in *Memoirs of a Bastard Angel*, Norse cites "an epidemic of jaundice" that swept the foreign colony. "A little known Canadian poet . . . also caught it, but quickly recovered. His name was Leonard Cohen. He played the guitar and sang folk songs in a beautiful voice and we read each other's poetry aloud. We also exchanged our books with inscribed copies. 'For Harold Norse, true poet,' he wrote in his copy of *The Spice Box of Earth*. I showed him my copy of the sniffling keyholes [a raunchy part of Norse's novella *Beat Hotel*] as we smoked pot on his white terrace in the sun. With trembling hands, Leonard gave me some freshly written typescript pages. 'I owe this to you,' he said, 'thanks to your keyholes.' He watched nervously as I read. It was the best innovative prose I had seen since *Naked Lunch*. It became Leonard's novel *Beautiful Losers*." If Norse's account is accurate, it suggests that Cohen had begun work on the second novel much earlier than is generally thought.

Patricia Amlin, the American artist who had precipitated the breakup of Ihlen's marriage to Axel Jensen, had also returned to Hydra.

PATRICIA AMLIN: I used to go for tea at Leonard's place. Leonard was like a big brother. He included me in his home life. I felt like I was his little sister. He let me stay at his house when he wasn't there. Leonard, to me, was rational, loving, kind and good, funny, intelligent. I really enjoyed the times with him. He covered me with a blanket of some kind of safety. He never hit on me on Hydra. When I saw him later in New York? That's not important. I remember Leonard telling me about LSD and how I had to do that and see different colours—he mentioned the hills of Montreal. I did it many years later and didn't see any colours I hadn't seen before.

Later, writing to Layton, Cohen pronounced *The Favourite Game* "fine, except for cover photograph . . . which is of the first novelist I never wanted to be . . . the face that haunts Hadassah meetings . . . Oh, Irving. So many minds to wiggle my finger in. To say nothing of the usual orifices. Everything breaking up here. Getting the intensity of first fucking by smashing the house down every second day and hopeless reconciliations. Getting a lot of fun out of life by seeing how far I will go in a beating. Lots of poems borning full-grown from my forehead . . . Gurdjieff was right when he shouted from his deathbed, 'abandon the system.'" "Irving," he later wrote, "will you understand what no one else will understand—that *The Favourite Game* is the third novel disguised as a first novel. Will you see it as a great detective story in which a body is lost in every paragraph?"

Cohen sold an excerpt of the book, entitled *Tamara* [a fictionalized version of Freda Guttman], to *Cavalier* magazine for $750—and spent it, raising the maid's salary and buying ice for the home (common in 1960s Hydra), airfare for Axel to visit his grandmother in Norway, antique earrings and dresses for Marianne, and white candles. An obsessive keeper of records, Cohen itemized the people he knew or had met on Hydra. These included Canadian writer Roger Maybank, who lived with his partner, Cypriot artist Marios Loizides; British cabinet maker David Goschen and his wife, Angela; Norwegian illustrator Tore Pedersen, a friend of Marianne's ex-husband, Axel Jensen; Swedish novelist Göran Tunström; Christopher Booker, a British journalist who cofounded the magazine *Private Eye*; Norwegian Lena Folke Olsson, with whom Jensen later had two children; and a woman named Mary Andrews.

BARRIE WEXLER: In his journal, Mary Andrews is the only one on that list he didn't write a few words about after the name—just an exclamation mark.

Other visitors that August included his cousin Edgar Cohen and his wife, Ruth, who were travelling with Montreal friends, the Sabloffs. Cohen had written to them in July to say that Hydra had become "touristic," and that he and Ihlen were headed to a village in the Peloponnesus for twenty days, but would return by August 1. He invited them all to dinner that evening.

RUTH COHEN: We ate on the terrace. Marianne was so soft. She moved so gracefully, a figure like a model's. And very gracious, the way she served us. It was a beautiful evening. We were there till two o'clock in the morning.

The next day, Cohen brought lunch to the beach.

RUTH COHEN: We weren't expecting lunch, and he just appeared with this big basket. Fresh fish, he picked it—tomatoes, olives, tzatziki, bread, small dishes. We were swimming in the cove. He was a very gracious and generous host. Marianne did not come to the beach.

By the end of September 1963, Cohen was back in Montreal—without Marianne. She'd returned briefly to Oslo to see Axel, then set off in search of modelling work in Paris.

ISRAEL CHARNEY: A gorgeous apartment. Marianne stayed at Madeleine's place for a time, then had a hotel room next door to mine. We were really good friends. Marianne was such a lovely soul. She had another boyfriend there—Joe Dassin, the son of the filmmaker, a major singing star. Leonard was a rake. He had that reputation. That was part of his poetry.

In Montreal, Cohen was introduced to a new romantic interest, Wendy Patten.

JULIANNA OVENS: It would have been late fall. He was carrying his guitar case and may just have given a concert or a reading. I introduced myself and mentioned Henry [Moscovitch], my boyfriend at the time, and Irving Layton. Then I introduced him to my friend Wendy, a tall, statuesque, drop-dead gorgeous blonde with violet-blue eyes, more beautiful than Grace Kelly, and a very nice person, very sweet. Their subsequent fling went on for at least three months.

WENDY PATTEN KEYS: It lasted longer. Julianna and I were walking down Sherbrooke Street and he came up and was hitting on us. I was in my third year at McGill. Then he realized he knew Julianna, so the three of us went off for a beer. Julianna spun off, and Leonard and I spent the rest of the afternoon and evening together. We became sweeties. Every night we were together was at a different place. We were at Claude Jutra's. We were at Robert Hershorn's. He stayed there a lot. Hershorn was like a guru, living in this dark house, hosting people. Leonard never called, but we'd bump into each other and go off and do whatever. I was in residence, so I'd have to pretend I was staying at a girlfriend's house for the night. He was almost thirty and I was about nine years younger.

JULIANNA OVENS: They were taken with each other. Wendy became invisible. She suddenly wasn't at classes. I would describe Leonard as a reticent person, not shy, but an observer, with an animal-like, instinctive feeling with respect to people, but always charming, in a real way. He was very authentic. There were no airs.

Patten, like many of Cohen's women, saw him intermittently.

WENDY PATTEN KEYS: It was off and on, because he'd run off to visit Marianne. I did bump into them once on Sainte-Catherine Street. It was very awkward. The whole relationship was very painful and terrible, actually. Partly because I knew he was with others, and because it didn't feel like we were making any permanent connection. He would never do that. I'd go to his readings. I think he wrote one poem about me. He read it at a reading and all my friends said, "Wendy, that's about you!" I think they're right. When he came back from Greece, he'd look for me at the Bistro. He was mad at me because I was not faithful to him, I suppose, when he was going off to Greece. So he wrote this rather nasty poem, which was not his wont. Usually, they're elegies to women.

The poem, "Why I Happen to Be Free," was published in *Flowers for Hitler* (1964). This is the relevant passage.

> *Forsaking the lovely girl*
> *was not my idea*
> *but she fell asleep in somebody's bed . . .*
> *I see her body puzzled*
> *with the mouthprints*
> *of all the kisses of all the men*
> *she's known . . .*
> *I walk through*
> *the blond November rain*
> *punishing her with my happiness*

WENDY PATTEN KEYS: [When I read that] I thought, "Well, perhaps I made more of an impact on him than I thought." Because at the poetry readings, I saw the women in thrall. He was able to throw out this net over his audience, effortlessly, and reel us all in. I'd be marching up and down the aisles thinking, "How do you know these words? And who are you?" That was uncomfortable. I constantly felt I was sharing him—and I was. It was tough because when you fall in love, you want that person entirely for yourself.

Although he was not yet performing as a singer, Cohen sang privately for Keys.

WENDY PATTEN KEYS: The first time I heard him sing, I said, "Leonard, I don't think this is going to fly." Boy, was I wrong.

Inevitably, Patten Keys met Cohen's circle.

WENDY PATTEN KEYS: Morty [Rosengarten]—he was a doll. Henry Moscovitch. Derek May—I went out with him too. It was a very lively gang. There was this crowd at the Bistro. I was part of all that. Leonard wasn't doing drugs at that time. I wasn't familiar with anybody of that sort because I came from the WASPy, English set. He stood out because of his extraordinary intellect and curiosity. He loved the fact that I was so WASPy. One day after going to the movies, *Fantasia*, we went to a deli. I ordered a BLT with extra mayo. He thought that was the most hysterical thing. He was kind to me. But the whole thing was quite painful, because I didn't know I was being manipulated by a master seducer. He was not overtly cruel and he had a great sense of humour. He took me to nice, tablecloth restaurants. I remember a Russian place on Crescent Street where we drank brandy Alexanders, trying to be grown up. It was playful, light—I wasn't pressing him too hard on a commitment. I loved his little smile, where the lip curls up. And he would snort—his version of a laugh. It was all completely adorable. He wasn't that great looking and didn't have a great body. A good lover? I guess so. He talked about his family, as a heritage, as the base of his faith, and as a weight. For me, it was nothing but exotic and fabulous and picturesque.

Another popular hangout was La Asociación Español, an after-hours club with flamenco dancers.

WENDY PATTEN KEYS: It went on till about six in the morning. I went with Leonard and others. Once, he and Henry Moscovitch took me and another friend to Ruby Foo's [a popular Chinese restaurant, owned by the Shapiro family]. They were very familiar with the whole operation. My friend was more virginal and these two men opened up a door for her. She still talks about it. Our relationship lasted a year and a half, with breaks for his trips to Hydra. He never wrote to me.

For a time, she took the Cohen relationship very seriously.

WENDY PATTEN KEYS: My father came up from New York to tell me, "You must drop this right now. For one thing, he's Jewish. And two, he's a poet and he'll never amount to anything." I saw my father crumbling before my eyes. He never recovered in my estimation. I said, "You're overreacting. We're not close to getting married and I'm really interested in all the things he's teaching me about the world and different ways of seeing things." My father wasn't buying it. My poor parents. A couple of years later, I eloped to Mexico with a black guy. The first night back, I went to see my mother. She said, "Even Leonard Cohen feels sorry for us." To this day, I don't know how he got that message to her.

In those years, Cohen's aura extended to gentile and Jew alike.

PATSY STEWART: I have a friend who calls it the Westmount Disease, our WASP need to achieve. Never good enough, never out from under the shadow of our grandparents. Wanting to impress, but without drawing attention to ourselves. The WASP paradox. That was why we, the bright, artistic kids, needed Leonard. The Montreal scribe who had to escape the same Westmount bonds, but with that Jewish chutzpah that we lacked.

BARBARA DODGE: At the time, Leonard almost prophetically altered the history of Montreal. So many people who were doing nothing—people in Canada don't think big—started changing their lives. I was one of them. Deeply impacted, not just by Leonard's success, which was surprising, but that he stuck to his guns, stuck to his amazing poetry, which wasn't even popular, and turned his poetry into songs and became this icon. There's still something about using your mental faculties to speak of deep truths, to question things, make investigation . . .

BARRIE WEXLER: As a fledgling writer, I had a different anxiety as it related to Leonard. The anxiety of influence. The struggle to escape from the ground he'd tilled before me. After all, he'd already said everything I wanted to say about growing up in Westmount. As a writer from the same streets, his oversized talent seemed to preclude the possibility of my own. While his example may have helped young, sensitive gentiles escape Westmount, when we became friends, he did everything he could to help me to escape him.

On October 12, 1963, Cohen—with Layton, F. R. Scott, A. J. M. Smith, Louis Dudek, Ralph Gustafson, D. G. Jones, Kenneth Hertz, Eli Mandel, Henry Moscovitch, and Seymour Mayne—arrived at the Glen Mountain Ski Resort, in the Eastern Townships, to attend a three-day poetry conference organized by John Glassco. The official record was eventually assembled into a book. Cohen was among twenty contributors, for which he received a cheque for three dollars.

WENDY PATTEN KEYS: I remember taking the train from North Hatley to Knowlton to meet Leonard, to go to this musty conference [and] being squished in the backseat with him and a bunch of other tweedy poets.

SEYMOUR MAYNE: Ron Sutherland played the bagpipes before every meal. One evening, in Mandel's room, [there was] Scott, Irving and

Aviva, Hertz, and, sitting in a corner, Leonard, talking about *Flowers for Hitler*. He proceeded to regale us with these new poems, which didn't sound anything like the poems in *The Spice Box*. The latter were lyrical, modernist, self-contained, very well crafted. The new poems were more abrasive, more spontaneous, not as traditional. He spoke with his characteristic sense of humour and self-deprecating irony. He had us all eating out of his palms.

ANN MANDEL: Eli told me that Cohen was very serious and very ambitious. He remembered Leonard standing up and saying that in ten years he'd be on the cover of *Time* or *Life* magazine—that he would be famous, but not necessarily as a poet. He was getting out of this provincial place.

It needs to be remembered that poetry in the 1960s was a small but lively alcove in Canada's house of literary culture.

SEYMOUR MAYNE: There was a discerning, loyal audience of poetry readers from one end of Canada to the other, maybe a thousand people. Journals published poetry. There were regular poetry readings to packed rooms. Robert Weaver's CBC program, *Anthology*, featured short stories and poetry. It's amazing how poetry was so accepted. Maybe thirty books of poetry were published a year in English Canada and they sold out their print runs.

It was almost at this very moment that a giant switch was thrown in North American culture, precipitating a continental convulsion. The long shadows of the Second World War had finally started to recede. A new generation was emerging, one that would be deeply impacted by the Kennedy assassination, the escalating war in Vietnam, and the British musical invasion. A variety of perception-altering drugs, from pot to serious hallucinogens, began to appear. The burgeoning counterculture was marked by sexual liberation, drug experimentation, and new musical forms. "It was almost," says Mayne, "a new Romantic period where people would value creativity."

Simultaneously, another switch was being thrown in Quebec, the so-called Quiet Revolution or *Révolution Tranquille.* Slowly but systematically, it stripped power from the conservative, monopolistic hands of the Roman Catholic Church, ushering in a wave of reform in education, health care, and other areas. An indication of the Church's stranglehold in education, for example, is that as late as 1963, 98 percent of the students at the Université de Montréal were still either priests or nuns.

When *The Favourite Game* was published that fall, Cohen was accused of writing autobiography. He denied it, maintaining that "I made it up out of my little head . . . While the emotions are autobiographical . . . the incidents are not autobiographic."

BARRIE WEXLER: Leonard felt that accusation held the torturous years a writer spends crafting a work of fiction in contempt. I did tell him, though, he'd brought some of this on himself, by choosing "Lawrence" as Breavman's first name—too much like his own name. When Leonard received copies of academic theses based on his work, he was amused. But when critics looked at characters in his novels as surrogates for himself and his friends, he was really pissed off.

Ever the contrarian, Cohen maintained that his book might be "lousy but it's true. Breavman is a kind of brilliant failure. He's not going to fare well anywhere. That's his charm. I think that's a good thing. I can't stand success. It's obscene." It's only a short, inversive leap, of course, from "success is obscene" to "failure is ennobling," a view he voiced as he ventured into the world of music. The novel also contained a hint that, even then, Cohen envisaged a creative life lived outside of the traditional norms. As Canadian critic Stephen Scobie noted in an insightful 1997 essay, if popular music could reach millions, Cohen—or his alter ego,

Breavman—could justifiably declare, "I no longer need my typewriter." Bob Dylan had convincingly demonstrated that, fusing music and poetry, an artist could achieve enormous success. By conventional standards, he might have had a terrible singing voice. But Dylan brought something else that Cohen and others recognized—emotional authenticity, or at least the illusion of it. Inevitably, Cohen's extended family devoured the novel. Some of its contents did not please them.

STEPHEN LACK: Leonard was in those days the family bad boy, because of the novel. It was bad enough he [wore] beards occasionally, but the scene between the doctor and his mother was a scandal.

In the novel, Lawrence Breavman observes his mother kissing Dr. Farley, his father's cardiologist, in the hallway of their home, while his father lies in a distant hospital ward. The inference the family drew was that Masha had been having an affair. In a letter to Ihlen that fall, Cohen acknowledged that "everyone I meet asks how I could do that to my mother." Masha Cohen, however, was offended by other aspects of her characterization. When Cohen returned home from Greece, he found her sick in bed, gasping, "Leonard, oh, Leonard. Why did you write those terrible things about your mother, just because I wanted you to eat?" The novel had mercilessly satirized her obsession with feeding him.

ARMELLE BRUSQ: Everything is written in the novel. In the evocation of his youth, you see already the mark of his destiny—the discovery of his power as an artist and the power of words. One of the first sentences is "the scar is what happens when the word is made flesh." It tells a lot. The flesh is sacrificed for the word. Of course, you don't know it's about destiny.

BARRIE WEXLER: I wanted to write my own coming-of-age novel, and told him he'd stolen Westmount. It was like trying to write a bildungsroman set in Dublin after Joyce. Still, he often used *The Favourite Game* as a kind of template to talk about craft. He'd learned a lot about the carpentry that goes into a novel from wrestling it to the ground. Funny thing was, he didn't think it was all that good. At least nothing that was going to define a generation the way *Portrait of the Artist* and *Catcher in the Rye* had entered the collective psyche.

The novel contained many memorable lines, among them this one— almost prophetic in view of his later involvement in Zen Buddhism: "We all want to be Chinese mystics living in thatched huts, but getting laid frequently."

During a promotional trip to Toronto, Cohen stayed at the Four Seasons Motel on Jarvis Avenue. One morning, he met eighteen-year-old university student Alice Freeman. She'd found him simply by calling him up.

ALICE FREEMAN: I stayed for two hours and we talked about absolutely everything. It was a terrifically intense conversation. I went through two complete packs of cigarettes. At one point, he picked up the guitar and sang a poem he'd set to music—it was the one from *Spice Box* that begins "Hold me hard light, soft light hold me." It was a totally beautiful moment. You have to be very alert with Leonard because his mind slides back and forth in subjects and in time, and even in the language he's thinking in. He's so intense. After I went home, I got into bed and slept for the rest of the day.

His romance with Wendy Patten notwithstanding, Cohen was trying to repair his relationship with Ihlen, still in Paris. An October 23 letter cited an angry long-distance call, but reported that his friend Rosengarten had a spare room for them in his country house. Two days later, Cohen wrote again, accusing her of wanting to hurt him by making him jealous, yet also insisting, "I don't give out guarantees [of commitment]. I have no solutions . . . You know who I am." The last phrase would become the title of a song on his second album, with lyrics that allude to abortion. "I need you to carry my children in / And I need you to kill a child."

BARRIE WEXLER: Marianne used to say that Leonard was always up front about his unwillingness to commit. She knew he was ambivalent at best. But it's not what she wanted to hear.

On December 15, Cohen appeared on a panel at Montreal's Jewish Public Library to discuss the future of Judaism. His remarks there—and in a second address six months later—limn his relationship to the community and his understanding of his place within it. Stressing the distinction between priest and prophet, he cited poet A. M. Klein as the archetype of the priest because he "was too much a champion of the cause, too much the theorist of the Jewish party line." Long ago, Cohen surmised, "There must have been . . . men who were both prophet and priest in the same office . . . I love the Bible because it honours them." Today, he said, there were only priests protecting largely obsolete ideas. "The God worshipped in our synagogues is a hideous distortion of a supreme idea—and deserves to be destroyed. I consider it one of my duties to expose [the] platitude which we have created."

BARRIE WEXLER: Leonard once quoted a line of Henry Miller's. "The Jews used to talk to God. Now they talk about God. It's not the same."

Cohen scholar Win Siemerling later researched the speech, finding a document called "Loneliness and History: A Speech Before the Jewish Public Library" among Cohen's papers at the University of Toronto.

WIN SIEMERLING: "Loneliness and History" is interesting because Cohen hadn't talked much about Klein. Even when I asked him about it [years later], he said he had a bit of protective amnesia about it. For him, Klein had used the pronoun "we" and become a spokesman for the Montreal Jewish community. Ultimately, that had become a problem for Klein. Cohen chose his role [as prophet] in contradistinction to Klein.

BARRIE WEXLER: The adjective—protective—is factual, the noun—amnesia—isn't. Leonard remembered everything.

By the time Siemerling interviewed Cohen in 1990, he had substantially moderated his opinion.

LEONARD COHEN: I understand [Klein's] position much better now. Community is a lot more fragile than I understood then, and a lot more valuable. To undertake the defence of a community is a high call, in no sense a betrayal of a personal destiny.

SEYMOUR MAYNE: I don't think Mordecai Richler and Cohen understood Klein, who grew up in the twenties and thirties—the Depression, anti-Semitism from the Catholic right wing in Quebec. Then came the Shoah, which had a tremendous effect on Klein. It seared his imagination. There was a great fear that what happened in Europe could happen here too. Jews felt uneasy. I don't think Cohen and Richler appreciated that. Those who came from Europe were *sha shtil*—don't be too loud, because the gentiles will turn against us. Klein knew he had to be a voice for his community. So I defend Klein.

Cohen's perceived attack on the community provoked a furor, complete with demands for further discussion. A second session was organized the following Saturday, and a packed house turned up; Cohen failed to appear, later saying his invitation had not been confirmed.

SEYMOUR MAYNE: Someone attacked him and I attacked the person who was attacking him. Because he along with Richler and Layton were

being attacked as self-hating Jews, as people who did not appreciate their Jewish heritage. This is the key—thirty thousand Holocaust
survivors came to Canada after the war, with a tremendous drive to
succeed. They didn't understand why Richler or Cohen or Layton wrote
satirically of the rising new middle class to which they belonged. To
them, it echoed the anti-Semitic caricatures they had faced in Eastern
Europe. That was the Jewish zeitgeist in Montreal. The deep wounds of
the Holocaust were still there. They didn't understand that these writers
were confident enough to satirize their fellow Jews—because it was
focused, as Layton said, "not on monotheism but on moneytheism."

While Cohen was in Montreal, writer Bim Wallis and his wife occupied
his house on Hydra—rent-free.

BARRIE WEXLER: In the sixties, even when money was tight, Leonard
never rented his house, not even for a night.

In a December 1963 letter to Wallis, Cohen reported that the University
of Saskatchewan wanted to buy his manuscripts and letters. In the end,
Cohen sold his papers to the University of Toronto for $3,500, but only
after his alma mater, McGill, inexplicably turned him down.

BARRIE WEXLER: I think the issue was money. U of T came up with
some dough for his early notebooks, poems, and drafts of his short
stories and novels.

LIONEL TIGER: We corresponded as well. I was thinking about writing *Men
in Groups* [Tiger's subsequent best seller] and sent him a couple letters
about it. He encouraged correspondence. Even then, he was aware of
what his reward was for supplying his correspondence to [an archive].

*   *   *

It was in January 1964 that Cohen sent his now famous telegram to Ihlen. "Have apartment. Need wife, child. Tell your mother will protect barnet [it means baby or child in Norwegian] with my life. Come now. Love Leonard." Soon after, they arrived.

AVIVA LAYTON: That was an impulse. He didn't really mean it. It was not good.

Cohen had rented a third-floor coach house; his friend Robert Hershorn lived in the property's main house.

ARNIE GELBART: In their kitchen, he had a fridge, which was a "Leonard" fridge—that was the brand name.

JUDY GAULT: Marianne just seemed like a nice, ordinary blonde—ordinary, but I mean that as a compliment.

ARNIE GELBART: Marianne was lovely. The thing about Leonard is, his graciousness was always natural and he was always funny, hilariously funny, self-deprecating, playing with language. Whatever depression he had, I never saw it. He was just a young artist, writing and starting to play the guitar.

MICHELE HENDLISZ COHEN: Marianne was beautiful, but she did things that—well, she had strung up this long thread, and at intervals there was a little red heart. It was a little bit twee. And she had celery standing in a glass. I'd never seen that. The house, a small flat, was extremely clean and had all these pretty things.

SEYMOUR MAYNE: Steve Smith and I would walk from the campus to visit Leonard. [Officially] we came to see the *rebbe*, but actually we came to see the *rebbetzin* [rabbi's wife]. Marianne was gorgeous and always nice to us, served us coffee, tea. Because she was stuck at home and he was off, gallivanting. One night, we were staying for dinner and Leonard comes in, slightly inebriated, two groupies on his arms. Marianne was not too happy. I shut my mouth, but I could feel a little tension in the air.

Smith's sister, Sheila Walker, had met Cohen at one of his McGill poetry readings.

SHEILA WALKER: It ended about 11 p.m., and he said, "Let's go to a coffee shop. This is too early." We went to someplace on Stanley Street and he read again there. I was taking Louis Dudek's course with Steve—Marianne used to come into that course to cry on Steve's shoulder, because I guess Leonard was doing a fair bit of screwing around. She turned to my brother for comfort.

MICHELE HENDLISZ COHEN: Steve had visited Cohen on Hydra. When Leonard came back with Marianne, we had dinner there. I had my first smoke of pot there. Leonard was very ironic, but in the most amazing, gentlest way possible. That's when I learned what the word "charismatic" means. He was charismatic then, when he was still just a little Jewish poet who read poetry to Jewish ladies' groups.

SHEILA WALKER: One time, Leonard and Marianne were going out with my brother Steve and Michelle. My boyfriend and I babysat at their place on Pine Avenue. Axel barely spoke English and he had this little [toy] gun under his pillow and he started to cry. I went in and he pulled the gun on me. When Leonard came in—he was a very talkative, gregarious guy—he wouldn't let us go home. We had to stay and talk until about two in the morning.

On Ihlen's first visit to Cohen's boyhood home, he gave her two pendants—a miniature gold ballerina, and the gold key from his high school graduation. But re-creating the romantic idyll of Hydra in Montreal proved difficult.

AVIVA LAYTON: The minute Marianne arrived, the fantasy became a reality again, and it wasn't on a Greek island. They were really having a hard time. So they'd go to New York for a weekend to work it out and leave Axel with us.

BRANDON AYRE: He told me they were driving to New York and the Beatles were on the radio and he thought, "Fuck, I can do that."

On another occasion, Cohen's friend Hersh Segal volunteered to take Axel to the Laurentians.

HERSH SEGAL: I had a young son, Phillip. To give them a break, I'd take both boys to my country house in Saint-Hippolyte. There was a horse farm nearby and I'd take them riding.

AVIVA LAYTON: I knew something was funny, because Axel would take one of Irving's pens or pencils and write his name on the wall. If I'd left him alone, he'd write it all over our furniture. It was compulsive. I thought he was probably very difficult for Marianne and very difficult for Leonard. [Axel] was a rambunctious, very unhappy, and incipiently disturbed boy.

BARRIE WEXLER: Some years later, Marianne sent Axel to visit Cohen in L.A. I recall hearing Axel had set fire to the house. When I met him a few years later, he'd occasionally behave strangely, be withdrawn and irritable. Genetic propensity plays a significant role with mental illness. His father, Big Axel, was a borderline schizophrenic and Marianne was concerned, even then.

One day, Cohen and Ihlen took photos of themselves in a coin-operated booth located inside St. Joseph's Oratory on Mount Royal. The building contained a shrine to Saint André, Montreal's most famous priest. His heart is preserved as a relic in the oratory's museum. It's not clear if Ihlen was with Cohen one spring weekend in New York, but he turned up at the Café Au Go Go in Greenwich Village one night.

AVIVA LAYTON: I had run away from Irving and was in New York with Dr. Joey Schwartz. Lenny Bruce was performing. The place was empty. But a few tables over from us—there was Leonard, sitting there. He'd been there the whole time. Leonard was *laughing* and understood exactly what Bruce was doing. We were the only three people in the room.

It's likely that there were at least a few more, because vice squad officers were routinely attending Bruce's shows and, on April 3, 1964, arrested him on charges of public obscenity. He was subsequently convicted.

Despite Ihlen's presence, Cohen continued to pursue women, often meeting them at the Bistro, formally known as Chez Lou Lou, on Mountain Street. There, his entourage gathered—Morton Rosengarten, Robert Hershorn, Derek May, filmmaker Don Owen, [artist] Vittorio Fiorucci, Israel Charney, Arnie Gelbart, and a nonstop parade of young, attractive—and attracted—women.

LEONARD COHEN: Le Bistro's like an irresponsible sanctuary. You aren't sure whether the hounds are waiting inside, or whether you've just left them.

LINDA GABORIAU: Those were wonderful, dynamic days in Quebec culture. It's not surprising that Leonard vibrated to that. Poets, painters, thinkers, writers, theatre people would all gather at the Bistro.

ARNIE GELBART: There was a bar at the front and a restaurant at the back. The Bistro was more alcoholic than caffeine, but a very pleasant place to drink. People would spend afternoons there. You'd walk over from McGill. Up the street was Trafalgar School, a private girls' school. The girls would come cruising down in their short skirts—all the good-looking young women, artists and actresses. That was the milieu.

MUSIA SCHWARTZ: That's where I met Leonard for the first time. My first impression was to a large extent shaped by the first thing I heard him say. I'd been writing a biographical thing. Leonard took the page and read it and said, "Oh my God, that's frightening. We have the same sensibility." Except he had talent, which I didn't have. Was it Jewish? A certain sensitivity? A discriminatory way of looking at things? And we became friends—not like with Irving [Layton], who was my best friend, ever, for half a century. They were very different. Irving needed people—not Leonard. He was very private, more aloof. I was aware of his reputation, but I felt no attraction, nor on his part any pursuit. Our talks were either completely intellectual or as buddies—no sexual tension at all.

ERICA POMERANCE: At the Bistro, you could get French baguettes and sit at marble-topped tables, all very *parisienne*. People looking for Leonard would go there. There was a piano player named Graham [McKeen], the journalist Nick Auf der Maur, [sculptor] Armand Vaillancourt and his partner, Suzanne Verdal, Derek May, of course, and his girlfriend, Patricia Nolin, an actress; graphic artist Vittorio Fiorucci.

CHERYL SOURKES: Leonard had his table there. You knew he was troubled. There was a very charged atmosphere—cool but controlled, kind of witty—"we are important people and everybody else should shut up and listen." But since I was a decade younger, it was interesting to hang out. He was still a poet, not a musician.

LINDA BOOK: Montreal artist Susan Scott, who knew him a few years later, said Cohen would hold court, and was the most hugely arrogant, self-absorbed individual. None of the vulnerability or seasoned wisdom we associate with him now was present. This was a guy struggling to be successful. Very charismatic. People hung on his every word, because he was so avant-garde and erudite, those dark swarthy ways, the brooding loner who happened to be good looking.

Another popular watering hole was the Boiler Room on Crescent Street.

MIRIAM WAGSCHAL: That's where we met Leonard. He was mysterious, funny, not depressive. He had this old leather jacket—really worn. He drove me home once and said nice things about my work. Irving Layton once said to me, "I know two geniuses, you and Leonard." I wasn't really part of the scene because I was ten years younger. He wasn't really my type. But I loved his work. He was a deep person.

It was at the Bistro that year that Cohen marked a café wall with a famous piece of graffiti—"Marita, Please find me. I am almost 30." Ostensibly, it referred to Marita La Fleche, whom Cohen had hit on, only to be rebuffed with the line, "On your way, young man. Come back when you're thirty."

ARNIE GELBART: I was there the afternoon he wrote that.

PATRICIA NOLIN: I was there too. I thought, "This is nice, delicious." I was sitting next to Derek. I was twenty-four.

CAROL ZEMEL: The inner group included Leonard, Hershorn, Derek, and Morton. Derek was a mensch. Morton was from childhood, a sweet guy who should have been a more successful sculptor than he is. Hershorn was insufferable. There aren't many men I've met that you just don't want to be in the same room with. He was not stupid, but he was bumbling. It was hard to enjoy his social generosity, or take in his wisdom and insight—and he had all of these—because the drug use was so constant. He always seemed befuddled and on-the-mark at the same time.

FRANCINE HERSHORN: Everyone was impressed by Robert. He was very bright, very interesting. You could talk to him for hours.

HENRY ZEMEL: Derek was very British. He wanted to be a pilot, but they wouldn't accept him because he wasn't of the right class. He was always the handsome one. That's what they called him.

ISRAEL CHARNEY: I was crazy about Derek. He was a really talented painter before he went to the Film Board. A really handsome guy. The girls were crazy about him.

CHERYL KENMEY: Derek was a shithead. Later, he was my tenant. So was Henry Zemel. The two of them were assholes. Nasty business. Henry would contradict you on principle.

BARBARA DODGE: Derek was another cunning, cool, suave guy, trying to seduce us, the young girls. I wasn't interested. I wasn't a floozy.

PATRICIA NOLIN: Leonard, the alpha male, was the centre of gravity. My husband, Derek, the gypsy. Hershorn, the boy—because he was this big, overgrown boy, with black, doe eyes and long eyelashes. I saw the child in him. I liked Robert. He was very intelligent, hospitable, and kind. And Morton—the mensch. He was a big fan of the *I Ching*. They taught me that, and they taught me about being a Pepsi [a derogatory term for French-Canadians]. I wasn't happy about that at all.

ARNIE GELBART: Leonard didn't behave like an alpha male. He didn't have to impose himself. His presence, his wit—people gravitated around him.

PATRICIA NOLIN: My favourite Cohen song is "All the Lonesome Heroes," which I'm convinced is about them. It's from those nights of hanging together. That's who they were—four lonesome heroes. That's who the song is about. It's all there. That song is the genesis.

> *A bunch of lonesome and very quarrelsome heroes*
> *Were smoking out along the open road . . .*
> *I'd like to tell my story*
> *Before I turn to gold*

Decades later, Cohen reflected on this period.

LEONARD COHEN: In Montreal, we always thought we were famous. In a sense, we were more famous to ourselves then than afterwards. Afterwards, you begin to realize—what is your fame compared to Muhammad Ali, to Marlon Brando? When you were young in Montreal, and nobody knew who you were except the four other poets, then you really felt that your fame had some weight.

ARNIE GELBART: Vittorio [Fiorucci] was more of a man needing to be heard, be the centre of attention. He and Leonard competed for the favours of young women. They didn't have a great opinion of each other.

DAVID LIEBER: Vittorio's appetite was for real. He was the real Don Juan. And he never had nice things to say about Leonard. He used to laugh at him and make fun of his pimples, and of his sitting in the Bistro writing poetry.

ISRAEL CHARNEY: What a great figure Vittorio was. Totally brilliant, full of panache and passion, joie de vivre. They were on the same turf, he and Leonard. Vittorio had a different way. He had long relationships with his women.

PATRICIA NOLIN: Every man, every male, was a rival to Leonard. Derek and Leonard had a great rivalry. About women—oh yes. It was unsaid, and most of the time unconscious. These men—they could have any woman they wanted. They didn't have to do anything. Leonard used to say he wasn't as handsome as Derek. Leonard was preoccupied with his looks. A narcissist? No. It never struck me at the time. I was dealing with a seducer, of men and women. He would seduce anybody he wanted to seduce. Anybody. He seduced Morton and Derek and Robert. They were all under his spell, definitely. He was the alpha. I would see him seduce the man at the Greek restaurant, the man behind the counter, the lady at the Hotel de France. I lost track of him after he became a star, and I'm glad I did.

One day, Cohen asked an acquaintance, musician Michael Nerenberg, for a favour.

MICHAEL NERENBERG: I had a two-hour tape of Bob Dylan appearing at Finjan [a Montreal folk club] in July 1962. Leonard wanted to hear it. So I played him the tape, and at the end, he asked me if I could show him how to make a C chord—the first chord a guitarist usually learns. From that, I inferred [incorrectly] that I might have shown Leonard Cohen his very first chord. Why did he need to learn the C chord then, if he had already been playing guitar for ten years? That's a big question. I've never solved it. But he came for Bob Dylan, not for me. Leonard had a very polished veneer of civility and, as a smart-assed Jew—his background was pretty privileged, and I was poor working class—I was always looking for a way to puncture it. And truth be told, he just happened to be a very nice, humble guy. One-on-one, he was as humble as could be, without appearing unctuous. He was just like a nice guy.

In 1964, Cohen met Henry Zemel, a quirky, brilliant mathematician and physicist, also interested in spiritual growth and exploration.

HENRY ZEMEL: Leonard liked me. He was my best friend. I had other friends, but he really wanted me to be something. He saw something in me that appealed to him. He tried to educate me, in my deficiencies, which is very unusual. He actually wanted to teach me things—how to tell a story, how to write poetry. I can't think of other friends who did that. I'm not an easy guy to instruct. It wasn't "read this book." It was more about process, because I could never re-create a story. I was always starting over, so the story was always different. He tried to teach me to remember what I'd done before—a number of things like that.

Meanwhile, the storm clouds of Quebec nationalism were gathering. In 1964, the Liberal government ushered in sweeping reforms and withdrew from almost thirty federal-provincial programs. When Queen Elizabeth II visited Quebec City in the fall, anticolonial demonstrators turned their backs on the royal procession. Several protesters were beaten by police. The day is now regarded as one of the seminal events of the Quiet Revolution. It wasn't exactly quiet. Between 1963 and 1970, the Front de Libération du Québec (FLQ) detonated more than ninety-five bombs in homes, mailboxes, train stations, department stores, police depots, and at the Montreal Stock Exchange.

BARBARA DODGE: The first terrorist attacks in North America were in Quebec. A bomb, twelve sticks of dynamite, went off two blocks from Leonard's childhood home and blew out every window in the front of our house [on Sydenham].

Despite rising separatist sentiments, the artists, English and French, frequently all hung out together, smoking dope, drinking, and swapping partners.

ARNIE GELBART: Mores were changing. French-Canadian women were looking to hang out with artists and writers. People had a lot of girlfriends. The movie world was happening—here, long before it happened in Toronto, because of the National Film Board, in part.

Another member of Cohen's arts-oriented set was Carol Talbot-Smith.

CAROL TALBOT-SMITH: I remember a party—[singer] Pauline Julien had just come back from Paris. Armand Vaillancourt was going after Julien because her accent wasn't Quebecois. Leonard was egging them on. He'd throw out things in *joual* [the French dialect of Quebec], just to get a reaction. Another time, I remember him throwing paper spitballs. I threw [one] back and we started talking.

Cohen was a frequent visitor to local museums and would go with Morton Rosengarten.

CAROL TALBOT-SMITH: Leonard had a real fixation on a Julio González sculpture hanging in the Montreal Museum of Fine Arts. He used to plot how to liberate it from its shackles on the ceiling. I was sitting one day with Leonard on the stairs, and he was going on and on and on about how he was going to finally become the owner of this González piece.

At the time, Cohen was favourably disposed to the burgeoning expressions of Quebec nationalism. "The revolution in Quebec," he said, "is a healthy indication of an awakening people."

LEONARD COHEN: All people realize . . . that the original concept of confederation as a partnership has to be reestablished . . . The revolution is irrational, as all important things are, and based on humiliation, partly. You feel a people assuming its dignity.

Still, Cohen was careful to hedge his bets. Part of this reflected his understanding that political revolutions tend to manifest the evil they were meant to replace. But part of it too was a recognition that, as his friend Ruth Roskies Wisse would later write, "to be a popular songwriter was to court the broadest possible public and to avoid giving it offence." Soon, in public at least, he was adopting more centrist positions.

LEONARD COHEN: I love Trudeau. I love René Lévesque. I love the fleur-de-lis. I love the maple leaf. I love the idea of an independent Quebec. I love the idea of a Canada from ocean to ocean. What can I tell you?

Years later, looking back on the period, Cohen told screenwriter Tony Babinski that he'd been "in sympathy with the separatists. I thought they had a noble cause." In fact, Cohen acknowledged that he and filmmaker Claude Jutra had once telephoned another young director, Denys Arcand, and suggested that he help them plant bombs. Presumably, it was a call made in jest because Cohen also was "in sympathy with the federalists. I could understand both positions." As separatism acquired more militancy, his views changed. "Some of these people were supposed to be our friends," he said. "But we'd be sitting with them, and they'd point at us and say: 'You know, you Jews. You Jews.' We hadn't heard that kind of language since 1944."

SEYMOUR MAYNE: For the Anglophone culture in Montreal, which had been very vigorous, French nationalism was a challenge. For younger Jews, who began to leave, it seemed to be a form of the nationalism that had oppressed Jews in Eastern Europe.

*   *   *

Among the many women Cohen romanced in this period was Erica Pomerance, a literature student at McGill.

ERICA POMERANCE: Leonard would visit the campus and hold forth. He'd read poetry or lecture—he was already a bit of a mythological figure. Sometimes he'd bring his guitar and sing.

CHERYL SOURKES: When he sang, it was very tentative. He was learning and modest about learning how to do things with the guitar from others younger than himself. He was apprenticing. He had more confidence as a poet.

FRAN AVNI: We all sat at Leonard's feet. I just remember his presence. I was mesmerized, not just by Leonard, but the whole ambience, coming as I did from such a conventional family. Our contact was vicarious. I was extremely shy.

ERICA POMERANCE: My first meeting with him was at the Fifth Amendment, a folk club on Bleury Street on the second floor. One of the American blues greats was performing and Leonard was with his friend Hershorn. Our tables were adjoining. He turned to Robert and said, "Doesn't she look like Freda?"—Freda Guttman, who had been his girlfriend. Then he started coming on to me. We ended up becoming "friends."

CAROL ZEMEL: Erica Pomerance—give me a break. She was a major groupie. She thought he was the great one and only. He isn't the great one and only. He's a great songwriter and a wonderful poet and that's it.

FRAN AVNI: I knew about the affair, of course. Erica was a stunningly beautiful girl—really exotic. She looked like a First Nations person. She had an electric energy and was a brilliant writer and thinker. She was nomadic.

ERICA POMERANCE: The first few times, I resisted the romance. He was attractive, but I was eighteen or something, a virgin. But eventually, you know, you succumbed. I was seeing him while he was living with Marianne off Pine Avenue. He took me there a few times. Marianne was a wonderful person, blond and very Nordic, graceful, feminine, very gentle. She had a strong mind, but was more soft-spoken. I didn't ask too many questions.

FRAN AVNI: Erica had a real, caring friendship with Leonard. She attracted people of incredible energy and talent. She was a magnet for people, as was he. And he mentored her. She'd send him her work and he'd comment.

ERICA POMERANCE: He became my mentor. If I was looking for direction, I'd talk to him or think about him. He was my guiding light, because he'd done the same thing as me—left a respectable Jewish family and explored new cultural horizons. I had to break away from my family and he had to break away from Mommy. He really understood where I came from.

BARRIE WEXLER: What he did for Erica, he did for me and many other people. He was extremely generous that way.

CHERYL SOURKES: A friend of mine once asked me if Leonard had ever hit on me. I said no. She said, "We must be the only two women in Montreal [that he didn't hit on]."

CAROL ZEMEL: Everybody loves Leonard. The songs and the poetry are brilliant, magical. I've always found them wise, insightful, meaningful, beautiful in the most contemporary Jewish sense—inspiring and deeply moving. You can listen to them over and over and they make you cry. It was the private behaviour and posture of the man that I disliked. The person, who was always merged with the songs, was less attractive. The womanizing was intense. It drove me crazy over the years, And all the men around him were treated to the women, whether they were married men or not. It was one of the ways he held men in his thrall—there were always women around. If he wasn't sleeping with them, he shared them.

PATRICIA NOLIN: It was scary, because he had a lot of influence on the other men. And Carol suffered. So did I, in a way, but I reacted differently.

CAROL ZEMEL: It was all one big groupy Jewish art scene. It makes me nauseous. The fact [that he never married] is interesting. If he affected a pose of humility, he needed to, because humility was probably the last thing he could manage. I'm not saying none of it was authentic, but it was a posture. He was a highly moralizing, highly judgemental man.

BARRIE WEXLER: Leonard was the least moralizing person I ever met.

ERICA POMERANCE: He always used his powers of seduction when he found an attractive woman. I don't think he was a sexaholic, but his persona was very seductive. He loved to seduce women, but he was seductive to everybody. He always had an unusual way to say something or make an observation. He was poetic in his daily discourse, without being pompous. He was not pompous—a cool guy.

Cohen during a visit to his cousin Robert Cohen, who was recuperating from mononucleosis, at his home on Roslyn Avenue, 1948. (*Courtesy of Robert Cohen*)

Cohen with friend and Zeta Beta Tau brother Mark Bercuvitz, receiving the McGill University fraternity's Pledge of the Year award from Arnie Tepner, 1952. (*Courtesy of Mark Bercuvitz*)

Cohen at the 1956 wedding of his stepsister, Roz Van Zaig. Back row: Henry Ostrow, Cohen's stepfather; Cohen's girlfriend Freda Guttman; Roz Van Zaig; her husband, Eddie Van Zaig; Cohen; Victor Cohen, Esther's husband. Front left, Masha Cohen, Cohen's mother; front right, Cohen's sister, Esther Cohen. (*Courtesy of Roz Van Zaig*)

Cohen's friends Irving and Aviva Layton, camping in the Laurentians, north of Montreal, summer 1958. (*Courtesy of Aviva Layton Collection*)

Cohen entertaining at Douskos Taverna, Hydra, October, 1960. Australian writer Charmian Clift is on his left; writer-poet Charles W. Heckstall is on his right. (*Photo by James Burke/The LIFE Picture Collection via Getty Images*)

Cohen with Marianne Ihlen and her son, Axel Jensen Jr., at the port on Hydra, October 1960. Also at the table, Australian authors George Johnston and his wife, Charmian Clift, and an unidentified bearded young man. (*Photo by James Burke/The LIFE Picture Collection via Getty Images*)

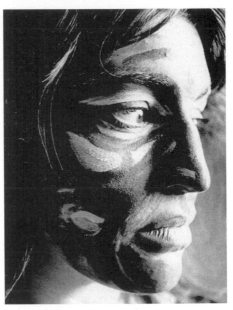

Wendy Patten Keys, a McGill University student and Cohen's girlfriend from fall 1963 into 1964. (*Courtesy of Wendy Patten Keys*)

Erica Pomerance, Cohen's occasional girlfriend in the mid-sixties. Photo from her album cover for *You Used to Think*. (*Courtesy of Erica Pomerance*)

Cohen's friends Carol and Henry Zemel with National Film Board director Arthur Lipsett in the background. Montreal, circa 1966. (*Photo by Judy Sandiford, courtesy of Carol Zemel*)

Cohen's friend Robert Hershorn with his wife, Francine Hershorn, circa 1966. (*Courtesy of Francine Hershorn*)

Cohen poses for a publicity shot during his visit to Edmonton, December 1966. (*Photo by Rocco Caratozzolo. Courtesy of Kim Solez, MD.*)

Cohen with Judy Collins, the woman who kick-started his music career, backstage at the Newport Folk Festival in Newport, Rhode Island, July 1967. (*Photo by David Gahr/Getty Images*)

Cohen with his then girlfriend, Joni Mitchell, backstage at the Newport Folk Festival, July 1967. (*Photo by David Gahr/Getty Images*)

Cohen in sunlit repose in Sausalito, California, summer 1968, during a visit to his friend Marcia Pacaud. And, cross-legged, Cohen's oldest friend, Morton Rosengarten, on same visit. (*Photos courtesy of Marcia Pacaud*)

Cohen serving as best man at the January 1969 wedding of his friends Steve Sanfield and Jacquie Bellon, at Rinzai-ji Zen Center, Los Angeles. The wedding was officiated by Joshu Sasaki Roshi, who would become Cohen's friend and teacher. And Cohen at post-nuptial reception with Jacquie Bellon. (*Photos courtesy of Jacquie Bellon*)

Cohen's friend Athenian weaver Despina Politi. Portrait taken by unknown photographer at the Louvre Museum, Paris, circa 1968. (*Courtesy of Barrie Wexler*)

Cohen's friends Pandias Scaramanga and Barrie Wexler, playing chess on the Writers' Rocks near Kamini, Hydra, circa 1970. (*Photo by Despina Politi, courtesy of Barrie Wexler*)

Cohen on terrace of his Hydra home with Barrie Wexler, circa 1970. (*Photo by Suzanne Elrod, courtesy of Barrie Wexler*)

CHERYL SOURKES: I wouldn't have let [seduction] happen. He would have had too much control. He was so much more sophisticated and mature. He liked younger girls. He loved the idea that I was younger. I wouldn't tell him how young, but he just kept pushing. He probably didn't have what he wanted when he was eighteen, and so, at twenty-nine, was trying to make up for [it]. But he was irresistible.

ERICA POMERANCE: I was never his official girlfriend, but we had a few trysts. It lasted, off and on, for a few years. He had his own room in his mother's house, and there was the Hotel de France, a seedy hotel on Sainte-Catherine Street. He liked places that gave him the flavour of bohemian life.

PATRICIA NOLIN: I don't think they had a relationship, he and Erica. *Ce n'est pas possible.* There is such a thing as people fantasizing and believing themselves. She was an infatuated teenager and hung around him. But Leonard always liked those poor things. The Hotel de France [was] a real dump. Derek and I visited him there. It was winter. He was writing. He ordered from the front desk—tarte au sucre, sugar pie. They adored him [there]—he was like a king, an emperor. So it comes up to the room and he tastes it and it's disgusting, of course. It tasted awful. So he took a second bite and it's awful, but he says, "It has a good feeling in the mouth." Of all the things I remember about Cohen, that I've always remembered, is this way of seeing things: okay, it's the worst tarte au sucre ever, but it has a good feeling in the mouth. And it was true—the squishy caramel did have a good feeling in the mouth. That's a philosophy I kept. If Leonard Cohen was ever a guru for me, it's that sentence. It's another version of "there is a crack in everything"—yes, yes! It's the same idea, in 1964. But even then, I thought it was a pose—this Westmount man going to this cheap hotel. It was a persona. But you forgave Leonard almost everything because he had so much charisma and charm.

On several occasions, Nolin accompanied Cohen to the System, a movie theatre at 539 Sainte-Catherine West.

PATRICIA NOLIN: We'd go in the afternoons, which was ridiculous—none of us really had jobs. It was a really run-down place, full of strange men. There were three movies, back-to-back—really horrible movies, cowboy movies, B movies, zombie movies. I'd go with Leonard and Derek, maybe Marianne. It tickled us pink to see those movies—with popcorn. [One day] we were waiting for the film and Leonard goes to the front and says, "The reason I brought you here this afternoon is to inform you that the hatcheck girl has syphilis." That cracked me up.

ERICA POMERANCE: He was always well dressed, very simply, but dapper, just so. He loved to go to the Greek restaurants. He was quite a gentleman. One year, on his birthday, we walked across Mount Royal and ended up at his house. He was quite unusual, even then practically Buddhic. He'd meditate and put a rose on his chest. We talked about books, ideas, philosophy, religion, but sometimes he just was quiet. He tried to tempt me with hash. At first I wouldn't take it, but then I started smoking. I was just this wide-eyed young Jewish girl, totally under his charm.

Pomerance later discovered that her best friend, filmmaker Tanya Ballantyne, later known as Tanya Tree, was also having an affair with Leonard.

ERICA POMERANCE: Sexually, I did not find him experimental. His was more of a Zen sexuality. He fused with his partner. Very often, he was completely—I don't want to say catatonic—but he would wait for the energy to inhabit him. But he enjoyed intimate encounters. He was an intimate person. When he invited you into his world, he was intimate in a deeper sense of the word, beyond the physical. He joined the physical and the spiritual. Tender? Very. But on a certain level, reserved as well. He was a very private person, but also very welcoming. You couldn't go beyond a certain point with him. He kept a certain aura around him that protected him or kept him from being deflected, or distracted from his own trajectory.

CHRISTOPHE LEBOLD: Women feel in him the heavenly part and the obscure part, this talent for opacity and absence, this aptitude to remain always elsewhere, even in their company.

BARRIE WEXLER: With Leonard, you couldn't go beyond a certain point. If you did—I'm talking emotionally, not sexually—which on rare occasions I was able to, the next morning it would be back to square one.

Another former lover of Cohen's recalls attending a party at Hershorn's house. They ended up in one of the bedrooms, but in the middle of their lovemaking, Cohen actually fell asleep. The woman quietly made her way home by herself. Meanwhile, Cohen's friend Henry Moscovitch had suffered the first of what would become a series of psychiatric disturbances—and been hospitalized in the Douglas hospital in Verdun.

JULIANNA OVENS: We had broken up and I lost contact, until I heard he was seriously into drugs. Then a friend informed me Henry had been hospitalized in a near-catatonic state. I remember running into Leonard, who mentioned Henry was not doing well.

PETER VAN TOORN: He was totally catatonic. He'd been an active, sporty man. I said, "Henry, let's go for a swim." And he'd be listless. But Christ, did he know good stuff [literature]. I did see him slowly go a bit off his rocker.

HOWARD ASTER: Henry was taking a lot of drugs. I understood Cohen gave him LSD in Montreal, but I think that was later.

CAROL ZEMEL: Henry was a Layton clone. a Layton wannabe. He loved Layton. Layton was the guru. Overweight. He could see almost nobody unless they were ready to kneel at his feet. Layton himself was a blowhard, insufferable, so obnoxious, loud, boisterous, commanding.

BARRIE WEXLER: Leonard told me this story after Moscovitch was released. Henry says, "Cohen, I've had this revelation. I'm the Chosen One. You have to worship me." Cohen replies: "You know, Henry, if there's any man I'd worship, it would be you. But I just can't kneel before another man." . . . "Come closer." . . . Cohen takes a step . . . "Closer, closer." . . . Henry proceeds to move his hands over Cohen's head, as if trying to catch some invisible, luminous strands, and starts reeling him in. When they're eyeball to eyeball, Cohen begins to see flashes of scenes from his life with great clarity, penetrating insights. After a minute, Moscovitch lets him go . . . "*Now,* are you ready to worship me?" . . . Leonard, dazed, just shakes his head. Henry storms out, vowing never to see Cohen again. Two weeks later, Leonard is walking down Mountain Street and spots Henry sauntering towards him. He's about to call out, but Henry looks right through him, as if he isn't there.

DORIAN MILLER: Henry gave me that blessing constantly . . . "Dorian, you'll be never frozen, never burnt. You'll never starve to death." Sometimes, it moved me to tears. But Henry was totally possessed by demonic voices. This wasn't an illusion. I'd say, "Henry, why can't you save your poetry?" . . . "Oh no. The voices tell me to rip them all up." . . . "Why did you scrape your eyebrows?" . . . "The voices told me to. They make it hell for me." This was not his imagination. It was demonic entities, as real as anything.

In another conversation with Cohen, Moscovitch said, "Leonard, I'm sorry I had to shoot your father."

DORIAN MILLER: Leonard says, "You shouldn't have done that, but I'm sure it's okay." . . . "Oh, thank you, Leonard." Then Henry says, "I'd love to make love to you. How big's your penis?" . . . "Well, Henry, it's about seven or eight inches—limp." Gross guy talk—Leonard was really good at that too. But he was so generous. Henry liked to smoke up—pot. Leonard would say, "How's Henry doing? Here, take forty [bucks], take twenty. I want Henry to be happy."

CHERYL SOURKES: Henry was my boyfriend then. He had a schizophrenic crisis—I was with him at the time and he ended up kissing my boots, in winter. I distanced myself from him. I think LSD pushed him over the brink. He went from having this amazing mania to being seriously off-balance. He always had a big heart, an incredible mind, precocious. It's like he lived all of his life in that youthful time. He was amazing to be with. He was a visionary—he was. In those days, Henry was widely known as Freaky. He was a JewBu—a Jewish Buddhist. Henry and Leonard had a strong connection. Their hanging out was just ideas upon ideas, incredibly rich associations.

MICHAEL NERENBERG: Leonard called Henry "the Buddha." Henry walked a fine line between madness and genius. A beautiful guy.

MUSIA SCHWARTZ: Henry—poor soul. A good Jewish boy. He had an obligation to be a rebel and an outsider. He wasn't by nature, but he felt it was his destiny.

DAVID SOLWAY: Henry was brilliant. He'd published two books of poetry before he was twenty and had read everything by the age of nineteen, but he went off the deep end. He ultimately committed suicide.

Approaching his thirtieth birthday, Leonard Cohen recognized that the zeitgeist was in upheaval, convulsed in virtually every political and social domain. Characteristically, he was somehow able to immerse himself in it and yet stand apart—his distance enabling him to portray this shifting landscape on the pages of the ambitious new book he was working on: *Beautiful Losers.*

CHAPTER EIGHT

Is There Any Fire Left?

It was as if he was a light to which people came.

—Michele Hendlisz Cohen

Cohen's persona applies to what is written about him—not what he wrote. You have to separate the two.

—Howard Aster

Drugs were among the most prominent features of the high-octane world of Montreal's midsixties youth culture. Cohen, always prepared to push his personal limits, was an early adopter.

SANDRA YUCK: Montreal was a melting pot, every race, every persuasion. Anything went and drugs were rampant. Mostly ganja and grass and mushrooms. For us, having a party meant the canapés were celery with magic mushrooms, fermented inside and sprinkled with cocaine and then champagne.

BARRIE WEXLER: I once asked Leonard if he'd ever had a bad LSD trip. He said he hadn't, that he didn't even hallucinate that much. He then told me a story Ram Dass had told him. Ram Dass [then Richard Alpert] had gone to India to see if he could attain enlightenment beyond what he'd experienced with psychedelics. He decided to test a Hindu mystic by giving him acid. After an hour, when there was no apparent change in the guru's teaching, Alpert asked why the LSD was having no effect. The guru replied, "I can make it have an effect, if you like." Ram Dass asked, "What effect is that?" The guru said, "See that grove over there? I'm going to transfer half of what you gave me to those trees." He turned to the trees, which immediately began to crack and then fall. After telling the story, Leonard said, "If you're spiritually aware, nothing happens."

BARBARA DODGE: There was a Moroccan restaurant on Crescent Street and at 3 a.m., they'd bring you steaming platters of bastilla [an appetizer] and hashish. Everybody was plastered. You lay around on cushions and smoked *kief.*

SANDRA YUCK: We were all stoned much of the time. Speed was the first drug we all got hooked on, Benzedrine, a pill you swallowed several a day, to study, to work, go out, stay up, followed by hashish and marijuana, then the hallucinogens, then cocaine, if you could afford it. Leonard was part of that whole scene, but I never indulged with him. I was in awe of his talent. I had a crush on him. He was extremely attractive, but I never thought I had a chance. There were so many people fawning over him. He was a very, very intelligent and soulful person. He had an aura that was very nice. Alfie Wade was part of the group. Alfie supplied a lot of us. I dropped acid three or four times a day. It fuelled my creativity. You could get it on the McGill campus, on Saint-Antoine Street, Crescent Street. The African-American guys would come around with drugs. I used to travel with a portfolio—mushrooms and cocaine—and was never checked.

Wade had known the Cohen circle from his days at Westmount Junior High School.

ALFIE WADE: We all kinda mingled there. Then we got separated because, by the time I was fourteen, I was seduced by the bebop. I left Montreal in 1959 and came back in 1965, and hooked up with [bar owner] Johnny Vago at Don Juan discotheque and later the Winston Churchill Pub. All my old pals were customers—Leonard, Robert, all these cats from high school. We used to hang out on Stanley Street. On Friday nights, *shabbas*, we'd gather at Robert's house for dinner or the family's place in the Laurentians. We were trying to figure out the meaning of our existence. Leonard wasn't yet into music. He was amassing human capital and popularity. We were all seeking, talking about *The Conference of the Birds* [a Persian masterpiece by poet Farid ud-Din Attar] and Gurdjieff and Ouspensky, and were deeply into the whole spiritual thing. Robert would get up and recite long passages from *The Conference of the Birds* and tell Sufi jokes that had us on the floor. We were the local intelligentsia, exchanging ideas.

FRANCINE HERSHORN: That was their favourite book, *The Conference of the Birds*. Robert swore by the story. Birds were compared to human beings. It was a mystical book. Robert was really fond of Persian and Sufi literature—the short stories of Idries Shah. He used to write book reviews. He and Leonard wrote letters to each other that were published in the Montreal newspaper, just for fun. He was bright, a force of nature, a special soul. Anybody who came to him for help in financing a play—he'd put money into it. He was an artist himself at heart. He would have liked to have been an artist, but he didn't want to give up the money.

ALFIE WADE: At one point, we came upon the *I Ching*—the Chinese book of changes. I was not in any way surprised that Leonard wound up in Zen, because this is what we were all looking at. All the Jewish cats turned full circle—Robert rediscovered Judaism and Leonard too. There was a lot of that polarity.

FRANCINE HERSHORN: Robert and Leonard—they were both into the Cabala. Later, Robert became religious and followed a Lubavitch rabbi. Wore a *tallis*, put on *tefillen*.

ISRAEL CHARNEY: LSD arrived in '63, '64. It started with morning glory seeds. *Time* magazine ran a page on it about then. I was in Paris and ran out to the bird food store and ground them up.

PATRICIA NOLIN: We took psilocybin, the real thing. It was positive. In my case, it came from private biochemists. After Expo '67, the drug scene got bad, because they started putting methamphetamines in the LSD, and the marijuana started getting adulterated. Before that, it was completely pure. I don't think I did LSD with Leonard, but we did do morning glory seeds, the heavenly blue type. If you crunched them, they'd give you hallucinations.

At some point, Cohen returned from a pilgrimage to Mexico with what he said was enough LSD "to disturb the social equilibrium of the entire city." Soon after, he was sharing the drug with friends.

AVIVA LAYTON: I had my first LSD experience with Leonard. It wasn't recreational. He was so generous. He stayed with me the entire day, while I was raving and rambling. He told me the batch of LSD had been isolated in a rusty bathtub in Zihuatanejo by Timothy Leary himself. Very strong and very, very pure. He had a sheet of paper with one of his poems on it, and on the corner of the page was the LSD, which made the whole thing more mystical. He put the tiny corner of the page in my mouth and I sucked on it. It must have taken me ten minutes to really start flying. Leonard had the radio on and [we heard] the weather forecast talking about "the high today." I said, "See? Everyone's getting high." At one point, I felt I would be lost forever and Leonard took my hand and tethered me and I hung on to him so hard that I bruised his hand. But he never took his hand way.

DAVID SOLWAY: I didn't even know what LSD was—I was so innocent. Leonard was sitting cross-legged on the floor. Irving was there and Marianne was puttering about. I felt I was in the midst of gods. They were taking this white powder out of a box and Leonard was sniffing it. He was high much of the time, apparently. He offered it to Irving and Irving refused, at first. Finally Leonard persuaded him to sample this magical white powder. After about twenty minutes, Leonard seemed to be soaring into the stratosphere. But Irving was perfectly normal. Nothing seemed to have happened to him. Leonard said, "What do you think, Irving?" As if to say, have you been transported to magical realms? And Irving said, "I've always been there." I thought that was the most wonderful put-down.

ANNA POTTIER: The way I heard it, Irving sneezed and all the powder went flying. I think that was Irving's first and last experiment with LSD. He blew it—literally.

AVIVA LAYTON: Irving didn't want to do it, but Leonard came and gave Irving LSD and Irving said, "Nothing's happening." He gave him a little more—"Nothing's happening." Leonard said, "Wait, Irving. Wait." After about an hour—we were in the living room and we had bookcases, floor to ceiling—Leonard asked, "Is anything happening?" And Irving said no, but all the books are coming down and kneeling in front of me. Leonard and I started to laugh. So Leonard said, "It's working." And Irving said, "No, it happens all the time. They always bow before me." But he said he didn't get high at all. He said, "This is what my head is like."

In Cohen's own account, as told to Layton biographer Elspeth Cameron, the LSD had transported Layton "to a gathering of greats . . . Plato. Shakespeare. His mind was so pure. Filled with such light and understanding of himself and this world of spirit. His was a classical beatific vision."

One afternoon, on the McGill campus, Cohen debated the merits of hallucinogens with his former professor Louis Dudek. Cohen argued in favour, Dudek against; Ruth Roskies Wisse played the audience.

RUTH ROSKIES WISSE: Leonard declared himself surprised that, as a poet, Louis would forgo the chance to expand his mental experience. How could he take a stand against something he had not even tried? Louis pointed to his head: "Look! I have up here the most intricate machine in the world. Why would any sane person take a hammer and smash the thing to pieces for the sake of a new adventure?" Not destruction but creation was at stake, replied Leonard. But when he began to describe the beauties of one such trip, Louis grew impatient. "I go home and I lie on the sofa listening to Mozart. There I experience all the adventures in beauty that I want for." This was the only time I'd ever seen him angry with Leonard, like a father grown impatient with his son. In truth, Leonard was no longer the same poet Louis had launched. He had started out as the casualty of a mythic struggle. Now he was turning into a casualty of his times.

In February 1964, Cohen took his poetry and music act on the road, performing with guitarist Lenny Breau in Winnipeg and later in Edmonton. In Winnipeg, he also did a solo poetry recital at the University of Manitoba.

NAOMI BERNEY HORODETZSKY: I'd never heard of Leonard Cohen. It was an emotional performance. He seemed very laid-back, almost depressed.

He was wearing all black, including a black turtleneck. His delivery was almost monotonous. He was evoking an atmosphere of depression. There was no singing. The hall was not completely full. But I became a big fan.

Cohen also read poetry that year at l'Hibou in Ottawa.

PETER HODGSON/SNEEZY WATERS: He was quite amazing. People lined up around the block. Half were women. Same with Irving Layton—he would sell out. Poetry was as big as people singing Bob Dylan songs.

May 15, 1964, saw the premiere of *À Tout Prendre*, the film that Robert Hershorn had helped bankroll, at the Saint-Denis Theatre.

MANNY VAINISH: Robert had rented the home of John Wilson McConnell, the guy who owned the *Montreal Star*. Big old mansion on Pine Avenue. One day, they called me to a meeting with Cohen, [director] Claude Jutra, a fellow by the name of Lyons, from England—his family owned Lyons Tea—and Robert. The whole discussion involved whether Leonard would somehow participate. These guys all had little snuff boxes, and they were all around the table snorting snuff [ground tobacco].

Hershorn subsequently signed a coproduction agreement under the umbrella of his company, Orion Films, and initially invested $6,000.

ARNIE GELBART: Robert financed a large part of that film. I worked on it with Jutra. Leonard did the English subtitles. I think he did it gratis, or perhaps Robert paid him.

The first independently produced feature film in Quebec, it testified to the cultural upheaval that was occurring, containing a homosexual subtext and a scene showing—possibly for the first time in North America—a white man and black woman together in bed. Cohen himself made an uncredited cameo appearance early in the film. Jutra, playing the character of Claude, asks him, "What's the name of that woman?"—a Haitian singer. To which Cohen says, "I don't know." To the opening, the film's major figures came dressed in suits fashioned by Hershorn's Hyde Park Clothes.

ROY MACSKIMMING: It had the air of a premiere—crowds of people on the sidewalk, limousines, a big cultural night in Montreal. Waiting for the film to start, Irving leaned forward and in his loud voice said something to Leonard, about two rows ahead. Leonard looked around, mortified, and said, "Irving, speak French tonight." And Irving said, even louder than before, so that everyone would hear, "But, Leonard, I don't speak French!" That was Irving deliberately trying to get under Leonard's skin. Leonard was swanning around, with all these young Quebecois actresses, trying to play the part of the suave, cosmopolitan bilingual.

Cohen did one more favour on behalf of Jutra and Hershorn later that year. He called the Academy of Motion Picture Arts and Sciences to inquire about entering the film for an Oscar nomination. Fifty years later, Belgian scholar Francis Mus excavated the amusing transcript of that conversation.

FRANCIS MUS: Cohen says, "I would like to enter a film in the foreign film category. The title is *À Tout Prendre*." . . . "A what?" . . . Cohen: "It's a French title. I'll spell it. A-T-O-U-T" . . . "Yeah, I got that. A trout what?" . . . Cohen: "Not a trout. Listen. This is French." . . . "We already have our French entry." . . . Cohen: "But this is a Canadian film." . . . "Canadian films are considered American films." Cohen: "All right, I'd like to enter it as an American film. The title is *À Tout Prendre*." . . . "But that's a foreign language." . . . Cohen: "Not in Canada. It's an official language. Five million people speak it every day. And most of the features made in Canada are in French." . . . "Oh." . . . Cohen: "So what category should we enter it under?" . . . "I really don't know." . . . Cohen: "Could some decision be made?" . . . "I suppose so. Anyhow, you're too late this year."

That summer, Cohen's poem "The Kite Is a Victim," from *The Spice Box of Earth*, was scheduled to be read on CBC-TV by the actor Paul Hecht.

ISRAEL CHARNEY: They needed visuals, so on a windy Sunday, we organized an event out at Morton's place in Ways Mills. This potter up the hill had a field and I had a World War II emergency kite I'd bought in London in 1963. Hecht flew it. Leonard was present, though he stayed in the kitchen. Did I ever see Leonard depressed? That's probably where I first heard the word.

Cohen might have been depressed because of Charney. In a letter to Ihlen at that time, he wrote, "Israel is back in town. I hardly know the boy and I'm at a loss to know why he regards me as a mortal enemy . . . perhaps you know." The last line is almost certainly sarcasm—Cohen again implying her infidelity.

*   *   *

The Cohen coterie spent many weekends at Rosengarten's retreat, a former buttery he had turned into a studio.

PATRICIA NOLIN: I see those guys in Ways Mills making music. Morton played the banjo. Derek played the harmonica, faking it. Hershorn played the guitar. What did we do? We danced, listened to music— we played Booker T. & the M. G.'s' "Green Onions" a lot—smoked pot. When I think about that time, the word that comes to mind is "insouciant." We laughed a lot. That's what I remember most. I laughed a lot with Leonard. He was extremely funny. His laugh was contagious and it was real, not phony.

CAROL TALBOT-SMITH: There were a lot of laughs. One day, I was about to apply for teacher's college and I bumped into Leonard and Morton. They insisted on taking me for a drink, where they tried to get me drunk enough to change my mind. Their argument was that if I became a teacher, I'd lose my creativity. They didn't dissuade me. I became a teacher and a principal. But Leonard was always fun to be around. You knew, even if you started with something dark and serious, there'd be fun with it. That's how he was. Yet my sense is he was a loner. Anyone trying to get information from him would not get a lot that he didn't want to give. And they wouldn't get it from the people around him either.

The bonhomie was genuine in the moment, but also a facade. Some sense of Cohen's turbulent inner life and his tumultuous relationship with Ihlen was captured in another letter written to her in late June, 1964. "Sick with the dishonesty between us," he asks, "what are you doing in Hydra? What are you really doing? . . . There is something I have to learn about you and that is whether you want to love me or destroy me." By then, Cohen was hard at work on the novel that would become *Beautiful Losers*.

LEONARD COHEN: A friend of mine, Alanis Obomsawin, who's an Abenaquis Indian, had in her apartment a lot of pictures of Kateri Tekakwitha. I inquired about them and over the years began to know things about her. Then she lent me this book, which I lost, a very rare book on Kateri Tekakwitha [*An Iroquois Virgin, Catherine Tekakwitha, Lily of the Mohawk and the St. Lawrence, 1656–1680* by Edouard Lecompte]. I had it with me in Greece and I also had a copy of . . . a 1943 Blue Beetle's comic and several other books. I sat down in this very desolate frame of mind and said, "Well, I don't know anything about the world. I don't know anything about myself, I don't know anything about Kateri Tekakwitha or the Blue Beetle, but I've just got to begin." And I began.

BARRIE WEXLER: He didn't lose the books. They were pilfered by someone staying at the house. The shops on the port weren't the only place people collected souvenirs from.

ARNIE GELBART: Alanis was the inspiration, because she told him about her antecedents and he became interested in Kateri.

ISRAEL CHARNEY: Kahn-Tineta Horn might also have been a model for Leonard. She was a Mohawk activist. I was at Leonard's place one day and we'd smoked up. Leonard was going to be a judge at this beauty contest at Kahnawake, the Mohawk reservation on the other side of [Montreal's] Mercier Bridge. So he says, "Come along." This huge stretch limousine showed up to take us to the event. It reminded me of summer camp. These girls, all natives—and we were the judges. I was a judge too, Leonard, a couple of nuns in habit, and Marius Barbeau, this really old Quebec ethnographer. What a goofy scene. There were two Jewish social workers there.

It was not Cohen's first visit to the reservation, then known as Caughnawaga.

LEONARD COHEN: My father used to take me [there]. Before I ever heard of Kateri Tekakwitha. I used to go with him Sunday afternoons and we'd watch the dances of the Indians. Strange that I found out later that Kateri's remains are buried there. It's not remote. I always loved her.

One day during this period, Gelbart claims, he became one of the first— perhaps *the* first—to hear the poem "Suzanne," the basis of the later song.

ARNIE GELBART: He actually read it to me, the day after he finished it. We were walking in old Montreal, down Bonsecours Street. Because I knew Suzanne [Verdal] and her former partner, Armand Vaillancourt, and he generously passed his woman on to Leonard.

There are various accounts of the song's origins. One 1974 newspaper article said Cohen composed it in Café Prag, a basement coffee shop on Montreal's Bishop Street, which opened in 1964.

DOUGLAS COHEN: I remember he phoned me from some café and asked me what I thought of it. He'd just finished writing it and he sang it, and I said, "I think it will work."

JUDIT KENYERES: Café Prag was one of the most wonderful hangouts. There was no alcohol, but there were wonderful baguettes and sandwiches. Different musicians and poets would perform and pass the hat. We had both English- and French-speaking artists, so it had a very unusual flavour.

There, one evening, Judit Kenyeres met Cohen.

JUDIT KENYERES: I was his waitress, thrilled and trying not to show it. He didn't read that night, but when they were leaving, I was near the exit and he came up and stroked my face and said, "You have a very beautiful face." I just melted. I was so excited. I haven't forgotten it. Another time, I saw him at the Bistro. It was his birthday and he was handing out chocolates.

BARRIE WEXLER: That's another tradition he picked up in Greece. In any small shop, if there's an open box of cookies or chocolates on the counter, you know it's the owner's name day.

Among the women Cohen was seeing during this period was Francine Loyer, a friend of Gelbart's and, a few years later, Robert Hershorn's wife.

ARNIE GELBART: She was a very cute girl. I know I brought her to Leonard's room at the Hotel de France. We'd gone out for dinner. She stayed and I left. Then she met Hershorn, who was then dating Alanis, though her name was Hélène Robert.

DAVID LIEBER: Francine was a bit of a siren. She was always hot.

BARRIE WEXLER: I was once at Francine's apartment on Nuns' Island. The phone rang and I could hear his voice at the other end. "This is Leonard Cohen." A pretty formal greeting for someone I'd thought she'd had an affair with. But that was Leonard.

CAROL ZEMEL: Francine was a very enterprising woman who started working for Hershie Segal [at Le Château] and worked her way up from there.

HERSH SEGAL: I shouldn't say this because I was married at the time, but Francine was a girlfriend of mine.

FRANCINE HERSHORN: I was working for Le Château as a designer when I met Robert. I hired Marianne as a model for the clothes—her picture was in the newspaper—and she became a salesgirl for a bit.

On June 7, at the Jewish Public Library, Cohen sat on another panel to discuss Jewish affairs. His address enunciated a viewpoint that lay at the heart of his work.

LEONARD COHEN: The world is hostile not only to the Jewish writer . . . the world is hostile to . . . any man who will hold up a mirror to the particular kind of mindless chaos in which we endure. That is the glory of the poet . . . the writer . . . the Jew: that he is despised, that he moves in this mirrored exile, covered in mirrors . . . To me, his destiny is exile and his vocation is to be despised.

Calling Judaism "a direct confrontation with the absolute," he compared its present spiritual life to an unclean oyster.

LEONARD COHEN: There is an awful truth . . . we no longer believe we are holy . . . This is the confession without which we cannot begin to raise our eyes: the absence of God in our midst . . . Let us encourage young men to go into the deserts of their heart and burn the praise of perfection. Let us do it with drugs, or whips, or sex, or blasphemy, or fasting, but let men begin to feel the perfection of the universe . . . We need our dirty saints and our monstrous hermits. Let us create a tradition for them, for they light the world.

SEYMOUR MAYNE: Cohen is generalizing. Study remained. Jews wanted to be successful, establish themselves, and build their big cathedral synagogues, as if to say to their Christian neighbours, "We have arrived and are proud of it." The large synagogues, the new plutocrats—he was right to criticize it, but there were other streams in Canadian Jewish society.

Ruth Roskies Wisse was more disappointed by the path Cohen chose to take.

RUTH ROSKIES WISSE: I discovered that the affiliated Jew is the iconoclast of every age, and . . . when I realized that neither Leonard nor anyone else would be the sufficient truth teller of my generation, I began to . . . have regrets about him, who cast himself as love's solitary survivor so that he would not have to bear the weight of his and my lonely community, or of the tattered culture that belongs to us all.

By July, Cohen returned to Hydra, but stopped in Toronto to see his friend Alfie Magerman before catching a flight to Greece.

BARBARA MAGERMAN: We went to hear him read at the North York Public Library and he came back to the house. He really did not look well. He had a head cold. He was coughing, his nose running, pale, undernourished. We gave him a roast beef meal. I thought he must be feeling so sorry for himself. But he couldn't wait to get out of there. Alfie took Leonard to the airport and he took my infant son, Ken, with him, in the back. They get near the airport and Leonard says to Alfie, "Why don't you come with me? Ditch all this." And Alfie pointed to Ken and said, "Leonard, what about him?" And Leonard said, "Oh, someone will find him, don't worry." I was shocked when he told me.

On Hydra, Cohen made a new friend—another sui generis character, Alexis Bolens. A bon vivant, raconteur, gentleman with courtly, old-world manners, Bolens had once been a soldier of fortune in South Africa, Biafra, and other war zones. According to Barrie Wexler, he was also the island's master of ceremonies when it came to sexual escapades.

ALEXIS BOLENS: Leonard and I were competitors, always chasing the same girls. We had completely different styles, of course. I had a macho approach. His was poetic, romantic. I used to call him the Wailing Wall.

Among the women Cohen romanced on Hydra that summer was Greek painter and writer Nana Isaia. Her memoir of the period, *The History Then and Now*, uses him as the principal character, named Ais—pronounced Ice. In the memoir, Isaia says that on Hydra, everyone was in love with Cohen, women and men alike.

That fall, McClelland & Stewart released *Flowers for Hitler*, Cohen's third volume of verse. On the dust jacket, Cohen insisted, "There has never been a book like this, prose or poetry, written in Canada. All I ask is that you put it in the hands of my generation and it will be recognized." One poem—"Queen Victoria and Me"—was later adapted to musical form as "Queen Victoria" on the album *Live Songs*. The epigraph for the book was a quotation by Holocaust survivor Primo Levi: "Take care not to let it happen in your own homes."

LEONARD COHEN: [Levi is] saying, what point is there to a political solution if in the homes these tortures and mutilations continue? That's what *Flowers for Hitler* is all about. It's taking the mythology of the concentration camps and saying, "This is what we do to each other." . . . There's no point in refusing to acknowledge the wrathful deities. That's like putting pants on the legs of pianos like the Victorians did. The fact is that we all succumb to lustful thoughts, to evil thoughts, to thoughts of torture.

BARRIE WEXLER: Levi's core conclusion is that most men, given the right—or I should say wrong—circumstances, are capable of doing what the Nazis did. That realization eventually led to his suicide.

IRVING LAYTON: The Holocaust is pivotal to Leonard, although he doesn't talk about it. His is a spiritual quest, with as much skepticism as faith. What I most admire about Leonard is that he keeps that dialectical tension . . . Leonard has refused all the grand consolations—all the isms, the solutions of the day. He'll taste them and maybe he'll delude himself he's got hold of something, but a few months later, he has spat it out, albeit gently. He is one of the few writers who has voluntarily immersed himself in the destructive element, not once but many times, then walked back from the abyss with dignity to tell us what he saw, to put a frame around the wind.

RUTH ROSKIES WISSE: *Flowers for Hitler* advertised his readiness to joke about the moral categories of good and evil, villainy and martyrdom.

SANDRA DJWA: Cohen wants to bring a guilty world into recognition of itself: "I wait / for each one of you to confess." But the confession Cohen demands is one which accepts personal responsibility for evil as the natural corollary of being human . . . The modern antihero accepts evil as part of existence and immerses himself within it.

The most scathing criticism came from Cohen's former mentor, Louis Dudek. Reviewing *Flowers for Hitler*, he called it "almost unnecessary . . . [His] rudderless wit and fantasy save these poems, but even this liberated imagination is filled with reeling despair. The centre of the mind is never found. The heart, as he says, is never reached."

Cohen's young friend, poet Steve Smith, died in September 1964, not long after his first book, *God's Kaleidoscope*, was published in Dudek's McGill Poetry Series.

SHEILA WALKER: Dudek came to see [my brother] in the hospital and told him the book was being reprinted. I think it was one of the last things he heard before he died.

Smith's girlfriend, Michele Hendlisz Cohen, was at his bedside when he died.

MICHELE HENDLISZ COHEN: It was such an awful event. He was in a lot of pain. The doctors had said he had five years. The rest is a fog of tears. I've never managed to really absorb it. I remember taking the book around to bookshops. It was almost cathartic.

SHEILA WALKER: It was horrible. I've never gotten over it. In those days, they didn't know how to treat dying people. They wouldn't give him painkillers because they thought he'd become an addict. Steve really liked Leonard. I liked him. We all liked him. Steve died a week before school started. At McGill, a week later, everyone was walking away from me because people didn't know what to say. But Leonard grabbed me and we sat on the grass together and [he] said he felt really bad about Steve obviously. He said he wanted to dedicate a book to my brother, but the one he wanted to dedicate [*Flowers for Hitler*] was already at press, so he said he'd dedicate the next one [*Beautiful Losers*]. And that's what he did. What a sweet guy. I remember Irving Layton at the funeral pounding on the hearse, saying "Steve didn't want to die and it didn't have to happen."

MICHELE HENDLISZ COHEN: Leonard did not come to the funeral—he was out of town—but I saw him [later] on campus, and he was very gentle and very nice. He was going to be reading poetry and invited me to come. After the talk, we went to Pine Avenue, where Leonard was staying. Marianne was gone. It was a beautiful room. This is when his charisma became almost palpable. He was sitting there in one of the armchairs and it was as if he was a light to which people came. They came into the room and they went straight for him. And he wasn't talking loud. He wasn't doing anything. He was just *being*—it was just extraordinary. Magnetic. And he never exploited it. And it was men and women. It wasn't that you fell in love. It was like moths to a flame. You just kind of went, and his voice was quiet and his gestures were delicate. He wasn't the sort of person to talk about himself, not narcissistic at all. He was more the kind to take up the present and joke about it, make comments, and with his friends, create a kind of sparring. I didn't think of him as a famous person. I wasn't attracted to him because of what he represented. He was just another poet, in my line of poets.

Sometime later, when they next met, Cohen gave her a short poem.

MICHELE HENDLISZ COHEN: It's four or five lines, and it says, "Montreal love story," something blah blah blah and—this is the line I love—"nothing ruins the grace of the weather." I haven't lost it. I have carried it through all my meanderings. I can't remember if he wrote it in my presence, probably so, but it's never been published.

CHERYL SOURKES: Pretty well as soon as Steve died, Leonard hit on Michele, and they got involved. I don't think it lasted that long. He helped her through her widowhood.

MICHELE HENDLISZ COHEN: Leonard cared and he didn't forget. He was very gentle. After Steve's death, it took me a long time to be both emotionally and physically able to love. Leonard completely understood that. We tried to be lovers, but it didn't work because I felt so guilty. I felt I was betraying Steve, because he'd been my first lover. I felt there must be all kinds of eyes looking. Even though I slept with him, I did not see myself as his girlfriend. And I told him that I couldn't love and he said fine. We took a bath together. I think we saw each other four or five times. It was quite intense. But Leonard did help, because he was there. He said nothing about Marianne. And I didn't ask.

CHERYL SOURKES: One night, at Michele's house, two in the morning, Leonard phoned and said, "What are you doing?" She said, "I'm here with a friend." He said, "That's funny, I'm here with a friend too. Why don't you come over?"

MICHELE HENDLISZ COHEN: We did not hesitate. The fact that the hotel was on Sainte-Catherine East was part of the frisson. In 1964, east and west were culturally so separate.

CHERYL SOURKES: We got in a cab and went to the Hotel de France. That night is completely indelible in my mind. Morton and Leonard were very frisky, jumping all over. I don't know what Michele and I did, except appreciate their brilliance. They held up a package of

Rothmans cigarettes and said, "In the future everything's going to be this size"—the size of a cell phone. We stayed the night. I don't think they were after group sex. They got very stoned and we were very stoned, some kind of weed or hash.

MICHELE HENDLISZ COHEN: There were several people on this bed, not just Leonard and Morton. The women were pretty quiet, but the fire between the men . . . The women left about 4 a.m., but I didn't. There was another night that ended in some delicatessen on Sainte-Catherine. Leonard, to my amazement, was able to eat borscht with sour cream at five o'clock in the morning.

CHERYL SOURKES: Morton and Leonard—they were an amazing duo. They sparked each other, inspired each other. They just tripped off, in brilliant riffs. It's part of the Jewish thing—the oral tradition, punning, associations, very Talmudic. I think Leonard is shaped very much Talmudically. But how he got to where he went so quickly, how he learned so much about the wider world when he was raised in Westmount—how did he know about the wide world?

In October, four Canadian writers—Irving Layton, Leonard Cohen, Earle Birney, and Phyllis Gotlieb—embarked on a cross-Canada tour to promote their new books of poetry. A government grant helped underwrite the cost and the National Film Board commissioned a film based on it. Reviewing one appearance in Toronto, the *Toronto Star*'s Ralph Thomas described Cohen as "the wry, very sensitive young man who's driven to a hundred neuroses by an impossibly stupid world." In Toronto, Cohen met Maureen O'Donnell, a young writer.

MAUREEN O'DONNELL: I went to a reading, and during the brief encounter that we had, he gave me the worst advice ever, which he prefaced by saying: "I'm going to tell you something very important." I reached for my chisel and my tablet. "No matter how much you love something or how carefully you build it, if it stands in the way of experience, destroy it!" Did he hit on me? I certainly hope so. Did I follow up? No. Even then I knew that travelling poets and itinerant musicians were not good for a girl.

Interviewed by the *Montreal Star*, Cohen defended the poetry tour, which some critics had compared to a cheap vaudeville act. Vaudeville, Cohen retorted, "is a precious human activity and I like to live like a vaudeville artist—on a banana peel." It's a line that perhaps foreshadowed, by twenty-four years, the famous banana photograph used on the cover of his *I'm Your Man* album. Years later, Cohen acknowledged that Louis Dudek took a dim view of this PR campaign for poetry.

LEONARD COHEN: Dudek resented what Irving and I were doing. He thought this was a crime against poetry. He sincerely believed it belonged in the ivory tower, where it couldn't be blemished. But over time, he realized he was wrong. And he copped to it publicly when he presented me with my honorary degree at McGill [in 1992].

Cohen's friend, director Don Owen, later claimed the hectic schedule of one-night stands made it almost impossible to shoot the film. He shot a few sequences, but spent most of his time getting stoned with Cohen. When the NFB sent Owen to Nigeria on another project, Donald Brittain took over. Brittain soon realized the film would have more appeal if it focused on Cohen alone. Birney and Gotlieb were flat, cinematically; and Layton was arguably overexposed. When *Ladies and Gentlemen, Mr. Leonard Cohen* was released the following year, Cohen did his diplomatic best to blunt the implications of that decision, saying "for some technical reason, only the parts of the film that dealt with me seemed to have been good."

In one segment, Cohen and Layton were interviewed by broadcaster Pierre Berton. The scene provides an extraordinary glimpse of the

Cohen-Layton dynamic. Layton is characteristically pugnacious; Cohen responds with detached coolness, speaking in riddles. But both are hiding behind personae. When Berton asks Cohen, "How can you be a good poet and not care about anything," Cohen says, "No, no. I do the poetry and you do the commentary." Berton refuses to let go. "How can you write poetry if you're not bothered by anything?" To which Cohen replies, "I'm bothered when I get up in the morning. My real concern is to discover whether or not I'm in a state of grace. And if I make that investigation, and discover that I'm not in the state of grace, I'm better in bed."

HOWARD ASTER: Cohen learned how to create a public persona—a false persona. He played games with his public and with the media. He did it all his life. He was a master. He learned that from Irving, the first Canadian poet to do it. Of course, you end up fooling yourself every now and then. Cohen's persona applies to what is written about him—not what he wrote. You have to separate the two. The conundrum is, how do they fit together?

LEONARD COHEN: The persona that the guy develops to protect himself in the world is another question. What kind of image you really go into collusion with and encourage is another thing from a man sitting in front of a blank canvas.

PICO IYER: One of the fascinating riddles is how he was able to steal the show as a slightly nerdy, nervous-seeming poet on the make and, thirty-five years later, would steal the show again as this poised, grave, black-clad monk. [His friend] Nancy Bacal has this wonderful line about Leonard having "the gift of leading from behind." He certainly had the gift of commanding the room in a subtle, unobtrusive way.

One night, Cohen told Hendlisz that he was leaving for New York but wanted to give her a gift. What would she like?

MICHELE HENDLISZ COHEN: It was after we had spent time together and I, a naive twenty-year-old, with chutzpah, asked for a leather coat. He didn't flinch. He got his friend [Hersh Segal] who ran Le Château, and I went over there and designed my coat. I still have it [fifty-four years later] and I still wear it.

From New York's Gotham Hotel, Cohen wrote to Ihlen, saying all his press attention had left him depressed, but he had thrown the coins of the *I Ching* and had come up with the same answer as she had—presumably to continue their relationship. Notwithstanding, when Cohen returned from New York, he booked a room at the Queen Elizabeth Hotel and called Hendlisz.

MICHELE HENDLISZ COHEN: I went over and the door wasn't shut, so I went in. He was standing at the large bay window, looking out, mostly at stars. I just went to him and we stood there for at least five minutes, if not more, not talking. He was the kind of guy you could do that with.

*   *   *

By January 1965, Cohen was back on Hydra, after spending a few days in London. In a March 3 letter to his uncle Lawrence Cohen, he apologized for an earlier criticizing missive, and asked him to "tear the letter up and chalk it up to the panic of a man who has tried to write the history of the world in three months and who is pretty nervous that nobody is going to want to read it." Soon after he arrived, he made new friends—poet Jack Hirschman and his wife, Ruth Seymour.

RUTH SEYMOUR: I didn't have a strong first impression. Jack and I knew Irving Layton, who left you with a very strong impression. Leonard didn't give you that impression. Jack was the figure of a poet, lean and tall and striding along the *agora* in his long coat. Leonard—as he once said to me, "I look like I sell real estate." But he struck me as extremely intelligent, a literary person. We spoke Yiddish together. He was with Marianne—she was stunning. I liked her right away. Her son, Axel, and my daughter bonded. Leonard was just beginning to focus on music, but he didn't have a good voice. We knew the same Yiddish songs. One night, we spent the whole evening singing them. "Can you top this? Do you know this one?" But it was inconceivable to me that he would become a singer.

JACK HIRSCHMAN: Leonard was writing *Beautiful Losers*. We smoked hashish. One of the reasons we got close was our kids were the same age—David, Celia, and Axel. There were no cars—the kids were utterly free to run around.

CELIA HIRSCHMAN: All the children were together and all the men taught. There were three men—Leonard with Axel, an American professor with three children—Sam Fisher—and my father, with myself and David. It was homeschooling long before homeschooling was in fashion, because there was no one to teach us.

JACK HIRSCHMAN: I remember a hashish-hazy evening. There was a guy named Ian who lived at the top of Hydra and there was a little theatre and there were poetry readings. Leonard read there. The one umbrage I took with him, that really disturbed me, which I only learned later—all right, we were all young and we were crazy too—but he and Marianne gave LSD to Axel.

RUTH SEYMOUR: This happened after we left the island. They had split up and Marianne allowed Leonard to take Axel to Mexico. That's where he gave Axel psilocybin. Marianne believed that when Axel came back, he wasn't the same anymore. But I think we were the only ones who had taken LSD—[others] had taken mescaline, but not LSD. It wasn't easy to get on Hydra. They did hash.

Although both Hirschman and Seymour heard this story, it's extremely unlikely that it's true. Ihlen herself later offered what is probably the accurate account.

MARIANNE IHLEN: Axel, unfortunately, at the age of fifteen, during his first meeting with his father, was given LSD and got very sick.

CAROL ZEMEL: Marianne had sent him to see his father, who took every drug in the world and shared them with Axel. [Axel] was later diagnosed with adult-onset schizophrenia. To some degree, she blamed the ex-husband for [his condition].

BARRIE WEXLER: It makes zero sense that Leonard would give a child a hallucinogen. Not only was Leonard not irresponsible. He was also protective. He kept drugs, including weed, away from me—and I was in my early twenties—knowing I didn't do them. Hirschman and Seymour likely heard the story from each other.

AVIVA LAYTON: Leonard would never do that, not in a million years. Big Axel took him to India and gave it to him there, and when he came back, he was never the same.

Years later, Zemel saw young Axel again, during a trip to Norway.

CAROL ZEMEL: He'd been hospitalized—institutionalized. He could get a day pass. We picked him up and went for a drive. He was twenty-something, smoking. He barely would talk to me. It must have been terrible. But Marianne had this quality, maybe stoicism. She was ultimately a very resourceful woman. She remarried. [But] she never got over Leonard—never, never.

Cohen was still on Hydra when he likely heard the news that an old friend, Nancy Challies, had committed suicide—shooting herself in a bathroom—in Montreal, age twenty-one. Her tragic story later inspired his song "Seems So Long Ago, Nancy." Challies had been forced to give up an out-of-wedlock child for adoption. Years later, Cohen told her nephew, Tim Challies, that while he had never been close to Nancy, he remembered her "beauty and bravery . . . Many young women of the time came up against the hard limitations of family and society, although not every confrontation ended so sadly." In another interview, Cohen concluded that Challies had been almost a heroic figure, a prototype for another generation. "Twenty years later, she would have been just the hippest girl on the block. [Then], in a certain way, she was doomed."

It is almost impossible to locate the precise moment when the notion of becoming a singer first formed in Cohen's mind. What is clear is that by the midsixties, while living on a remote Greek island, he was very much aware of Bob Dylan and the impact he was having on pop culture.

JACK HIRSCHMAN: I was very struck when I met him—Leonard was extremely ambitious, expressly, to overtake Dylan. He was very conscious of Dylan. I didn't know who Dylan was. He wrote a poem full of rage and he excluded it from the Penguin edition. I asked him later, "Why did you leave out those poems of rage?" Because he had changed the poems of rage at the beginning of the war in Vietnam to songs in the Penguin edition. And his answer was he didn't want poems of rage. He wanted more light stuff, which I thought was really compromising. Because for me, Vietnam—that was the war of my adult life.

RUTH SEYMOUR: At that time, Leonard was a vegetarian. One day, just before Easter, he said, "I want to take you guys someplace." He arranged to take me and Jack, and Demetri Gassoumis and his lady friend, Aniskha, and Marianne, on this walk. He would not tell us where he was taking us. We kept walking and walking and finally came to a wooden shed. Then we saw horses pulling a cart full of lambs. The drivers had to beat the horses with whips to get them to go. They didn't want to go, because they were taking the lambs to a slaughterhouse, where they would slit their throats. The lambs were watching this, but obviously did not understand the concept of death, so there was no panic. But the horses understood it and certainly the dogs. It was Easter and this was the paschal lamb—what you traditionally eat in Greece. The women were quite horrified. We discussed whether to buy a lamb and try to save one. This led to a great discussion, because we were all transient people and who would ultimately take care of the lamb we might save? Leonard did this out of a moral sense—watch the slaughter.

The lambs-to-slaughter metaphor appears in several Cohen works: "The Glass Dog," in *Flowers for Hitler,* in "Stories of the Street" on his first album, *Songs of Leonard Cohen.* The image appears three times in *Death of a Lady's Man* and again in "Amen," a song from his 2012 album, *Old Ideas* ("When the filth of the butcher / Is washed in the blood of the lamb"). It wasn't until the mid-1960s that the island's slaughterhouse was converted to a nightclub, called the Yacht Club. Cohen used to joke that disco goers were dancing on the slaughterhouse floor.

Cohen welcomed other friends to Hydra that summer—Irving and Aviva Layton.

AVIVA LAYTON: I arrived in Piraeus and Leonard came to meet me— Irving wasn't coming for three weeks. Typically Greek, they locked all our luggage in a hold and couldn't find the key. We had to stay on board till the next day. Leonard came on board and we stayed up the whole night dancing and drinking ouzo or retsina. We learned

Greek dancing. Travelling, I'd met a woman who became my life-long friend, Julie Copeland, beautiful and exquisite and long-legged. Leonard was very taken with her. I once asked her if she ever went to bed with him and she said no. But he flirted and danced Greek dancing with her all night.

JULIE COPELAND: It was May. We did indeed dance all night. Leonard was doing a bit of a line for me. It was pretty obvious. But I wasn't taken with him. He was being charming, as men are. He certainly knew the Greek dancing.

On Hydra, Copeland thought Cohen was preoccupied.

JULIE COPELAND: He was very quiet, quite an introvert. He seemed to me rather miserable, a depressed sort of character. He was very frustrated with his writing and had thrown, or tried to throw, his typewriter out the window. Marianne wasn't there. We were in her house. We stayed up drinking at night in the port, but Leonard wasn't often there. He wasn't a party man. He came across as very intense, very serious. There was a gloomy dark atmosphere around him.

The Laytons too had stayed in Ihlen's old house.

AVIVA LAYTON: I don't believe in any of this, but Marianne's house was haunted. I spent a couple of nights there and [told] her, "I feel there's somebody in the house with me. I'd hear somebody tapping on a type-writer and steps on the wooden stairs up to the bedroom. And on the terrace I heard a man's voice saying, "Throw your baby off the cliff." And Marianne said, "That's him—the ghost that lives in the house."

BARRIE WEXLER: Marianne saw ghosts everywhere. She used to tell stories about haunted houses and church bells ringing on windless nights.

She was quite superstitious. At her farmhouse in Larkollen, there was an old book—a Norwegian almanac, full of mystical symbols, that gave advice on the most auspicious time to have babies, plant crops, even cut your nails. She took that almanac fairly seriously.

Aviva Layton soon discovered that life on Hydra, with all its peculiarities, only seemed like paradise.

AVIVA LAYTON: Since paradise can't exist without the lurking snake, it inevitably became hellish. It ended up being a fucking nightmare. The sixties were dangerous times for relationships, and Greek islands were quadruply dangerous. Beautiful, wild women came—that's what happened. They swarmed around Leonard. In a way, how could [he] say no? You're sexual, vibrant, young, lusty, and women are there, ripe for the picking. The women would just throw themselves at Leonard and that wave lapped over onto Irving. And the island could be suffocating, because everyone knew. It was all falling to pieces for everybody. Paradise has the snake and it's going to bite you on the ass. The kids were going bonkers. Relationships were unravelling. Everyone was sleeping with everyone else. Open marriages. It really was a painful, emotionally dangerous time. We became the children and our children had to be the adults. But the children became basket cases, like Axel or Irving's daughter, Naomi. It looked like the perfect place for children. It was hell for children.

JACK HIRSCHMAN: There was wife-swapping. Ruth had a thing with Leonard's closest friend, [George] Lialios. And I had known another woman on the island. Everyone was pretty crazy.

BARRIE WEXLER: In those days, we slipped effortlessly in and out of each other's beds as easily as you changed the sheets, and far more often.

RUTH SEYMOUR: One wife, Nancy, with two little children—she flipped out. A straight couple, compared to everybody else we knew. I remember going down to the port in the morning and she was in a café full of guys, expats, and it looked like a dog in heat. It was scary in a way. Finally, her husband took her away from the island. Demetri Gassoumis's [future wife] Anishka had arrived, saying she was going to break up every marriage on the island, but she only ended up breaking up one—Demetri's.

Ultimately, many lives would shatter on the rocks of the Hydriote idyll. There were two suicides in the Johnston family, two more in Alexis Bolens's. Alcoholism would first claim the talent and then the life of Anthony Kingsmill. Bill Cunliffe would suffer the same disease. Welsh painter and writer Brenda Chamberlain also took her own life. And there would be uncounted broken marriages and severed relationships.

BILL POWNALL: People make a big thing about the decadence of Hydra. That was the time. It was going on in London—the sexual revolution, the pill, the whole bloody works. They say Hydra broke up marriages. But only one in three marriages last[s] anyway. And quite a lot of people just worked. The Johnstons, whatever else they did, got the work done. Leonard worked and was reclusive. And I was reclusive. That was one of the things Leonard liked about Hydra. Nobody bothered him. Everyone liked and admired him and left him alone. Greeks would call him "my brother."

BARRIE WEXLER: Hydra practically institutionalized infidelity. The only issue Leonard had with attached women sleeping with other men was when the woman in question was attached to him. Marianne gave almost as good as she got when it came to unfaithfulness. Leonard's relationship with her as his so-called muse is often misunderstood. For Cohen, a woman's inspiration had as much to do with her betrayal as anything else. I never really believed him when he said that if he knew where the good songs came from, he'd go there more often. After his volatile relationship with Marianne, he knew very well where the good songs came from.

RUTH SEYMOUR: More than infidelity, madness was the thing to be careful about. People were en route to India to find truth and beauty. People talked like that and believed it. It was a time of much more innocence, because people still believed you could speak about truth and beauty and go on a search.

The Laytons later began to spend summers on Lesbos; Cohen would occasionally visit. Even there, women pursued him, including Montrealer Niema Ash, who had been Layton's student at Sir George Williams University and had run the folk club, Finjan, where Bob Dylan had appeared.

AVIVA LAYTON: Niema was once my closest friend. She was like my sister. But on Lesbos, Niema would stalk Leonard with her little camera and take photos of him everywhere. She would pop up and shoot. One day Leonard said, "I can't stand it. Let's go and expose the film." And once we saw her leave her little rented room, we went into it through the window and found her camera and he took all the film out. We never told Niema that story.

Cohen was working hard to finish *Beautiful Losers*, writing on his terrace while listening to U.S. Armed Forces radio and to Ray Charles's *The Genius Sings the Blues* on a portable record player. The disc is said to have ultimately warped in the sun.

LEONARD COHEN: I wrote a minimum of four hours a day and a maximum of twenty. The last two weeks I worked twenty hours a day. That was when I flipped out.

ANNE COLEMAN: He later told us how he'd written it, with the blazing sun incandescent on the page—heat and sun creating a kind of madness.

When he finished, Cohen fasted for twelve days and began hallucinating. His temperature climbed to 104 degrees. It took protein injections and two months of bed rest for him to recover, nursed by Ihlen and their housekeeper, Kyria Sophia, who prepared homemade nettle soup.

BARRIE WEXLER: The whole last year was nonstop. He'd been doing acid and huge amounts of speed, which George Lialios brought in from Athens. He'd lost a lot of weight [he was said to have dropped to 116 pounds] and was operating on very little sleep. His fast afterwards had as much to do with the cumulative effect of amphetamines as it did with any sort of purification trip. Marianne said he was beginning to shut down. There was no medical clinic on the island. She had to practically prop him up on the ferry on the way to the emergency room in Athens. She said that during the preceding year, he'd had a premonition that he was going to die or thought he was dying—I'm not sure which—and was driving himself to get the book done.

It was during this period that Cohen, on an LSD trip, painted the mantra "I change I am the same" on the walls of his downstairs bedroom. Ihlen later had the room painted over. After he recovered, Cohen met another aspiring writer, Montrealer Charlie Sise, scion of a prominent Westmount family.

CHARLIE SISE: He had just finished *Beautiful Losers*. He told me finishing it was like a nervous breakdown. He wrote a lot of it on another island, not close by. I'd been travelling for three years, so I asked him about Henry Moscovitch and other Jewish friends in Montreal. He said, "Henry's been through a lot. You might have trouble recognizing him. He's a bit of a blimp." He took me up to the house to meet

Marianne and Axel. I was struck by how bare it was, so Spartan. It hit me hard.

BARRIE WEXLER: I never heard that he went to another island—not from him or anyone else. Leonard wasn't trying to get away from Marianne and Axel. It was the exact opposite. He told me that he not only couldn't have written the book if she hadn't been there to feed and take care of him. He would have died from all the drugs he was taking.

Another day, Sise told Cohen he was looking for cheap furniture, and complained about the port merchants gouging him.

CHARLIE SISE: Leonard sat back in his chair and said, "Well, we're all Levantines. We shouldn't be surprised." Then he said, "You *are* Jewish, aren't you?" And I said, "Not really." He smiled—he had a beautiful boyish smile—and said, "I'm sorry. I have an impeccable ear. You're talking with a middle-class Jewish accent." I explained my WASP background, boarding school, the whole bit, but if I had a Jewish accent, it came from my friends at McGill. He leaned back again and said, "This gives me a whole new impression of you. Before, I wasn't that sure you'd have much to say. Now when I see you're carrying these two incompatible speech patterns, that has to produce friction, dialectic, ferment that can lead to poetry and novels." He encouraged me to keep writing.

By August 1965, Cohen was back in North America.

HENRY ZEMEL: In Greece, he had two suits made—one for him and one for me. Beautiful suits, like cotton, not fine-tailored. I refused it. It was too nice. I could not accept the gift. Was he appalled? Who the fuck knows? He did something generous and I said, "I can't take it." Talk about a schmuck, huh?

Cohen also reconnected with Moscovitch.

BARRIE WEXLER: Henry, who had the physique of someone who had never seen the inside of a gym, said, "Cohen, how come you're so thin?" Leonard replied, "Henry, you'd be thin too if you lived on seaweed and amphetamines." And in fact, for years, his favourite snack was seaweed wafers, transparent green crisps that tasted like the Aegean.

Cohen, meanwhile, was thinking ever more seriously about a career in music. Journalist Barbara Amiel remembered him on a couch in Toronto's King Edward Hotel composing tunes on a mouth organ and singing his poems. "In an adjoining bedroom," Amiel later wrote, "a naked couple twisted and moaned through the songs." Cohen chose to interpret their noises positively. "I think I'm going to record myself singing my poems," he said. Amiel winced at the sound of Cohen's nasal voice. "Please don't," she replied.

One song Cohen likely sang that day was "Suzanne," the song that would effectively launch his music career a year later. Cohen had met contemporary dancer Suzanne Verdal when she was the partner of Montreal sculptor Armand Vaillancourt, in the early 1960s. By the time he visited her at her loft apartment on the waterfront, they had parted.

MICHAEL HARRIS: Armand—a very crazy fucker. Absolutely wonderful. Larger than life at all times, the same presence and theatricality as Leonard and Layton. I always believed they were imbued with a kind of theatricality—not just to do with clothes or swagger or elegance, but a theatricality that they believed in and lived. That is how the light gets in. They very seldom dropped that theatre.

ALFIE WADE: I watched that trilogy, man, that activity of Leonard, Suzanne Verdal, and Armand. All that hippy-dippy stuff going on at

Le Vieux Moulin. I felt for Leonard, man, because he was quite taken with Suzanne, but Armand was a burly French-Canadian sculptor. He wasn't happy about that.

ERICA POMERANCE: Suzanne Verdal was then a mother—she had her daughter, Julie, with Armand. She was never really a lover of Leonard's. It was an occasional thing. She was his muse for that song. She and Leonard both left unclear the exact nature of their relationship. He said they were just friends, possibly because she was Armand's girlfriend, and had had Armand's child. And he respected that. Suzanne later had two other children.

LINDA GABORIAU: Suzanne was very much as described in the song, a wonderful, sensual dancer with feathers in her hair. One day, she arrived on our doorstep with her daughter and said, "I have to go to rehearsal. Can you take care of Julie? I'll be back in three hours." She came back a day and a half later.

SUZANNE VERDAL: Leonard heard about this place I was living, with crooked floors and a poetic view of the river. We had tea together many times and mandarin oranges. [Leonard] was drinking me in more than I even recognized. I just would speak and move and encourage and he would just sit back and grin while soaking it all up, but I felt his presence really being with me. We'd walk down the street for instance, and the click of his boots and my shoes would be in synchronicity. We'd almost hear each other thinking.

Back in Montreal, Lionel Tiger came to visit.

LIONEL TIGER: I met him at his apartment—rented furniture, rooming house kind of thing. "Hey, Leonard," I said, "what have you been doing?" He says, "I've been writing songs." I say, "What kind of songs?" He says, "Anyone who asks me, I sing them all." So he sang me several, including "Suzanne." At first, I thought it was about our mutual friend Suzanne Grossman, a beautiful Swiss-Canadian actress, who visited him in Greece. Were they lovers? I hope so. She thought highly of Leonard. We were all at that epic period of life where everything is unfolding and everything is possible.

Cohen and Tiger went for a long walk—almost as far as the city's botanical gardens.

LIONEL TIGER: We talked and talked and talked. Not so much about politics, but we were always concerned about fairness, candour, and the uncertainties of living. And we discussed precisely what it was you did to get to what he became—the integrity of the work, the fact that it would take him two weeks to write a single line, the intimations of craft.

During a weekend with Morton Rosengarten in Ways Mills, he went to a party at the lakeside cottage of his friend Judy Gault in Ayer's Cliff.

ANNE COLEMAN: We're on the veranda. It is a warm evening. I'm talking to two young Australians, and I notice Leonard a few feet away, talking to someone else. I'd met him a few times, but don't really know him. He breaks off his conversation and moves to where I'm standing. His eyes gleam up at me for a moment—up, because he is considerably shorter than I am—and then he places his hand gently on my tummy and strokes me, watching his hand while he does this. Then his eyes gleam up again and he steps back and continues his conversation. I turn back to the Australians. There is a feeling of something unfinished. It was one of those sixties moments—so typical of a party at that time. Nowadays it might be seen as sexual harassment. It certainly wasn't. There wasn't anything about Leonard that seemed as though he would be doing something that wasn't welcome. It was a sensual appreciation.

Cohen's friends were becoming aware of his musical ambitions, including Phyllis Webb.

PHYLLIS WEBB: One night, driving around, we parked—I think on Peel Street—and he told me he wanted to be a singer. I was so amazed, because I thought of him as a poet. He also introduced me to pot. We had some and then went for Chinese dinner. He was chattering away and said, "Aren't I being brilliant?" And I said, "No." It was the first time I'd ever been stoned. The food did taste wonderful. Walking me home, I began to come down and he was very kind. He was warning me about depression after pot. I sensed he'd done this quite a bit. I didn't find him terribly amusing. He was a very serious young man at that stage.

An aspiring poet from Calgary, Barry McKinnon, had moved to Montreal to study with Layton. Eventually, he met Cohen—once. His girlfriend, Joy, had phoned from the Bistro to say that she was drinking with Cohen and artist Graham MacIntosh.

BARRY MCKINNON: She described Cohen as slouched, sunken, and skinny in a black turtleneck sweater, suffering bad acne, and not very attractive. [When] Joy finally recognized him, she got on the phone immediately. "I told him you wrote poetry. He says come down for a drink." I paced the apartment for a long time before deciding to head down to Mountain Street. When I [arrived], Cohen was leaving. We passed each other, but did not speak. But I also knew that this might be our only chance to meet, so I followed him to the Ritz-Carlton hotel. As he was going up the steps, I called: "Leonard, I was supposed to meet you. I'm Barry." He smiled and we entered a long and awkward pause until he said, "Well?" In my nervousness I blurted out: "I hate poetry!" He laughed and said, "That's the spirit!" We decided to meet again in two weeks at the Bistro. He was with [Marianne] and Axel, and MacIntosh. The meeting was not what I anticipated. Cohen and I barely spoke. Small talk went nowhere, as did any attempt at serious talk. "What's the cause of the quarrel between Layton and Dudek?" I asked. Reply: "Oh, I don't really know." After a few dead-end attempts, I started yakking to Graham, who guzzled up the beer I ended up paying for. Soon my ten dollars was gone. I met Joy and walked home, drunk and disappointed in the anticlimax of my only meeting with the famous writer partly responsible for luring me to Montreal.

One day, Cohen bumped into Michele Hendlisz Cohen on Mountain Street.

MICHELE HENDLISZ COHEN: He said, "I'm singing Judy Collins's songs." I was surprised. I went to see him [perform], somewhere downtown, and was taken aback. He had such a different style. I never saw him again, except once in concert in London. I didn't go backstage. He'd moved on. What would I say, "Bonjour"? But what I thought was wonderful was that he never betrayed the poetry for the song. The songs remain poems.

That winter, Derek May asked Cohen to help with a short experimental film he was making for the NFB, *Angel*. Cohen wrote the music, played by the Stormy Clovers. The film's narrative, insofar as there is one, is a vignette about seduction. A male character, played by May, attempts to persuade a woman, an angel with wings, to stay in his life. Cohen also provided the voice-over reading of the man's dialogue. The woman was played by actress Patricia Nolin, May's girlfriend.

DAVID FOUGERE: "I know the stars are wild as dust and wait for no man's discipline, but as they wheel from sky to sky they rake our lives with pins of light." This was the lyric that went with the music. The mouth harp was played by Leonard's friend Henry Zemel. Derek had a budget for audio recording, a certain number of hours. The Clovers had a tense and quarrelsome day. After eighteen or twenty attempts, there was no usable track and all the studio time was used up. Robert Hershorn came to the rescue. He had a good-quality reel-to-reel recorder. That's where some of the soundtrack was recorded— in Hershorn's living room.

Cohen was there that day as well.

DAVID FOUGERE: I remember climbing stairs to Robert's front door. I said to Leonard, "Are you sure this is all right? We're not imposing?" He said, "You're really hung up on that one, aren't you?"

Meanwhile, Cohen's relationship with Ihlen had hit yet another bumpy patch. She was planning to go to London, and did. As 1965 drew to a close, he wrote to her, again declaring his aversion to "a contract," and again suspecting infidelity. "I hope you're not keeping anything from me," he wrote. "Are you being straight with me? . . . Is there any fire left?"

CHAPTER NINE

I Must Be a Singer

I once said to him, when I thought I'd given up music, "It's just pop music. How serious can you take it?" And he said, "To me, it was always a matter of life and death." And he was dead fucking serious. I thought, "Holy shit. That's why you're Leonard Cohen and I'm not."

—Brandon Ayre

I see Leonard as the white mouse they put down into a submarine to see if the air is foul. He is the white mouse of civilization who tests its foulness.

—Irving Layton

In January 1966, Cohen's friend, the poet and judicial scholar Frank Scott and his wife Marian, hosted a party at their Westmount home at 451 Clarke Avenue, to celebrate the new year. Guests included members of the Montreal poetry elite—A. J. M. Smith, Irving Layton, Louis Dudek, Al Purdy, Ralph Gustafson, and thirty-one-year-old Leonard Cohen. By then, Cohen had published three books of poetry and a novel; another poetry volume and his second novel were due out that year. On paper, his career was flourishing. Yet Cohen was deeply dissatisfied. Although his work was selling reasonably well, he was struggling to earn a living. Other writers survived by taking teaching jobs, which typically provided a stable base income and health care benefits.

MICHAEL HARRIS: Layton was teaching. I was teaching. When others came along, David Solway, Peter van Toorn, they taught. In fact, everybody ended up teaching. But Leonard sang. He had an advantage—the family money that enabled him to go to Greece.

Unable to envisage himself in the cloistered world of academe, Cohen, more and more, was turning his attention to music and the question it implicitly posed—could he successfully transform himself from poet-novelist to troubadour?

HENRY ZEMEL: He wanted to earn enough money commensurate with his status. His status at that time was bohemian—he wanted money to be a bohemian. Travel was just part of the status—that's what was underlying it. Once, he drove to the airport and, instead of parking far away in the cheaper lot, we parked close and paid more. I said, "Leonard?" And he said, "Well, you know . . ." That was about status. That was where he was at.

As the story goes, Cohen—that January day—introduced his friends to the music of Bob Dylan and allegedly announced that he would become the Canadian equivalent. The others had barely heard of Dylan, so Scott left the party, returned with two newly purchased Dylan albums—*Bringing It All Back Home* and *Highway 61 Revisited*—and played them for the group. Later, Cohen denied making the boast.

LEONARD COHEN: I'd never say that, any more than I'd say I want to be the next William Yeats. I had a record of Bob Dylan, and I brought it to this party . . . I said, "Fellas, listen to this. This guy's a real poet." It was greeted with yawns. I said, "No, I insist, let me play it again." They said, "Do you want to be that?" That's how it arose. But it's not my syntax. Anyway, they didn't like it. But I put it on a few more times, and by the end of the evening, they were dancing.

SANDRA DJWA: That was untruthful, because that story came to me through three different sources, Louis Dudek, Frank Scott, and I think Marion Scott. So I'm quite sure he said it.

AVIVA LAYTON: Frank Scott didn't go out on New Year's Day to buy records. The shops weren't even open. Leonard brought the Dylan record. It was an evening. And he definitely did not say at Scott's party that he'd be the next Dylan. He may have said it elsewhere. But he often said to me and others that he wasn't interested in academia. He was interested in the marketplace.

MORRIS FISH: I distinctly remember Frank telling me that Leonard had told him that one of the most important poets in America was Bob Dylan. Then Scott got interested in that. The relationship between Leonard and Frank Scott was interesting. Partly, it was Frank being a mentor to Leonard, and partly the other way around.

His poetry friends may not have realized it then, but other friends knew of Cohen's musical ambitions.

PATRICIA NOLIN: I was a huge fan of Dylan, listening to him a million times a day. And Leonard started this shtick—"I can't make enough money as a writer." I even told him—"But, Leonard, Dylan is already there." He didn't like that. I thought he'd fail. I couldn't imagine anybody writing those songs better than Dylan, but he ended up doing it just as well and sometimes better.

One day, when Cohen's distant cousin Sylvia Spring came to visit, he told her he was thinking of focusing more on songwriting and singing.

SYLVIA SPRING: He sang "Suzanne" for me—just the two of us in his apartment. He said, "What do you think?" I said, "Well, Leonard, you're a wonderful poet, but I think you should forget about singing. You don't have a great voice." He said, "Thank you very much." But I was in awe of Leonard. He always spoke in riddles, metaphors, parables. He was very enigmatic. He was very moody, I knew that. He didn't call it depression. He said he had down times when he needed to be alone.

CHERYL KENMEY: I told him he'd never make it. A chuckle is what I got.

SEYMOUR MAYNE: I didn't see music as a distraction. I saw it as a way for him to redirect the underground stream of his creativity. Some of his lyrics are of the same strength and power [as] his earlier poetry.

HENRY ZEMEL: That's what he came back from Hydra to do—to take his poetry into music. That's what he told me: "I came back to go into music." I said okay. He didn't have any feel for it, he thought he had a terrible voice, but he was going to do this. This was going to be his career.

ALFIE WADE: Leonard came with his guitar to Robert's [Hershorn] pad and proposed what he wanted to do. I'd just come back from New York after working with Gerry Goffin, Carole King, Bobby Darin, Paul Anka. I said, "You need a little bit of that and this." We pitched Leonard ideas.

BERNIE ROTHMAN: I wasn't surprised. He was not an inordinately talented musician, but he loved doing what he did. Whenever there was more than two or three people, he'd get out his guitar and serenade us, anywhere. He sang one of my songs in a prison once—"The Closed-in Blues."

Cohen's insistence that economic necessity had dictated the transition wasn't the whole story.

BARRIE WEXLER: It wasn't just that poems and novels hardly paid. Leonard never thought he'd be spoken of in the same breath as T. S. Eliot, Ezra Pound, and e. e. cummings—or even first-rate poets like Sylvia Plath, Langston Hughes, and Allen Ginsberg. He used to say, "Many are called, few are chosen." He knew he was good, but didn't think he was great. That, in part, is why he applied his talent to song. There, a minor poet—no small thing in itself—could become a major lyricist.

Initially, Cohen approached Albert Grossman, then managing Bob Dylan, Janis Joplin, and Peter, Paul and Mary. Grossman rejected him, as did other managers he approached.

BUFFY SAINTE-MARIE: A lot of people just didn't get it with Leonard. Joni Mitchell too. People were looking for good music, but some of the entrepreneurs were not letting it through. It was "my artist" or "my stable" or "my money." Leonard and Joni were not naturals for that scene. But he had no [pretense] he was going to be a singer. His description was, "I have a very human voice." He didn't need anything more than the exact voice that he had.

A year earlier, Robert Hershorn had introduced Cohen to Grossman's executive assistant, Mary Martin—the woman who had introduced Dylan to Levon Helm and the Hawks, later known as The Band.

MARY MARTIN: [I'd] worked with Dylan and seen how he really did change a whole generation. Leonard's stuff was not as earth-shattering, but it was a comfort to those who really felt the need for romance.

Martin, who soon struck out on her own as a manager, started to help Cohen even before leaving Grossman's employ. Together, they hatched plans to set up a company, Stranger Music, to publish his songs. That same January, she introduced him to Judy Collins.

JUDY COLLINS: I knew Mary from Greenwich Village. She had talked about Leonard and said, "He's so brilliant, but he's going nowhere because nobody can understand his poems." Then she called me and said, "You'll never guess who wants to play you his songs." They both knew that I didn't write my own songs and had recorded many songs of my contemporaries.

Collins had already recorded four studio albums, using the work of Dylan, Eric Andersen, Phil Ochs, and Gordon Lightfoot.

JUDY COLLINS: At that point, he would not sing them himself. Leonard, myself, my boyfriend Michael Thomas, and my friend Linda Liebman went out to dinner at Tony's, a lovely Italian joint on Seventy-Ninth Street. I said to him, "What about these famous songs you write?" The next day he came over—there was just Michael and me there—and said, "I can't sing or play guitar and I don't know if this is a song." But he sang three songs, "Suzanne," "Dress Rehearsal Rag," and "The Stranger Song." I fell off my chair at all three, but it was "Suzanne" and "Dress Rehearsal" that I recorded soon after.

In fact, Collins, then finishing her fifth studio album, *In My Life*, was looking for additional material.

JUDY COLLINS: I thought we were done and Jac [Holzman, cofounder of Elektra Records] said to me, "We're not done. We still need something." After I heard Leonard, I called Jack and said, "We found our something." Jack fell off his chair too. Leonard's songs landed on that album at a particularly fortuitous time. Record company executives were beginning to get the idea of how, where, and when to sell records.

Collins said later that what impressed her about "Suzanne" was that it was "so different and so evocative of something almost ethereal," yet grounded—"present and mystical at the same time. 'Suzanne' was one of the greatest songs I ever heard. All my songs seemed naive by comparison." The following year, on her *Wildflowers* album, she recorded three more Cohen tunes: "Priests," "Sisters of Mercy," and "Hey, That's No Way to Say Goodbye."

JUDY COLLINS: It's no understatement to say that [my endorsement kickstarted his career]. And he knew it and he always thanked me for it.

Marianne Ihlen, however, did not. Years later, Collins received a letter from Ihlen, which said, "You recorded all his songs and I just want to tell you that you ruined my life." Ihlen might also have blamed British singer Noel Harrison, who also covered "Suzanne" in 1966. His up-tempo version reached number 56 on Billboard's Top 100 and also seeded Cohen's reputation. Collins's arranger for both *In My Life* and *Wildflowers* was twenty-two-year-old Juilliard graduate Joshua Rifkin. *In My Life* was recorded in London in the summer of 1966.

JOSHUA RIFKIN: I arranged "Suzanne," but the arrangement was dropped. Judy and Bruce Langhorn, a wonderful guitarist, [did another version]. I was disappointed, but that's the biz. I did "Dress Rehearsal Rag" and other songs in London. Musically, for a hard modernist like me, it was minimal, which is not necessarily a criticism. More positively, the music was a vehicle for Leonard and the words. But looking back, I'd say he managed just to get the right thing. I was never a great fan—I couldn't go with the spiritual stuff—but anybody who created "Everybody Knows" is simply one of the immortals.

For *Wildflowers*, Rifkin arranged two other Cohen songs, "Sisters of Mercy" and "Hey, That's No Way to Say Goodbye," in Los Angeles.

JOSHUA RIFKIN: Leonard's version is super laid-back, almost catatonic. Judy was more up-tempo, and she had the vibrato voice. I used flugelhorns. I had this sense of colours that would blend and meld. The other song is very sparse, almost hymn-like, and I wanted to go with that, not against it.

On February 12, Cohen attended the Saturday-evening wedding of his friends, art history student Carol Moscovitch and Henry Zemel, a mathematician, physicist, and aspiring filmmaker, at Shaar Hashomayim Synagogue.

CAROL ZEMEL: Leonard sat in stony grumpiness throughout. He sat as if he was at a funeral of his best friend. Every time I looked at him, I saw this depressed man. Marianna wore a beautiful, floor-length, long-sleeved, buttoned-up, lavender-coloured sweater. She looked gorgeous. She always looked gorgeous. She had all of the beauty and immaculateness of a Scandinavian princess. In her home, everything was perfectly in order, perfectly clean.

HENRY ZEMEL: I was pretty far out, man. Pretty smashed.

Later, the Zemels hosted dinners for the entourage at their Westmount apartment, "a new bride, learning to cook."

CAROL ZEMEL: By the way, we had no chairs. We were so hip that we sat uncomfortably on the floor. Leonard didn't bring dates. Either Marianne would be there or he'd come alone.

By then, Cohen was bringing music to his poetry readings. On February 14, he and Irving Layton appeared at New York's 92nd Street YMHA. Cohen read several poems, part of the forthcoming *Beautiful Losers* novel, and sang "Suzanne" and "The Stranger Song."

AVIVA LAYTON: It was a fabulous evening. Frank Scott was there too.

Cohen's former valentine, Wendy Patten, was in the audience.

WENDY PATTEN KEYS: My mother came with me. Some of [the poetry] was erotic. My mother was quite startled. We went to the VIP reception. I would bump into him [later] in New York at parties—there was one for Fassbinder he came to—and it was quite exciting for me. I guess I was still holding on to something.

In New York, Cohen stayed at the Penn Terminal, on Fourteenth Street, a seedy hotel where he had written "Hey, That's No Way to Say Goodbye." That same winter, Cohen got a phone call from his cousin, journalist Sylvia Spring—her aunt was married to Bernard Cohen (a cousin of Leonard's late father) who had written two right-wing tracts, "A Case for Conservatism" and "Law Without Order." Spring had been commissioned by the CBC to interview Layton.

SYLVIA SPRING: We bonded on that. We both didn't like this right-wing jerk. But Bernard didn't care for Leonard either. He thought he was a phony poet, who did all of this to get girls. I said, "I hear Irving's a womanizer." Leonard said, "He's an old man. He's harmless." I go to the interview and I'm sitting on Irving's bed, because he tells me the only plug that will work for my tape recorder is in the bedroom. And he's trying to touch me. I got up and started circling the bed and he starts circling after me. At one point, I was running around the bed. Eventually, I had to leave. I didn't get the interview. I phoned Leonard and said, "You should have told me!" His reaction was "Oh, you should have given him a bit." Like my body was a charity.

AVIVA LAYTON: I think it was Mordecai Richler who said, "Irving screws everyone with a pulse and they don't even have to have a pulse." Leonard was more discriminating. But he did once chase [poet and novelist] Gwendolyn MacEwan around our dining room table, without recognizing that she was terrified of him. She went absolutely white. We were all screaming with laughter, which was really cruel, and then we saw that she was seriously disturbed.

It was a rare instance of Cohen failing to read the mood of the woman he was pursuing. On February 20, he and Layton attended a Bob Dylan and the Hawks concert at Montreal's Place des Arts—an event that can only have crystallized his musical ambitions. Cohen himself would later say it wasn't so much Dylan's originality that first impressed him, but "his familiarity . . . Dylan was what I'd always meant by the poet—someone about whom the word was never used."

JORGE CALDERÓN: On the 1993 tour, he told me, "When I first saw Bob Dylan, I said to myself, 'I want to do this. This guy is doing it. This is what I want to do. I can do that too.'"

One of Mary Martin's first clients—her star account at the time—was a Canadian folk group, the Stormy Clovers, a quintet fronted by Susan Jains (née Susan Jane Gemmell). A graduate of the University of Toronto, Jains soon started covering Cohen's songs.

MARY MARTIN: Susan was an amazing, dynamic, and determined woman. She really had a vision. She was musically sound and had an inquiring mind, almost intellectual. It would be natural that she'd be drawn to Leonard. The role the Stormy Clovers played with Leonard's songs probably happened by Susan's dogged persistence. It was Susan marching to her specific drumbeat and her need to identify with something that was romantic, like Cohen's words. Susan probably understood that vision was more important, almost, than anything else.

PETER HODGSON: Susan and the Clovers were the people really putting his songs out there. Susan admired his songwriting. They turned people on to his music. He would be quite indebted to them for doing it.

CHRIS NUTTER: I loved Susan. Everybody loved Susan. She was wonderful. They used to call her Poppy. She'd spent much of her childhood in an iron lung, with polio, but at sixteen she was hosting a CBC-TV show. I never met anybody as good at entertaining an audience.

HENRY ZEMEL: The Stormy Clovers and Leonard used to come over to my place and play. I fixed up this music room—it had a real great sound. I played with Leonard many times there, the two of us alone. I played drums, flute, Jew's harp. I had some strange instruments lying around. Arthur Lipsett made instruments and I had ordered some from China.

DAVID FOUGERE: I was playing bass for the Stormies. It made sense to put a songwriter together with a band that liked his music. We came up with our own way of doing the song, but never changed a word or a chord. I remember the first time we met—on a sidewalk in Montreal. He was with Marianne—they were just radiant together. I was just an unwashed kid from Galt, twenty-two years old. I had no idea there were such people in the world. Leonard had a compelling presence. He was a role model. He was always immaculately dressed. His songs were powerful and beautiful. It took a lot of courage for him to make the leap from living room to concert hall. Invariably, he would win the audience over. They could let go of some of their sorrow and grief because he showed the way.

IRWIN BLOCK: I first heard "Suzanne" when the Stormy Clovers performed in 1966 at the Venus de Milo room, above Dunn's Delicatessen, and was struck by its poetic beauty and imagery. Susan Jains sparkled and almost seemed to make Suzanne appear onstage.

CHRIS NUTTER: I was walking along Sainte-Catherine Street and heard this music. I ran in and saw a friend—Mark Ranger [a roadie for the Clovers]. They asked me if I played an instrument and I said "oboe," so I was recruited.

PETER HODGSON/SNEEZY WATERS: They played at Le Hibou in Ottawa and at the Venus de Milo—the VD room, we called it—near the train station. The railway workers came in after their shift and they loved Susan. One night, she was singing and a guy in the back was singing along with her and the crowd told him to shut the fuck up. That guy was Leonard.

MARK RANGER: He'd come to hear her sing. This is a bar where people were drinking, right? But when she sang, you could hear a pin drop. Was there a relationship with Leonard? There was a relationship between Susan and many people, but I could not verify that [one].

DAVID FOUGERE: Leonard and Susan were just friends, as far I know. If there was anything romantic, I wasn't aware. Both were in other relationships at the time. Then again, if there was something, would they say, "Let's tell the young bass player?" All kinds of guys had a crush on Susan. And with good reason. She had intelligence, a great sense of humour, a lot of vitality, and, usually, a short dress—an exuberant personality, very sociable. She'd step up to the microphone, smile mischievously, and burp. She read Doris Lessing. She was liberated before liberation was invented.

PETER HODGSON: I could imagine Leonard was obsessed with her. She was very attractive, physically and spiritually. She had a spell, an aura. [Hodgson and Jains would later marry, though the marriage lasted only a few years.] I never asked her if she and Leonard were an item. But I couldn't imagine who was more spellbound about the other. She loved to hear him sing.

CHRIS NUTTER: I imagine there probably was [a relationship]. It was wonderful to behold them [in conversation]. He was very witty. [Guitarist] Ray Perdue and Susan were on and off, arguing with each other about drugs. There were too many drugs. One night, we had to carry Ray offstage and take him to the hospital. We used to go—the Stormies—to visit Robert Hershorn. Visit, have drugs. Susan was the kind of person Robert would have loved. Extremely smart and very entertaining, very funny. That's where my first acid trips came from. Leonard was often there and he came down to the VD quite a lot.

Indeed, even then, Jains had developed a serious drug habit.

MARK RANGER: Susan carried a purse, but she had another bag, quite big, full of pills. She took a pill to wake up, a pill to eat, a pill to go to sleep, a pill before a concert. She later became totally paranoid. Leonard had a big party at his place. The band was invited. And there was LSD, like Kool-Aid, going around. Ray and Susan were okay, but David Fougere [D. D. Fraser] and Pat Patterson, the drummer, had a bummer of a trip. And Leonard was devastated that these two guys were not having a good time. He was really sorry about that and expressed himself to them. [Much later], when Susan was in bad shape, Leonard was always very supportive.

DAVID FOUGERE: There *was* a big party at Leonard's, but not with LSD. However, on a separate occasion, in the same apartment at 3657 Aylmer Street, Pat and I took a trip, with Leonard and Marianne as guardians. Having read Huxley's *The Doors of Perception*, I persuaded Leonard to let me try LSD. Pat was curious and came along for the ride. It was Pat who had a bad trip. Some people shouldn't mess with that stuff. I went to paradise and laughed for many hours. I was not aware until afterwards that Pat had fallen into fear and had to be rescued by Leonard. But Leonard and Marianne were sober, responsible, and kind throughout this experience.

Trying to land the Stormies a recording contract, Martin brought them to New York. According to Mark Ranger, the deal was conditional on jettisoning Fougere and Patterson.

MARK RANGER: And Susan said, "No, it's all or none."

MARY MARTIN: The sad thing was that we couldn't get the world to understand the talents of the Stormy Clovers. I don't know why, I really don't.

Later, there was speculation that Jains might have resented the fact that Cohen had allowed Collins to record the song they had first sung and popularized.

CAROL ZEMEL: Susan, I think, had bitter feelings about Leonard. I don't know the details.

PETER HODGSON: I never heard her diss Leonard or say, "Oh fuck, I should have been there, instead of Judy Collins."

DAVID FOUGERE: The Judy Collins version was far more beautiful than ours.

With the status of the Stormy Clovers album in doubt, Cohen offered the recording rights to "Suzanne" to Penny Lang, another young folk artist. It was already part of her repertoire. MCA Records proposed setting Lang's version against an electric, full-band arrangement. Lang, an acoustic purist, refused.

PENNY LANG: Maybe it was foolish, in hindsight. But I don't think I could have handled the kind of success it would have brought me. I probably would not have lived. They called it manic depression then. I'd go from being very high to crashing into severe depression.

GEORGE FERENCZI: Later, while he was staying at the Chelsea, Leonard wanted Penny to teach him to play guitar better, but she wasn't interested.

PENNY LANG: When Leonard called he said, "I'm Leonard Cohen. I was told you'd teach me guitar." I said, "Not today. I'm very depressed," and hung up on him. It was the last time we spoke. I didn't know who he was, and I wasn't a guitar teacher.

Lang subsequently spent months in a psychiatric ward at Montreal's Royal Victoria Hospital, and eventually recovered. She died about three months before Cohen in 2016. The Stormy Clovers disbanded in 1968. Susan Jains died June 19, 2010. According to an obituary notice, she had fallen victim in midlife "to the torment and confusion of mental illness," and thereafter had lived "a vagabond existence."

On March 29, 1966, McClelland & Stewart publisher Jack McClelland hosted a party at Toronto's Inn on the Park to honour the publication of *Beautiful Losers*. The guest list was a veritable who's who of Canadian culture—Pierre Berton, Austin Clarke, Adrienne Clarkson, Robertson Davies, Timothy Findley, Northrop Frye, Robert Fulford, George Grant, Peter Gzowski, Marshall McLuhan, and members of the Stormy Clovers. The book went on sale soon after, at a then-steep price of $6.50—needed, the publisher maintained, to offset costs of promotion. McClelland's fears that its sexually explicit content would offend retailers proved prophetic. Both Simpson's, a department store, and W. H. Smith, a bookseller, declined to carry it.

Critical response ranged from celebration to denunciation. Desmond Pacey called it "the most intricate, erudite, and fascinating Canadian novel ever written." A *Boston Sunday Herald* reviewer wrote that the novel was "explosive, a fountain of talent . . . James Joyce is not dead . . . He lives in Montreal under the name of Cohen . . . writing from the point of view of Henry Miller." *Toronto Star* critic Robert Fulford described it as "a book of ravings, some sacred, some profane . . . the most revolting book ever written in Canada, [but] at the same time it is probably the most interesting Canadian book of the year." The distinguished critic Leslie Fiedler said *Beautiful Losers* was either one of the best or worst novels he'd ever read—he wasn't sure which. And critic and poet Dennis Lee described it as "funny, dirty, lyrical, trendy, self-indulgent, often incomprehensible." Cohen himself described the book on its jacket flap as "a love story, a Black Mass, a satire, a prayer, a tasteless affront, an hallucination, a bore, an irrelevant display of diseased virtuosity . . . in short, a disagreeable religious epic of incomparable beauty." To help market it, he approached his friend Hersh Segal.

HERSH SEGAL: My Le Château [clothing store] on Sainte-Catherine had a wooden arched front. He got book covers and we stapled [them] around the door. He went up on the ladder. He was doing it. It didn't help too much.

BARRIE WEXLER: I remember admiring the window display—hardcover books, about a dozen, with open copies on top of the mounds. Covers were also tacked to the wall with pins from the shop's tailor. I brazenly announced to Mr. Segal, as I called him, that I was working on a novel myself, and one day there'd be a stack of my own books in his window. In Montreal, there was no higher pedestal.

In a 1967 essay cowritten with poet Al Purdy, Sandra Djwa suggested that Cohen's novel offered a "case study of the young hero and his *saison en enfer*. The division of the romantic *femme fatale* into her opposite but complementary aspects of innocent and destroyer (Catherine and Edith) are familiar features of Decadent literature, as is the presentation of the satanic, often homosexual, friend and alter-ego."

SANDRA DJWA: Maybe these two female figures are really part of the Jewish conception of women, the mother on the one hand and the madwoman as the antithesis. [Leonard] may have had some scores to settle with his mother. But the vision of the woman figure runs through his work and in this mythic structure there's always a male friend, not necessarily a homosexual. Is there such a thing as a typical Jewish intellectual—highly introspective, highly critical, and highly intelligent? It's the play of the mind I find so interesting in Cohen, so attractive. And he's a little sardonic.

BARRIE WEXLER: Similarly, the Breavman/Krantz relationship in *The Favourite Game*, and F's with the unnamed folklorist in *Beautiful Losers*, stand on the shoulders of the bond between David and Jonathan in the book of Samuel.

Cohen later inscribed a copy of the novel to Djwa—"For Sandra, who explains me better."

CHANTAL RINGUET: Today, I don't believe it would be published. It's a totally different Montreal and a totally different configuration of Canada. This was the time of the two solitudes. It's a bit dated today. It's really an experimental novel. It took two generations to accept that it was an important novel.

The term "cultural appropriation" was not in currency in 1966, but there is evidence that Cohen felt a backlash from his aboriginal friends, including Alanis Obomsawin.

VIVIENNE LEEBOSH: Alanis would have been offended. She was offended all the time—not that I blame her. But sparks would fly.

DENNIS LEE: A non-indigenous who wrote Catherine as Leonard did would get torched today.

SANDRA DJWA: There would have been some blowback about it. He was being a little cautious. I notice his Catherine Tekakwitha has a *C* rather than a *K*, for Kateri, and his Charles Atlas became Charles Axis—so maybe he was making a kind of a bow—"hey, I'm not using the same names."

BARRIE WEXLER: Politically incorrect? That's irrelevant. The book will be read long after most gender-free, nonsexist contemporary novels have been forgotten.

LINDA GABORIAU: [Today] *Beautiful Losers* never would have come to be. It couldn't have gone where it went to in our collective consciousness.

PATRICIA GODBOUT: To me, it's not appropriation at all. He's putting that figure even more on the pedestal, eroticizing her.

Cohen owned up to his offence some three decades later, when attempts were made to turn the novel into a feature film.

JACOB POTASHNIK: He told me, "When the book came out, I got slaughtered by the native community. Alanis—Alanis Obomsawin." I said, "But isn't she a friend of yours?" "Yes, but there was a lot of criticism."

TONY BABINSKI: I don't think it's about cultural appropriation. The depiction of aboriginal communities in the book is not ennobling. His depiction of women is terrible. It's a misogynistic, kind of creepy book.

CAROL TALBOT-SMITH: It didn't bother me at that point, even though I'm half-indigenous. I didn't know enough about my aboriginal history. Today, I would take umbrage.

BUFFY SAINTE-MARIE: There was so little written about indigenous people in those days. People didn't know who Kateri was. Indigenous people didn't know who she was. Catholics didn't know who she was. So Leonard shone a light on her for a huge audience.

BILL POWNALL: That "God is alive, Magic is afoot" section is pure poetry. The whole book is worth it for that, though it is a bit of a mess. It reads like it was written on speed, which it was.

HENRY ZEMEL: *Beautiful Losers*—whatever that's about. It's like nonsense. We didn't talk about it much. He himself would have said it's unreadable. I felt that at the time, but did not say it.

TONY BABINSKI: *Beautiful Losers* is really a hysterical cry for some kind of grace. However, it's an anomalous work. It's an exclamation point rejection of our more conservative literary tradition. Also, it captured the anguish of Quebec's Quiet Revolution, when so many structures, including the Church, were being challenged. It's totally of a piece with the deconstructionist approach of the Automatistes, a group of Quebecois painters and poets who had proclaimed an anarchic, revolutionary ethos. There are passages that read like they were plucked right out of the Automatiste manifesto.

Years later, in conversation, Babinski mentioned this theory, "and Leonard started visibly."

TONY BABINSKI: I had touched something in him. He said I was the first person to spot it. He and Morton Rosengarten practically lived in the cafés with these people. They would adopt the opposite position, just for the hell of it. He said they were "life-and-death struggles." Once, one of them approached Cohen and said, "Elvis Presley is a better poet than you because he said 'Love Me Tender' and you would have said 'Love Me Tenderly.'"

BARRIE WEXLER: Cohen didn't adopt the opposite position for the hell of it. He had great respect for language and resisted its corruption. The amazing thing is that by using correct grammar and phrasing, he managed to achieve the same immediacy and accessibility as the radical Automatistes.

*   *   *

Cohen's transition from poet-novelist to troubadour continued through the spring and summer of 1966. On May 8, he appeared on CBC Television's *This Hour Has Seven Days*. The sexual chemistry between Cohen and his interviewer, Beryl Fox, is almost palpable, but it never led to consummation. Fox asked Cohen if he had ever considered changing his name. "Yes," he replied, clearly putting her on. "I've thought of changing it to September." "Leonard September?" she asked. "No. September Cohen."

CAROL ZEMEL: I remember we joked about that name more than once. We all thought it was absurd.

HENRY ZEMEL: He was calling himself September Cohen before that. It was like a joke—shtick. Hey, man. It's a good idea. September Cohen.

Cohen wasn't being entirely facetious about the name. Two decades later, he wrote two letters to an imaginary, yet-to-be-conceived child of a woman he was seeing, proposing to call it September Cohen.

In late May, Cohen was back in Toronto to appear on *Take Thirty*, a CBC afternoon show. Wearing a dark grey, double-breasted suit and a black turtleneck, he was interviewed by host Adrienne Clarkson—the start of a fifty-year friendship. He read a poem and sang—both solo and with the Stormy Clovers.

ADRIENNE CLARKSON: Leonard was the best-dressed man I've ever seen. He was so well brought up. His posture was perfect. That calm, fine head. It would be a cliché to say he is the magus, the priest. I always believed that he is the prophet for our time. He didn't announce the sixties. He *was* the sixties. How would I characterize that? By using the word "loose." A flexibility, a suppleness. A subtlety with curves and softness, an inner strength. In all the years I knew him, Leonard remained as constant as the rising and waning moon.

During that Toronto visit, Cohen's friend Phyllis Webb arranged for him to recite seven poems for a radio broadcast promoting the work of Canadian poets, and featured him in a profile on *Ideas*. But general skepticism continued to greet Cohen's plans to turn to music, professionally.

ERICA POMERANCE: I remember jamming with him one afternoon at the home of Patricia Nolin's mother, in Old Montreal. I never was too impressed with his singing voice. I thought his future was really as a writer, because he'd come out with *Beautiful Losers*.

VERA FRENKEL: Leonard's transition seemed a natural progression. I wasn't a great fan. But if it pleased him to do that, it seemed fine. I didn't have any allegiance to poetry on the page. Poetry at its best is an oral tradition.

Cohen's friends in the poetry circle monitored his development.

DAVID SOLWAY: Leonard became less of a poet and more of a songwriter/singer, a different world. I remember Irving [Layton] saying, "Leonard is no longer in the poetry game." I think Leonard had Irving's blessing for whatever he wanted to do. But as a result, Irving said, the mantle [First Jewish Poet of Montreal] should pass to me, the fourth in the series, after Klein, Layton, and Cohen, although it should have been passed to Seymour Mayne or maybe Henry Moscovitch. That discussion was part of the Jewish Montreal poet's syndrome.

BARRIE WEXLER: Irving characterized Cohen as a twentieth-century troubadour who had swapped the lute for a guitar because it had nine less strings.

When asked about it in 1983, Cohen said, "mantle suggests the leadership of a generation."

LEONARD COHEN: Perhaps A. M. Klein wore it for a while, if there is such a mantle. Irving Layton could put it on and wear it forever. I doubt if he would want to. It's hard to say who has it. It's really in shreds. I mean everybody has a piece of the true cross today, and probably that's the way it should be. There is a mantle in the sense that there is a living tradition. But this living tradition is not specifically Jewish. It has a Jewish element. It's appropriate that the Jewish writers approach it through the Jewish gate. The gifted ones among us keep the torches lit.

Cohen spent many evenings with his friend Henry Zemel, who had taken a job at the National Film Board.

HENRY ZEMEL: Leonard and I were into walking and talking, long walks on Sainte-Catherine East, and then back, four-, five-hour walks, till three or four a.m. We talked about politics, women. Leonard was very interested in Judaism, religion, and the Bible, but in a very real way, not a phony way. It was always interesting, the way he amalgamated aspects of Christianity and Islam into his way of seeing things. In our apartment in Westmount, I made drugs. He'd come and play music.

CAROL ZEMEL: The Film Board fired him after maybe three months.

HENRY ZEMEL: I was a total goofball. I didn't fit in. I alienated everyone for no reason. I was high, man. I didn't understand that you're not supposed to say anything.

VERA FRENKEL: Carol suffered, because Henry was attached to Leonard. Carol resented Leonard. And whatever affection Leonard had for drugs, he shared with Henry. For Leonard, Henry was a follower. He forgave Leonard everything. If Leonard had doubts of any kind, Henry would massage him.

ISRAEL CHARNEY: I never really could understand that relationship. Henry was almost like a groupie—and Leonard must have needed a foil. Henry was brilliant in his own right.

CAROL ZEMEL: What did Leonard get? A very smart Jewish guy. Argumentative in a good way. A really slavish admirer. Who else was

Leonard close to then? Derek and Morton, who was living in the country, and Hershorn. And a few women from his childhood—Nancy Bacal and Yafa Lerner.

HENRY ZEMEL: Carol didn't like him. Did we argue about him? We spoke about him. He came up in the conversations—how's that?

CAROL ZEMEL: Most of the time, Leonard was never anything but simply cordial. But he was a competitor for the attention of my husband. He seduced my husband away from me. That says as much about my husband as it says about Leonard.

On one occasion, however, Cohen, in her judgement, misbehaved.

CAROL ZEMEL: Leonard had rented an apartment on Aylmer. One day, we went over there, Henry and I. Marianne was not there. Suddenly Henry says, "I have to go somewhere." I don't know where. Maybe to get drugs. He left me there with Leonard. And Leonard could not talk to me—could not have a conversation. And this is really humiliating for me. At one point—I don't know if he'd been drinking or smoking dope, because everybody did all the time—but he sat on the floor and I sat on the couch, and he took a blanket that you cover a couch with, and put it over his head. And that's how he sat, in silence. Was he depressed? Who gives a fuck? He sat there and hid from me, under a blanket, for twenty minutes, a half hour. I was beside myself. I didn't know what to do. I should have just left, but I didn't. Who is this man to behave this way? This was a judgement on me. He was unable to have a conversation with me.

BARRIE WEXLER: For some reason, Leonard never threw a blanket over his head with me, literally or figuratively. Why? I guess it was what he thought I needed. He certainly wasn't doing it for himself.

Ihlen was not present because, to gain perspective on their relationship, she'd gone to Mexico, to Tepoztlán.

MARIANNE IHLEN: To alleviate everything, I left to visit my old friend [John Starr Cooke, an American mystic]. I took little Axel with me. It was a very strong experience, among the Indians. I had a feeling I was very close to God. I was almost convinced I would never come down that mountain. So that was my sojourn from Montreal, when the world was in danger of falling apart.

BARRIE WEXLER: She said she took the trip hoping that the time apart would create a space for them to reconnect when she got back, which briefly it did.

In Mexico, Ihlen took LSD for the first time, thinking it might offer "some way out of the dead end in which I found myself." The experience was traumatic. "Ceilings and walls were no longer where they had been; the floor vanished. Characters from fairy tales appeared." Aspects of her trip were so terrifying that she thought she would die. On a second trip, she saw her face disintegrate in a mirror . . . Later, she acknowledged that the simple solutions she'd hoped for did not exist. She never used acid again. Among other souvenirs, Ihlen returned with a woven Mexican blanket.

MARIANNE IHLEN: Leonard and I sat under that blanket awhile. Then we actually began sitting still, both of us, and letting everything settle down. We had had so many retreats, and we tried and we tried. Neither of us really felt like giving up completely.

One evening, the couple hosted a party at their apartment.

IRWIN BLOCK: It was a hootenanny. About twenty people, including his sister, Esther, most sitting on the floor. In spite of my expectations of a wild and crazy party, it was a slow, tame evening of song and quiet talk.

DONALD WINKLER: Gary Eisenkraft, who ran the New Penelope club, was invited over to hear a sampling of songs and give feedback. When Gary came back, I asked him how it had gone. He paused, and said: "Well, I tell you . . . I wouldn't book him." And I guess he never did.

DAVID FOUGERE: That's the first time I heard "Suzanne." The small living room was crowded—the only place I could find was under a table. Leonard sang the song and we were spellbound. It was mesmerizing, astonishing. I'd never heard a song like it before. When it came to an end, the room was utterly silent. I wish I'd remained respectfully silent, but I said: "Play that again! I came out from under the table to hear that song!" Or some dumbass remark like that. At least it helped us to get over being poleaxed and gobsmacked by its incredible beauty. Marianne gave a gift to Pat [Patterson, the drummer] and to me—a little Mexican charm on a turquoise string to wear around the neck "for good luck and protection."

Among the women Cohen saw while Ihlen was in Mexico was novelist Diane Giguère, also a member of the McClelland & Stewart writing stable.

DIANE GIGUÈRE: I guess we met through Jack McClelland. He was still with Marianne. He was smoking marijuana. He told me he sent his poems to Jack on wrapping paper, written by hand. He never discussed becoming a singer. He was quite devastated by the criticisms of *Beautiful Losers*. He was on drugs. It was practically a religion for him, and I don't like drugs. I was drinking, but I stopped not long afterward. He went on with his life and I went on with mine. We saw each other through the years—occasional, not serious. I liked him a lot. He was like a brother. I loved his sense of humour. He had a great, dry sense of humour when he was young. He wasn't infatuated with himself at all. He was rather poor, though his mother had a house in Westmount. He had a little apartment and was living with little means. I found him very brave. He invited me to Greece, but I never went, because there was no electricity.

One summer weekend, Cohen drove to the Eastern Townships to see his friend Morton Rosengarten and his twenty-one-year-old girlfriend, Marcia Pacaud.

MARCIA PACAUD: Leonard was alone, not with Marianne. He'd written his first song and was singing it to us and discussing his plan to go into music. The atmosphere was very warm and relaxed. It was actually my first introduction to smoking a joint, which I believe Leonard gave me. I don't remember any particular impression he made, though I certainly liked him. It was a quiet, amiable country get-together of two dear friends, making music and laughter, good meals and camaraderie.

Although Pacaud only met Cohen a handful of times, he had an enormous impact on her life.

MARCIA PACAUD: Because of him and Morton, I spent a couple of weeks exploring Scientology, almost two years on Hydra, in Greece for ten, and then forty years in two ashrams in India.

From his earliest days as a camp counsellor, Cohen had evinced a remarkable ability to draw artistically inclined younger men into his orbit. Among that group was one he met that summer.

BARRIE WEXLER: We met in Murray Hill Park, the centre of gravity in the neighbourhood. Not long after he asked me why I started writing poems. I said because I figured it was a great way to get girls. Later, I noticed all the poem-less guys on the football team were scoring off the field. All I had was a pile of lousy poems. So I switched to Rimbaudian prose. Leonard said, "Why the hell did you do that? You figured it would be a great way to get boys?"

Cohen encouraged Charlie Sise as well, the young Montrealer he'd met on Hydra the previous year.

CHARLIE SISE: I took him a short story. He thought it was pretty good and sent it to *Parallel*, but nothing came of it. Then I showed him about thirty pages of a novel, and he was very impressed. He said, "You must have got that from William Burroughs." I hadn't read Burroughs. He said, "Well, Burroughs through me and *Beautiful Losers*." When I was leaving his apartment, he gave me twenty bucks because he thought I might need it.

Increasingly drawn into the vortex of popular music, Cohen was still hedging his bets. That summer, he began discussions with CBC Television about cohosting a nightly public affairs show.

ANDREW SIMON: I was a producer of a popular local current affairs show—*Seven on Six*. We had to replace our host, Peter Desbarats.

JULIANNA OVENS: They were actually looking for a second host or an alternate host. Peter was very busy with his love life and wanted free time. I worked on that show for three years, part of it for Andrew.

MADELEINE POULIN: I was seeing Andrew that summer, before going to Oxford, working as a news editor at the CBC. I saw Leonard again during that time.

ANDREW SIMON: Madeleine told me she'd gone out with Leonard before she went out with me. She told me he was a nice guy, but they didn't get along well enough to make it last—I don't know why.

In Simon's eyes, the ideal host was a bilingual, good-looking, articulate, personable Montrealer, with a sense of humour, an ability to write, and a background in broadcasting.

ANDREW SIMON: Leonard had no journalism background, but he had everything else, ideal in many ways. I met him two or three times for dinner at Café des Artists, on what was then Dorchester Boulevard, at the corner of Mackay. He was always well dressed—he wore ties— which wasn't characteristic of journalists of that era. By coincidence, I was between marriages and living [with Madeleine] immediately above the café. It had never crossed his mind to be a TV host, but he was fascinated by the idea.

The discussions weren't exactly a secret. In an interview with the *Toronto Star* published in late July, Cohen said, "I'd like to get close to the viewers, get them to participate, even send in home movies. And I'd like to help reestablish English Montreal as a community. English Montreal has felt very, very intimidated in recent years, and for good reason. These people feel they've been sort of wiped out." Simon was troubled by one recurring issue.

ANDREW SIMON: I worried whether his feet were in the real world. I had to explain that what we were doing was mainly topical, fast-paced journalism, interviews, panel discussions, documentaries, etc., focused on Montreal and the province. He absorbed all that and he was very much into LSD then, and not secretive about using it. He wanted to do an essay on what it was like to go on an LSD trip or other paranormal experiences. I'd say, "We're always open to new ideas, but really there has to be some news value." Separatism, political and labour corruption—this was our content. He definitely liked the idea of being on the air every day, and being even better known. Finally, we agreed in principle, agreed on a start date, and I got a contract drawn up—he would have been paid $12,000 to $15,000 a year—more than most CBC reporters. I said, "I'll call you in a couple days to sign and make a public announcement." So we were very close. We thought he'd lose interest in the supernatural stuff and focus on journalism, once he got into it. We did no trial run with him, no audition, as we usually did. We figured his name value would be enough—a judgement call.

JULIANNA OVENS: Oh no. Leonard was tested in studio and on the street. One day I got a call—Leonard wanted to meet. So we met on Sainte-Catherine in a coffee shop. He told me about the offer and wanted to know what Andrew Simon was like. I was honest—I said he had plus and minus points. But what I wanted to make clear to Leonard was that he would have a much more limited private life. People would be looking more closely at him. I said, "I think you could do it, but if you sign, it's a regular thing, no matter how you feel, you're in front of a camera, and the camera does not lie." We talked for three or four hours. He was concentrating and extremely sober. He was very bothered by what I told him. He said, "I don't think I can do this." He never once mentioned singing in that conversation. I do think I influenced him, by communicating how invasive to his sense of privacy, which was important to him, it would be. He said the screen tests had been fun. I said, "Yes, but you have to think about doing this five days a week."

BARRIE WEXLER: Except for the hours, Juliana's predictions came about anyway. Cohen grew to be recognized everywhere, his work endlessly scrutinized, his private life a topic of discussion. It was one of those forks in the road, and Leonard being Leonard, he took the path that had heart. In some ways, he embodied the insights of *The Teachings of Don Juan: A Yaqui Way of Knowledge*, which he and I discussed. There's an exchange between the author, Carlos Castaneda, and the Indian sorcerer. Castaneda, torn between becoming a full-time writer or an academic, says, "Don Juan, I don't know what to do." Don Juan responds, "All paths are the same, and all paths lead nowhere." . . . "So, how do I know which path to take?" . . . "Some have heart." . . . "And how do I know if I'm on a path that has heart?" To which Don Juan replies, "You *know*."

MADELEINE POULIN: It was suggested at the time that Leonard change his family name as host, to make it more neutral for Montreal's English-speaking audience. I don't remember if "neutral" was the word used. I think it was Andrew's idea. Leonard refused, of course. It all sounded weird even then.

ANDREW SIMON: I certainly did *not* ask him to change his name. I would never have done this.

JULIANNA OVENS: I never heard that, and I don't think it's possible, because by then he was already an established name, if not a star, yet.

Cohen appeared to tip his hand about the CBC offer in an interview with *Maclean's* that August, saying, "You have to stick to things you are uniquely good at. I don't know whether I'd be any good at interviewing people. I think I'm afraid of cameras."

ANDREW SIMON: Before the contract was finished, he called me one evening at eleven o'clock and said, "Andrew, I have to talk to you. I just went on a trip"—an LSD trip—"and I made a big decision."

"What is it?" "I want to be a songwriter, not a television journalist." "Are you sure? Songwriting is a very iffy existence." "I know, I know, but I have it in me. I have a need, and when I went on the trip, I realized that that's my calling. You're the first person I've told."

MADELEINE POULIN: He changed his mind towards the end of the summer. He told Andrew, "God did not mean for me to be a broadcaster." Leonard would take LSD every Saturday. He wanted Andrew and me to join him. But I didn't want to. Andrew didn't want to.

ANDREW SIMON: I have no recall of any invitation to go on an LSD trip.

MADELEINE POULIN: After that, I never saw him again. And LSD had something to do with it. It was as if he'd gone off in another direction and was lost, to me at least. It didn't surprise me that he became a singer. He'd sung for me. But I thought maybe he left something behind. To me, being a writer was above everything else. I felt he had abandoned something that perhaps was very precious for him. I appreciated his success, but had a feeling he wasn't very happy. I'm grateful that I knew him. He's a figure of our time and we shared moments. His music always touched me. He made me see things. I can relive his personality in my mind quite easily. His intelligence, yes, but great sensitivity.

Simon considered trying to talk Cohen out of it, but decided against it.

ANDREW SIMON: He had a strong personality. So I said, "Of course, if that's your real calling and you're convinced. But I'm really sorry. You would have made a fine host." A very short conversation, five or ten minutes. Perhaps being asked to be a TV journalist made him think about where he was going. It was a deeply felt decision. Very soon after, he moved to New York.

In the *Maclean's* interview, Cohen was candid about the effects of LSD and an advocate for its mind-blowing potential. "You get a fantastic single-mindedness when you are lying in one place hallucinating," he said. "For me, it ended a lot of things. I would like to say that it made me saintly." Comparing 1965 to the beginning of the Renaissance, he said, "A lot of people . . . feel the world has gone crazy, and they can't get their hands on what is happening. To get along, you have to become part of the chaos."

BARRIE WEXLER: In those days—his apocalyptic phase—he'd say to me, "We're at the dawn of a new religious age."

Maclean's also interviewed Ihlen, who bravely maintained that, while Cohen was absent six months of the year, "I don't feel alone wherever he is. I believe in him so much that it gives me tremendous strength. In the beginning I believed in marriage. Now I feel it is of no importance. I feel more married than I ever did before. It is very important for him to be alone." No doubt she wanted to believe that.

In November, after appearing on a new CBC public affairs show, *Sunday*, Cohen embarked on a tour of Canadian colleges. That same month—the month Judy Collins released her album with "Suzanne"—Cohen arrived in Edmonton. The trip marked a seminal moment in his transition from poet-novelist to singer-songwriter. Dianne Woodman, then McClelland & Stewart's Edmonton representative, handled the logistics.

DIANNE WOODMAN: Eli Mandel was teaching at the University of Alberta and was a good friend of Leonard's. Eli had a group of very talented grad students. They called themselves the Barbarians, after a poem by Gwendolyn MacEwen, "Breakfast for Barbarians." They were sitting around one night talking about Cohen and Mandel said, "Why don't we phone him?"

ANN MANDEL: Eli was teaching a graduate course in Victorian poetry. After class, we'd go out for beers or hang out in my apartment. We began to get the idea—let's phone somebody. Eli liked doing this, seeing if you could contact somebody. One evening, he said, "Let's try Leonard Cohen." It was probably 2 or 3 a.m. Eastern time, but he [eventually] reached Leonard and said, "Come to Edmonton to give a reading." After much urging, Leonard said, "Well, because you caught me in the middle of the night, when I'm serenading my lady and I'm in a good mood, I'll come."

DIANNE WOODMAN: I phoned Jack [McClelland] and asked him if M&S would pay and he said yes. So I booked him into the MacDonald Hotel. Normally, I'd have booked poetry readings, but when I talked to him, he said, "I don't want to read. I want to sing."

Woodman met him the day he arrived, in a blizzard.

DIANNE WOODMAN: He was wearing this green turtleneck sweater and a leather jacket—no coat. The first thing I did, I took him to the Army and Navy department store and bought him thermal underwear. He was very glad for that. [He was] nice, diffident almost. He wasn't an aggressive person, an angry person, a troubled person—he was happy. There was no depression.

Woodman arranged a concert for Cohen in the five-hundred-seat Tory Turtle, the largest venue on campus.

DIANNE WOODMAN: It was jammed—I mean, jammed. I had no idea. These kids were sitting on the floor, in the aisles, and he just held them in thrall, with his guitar. The emotional reaction of those kids coming up to him afterwards—some of them could hardly speak.

ANN MANDEL: The first thing he did was hand out joss sticks. He gave a really good reading. There was no music, though he did tell the audience he had a guitar with him.

DIANNE WOODMAN: Mostly, we hung out at the hotel, with Eli and his then wife, Mimi, and his students. He taught me how to eat raw oysters, off silver platters. I haven't had raw oysters since. Of course, he hit on me, but I was just this naive little Catholic housewife with four kids, putting her husband through medical school. What did I know? It wasn't a serious thing—just the requisite thing he had to do. He did the concert and a couple of gigs at the Yardbird Suite and then he wouldn't leave—he loved Edmonton.

ANN MANDEL: He had a kind of open-door policy at the MacDonald. Any kid could bomb into the hotel and go up to the room and hang out with Leonard Cohen. The MacDonald was then a very stuffy hotel and was beginning to get shirty about all these beatniks hanging around.

One night, according to Mandel, Cohen hosted a big party.

ANN MANDEL: There was so much booze and so many kids. It went on and on. Chivas Regal Scotch being passed around. It wasn't a cheap deal. Some people were getting very drunk. One student passed out on the bathroom floor—John Cook. We agreed to let him lie there. Leonard never hit on me, but he knew I was more or less involved with Eli, even though he was in fact married to Mimi.

MICHAEL DORSEY: At the last party at the Mac, I was singing Dylan's "Just Like Tom Thumb's Blues," and he told me when Dylan wrote the song, he looked in his mirror and saw Leonard and, at the same time in London, Leonard looked in his mirror and saw Dylan. He recounted this while kneeling in front of my chair, his elbows on my knees, his face inches from my guitar. A very intense gaze.

Cohen's version seems fanciful, since "Just Like Tom Thumb's Blues" was first recorded in August 1965, long before Dylan would have been aware of Cohen as a songwriter. It was during that Edmonton trip, however, that Cohen wrote "Sisters of Mercy." Accounts of its genesis are wildly conflicting. Cohen offered the most fulsome version in a 1974 radio interview.

LEONARD COHEN: I was . . . walking along one of the main streets . . . It was bitter cold. I passed these two girls [Barbara and Lorraine]. They invited me to stand in the doorway with them. Of course I did. Sometime later, we found ourselves in my little hotel room . . . and the three of us were gonna sleep together. Of course, I had all kinds of erotic fantasies of what the evening might bring . . . I think we all jammed into this one small couch . . . and it became clear that it wasn't the purpose of the evening at all. At one point I found myself unable to sleep. I got up and, by the moonlight, I wrote that poem while these women were sleeping. It was one of the few songs I ever wrote from top to bottom without a line of revision. By the time they woke up . . . I had this completed song to sing to them.

DIANNE WOODMAN: He was thrilled with that song, very excited. He didn't tell me the story. He just sang it for me—just the two of us. He sang a lot of his songs to me. He told me the lines in "Suzanne" about the sun pouring down like honey were about Greece. In the harbour on Hydra, there were broken columns and statues in the water, and in those days everyone threw their garbage there, where the children played.

According to University of Alberta professor Dr. Kim Solez, the song was written not at the Hotel MacDonald, but at the Hotel Alberta, because Cohen had been evicted from the former.

KIM SOLEZ: He'd been staying in the [MacDonald's] wood-frame annex, and got kicked out because of all the noise and all the extra people, and fire-code limits. It was becoming dangerous. It was also dangerous because he had this custom of candles. The hotel was upset about all these lit candles.

DIANNE WOODMAN: The hotel did not throw him out. I did. I said to him after a week, "You can't stay at the hotel. Jack's not going to pay for more than a week." I was looking after my boss. He said that was okay and he went to this *horrible* dive, the Alberta Hotel. And he stayed there for another couple of weeks. He hung out the most with Jon Whyte. [Whyte, a poet, publisher, filmmaker, bookseller, and publisher, died in 1992.] They had a few escapades I heard about.

ANN MANDEL: Jon was very interested in contemporary poetry and was a very adventurous poet. They would have had a similar view of the universe and [shared] their caring for avant-garde poetry.

Ann Mandel, however, maintains the song was written before Cohen left or was evicted from the MacDonald.

ANN MANDEL: The next part is John Cook's account. [After that party], he got up in the morning and staggered, literally, into the bedroom, and there was Leonard in bed with two young girls—Barbara and Lorraine.

MICHAEL DORSEY: I knew them as Basha and Lorraine.

DIANNE WOODMAN: Ann may be right, because I remember him singing it to me and I was never in the Alberta Hotel.

KIM SOLEZ: They were faculty children, undergrads. Their parents worked for the university. So they had a great deal to lose by revealing the story. One of them would have been willing, decades later, if the other one was, but the other one's family members did not know about this, and she did not want them to know.

ANN MANDEL: According to John, Leonard threw back the covers and they're all fully clothed and said to John, "It's not Montreal, you know." Later that day, Eli and I went over to the hotel. Leonard said he'd written a poem. He read it to us right there. Mimi was there. Whether he'd set it to music or not, I don't know. I don't think anything sexual happened at all. These were two women, students of Eli's, and they were both troubled in that sixties, angsty sort of way. Attractive, but not in an amazing way.

Solez contends Cohen later stayed at the girls' apartment many nights.

KIM SOLEZ: I'm not exactly sure if [that] night was chaste—as the song suggests—but I know that the day after wasn't chaste. He later said it was the first song he'd written completely from beginning to end and never edited. What I've concluded is that it was the music he wasn't happy with—because he later called the women from Montreal and sang it to them. But the lyrics were probably fine.

MICHAEL DORSEY: He stayed with two friends in a basement room beside mine, even when he was at the MacDonald. It was a co-op on 111th Street and 88th or 89th Avenue, I think. I don't know how much time he spent at the Alberta, but he did say he liked the ambience. Women liked him, and there were fans who hung. I can't remember him being mobbed as much as signing books after readings and music.

According to Solez, Cohen actually spent time with five women during his stay.

KIM SOLEZ: He only remembers the two in the song, but the other three were quite sure he would remember them for the rest of his life.

During his stay, Cohen was interviewed by the *Gateway*, the student newspaper. Asked if he thought Bob Dylan would have any impact on music or the general culture, Cohen responded: "I don't know. I feel like I created Dylan. The whole thing was the incantation of words to a string accompaniment." In another *Gateway* piece, in February 1967, Ralph Melnychuk recalled that Cohen's appearance had resulted in an "outburst of sexual energy by normally cool, level-headed and rational literature-oriented females [who] reacted to the poet like a mob of teeny-boppers leaving a performance of [the] Beatles . . . their normally violent energies increased to a state of almost Dionysian frenzy."

ANN MANDEL: You could see it at the reading. The young women were the ones going up to him afterward.

PATRICIA HUGHES-FULLER: There was something in the air. He became one of the first Canadian writers to step away from the academy and become a celebrity and a pop culture figure. His visit wasn't a celebrity experience for those of us there. It had a very personal feel.

Cohen's gig at the Yardbird Suite, a jazz and blues club, was also sold out.

MICHAEL DORSEY: He was just another guy on the road, more of a speaker than a musician, working the bugs, tricks, and techniques.

I remember he was unhappy with the pitch, mainly because he was singing so low that it's hard to keep the pitch and project at the same time. We talked a lot about music, practical stuff as well as a bit about philosophy and politics, but ultimately there wasn't much advice I could give him. Edmonton was pretty open back then, way less rigid and more discipline-blurring than other cities.

One Woodman memory challenges the official narrative.

DIANNE WOODMAN: He said he was in discussion with Bob Johnston, who had been Dylan's producer. He had chosen the songs he wanted to record. He was excited about it. And he was insisting that he have backup girl singers because Ray Charles always had the Raelettes. He wanted his own Raelettes.

Cohen made a second visit to Edmonton, likely in 1968.

ANN MANDEL: It was early summer, and we were standing in a backyard, a hot, prairie summer day, and Leonard is letting the mosquitos bite him and we're saying, "You know, you can slap those things." And he says, "No, I think they should feed on me." He did this kind of Christian business, being one with the universe. Irving Layton always claimed that Cohen was a crypto-Christian. He did have a bit of a Messiah thing going for him.

*   *   *

The decision had been bubbling up for some time, forcing itself upon him by degrees. He didn't sing particularly well, and his guitar skills were limited at best. But he could write as well or better than anyone, and if he had to rely on poetry and novels for his income, he'd starve. He could teach English, but the very idea was anathema. He could return to the family business, but that prospect was equally unappealing.

NAIM KATTAN: Leonard had a friend, a French writer, from France, who told me Leonard had confided to him that he wanted to be a poet and a novelist, but he didn't want to miss the opportunity to make a million dollars. I said, "That's crazy." But he said, "No, Leonard does not want to live in poverty."

SANDRA DJWA: The other thing, I suppose, is changing times . . . [In turning to music], he's making his bow to modernism or postmodernism. Maybe he felt he'd gone as far as he could go in that [literary] medium.

Edmonton marked the epiphanic moment. Cohen had sung before, of course—at summer camp and for friends—and always won polite applause. But Edmonton represented something entirely new—an audience completely in thrall, hanging on his melodies and every melancholic lyric. Literature could touch hearts too, but not so directly. At thirty-two years old, he had found his calling.

CHAPTER TEN

Never Finished, Only Abandoned

The fascination of Leonard was how he could come into the room and captivate by being quiet and invisible. He wasn't saying much but, partly because he wasn't saying much, when he did speak, it felt like something coming up from the deep, a polished pebble coming from a deep well, the deep well of himself.

—Pico Iyer

Once you've lived on Hydra, you can't live anywhere else, including Hydra.

—Leonard Cohen

Energized by his insight and its implications, Cohen wrote to Marianne Ihlen on December 4.

KIM SOLEZ: It's a pivotal letter and indicates that he realized he could not support himself and Marianne as a novelist and poet. He would have to be a singer-songwriter. He made that decision in Edmonton, based on experiences there, because it was his first real taste of celebrity, groupies, and standing-room-only audiences, people following him everywhere and mobbing his hotel room.

In the letter, Cohen writes, "I must be a singer, a man who owns nothing . . . I know now what I must train for . . . Darling I hope we can repair the painful spaces where uncertainties have us. I hope you can lead yourself out of despair and I hope I can help you."

DIANNE WOODMAN: When he was leaving town, he asked me to drive him to the airport and told me to meet him at a five-and-dime store. He took me to several of these stores and bought candies and toys for my kids—long chains of bubble gums, bats with a rubber ball attached, a couple of bagsful. My kids still remember that. He was very generous.

Soon after, Cohen flew to Winnipeg to perform in Taché Hall at the University of Manitoba—his first concert as a fully committed singer-songwriter. The student union's events coordinator had sent Cohen an invitation.

MENDL MALKIN: I asked if we could set up something like that again and the answer came back, "No, but he will come and perform." I was expecting a poetry reading and I was totally in the dark about what the show would be.

JACK BIDNIK: Leonard arrived alone, wearing a grey trench coat. Nobody came to meet him, so I and a few others greeted him and showed him to the backstage area. It was a small audience, about seventy-five. The atmosphere was a bit awkward because, although his songs had been sung by [Judy] Collins, few except the cognoscenti had heard of him. Then he handed me some sticks of incense to hand out, saying if the audience had these, we'd have half a chance. The sticks were soon lit, and I took my seat. Then someone noticed there was nobody to introduce him. This was ridiculous, so I got up onstage and announced, "Ladies and gentlemen, I give you Leonard Poet."

MENDL MALKIN: Jack also said, "You may be wondering why I'm introducing Leonard Cohen. And the reason is, I'm the only one here wearing a tie." He sang the whole concert—he did not read. Everyone was spellbound. It was magical.

MARTIN LEVIN: My strongest memory is of him singing "Suzanne." Hypnotic. Don't recall any Dylan betrayal effect, that he'd abandoned poetry for pop.

High school student Alan Mendelsohn also attended the concert.

ALAN MENDELSOHN: I was seventeen and we were all listening to the Beatles and Stones, the Lovin' Spoonful, a far cry from Cohen's haunting tunes. But I found it difficult to engage with him. He didn't [then] have that charming stage presence—more like a brooder, mysterious; I don't remember any patter. I don't remember him relating or flirting with the audience. But he had a mystique. He was alone onstage with his guitar looking the role of a bohemian. The audience was in awe, transfixed by his persona. He sang "The Stranger Song"—I wasn't sure what he meant but it sounded very deep.

After the concert, the NFB film *Ladies and Gentlemen, Mr. Leonard Cohen* was screened.

JACK BIDNIK: I recall watching him watching himself in his movie, thinking how unusual a scene it was. We had some conversation on schizophrenia in poetry. He was somewhat bemused when I told him I was in favour of it.

MENDL MALKIN: Afterwards, backstage, about thirty kids were asking questions. Someone asked him about building character and he recommended three things that were good for you—LSD, divorce, and a nervous breakdown. I don't think he was on LSD at the time. He was too coherent.

An insightful review in the university newspaper—by Michael Mitchell—noted that Cohen "made no attempt to put himself over . . . The audience was not graced with a smile, a sign of friendship, or any emphatic gesture . . . The result was that the words themselves became stark, powerful, and at times embarrassingly naked . . . The poetry spoke for itself. It alone was on exhibition. No attempt was made to sell it . . . It was an evening . . . devoid of the con." If the Leonard Cohen of 1967 had drafted a foundational mission statement for his music, it would have come pretty close to that.

BARRIE WEXLER: The Leonard Cohen of 1967 *had* drafted a foundational mission statement. I remember reading an unpublished manuscript titled *The Dictation*. It was dated Winter '72, but it had been worked on for several years prior. It contained an addendum, "How to Speak Poetry," published in an expanded form in *Death of a Lady's Man*, in 1978.

Among the many lines in the poem that echoed Mitchell's trenchant review were "There is nothing you can show on your face that can match the horror of this time. Do not even try." A few days later, Cohen arrived in Vancouver to give a concert at UBC.

SEYMOUR MAYNE: I arranged it. We paid his airfare. All he got paid was $500. That afternoon, I'd gone to get Leonard at Hotel Vancouver. He had just completed his bath. He was stark naked, coming out of a shower, thin, almost like a concentration camp survivor. Later, he would appear with a bronze goddess, some muse or nymph from mythology, one of whom always seemed to be with him.

PIERRE COUPEY: The concert was mesmerizing, the young and beautiful Leonard onstage, vulnerable. The gathering [afterwards, at poet Dorothy Livesay's house in Kitsilano] became a little boring. Where was Leonard? Sitting alone on the stairs, looking a little ignored and bored. Poor Leonard. Perhaps he was used to more Dionysian affairs in Montreal, Hydra? I went up the staircase and sat next to him.

SEYMOUR MAYNE: When Leonard arrived, he took a seat in my upstairs study. Peter Trower, the eccentric poet, pushed his way in, removed his boot, then his sock, pulled out a wad of dope, and passed it around. We bantered, but I was not keen on smoking in the house since that could lead to a bust. In fact, the party got out of control, and the police showed up.

PIERRE COUPEY: I took pity on Leonard and asked if he wouldn't prefer to see crazy Vancouver at night. Yes, he did. [But] how could I hijack the guest of honour, without incurring the wrath of the host? I called Rick Kitaeff, another Montreal expatriate and [club owner], and told him to make ready—Mr. Leonard Cohen was on his way. Seymour caught wind, and was, to say the least, not pleased.

SEYMOUR MAYNE: Eventually, a group from the party went off with Leonard to Kitsilano Beach to indulge in the weed. Leonard was off the next day. Leonard always came into your life quickly and he left quickly.

At Kitaeff's nightclub, Coupey recalls, there was a show—"the legendary Marcel Horne, aka El Diablo, a six-foot-six stunner, knife thrower, ladies' man."

PIERRE COUPEY: The climax was El Diablo's spectacular fire-breathing tribute to Cohen, a blast of flame from one end of the room to the other. Leonard smiled his complicated, shy smile. The other highlight was watching the women make heavy plays for Cohen, a parade of seduction, pure Fellini. Leonard conducted himself with perfect charm and grace, subtly deflecting every manoeuvre with the utmost kindness, the sweetest mercy. He was engaging, moody, amusing, and above all, charming, gentle, kind, and very self-contained. His intelligent curiosity, openness, and ability to be quiet and observe was palpable. He never once tried to be the centre of attention and yet always was. You sensed his deep self-reliance. Around 4 or 5 a.m., when I dropped Leonard off at the Hotel Vancouver, he had enough energy left to do an amazing comic dance—a kind of sideways Charlie Chaplin, Fred Astaire dance up the stairs, with a bow and a tip of an imaginary hat and a wicked grin. It was so sudden, impromptu. A gift, and then gone. Definitely a shaman, a trickster. A poet. If not *the* poet.

The following month saw the birth in Vancouver of the underground newspaper that would become the *Georgia Straight*. Its founders, including Kitaeff, later cited Cohen's visit as something of a catalyst. In an interview with the campus newspaper, *Ubyssey,* Cohen described himself as a cantor, "a priest of a catacomb religion that is underground, just beginning . . . and I am one of the creators of the liturgy that will create the church . . . It's not the idea of imposing a prayer, but that he creates the finest part of themselves." The interviewer was Sandra Djwa, then a graduate English student and later a distinguished writer and cultural critic.

SANDRA DJWA: We conducted it in the newspaper offices. Leonard was very perceptive, charming, even if a little high. He really wanted to talk. He saw me, if not as a kindred soul, as someone who would understand what he was talking about. I had absolutely no sense that he was out to seduce me.

At one point, Djwa observed that Cohen's work often featured two female figures, that of the beloved, the aspiring figure, the mother, and that of the madwoman, the destructive. "The whole structure seems to be that of the Orpheus myth."

SANDRA DJAW: I wondered whether these two figures are really part of the Jewish conception of women.

To which Cohen replied: "Absolutely. I've always honoured the wrathful deities and the blessed deities . . . One is dark and one is light, and the third that comes from it like a braid that takes its colour from both, like a salamander. That seems to represent me to myself . . . It's not that a man chooses the gods that he worships. It's the gods who choose him. It's only when we come closest to the gods that we engage in creation."

SANDRA DJWA: He was probably exposed to Genet, Sartre, and Céline through Louis Dudek's course at McGill, and probably read Burroughs and others in New York in the late 1950s.

The difference between them, Cohen replied, was that "I hold out the idea of ecstasy as the solution. If only people get high, then they can face the evil part . . . The thing about Sartre is that he never had his head blown off. The thing that people are interested in doing now is blowing their heads off and that's why the writing of schizophrenics like myself will be important."

SANDRA DJWA: Cohen began as a Romantic. You see a lot of that in *The Favourite Game*, the gentler soul. [But] he later really advocated a new aesthetic. The epigraph to *Let Us Compare Mythologies* is really revealing because he's quoting the Romantics [Keats's "Ode on a Grecian Urn"]—*"She cannot fade, though thou hast not thy bliss / For ever wilt thou love, and she be fair!"*—and then [adds], "He's talking about a girl, he said. He had to talk about something."

BARRIE WEXLER: For such a sharp-witted guy, some of what he said in those days was arrogant bullshit. A bit of Layton's bravado had rubbed off on him.

En route home to Montreal, in mid-February 1967, Cohen played a concert at York University.

ALICE FREEMAN: He mesmerized five hundred people. He walked onstage, lit incense, and said very quietly, "The person here in the most pain is me." Then he went into a soft chant and got everybody in a nice trance. After that, he talked and read and sang for three hours. Every single person worshipped him. It turned into a Leonard Cohen love-in.

When the concert ended, Cohen walked away, leaving his books, his incense, and his guitar.

ALICE FREEMAN: He vanished so successfully that the girl who promoted the concert couldn't find him to hand him his fee. He's always doing that, disappearing and deserting his people and his possessions. He's always alone, and he does almost all of his living inside his own head. He never really lives anywhere physically. I always wonder where he changes his clothes and what he does with his underwear.

BARRIE WEXLER: He travelled lightly so he could make a quick getaway. He used to say his tiny valise had a false bottom where he kept a change of clothes.

ALICE FREEMAN: He actually does see himself as a constant wanderer, a kind of travelling body of pain. The image of Leonard in pain, in danger, attracts a lot of girls. It isn't a big sex thing with most of them. They want to mother Leonard and protect him.

Back in Montreal, Cohen's friend Don Owen had begun work on a film for the National Film Board—*The Ernie Game*, featuring actress Judith Gault. Cohen made a cameo appearance, singing "The Stranger Song" at a party. It's doubtful that he had anything to do with the script, which is credited to Owen, but the film's theme—how a young artist can function in the world after being released from a mental asylum—would certainly have resonated with him.

JUDITH GAULT: Everyone thinks Leonard and I were lovers, but we weren't. We were almost like brother and sister. I just loved him. He was so friendly and so much fun. He didn't come on to me. But he had a lot of girlfriends. He'd just walk in a room and the women were all over him. He and Morton would crack jokes all the time, and discuss books they were reading. He was sad—there was always sadness in everything—but he'd always twist it and make everyone laugh. Don Owen wanted to be right in there with Leonard, because Leonard was a very special person. Don looked up to him. He would have liked to have been like him.

Finally, borrowing funds from Robert Hershorn, Cohen announced his intention to seek fame and fortune in music. En route to Nashville, revered home of country music—the genre with which he most identified—he stopped in New York City. His life was never the same.

BARRIE WEXLER: He originally intended New York to be a stopover on his way to Nashville. His manager, Mary Martin, may have had something to do with him staying.

PATRICIA NOLIN: It all went dark, fell apart, after Leonard went to New York. Everything came unglued. Sure, he came back, but it wasn't the same. Golden youth was gone, for everybody. The *légèreté*—the lightness—went away. It got testy between the guys. All of a sudden this man was on the road, free, having women—and the domesticity of the others. All hell broke loose at some point.

ISRAEL CHARNEY: Patricia probably knows. The fire did go out, and everybody's life took a different turn.

BARRIE WEXLER: Afterwards, whenever I was with Derek or Morton, you could feel that they were almost waiting for Leonard to walk through the door.

Among the legions of women who inhabited Cohen's life, many have been identified; many more have not. One of them is a Swedish prostitute he met in this period. Cohen talked about her in a 1972 interview. The woman, Cohen told journalist Roger Squires, claimed to have psychic powers; she told him he was dead but she would restore him to life. Cohen described her as "a teacher in the true meaning of the word . . . Her way of prophesying—and prophesying it was—was beautiful." At one point, Cohen decided to write a book about her, and took a tape recorder to her room. But when he replayed the tape, "nothing she said made sense, so I wasn't able to write the book." Cohen later credited the woman with putting him back on his feet.

Hoping to put Cohen's version of "Suzanne" in the hands of Columbia Records, Mary Martin arranged to record a demo—in the shower of her Bleecker Street apartment in New York.

TONI MYERS: Mary asked me to help. He stood in the shower so the acoustics would be better and we taped him. But "Suzanne" was really starting to catch on. I was at a Nina Simone concert at the Village

Gate—Leonard wasn't there—but it was very much a Black Power night and Nina was in her angry phase. And she did "Suzanne." I was shocked.

On February 22, 1967, Cohen made his professional debut in New York at the Village Theatre (later the Fillmore East). Introduced by Judy Collins, who had invited him on the program, he sang "Suzanne" to an audience of more than three thousand people.

JUDY COLLINS: I wanted him there, because I wanted him to sing. I said, "Look, you've got to." And he said, "No, no. I can't sing. I have a terrible voice." I said, "You don't have a terrible voice. It's a little obscure but it's not terrible." It was a big deal, this concert. So I pushed him onstage and he started singing and, about halfway through, he stopped and started to weep. People have told me this— they saw him sobbing onstage.

In Cohen's account, described in a February 23 letter to Ihlen, he struck a chord on his guitar, only to find it out of tune. He tried to tune it, but "couldn't get more than a croak out of my throat, managed four lines." Apologizing, he walked offstage, "the people baffled and my career . . . dying among the coughs of the people backstage." Cohen stood in the wings, overcome by a "curious happiness . . . I had failed . . . really failed, there is something so beautiful about total failure."

JUDY COLLINS: I was waiting in the dressing room. I said, "What happened?" He said, "I just can't do this." I said, "Let's go back and we'll sing it together. You must go out there." Which he did. And the audience went crazy. Because my recording was out, and they knew it, and because of it, they knew him.

Later, Cohen sang "The Stranger Song." "I hardly got the words out . . . but I finished somehow and I thought I'll just commit suicide . . . Everybody backstage very sorry for me and couldn't believe how happy I was, how relieved I was that it had all come to nothing, that I had never been so free." Characteristically Cohen, he finds the pinpoint of light in the darkness. "This damn hotel, loneliness, isolation, insomnia, the secular triumph that always just misses me—it's all made me calm and curiously happy, it's all mine at last, it's my kingdom." Surprisingly, Cohen never hit on Collins.

JUDY COLLINS: I didn't hit on him either. I wasn't interested in him. I was interested in the songs. I was completely over the moon about his writing.

At the end of March, Cohen—appearing with Norman Mailer—read poetry and excerpts from *Beautiful Losers* at State University at Buffalo and sang again, in conjunction with the campus's Festival of Arts. In the audience was graduate English student Michael Morgulis, already a Cohen disciple.

MICHAEL MORGULIS: Leonard, looking dark and Jewish, accepted the audience's applause and then did something no one expected. He picked up a guitar and said [words that were not exactly true], "I have never sung in public before, so please bear with me." He began with "Suzanne." Everyone recognized the song as a Judy Collins hit, but had no idea it had been written by Leonard. Before long, the audience was hanging on every note and word. It was hypnotic. This guy with an edgy voice reminiscent of Bob Dylan had reached out and taken their hearts. I was ecstatic.

In another letter to Ihlen, Cohen reported that he was abandoning plans for "sainthood, revolution, redemptive visions, music mastery." Although he called himself "just the ageing man with a notebook, happiest when alone in a Puerto Rican restaurant, coffee and Spanish juke-box," his nascent music career was taking flight. Hollywood was interested in buying the rights to "Suzanne"; he would later fly to L.A. for talks with director John Boorman, but nothing came of it. Buffy Sainte-Marie, he reported, was recording "The Stranger Song" and the singer Nico planned to record a new song he'd written for her, "The Jewels in Your Shoulder." He had offers from Expo '67, the Newport Folk Festival, and a proposal to tour forty American colleges. His own mood was uncertain—he walked the city "feeling either black or golden, dead to lust, tired of ambition, a lazy student of my own pain, happy about the occasional sun, thin and dressing very shabbily, hair out of control, feeling good tonight as I write my perfect friend." Meanwhile, Mary Martin had persuaded legendary record producer John Hammond to give Cohen an audience.

MARY MARTIN: Pop music is like opening a bottle of Perrier, drinking down the contents, and discarding the bottle. Until the next flavour is marketed—then we go and buy the next pop. Cohen emerged at a time when Bob Dylan was being a little silent. [The previous summer, Dylan had suffered a serious motorcycle accident and was still recuperating.] Perhaps the timing was right. But if there was a vacancy in the charts, there'd be a reason to fill that void with a new act, which was in the back of my pea brain. John was an amazing man. He really understood the power of the singer-songwriter. In those days it really was a team of people who really understood and liked Leonard and wished to see him be successful—John Hammond being spear number one, and Clive Davis another, and Bunny Freidus, the international girl.

JOHN HAMMOND: A friend of mine said, "John, there's this poet from Canada who I think you'd be interested in. He plays pretty good guitar, and he's a wonderful songwriter, but he doesn't read music, and he's sort of very strange. I don't think Columbia would be at all interested in him, but you might be." So I said, "Well, fine."

After lunch with Cohen, Hammond suggested they go back to the Chelsea.

LEONARD COHEN: So we went up to my room. It's hard to play for somebody, just cold like that; but if you could do it for anybody, it would be John Hammond, because he made it easy. If there was ever a man you could trust, it was John Hammond.

Cohen sang him "Master Song," "Hey, That's No Way to Say Goodbye," "The Stranger Song," "Suzanne," and a song about rivers that he never recorded.

JOHN HAMMOND: I listened to this guy, and he's got a hypnotic effect. He plays acoustic guitar, of course. He is a real poet and he's a very sensitive guy.

LEONARD COHEN: At the end of six or seven songs, he said, "You got it, Leonard." I didn't quite know whether he meant a contract, or the gift, but it certainly made me feel very good. He said he had to consult with his colleagues, but that he'd like to offer me a contract.

JOHN HAMMOND: I thought he was enchanting. That's the only word you can use. He was not like anything I've ever heard before. I just feel that I always want a true original, if I can find one, because there are not many in the world; and the young man set his own rules, and he was a really first-class poet, which is most important. They all looked at me at Columbia and said, "What, are you . . . ? A forty-year-old, Canadian poet? [Cohen was thirty-three.] How are we going to sell him?" I said, "Listen to him." And, lo and behold, Columbia signed him.

On May 22, 1967, wearing a flower in his hair, Cohen performed at a love-in at Toronto's Queen's Park, along with Buffy Sainte-Marie. By one account, he was again stricken with stage fright.

LESTER BROWN: We heard the poet Earle Birney, then Buffy sang and said she had a special guest with her. It was rumoured that Buffy and him were a number. She then called up Leonard. He started to sing "Suzanne." I don't remember if he finished his verse, but he definitely did not get past his first verse. Then he said, "I can't sing," and walked off the stage.

Other reports, however, say Cohen, wearing a brown suede jacket and turtleneck sweater, told the crowd of about four thousand that he loved everybody and said, "Spring called me here." Then he sang "Suzanne," "So Long, Marianne," and other songs with flowers behind his ear and also recited poetry. The following week, Cohen began recording his first album, *Songs of Leonard Cohen*, at Columbia's Studio E on East Fifty-Second Street. The engineer was Fred Catero.

FRED CATERO: I didn't know there was a Leonard Cohen or anything about him. I remember seeing this big mirror in the corner, a dress mirror, five feet tall. Leonard walks in with John and says, "Okay, set it up." John would sit down—he had this big cigar that he'd smoke—and the singer would sing and he'd say, "Isn't that mahvellous? Mahvellous." My impression was Leonard was a very introverted person—very into himself. He lived in his own world—just by looking, you could see that. Right away, I knew there was something strange about this individual. I put up the mike and he goes, in a subdued voice, "You see that mirror over there?" Yeah. "Bring it over here. Put it in front of me." I thought maybe there was some new technique I was going to learn, where the sound bounces off the glass. I say, "What's the mirror for?" So he says, deep voice, "When I'm playing and singing, sometimes I get lost and I look up and I see where I am." I said, "Okay." John didn't question it.

Catero eventually concluded that Cohen enjoyed playing mind games, and watching the reactions of people he was putting on.

FRED CATERO: We had this machine operator, Lou Waxman, in another room. He had this little station and looked through the window. Leonard went over to him and Waxman was a middle-aged, very square individual, no hipness. And Leonard says, low voice, "Listen, man, I just got out of an institution. Be careful, because Fred and I are going to kidnap you and fuck you." Lou was shaken—"Did you hear what he said?" And I think it was all [a game]. Leonard wanted to shake him, and Lou was one of those people you wanted to shake. People with problems like this have this genius streak in them. I was only in my midtwenties and don't think I had enough life experience to appreciate his work.

Cohen, for his part, later confessed to feeling overwhelmed.

LEONARD COHEN: I was somewhat intimidated. I didn't really know how to sing with a band. I really didn't know how to sing with really good, professional musicians. I would tend to listen to the musicians, rather than concentrate on what I was doing, because they were doing it so much more proficiently than I was.

Hammond then proposed laying basic tracks using only bass player Willie Ruff, who had a background in both classical and jazz.

JOHN HAMMOND: Leonard always needed reassurance of some kind, and he recognized that Willie was a supreme musician. It was a wonderful combination. Willie was not upset by the fact that Leonard couldn't read music. He just realized this guy was a genius of his own kind.

LEONARD COHEN: The support that Willie Ruff brought to those sessions was crucial. I couldn't have laid down those tracks without him. He supported the guitar playing so well. He could always anticipate my next move, he understood the song so thoroughly. He was one of those rare musicians that play selflessly, and for pure and complete support.

Later, Hammond conceded that the early studio sessions had been "terribly difficult."

JOHN HAMMOND: You couldn't get Leonard to work with other musicians because he felt they were all laughing at him. And they mostly were.

Progress on the album was therefore fitful.

JOHN SIMON: John Hammond would schedule a session, then cancel and reschedule a month later—which drove Leonard crazy.

Then Hammond suffered a heart attack and formally bowed out. When Cohen asked for another producer, CBS awarded the gig to John Simon, a hugely talented musician who had arranged a hit pop tune, "Red Rubber Ball." Simon was impressed by Cohen.

JOHN SIMON: Leonard's lyrics set him apart from most rock-and-roll acts because they were more finely crafted. The imagery was there, but the balance in the lines and the inner rhymes and scansion—everything was regular, schooled, studied. This was a guy who had read and written poetry. I'd be hard-pressed to think of somebody who had those kind of chops.

Still, Simon's desire to add instrumental textures clashed with Cohen's desire to keep the melodies simple and spare. Simon wanted to add strings and other backing tracks; Cohen was content with his voice and his guitar.

MARY MARTIN: One day, John said, "I don't understand why Leonard Cohen has a record deal." I thought, "Shit. How can you even think about that?" So a few things were very odd. Probably everybody got frustrated and, if you were a trained musician, [and] heard Leonard Cohen sing, perhaps it may have hurt your musical sensibilities. But then, you didn't want to hear what was being said. Leonard, on the other hand, didn't necessarily think playing at the Troubadour was necessarily the most important thing in the world. He didn't really like to perform in those early days.

JOHN SIMON: At one point, I suggested we go to my parents' house in Norwich [Connecticut]—they were away—to go over material. Leonard stayed up all night going through my dad's library. I slept. He didn't. He was a man, while the other rock acts I worked with were boys. He was an established poet. Real bright and clever with words. He had that finger-picking triplet style that was very impressive. Sort of a classical technique. I'm proud of the experimentation I did use—wordless women's voices instead of instruments, mostly Nancy Priddy, my girlfriend at the time.

Before Simon had even begun work on the album, Cohen invited him and Priddy to Montreal.

NANCY PRIDDY: We went for Expo '67. But I don't think we even went [to it]. Maybe we stayed in Leonard's apartment. If I met him, I don't remember him. I met someone—a friend. Maybe it was him. John and I had a fight there. John told me one time Leonard wanted to do acid. But I think the fight was about grass. I probably said, "You don't want to do that." What a prude I was then.

Work on the album continued to stall.

NANCY PRIDDY: John told me Leonard was very uncomfortable with what he was doing and it took a little longer than the record label appreciated. He never said anything about a disagreement, only that Leonard was having a problem with confidence, which you could understand, being his first album. Columbia had told John they would put no more money into the project. John came to me one night and said we have to go finish Leonard's album. So we went into the studio and I sang backup on "Suzanne," "Sisters of Mercy," and "So Long, Marianne"—every time you hear a female voice, that's me. I think John sang with me on "So Long, Marianne." It was very simple—just the two of us and the engineer. I didn't even get a credit. Before that, I knew nothing about Leonard. We'd sit in the studio and listen to his work. We loved Leonard's songs. Oh my God—the words, the words. We were just in awe, totally in awe. John told me the next day, he'd played what we had done for Leonard and he had really liked it.

JOHN SIMON: In spite of those differences in taste, there was not a speck of animosity between Leonard and me. In our time together he was cheerful, funny, very rarely dark. And, with his wit and intelligence, he was a joy to be around. About ten years [later], I bumped into him in the Algonquin Hotel. There was never anything but cordiality between us. It wasn't a messy denouement. He had his ideas—I had mine. I'm real happy with the charts I did for him that ended up on the album. I don't recall what the others sounded like. They probably weren't as good.

One day in New York, Cohen bumped into poet Ken Koch, an old friend from Hydra, on the bus.

KEN KOCH: I invited him over and he told me I should become a singer too . . . sing all my poems. It was wonderful because you met lots of women and made a lot of money and got to travel around. "That's great, Leonard" [but] "I can't carry a tune." He said, "That's good, that means no one else will be able to sing your stuff." And I said, "Okay, but also I don't play an instrument." He said, "You can probably learn—let's try." There wasn't anything that made noise except a vacuum cleaner. I plugged in the vacuum cleaner and I thought I'd be more in the mood to sing if I stood up on a chair. He said, "Sing one of your poems." I said, "There's no music to any of my poems." He said, "That's okay." I sang, with intermittent noise from the vacuum cleaner, "You were wearing your Edgar Allan Poe printed cotton blouse" in a hillbilly voice. Leonard interrupted me after a few bars. "You're not serious." There I was standing on a chair and playing a vacuum cleaner. He said, "I don't believe you. Who are you singing to?" "Leonard, I'm singing to you. There's no one else here." "No—who in the audience? Who do you want to go to bed with after the show? Who do you want to like you?" [I said], "Twenty-two-year-old women." "No. Everybody wants twenty-two-year-old women. Sing to somebody else. You know who I sing to? Fourteen-year-olds and forty-year-olds." I'm not sure those are the exact numbers—something like fourteen and forty. I said, "Okay, I'll try to sing to fourteen-year-olds."

Koch eventually conceded defeat, but said there's one way Cohen could help.

KEN KOCH: He said, "Anything, what is it?" "Put me on your record jacket." He promised. Months went by. I did receive his record—this girl, rising from flames, Leonard, his lyrics, and no tributes. And no Kenny.

Although Cohen seemed poised on the brink of stardom, his mother remained skeptical.

SEYMOUR MAYNE: One day, Layton and I are leaving Murray's Restaurant and who do we see but Masha Cohen. She says, "Don't do what my

Lennie did. Finish your PhD. Lennie never finished anything." He had dropped out of law school and dropped out of graduate school. I just looked at her. I thought, "God help us." Most of us would trade in our PhDs for his career. I met her three years later and she said the same thing. She couldn't see that what he was doing was valuable.

During production on the album, Cohen appeared at the Newport Folk Festival, July 16, 1967, in Rhode Island, along with Judy Collins, Arlo Guthrie, Joni Mitchell, and Gordon Lightfoot.

JUDY COLLINS: I was on [Newport's] board—the only girl in town. The guys on the board, they were a very hard bunch. I wanted a workshop, on the lawn in the afternoon, of singer-songwriters. And they said, "Oh no, no, no. We have fiddlers and all these things." I pushed and pushed and finally got both Joni Mitchell and Leonard on an afternoon program.

BILL FUREY: He really didn't like his voice. And he was very nervous to perform. Backstage, the producer said to him, "Okay, Leonard Cohen! You're on." And Leonard said, "I can't go on." . . . "Why not?" . . . "I have a terrible voice. I can't sing." And the producer said, "Nobody here can sing. If you want singing, go to the Met."

After meeting at Newport, Cohen and Joni Mitchell began a romance that lasted for almost a year.

VERA FRENKEL: It made sense that they would be drawn to each other. Both are keepers of the flame and they want to see how the other person lights it.

Collins herself was otherwise engaged at Newport. She recalls "having wild sex" with a man she didn't know.

JUDY COLLINS: Leonard was in the corner singing "The Stranger Song," not paying attention. I totally trusted Leonard Cohen. He was the most trustworthy person I ever met. I had to pass all my boyfriends past Leonard to see if he approved.

One weekend, Cohen brought Mitchell to Montreal. She fell asleep on Cohen's mother's bed and, according to her later song, "Rainy Night House," Cohen stayed up all night watching her, "to see who in the world I might be." The lyric calls Cohen "a refugee from a wealthy family / you gave up all the golden factories to see who in the world he might be." The song, Mitchell subsequently acknowledged, was written as a farewell to their relationship. In time, Mitchell voiced contradictory sentiments about Cohen. On the one hand, she conceded, he had been a major influence on her lyrics, and taught her to plumb the depths of her experience for material. On the other, she categorized him as a mere "boudoir poet" who plagiarized other writers' work, and said dismissively, "He owns the phrase 'naked body,' for example. It appears in every one of his songs."

JONI MITCHELL: I briefly liked Leonard Cohen, though once I read Camus and Lorca, I started to realize that he had taken a lot of lines from those books, which was disappointing to me.

BARRIE WEXLER: Leonard used to say, "Good writers borrow, great writers steal." He never said the line was his—I just assumed it was. Later, I read the quote was credited to T. S. Eliot. And later still, that Eliot confessed to W. H. Auden that he'd boosted the line from Picasso, who said, "Good artists copy, great artists steal."

JUDY COLLINS: It was not a terrific ending. Joni wrote "That Song About the Midway" about Leonard, so she says. Sounds right: the festival, the guy, the jewel in the ear.

Part of the lyric reads, "You were betting on some lover, you were shaking up the dice / And I thought I saw you cheating once or twice, once or twice." Mitchell's "A Case of You" is almost certainly about Cohen as well. It virtually quotes his mother Masha saying, "Stay with him if you can / But be prepared to bleed."

Five days later, Cohen appeared with Collins again, at the Rheingold Music Festival in New York's Central Park. In a sense, Cohen reimbursed Collins for her generosity.

JUDY COLLINS: That's why Leonard and I felt so grateful to one another. I pushed him on the stage and, according to him, made him famous, and he said to me, "I love that you're recording my songs and please don't stop. What I don't understand is why you're not writing songs." I went home to my grand piano and sat down and wrote "Since You've Asked" in forty minutes, [though] the next one took five years. But it was because he asked me and the way he asked.

AVIVA LAYTON: There were oceans of people. Judy introduced him and he was trembling with terror. He stopped midway through "Suzanne" and said the most beautiful thing—I wrote it down—"Today my guitar is full of tears and feathers."

One July weekend that summer, Cohen attended his friend Robert Hershorn's wedding to the former Francine Loyer, a dress designer and boutique owner.

FRANCINE HERSHORN: It was at Temple Beth Shalom, a Reform synagogue. We had a big party after at a studio where Leonard worked. We did the demo of his first album in our living room on Pine Avenue. Leonard had introduced me to Robert. He was big and scary at first—intimidating. They were the intellectual scene at the time. And I was ten years younger. They were very close, Leonard and Robert. They had a lot of fun together and used to argue about all kinds of intellectual subjects, all the books in fashion. They were big fans of the *I Ching*.

PATRICIA NOLIN: The first I heard of Rumi, the great Persian poet—from Robert Hershorn. Shams Tabrizi, the love of Rumi—from Robert Hershorn. He was very, very bright and intellectually curious and introduced Leonard to that stuff. I liked Robert, except when he nodded—from heroin. He was very funny, very curious about everything, very hospitable, a great host. He had great music. We hung around at his house all the time.

During one stay in Montreal, Cohen dropped in to see Irving and Aviva Layton. A bizarre scenario soon unfolded: Aviva's friend Niema Ash arrived after 11 p.m. with Jim Fjeld. Cohen complained that he couldn't get an erection and Ash offered to help. Irving Layton quickly wanted in on the action. Soon they were all naked.

JIM FJELD: Irving was fooling around and dropped his pants and showed his ass. That's how the ball got rolling. Niema was between them, giving them each a hand job, oh yes. Aviva was on my lap, naked, and aside from a bit of fondling, it never went further.

The session ended when the Laytons' son, David, wandered in from his bedroom.

JIM FJELD: Niema was very vivacious. She had a thing for any celebrity. A groupie—you could call her that. Leonard was an unusual person. He was very intense. He wasn't lighthearted. We all smoked a bit of pot, though maybe not that evening. Niema later called herself a channel between these two great literary figures.

In July, Cohen performed at Expo '67 in Montreal—his first full-fledged appearance before a hometown audience.

LEWIS FUREY: I was working at the Pavillon de la Jeunesse Musicale—my summer job. I knew his poems—an English poet who talked about the streets on which I lived. There were other Montreal poets, but to sell ten thousand books was real popularity. He was playing his guitar and everyone was sitting on the floor. It seemed like an in place to be. I wasn't that impressed—I was a bit snobbish about folk music at that point. It didn't really interest me.

CHRIS NUTTER: Leonard was sucking on a lemon before going on. I really liked his guitar skills initially. It surprised me that he knew how to do [rolling arpeggios]. I wasn't sure about his voice, but I did notice that he had a good ear, and that makes all the difference. Plus, sucking on the lemon helped.

FRANK VITALE: I was also working at the Youth Pavilion, cooking fries and burgers. He was eager and energetic. He handed out candles to everyone that were lit for atmosphere, then sat down with his guitar and sang.

Not long after, Furey—then still known as Lewis Greenblatt—called Cohen.

LEWIS FUREY: I had a collection of thirty poems and felt some urgency about publishing them, so the world could discover what a genius I was. I found his number in the phone book and he met me at the Bistro. I thought I'd just leave them and he'd call me later, but he ordered coffee and started to read them, on the spot. I sat there for an hour and he read them carefully and then talked about them, very generously. I remember asking him if he thought I should publish and he said, "Ya know, there's no rush." A way of being so kind. He was saying all the things I wanted to hear, to encourage me. And it started a relationship. He said, "Come and show me your next poems." He gave me his address and said, "Don't call. Just ring the bell."

BARRIE WEXLER: Cohen told people to drop by anytime, his entire life. It wasn't really a function of spontaneity as much as he simply didn't want to be shackled by appointments. If he was working, he'd just ignore the bell.

Another evening, Cohen watched the Stormy Clovers perform at Expo's Ontario Pavilion.

ANNE FOUGERE: We were at a table at the back. I lit a cigarette and the entire pack of matches burst into flame. I managed to blow them out, but I was horrendously embarrassed. Leonard just smiled. His goodness shone through. And it was not phony. It was that compassionate, Buddhist empathy. I felt his smile enter my soul to speak of forgiveness.

A few days later, members of the band and their partners hung out with Cohen in the backyard of his mother's house in Westmount.

ANNE FOUGERE: We were all on a blanket. I was sitting directly across from Leonard, gazing in awe at his profound eyes. I felt I was in the company of one of our universe's most incredible beings. I'd never met anybody with that intensity. He had that in his essence. I was too shy to speak, but as he spoke, I saw the colours, heard the music, saw the shape of his words. I was so mesmerized that I couldn't understand a word he said. My mind flew into the beauty of his poet's voice.

DAVID FOUGERE: That day, he spoke of a dream he had for the future, [of] a travelling band. They would gather before every performance to pray for light. He said, "I could see myself doing this for the rest of my life."

In his later years, Cohen and his bandmates often did exactly that—holding prayerful moments in the greenroom before heading to the stage. Fougere had written a tribute song to Cohen, "I Met a Good Man," and wanted to perform it for him. He recruited Chris Nutter to accompany him on oboe, and the two drove to Cohen's mother's house.

CHRIS NUTTER: We get there, there's a big fire truck outside and several firemen in the living room moving about in hats and slickers. The mother wasn't there. A young lady—beautiful, quiet, French, serious, sombre—was there. They were having a private thing. Leonard allowed us to come in and they had a break. The red light on the truck was flashing. Leonard opened the door a little and I said, "Happy fire, Leonard." He took us into the kitchen and gave us diet cola. The girl disappeared while Leonard dealt with us. He gave us a lecture on the importance of benedictions. Then we performed the song, in the living room. He'd been burning a chest of old love poems in his mother's fireplace and, as he admitted, had nearly burned down his mother's house.

ANNE FOUGERE: We arrived just as the firemen were leaving. Leonard was shaking each fireman's hand with sincerity, saying, "I could say you saved my life." We laughed as he explained that the fire had gotten out of hand. He surmised that the fire couldn't digest his poems.

DAVID FOUGERE: "I met a good man one time. He turned me on. I was sleeping at the time, and when I woke up he was gone. Never saw him again, but I've heard his songs. They say a good man has a hard, hard time just to get along." Those were the lyrics. I think we interrupted a date in progress. I remember him giving me fifty dollars before we left, which I did not want, but was too broke to refuse.

Other young artists came to seek his assistance or pay homage, among them David Solway, who was en route to Greece.

DAVID SOLWAY: I went up to his apartment and he said, "Why are you going?" And I explained—I had just discovered Kazantzakis and seen *Zorba the Greek.* Then Marianne said she had a house on Hydra and, if I agreed to tutor her son, Axel, she'd let me stay at her house. I'd just sold a script to the CBC, had $400 in my pocket—an airplane ticket—and now free rent. So this was the most important effect Leonard had on my life, through Marianne—enabling me to go to Hydra. I spent five years of my life in Greece—Hydra, Crete, Paxos, Corfu. I never did tutor Axel, though.

SANDRA ANDERSON: Leonard once told me he considered David Solway to be a better poet than either Irving or himself. Later, I asked Irving about his reaction to this. He said that it had some merit, but he felt it would be more accurate to say that David was a better wordsmith.

PETER VAN TOORN: I was applying for a Canada Council grant and called him up and asked if he'd give me a reference. He said, "Well, read them to me." I said, "I'm not a very good reader. Can I drop them in your mailbox?" So I did. And I got the grant.

Back in New York, Cohen got an anxious call one day from Barrie Wexler.

BARRIE WEXLER: I was still living with my parents. Things weren't going well. Lewis Greenblatt and I were planning to get a place together but hadn't yet found one. I called Leonard and asked if I could stay at his flat for a few weeks. He was noncommittal and said he'd get back to me. A few days later, a letter arrived, addressed to "Master Barrie Wexler." In those days, my parents thought he was a terrible influence. They didn't know much about him, except that he wrote poems, and didn't think he had much of a future. The Master Barrie honorific—I wasn't yet eighteen—had a modestly calming effect on my British mother. Inside the envelope was a vintage postcard of a girl at a vanity mirror and a one-hundred-dollar bill, a fortune in those days. On the back of the postcard, he'd written: "prefer not to disturb the dust. leonard."

Among the music journalists Cohen met that fall was Ellen Sander. Shortly after, they ran into each other at a party.

ELLEN SANDER: Unlike anyone else there, Leonard was wearing a suit and tie. He looked like a contented and curious fine-art collector, which I suppose he was. I complimented him on his costume and he lowered his voice and turned his head sideways towards me, saying, "When you're really broke, it's important to look rich." He couldn't help smiling on the word "really." We both laughed, me in my jeans, well-worn boots, and ninety-nine-cent lipstick. This was right in the middle of recording his first album, but we didn't discuss it. We just talked about personal stuff—moodiness, dislocation, New York, the tyranny of news. We were not terribly close, but he was always really sweet to me.

In August, Cohen and Joni Mitchell both performed at the Mariposa Folk Festival, north of Toronto. Cohen also chaired a ninety-minute session featuring new talent. Reviewing Cohen's performance, *Toronto Star* reporter Peter Goddard said he "sounded emasculated. But like the early Bob Dylan, Cohen's technical inadequacy on the guitar and his penchant for stereotyped chord changes took little away from his lyrics . . . His imagery is often flagrantly sexual though always in taste." Yet another reviewer said, "Cohen philosophized in soft, serious, almost monotonous tones, but thrilled those who are entranced by his writings."

Later that summer, Cohen returned to Hydra for a few weeks.

DAVID SOLWAY: Marianne was there with Axel, and Leonard was sometimes there, but often not, and Marianne would have an affair. So did Leonard, of course, but you know how we felt then—a man could sow his seed. He was a wild thing. Somehow, I remember from our conversations that this was Leonard's attitude—the man could have affairs, this was understood, but the woman would be faithful. I don't know if he knew about hers. But she did have a liaison with George Slater, who lived on the island and had lost an eye to a pool cue in a bar fight. All of that went on. The island was a mad place. What really struck me with great force is that one day, Leonard appeared with Marianne, walking by, hand in hand, and George walks by [in] the other direction. I happened to be there and saw the covert glance of mutual understanding exchanged between Marianne and George. I said nothing, of course. Marianne did not know I knew, but everyone on the island knew something was going on. The Greeks likely did not care. To them, all foreigners were crazy. But it hurt me. I couldn't say anything. There was this marvellous man—yes, with failings and flaws. So did Irving [have flaws]. So did I.

It was during that visit, apparently, that electric telephone lines finally were installed on the island. The birds began appearing soon after. Making Cohen a cup of cocoa, Ihlen later recalled that when she handed him his guitar, he strummed it and said, "Like a bird on the wire."

LEONARD COHEN: I had come there with some myth of having lost, abandoned, the modern world . . . Suddenly there was this symbol of modernity straight across my window. My window looked out at a beautiful lane where there was an almond tree in full bloom, and suddenly there were these horizontal violations of my perfect window, and of course, I was angry and disappointed. But I knew there was no point in entertaining these kinds of emotions because it was useful and we could have light and telephones. And while I was having these conflicted feelings . . . a bird came, probably the wire's first bird, because I think it had just gone up overnight. And the bird just perched on the wire, as if [it] had been strung there for that specific purpose. I believe that was the genesis of the song.

Ihlen pointed out that the birds looked like musical notes and suggested he write a song about it.

MARIANNE IHLEN: I gave him the guitar. We looked out of the window. We saw the birds landing on the wires. He had not been able to create or write or sing or do anything for weeks, and was in a very, very deep, deep depression.

BARRIE WEXLER: The almond tree belonged to his neighbour Elena. It cast a shadow through the window that flickered against the white-washed walls inside. He once described it in a poem, but I'm not sure it was published.

MAX LAYTON: You see echoes of my father in some of Leonard's stuff. "Bird on a Wire." "In the midst of my fever, large as Europe's pain. The birds hopping on the blackened wires were instantly electrocuted." That's what Leonard means by "like a bird on a wire." The two ideas would come together.

En route back to New York, Cohen chaperoned young Axel Jensen and his friend Athena Gassoumis, daughter of the artist Demetri Gassoumis, to Summerhill, the experimental British school; he had paid tuition for the first semester and a little more. He later wrote to Ihlen that he'd had a drink with its founder and principal, A. S. Neill, and, clearly trying to reassure her about the decision to send her son to boarding school at age seven, said "I'd trust him with my soul." He also apologized—for being "very hard" on her during their time together.

MARIA COHEN VIANA: She had sent [Axel] there at Leonard's request, because he wanted her to come to New York with him. Marianne had asked a woman who had a child of Axel's age to raise Axel. When she said no, Axel was shipped off to Summerhill, where he was bullied. That's why Marianne always blamed herself for Axel ending up where he did. She once wrote that there were more ways to lose a son than by death.

BARRIE WEXLER: Marianne blamed her son's mental illness on the LSD that Big Axel had given him in India when he was fifteen, not on his being sent to Summerhill.

In New York, the album recording sessions hit another snag. Cohen and John Simon were at an impasse.

CHRIS DARROW: Simon had added strings, and Cohen didn't want to sound like that. My guess is Simon was trying to minimize Leonard's [musical] involvement and make the arrangements *be* the song.

Soon Simon began to attend to other projects. According to Bob Johnston, who was working at CBS at the time, Cohen eventually asked for permission to finish the album on his own.

JOHN SIMON: That was okay with me. Subsequently, he ditched some of my arrangements and substituted some exotic instruments from a band called Kaleidoscope. There was no reason for that except, as

Leonard said at the time, "There's no accounting for taste." As brilliant as Leonard was, I don't agree with that. Your taste is influenced by what you heard growing up, the associations you made with it or heard about it from your peers and how it moved you—in a place a few feet lower than your brain.

Years later, Cohen would adopt a diplomatic line about Simon, maintaining that, after laying down guitar and voice tracks, and an occasional bass, "Simon presented me with the finished record, but I felt there were some eccentricities in his arrangements that I objected to. John Simon was great, and much greater than I understood at the time."

By this time, Cohen had met and become completely enamoured with the singer Nico, née Christa Päffgen, a disciple of Andy Warhol and an occasional member of Lou Reed's Velvet Underground. Nico spurned him, insisting she was only interested in younger men, but did offer friendship.

LEONARD COHEN: I was lighting candles, performing incantations, and wearing amulets, anything to have her fall in love with me, but she never did.

They likely met at the Dom, on St. Marks Place, the band's home. Though she also appeared at Max's Kansas City, a restaurant on Park Avenue South, the hot spot for hip culture.

BARRIE WEXLER: Max's was a scene out of a Fellini movie. A who's who of the New York art world with a smattering of rock and rollers. Warhol's underground "superstars," the nucleus of the inner sanctum in the back, would lounge around, half-naked in trashy underwear, wearing dog collars. Cohen described Nico as the Marlene Dietrich of nihilistic rock. He said it was perfect irony that the most beautiful woman he'd ever met should be completely disinterested in him.

At least two Cohen songs, "Take This Longing" and "Joan of Arc" ("such a cold and lonesome heroine"), are thought to be inspired in part by Nico. She may have inspired other lyrics as well, including "Winter Lady" and "Last Year's Man." An idealized form of her also appears in Cohen's *Selected Poems 1956–1968*. Later, Warhol called Cohen's first album "Nico with whiskers." Remembering a review that said Cohen's singing was like "dragging one note over the entire chromatic scale," Warhol said he "couldn't help thinking of all those hours he'd spent listening to Nico." In a subsequent interview, Cohen also said that he had made a film and two screen tests for Warhol with Nico. It's not known what became of those.

One night at Max's, Cohen was approached by Lynn Myers, a waitress who had just been fired. She later recounted her story to Yvonne Sewall-Ruskin for her book *High on Rebellion: Inside the Underground at Max's Kansas City*.

LYNN MYERS: I was really, really depressed and the only person I thought I could talk to on the entire planet, I decided, was Leonard Cohen. I'd never even seen the guy. It just came into my little drug-abused mind. I'd read all his books and really gotten into his music and I was obsessed. I only wanted to talk to Leonard Cohen and was convinced I had to find him. I was doing one of those manipulations that you do with God: "If there's really a God, you'll let Leonard Cohen save my life."

At the bar, Myers noticed a man staring at her.

LYNN MYERS: I just walked up to him and said, "Are you Leonard Cohen?" He said, "Yes!" I said, "I've been waiting for you," and I started talking. "I really need to talk to you, but I'm working and this is my last night." I go back to working my tables and at one point he comes up and says, "I'm leaving, leave with me!" I said, "I can't . . . I have to work until 4 a.m." This is what the insanity of drugs does. Just because I was fired, that had nothing to do with it, I was responsible. He leaves, and now I really start to cry. Here's the love of my life, God had sent him to me, and I let him get away. Well, he came back at four in the morning and got me. We left and drove around New York and went to a coffee shop and drank coffee and ate breakfast and sang songs and made out until around eleven in the morning.

That fall, Columbia Records hired a young woman to work in its international marketing department—Bunny Freidus.

BUNNY FREIDUS: Leonard was a pivotal character in my career [which lasted twenty-seven years]. I had seen a PBS documentary about him—*Ladies and Gentlemen, Mr. Leonard Cohen*—and was just entranced. I thought, "This man is an artist." I listened to it and thought, "This is really terrific. I don't know about America, but he's just so spot on for Europe." I came in after John Simon had left the project, but was aware of some dissatisfaction in the company on creative calls. I was aware of Leonard's frustration later, when he was ignored. But I decided he'd be the first artist I'd [take] overseas, do some interviews and get him known. It came out of my personal enthusiasm for this intriguing man. Everyone thought I was crazy.

One early morning, after a drink at the White Horse Tavern in Greenwich Village, Cohen returned to his New York home, the Chelsea Hotel.

BARRIE WEXLER: When he first registered, Leonard asked for room 205, where Dylan Thomas spent his final days. Staying there had become a ritual among up-and-coming. But the room was already taken, so he ended up in 424.

On this occasion—the event has usually been dated to 1968, but Cohen himself said it occurred in 1967—he met twenty-five-year-old Janis Joplin in the elevator.

LEONARD COHEN: I said to her, "Are you looking for someone?" She said, "Yes, I'm looking for Kris Kristofferson." I said, "Little lady, you're in luck, I am Kris Kristofferson." Those were generous times. Even though she knew that I was someone shorter than Kris Kristofferson, she never let on. Great generosity prevailed in those doom decades. She wasn't looking for me, she was looking for Kris Kristofferson. I wasn't looking for her, I was looking for Brigitte Bardot. But we fell into each other's arms through some process of elimination. The last time I saw her was on Twenty-Third Street. She said, "Hey man, you in town to read poetry for old ladies?" That was her view of my career.

Out of that experience would later come his song "Chelsea Hotel." On September 22, 1967, the day after his thirty-third birthday, Cohen had visitors at the Chelsea Hotel—folk singer Ramblin' Jack Elliott and Phyllis Major, whom Cohen had romanced on Hydra. Elliott, who was carrying a tiny Swiss tape recorder, had just been to watch the famous RMS *Queen Mary* sail out of the Port of New York for the last time—her one-thousandth Atlantic crossing. He had taped the proceedings.

RAMBLIN' JACK ELLIOTT: The other side of the tape is Leonard. He was lying on his bed with a battery-powered piano, ten or twelve keys, and he had it on his lap, singing a song. And I thought, "What fine poetry. Too bad he can't sing."

On October 22, the record still unfinished, Cohen went to hear Nico perform at the Scene, a basement club on West Forty-Sixth Street. The opening act was a West Coast–based band, Kaleidoscope.

CHRIS DARROW: Kaleidoscope was myself, Solomon Feldthouse, David Lindley, and Chester Crill. We were a very eclectic group, very popular, but didn't sell a lot of records. That night, we were opening for Nico, who I'd already met in L.A., just after she fucked Jim Morrison. German, detached, playing a Hammond B-3, not a great voice. But she went over really well. It was opening night, so Andy Warhol was there, Edie Sedgwick, his whole entourage, David Clayton-Thomas. It was a heavy night. Tiny Tim was the MC.

After their set, Darrow was approached by Cohen.

CHRIS DARROW: He was the palest guy I'd ever seen. He looked almost like a ghost. He was wearing a black leather jacket and carrying a black leather briefcase. He said, "I really like you guys. Would you be interested in playing on my album?" I had no idea who he was. The next day we were in his apartment, sitting on the floor—might have been the Chelsea. To be quite honest, he was not very good. We had to sit down with him and go through all the songs. A lot of it was out of time. Later, in the studio, there was no producer. His guitar skills? I don't think he hardly had any. I'm gonna be quite blunt about this—I think if he hadn't gotten us, that record would not be the record it was. We changed the tone of it in his favour. Because that record, James Taylor's *Sweet Baby James* [Darrow played on that as well], and the first Bob Dylan record [*Bob Dylan*] are considered *the* singer-songwriter records. Leonard was trying like mad to finish. I know we were paid scale to play, but I never saw a dime. I played on a couple of songs, mandolin on "So Long, Marianne," and bass on "Teachers." But there were no credits on the album. It was all done fast, chop-chop, because we were playing gigs at night. Everything was work. We weren't sitting around chatting. He had the songs, but we didn't think—how can I put it?—that he knew how they were supposed to go. He didn't fit into the equation of a singer-songwriter in 1967, and we did. I think Bob Johnston, who's also not credited, did the mixing. But we got along well. Leonard liked and understood what we were doing and went along with it. He was not imposing his ego—not at all. Chester Crill later called the record an abomination because too many things had been put into it. From the standpoint of technique, he's probably right. But otherwise, I disagree, because the songs off that album are the classics.

HARVEY KUBERNIK: Darrow was the guy that saved that record.

Richard Goldstein, interviewing Cohen for the *Village Voice* on the eve of the album's release, called him "a Visceral Romantic . . . He suffers gloriously in every couplet. Even his moments of ecstasy seem predicated on hours of refined despair." Once again, Cohen struck his default motif—troubadour. "I sometimes see myself in the Court of Ferdinand, singing my songs to girls over a lute." The other familiar note was gloomy self-effacement. "I think my album is going to be very spotty and undistinguished," he told Goldstein. "I blame this on my total unfamiliarity with the recording studio. They tried to make my songs into music. I got put down all the time . . . I thought I was going to . . . crack up . . . Around 30 or 35 is the traditional age for the suicide of the poet, did you know that? That's the age when you finally understand that the universe does not succumb to your command."

The back cover of the album, *Songs of Leonard Cohen*, featured the Anima Sola—a painting he'd found near the Chelsea Hotel. It depicted a young woman in chains surrounded by flames. Cohen described it as "the triumph of the spirit over matter." The front cover used a sepia shot from a railway station photo booth. In another interview, with the *New York Times*, Cohen returned to the theme of societal convulsion that he was witnessing. Although revolution was in the air, that spirit alone was not sufficient. Indeed, Cohen carefully distanced himself from the political left, arguing that it contained the seeds of its own fascist potential. Over the following decades, his private political views would move steadily to the right.

LEONARD COHEN: Revolutionaries, in their heart of hearts, are excited by the tyranny they wield . . . I'm afraid that when the Pentagon is finally . . . taken, it will be by guys wearing uniforms very much like the ones worn by the guys defending it.

Others saw Cohen as wanting to straddle both sides of the political divide. His friend Ruth Roskies Wisse would later recall that "Leonard took no part" in the student revolution of the 1960s. She termed his militaristic wardrobe and shaven head a "trivializing camouflage" that paid off.

RUTH ROSKIES WISSE: Aesthetically, temperamentally, he was as removed from the boorish radicals as a Romanov from the Bolsheviks. But still he saw his opportunity among the young. He concentrated programmatically on the first-person singular and cultivated an attitude of philosophical indifference, as though by opposing politics altogether, he could avoid having to take sides. For the public record, though, he fell right into step with the flower children's brigades.

A few weeks later, on January 27, 1968, Cohen, in London, appeared on BBC's *Once More with Felix*, with Julie Felix, then the queen of Britain's folk music scene. They sang a duet of "Hey, That's No Way to Say Goodbye."

JULIE FELIX: He'd sent me a copy of his album. I talked to my producer, Stanley Dorfman, and asked him if Leonard could be on the show. He was Jewish too, so there was a kinship there. We were both at the same level of inadequacy on guitar. We spent time together then. He was still with Marianne. We talked about Axel. He said, "Come and stay with Marianne and me in Hydra." Later, I was on my way to a music festival in Split, so on the way, I went to Greece.

Songs of Leonard Cohen ultimately reached number ten on the British charts and helped him establish a significant profile in Europe.

HARVEY KUBERNIK: Leonard understood media. He did his first interview with *Melody Maker.* He knew about England as the gateway to Europe.

HERSH SEGAL: One day in Carnaby Street, some very with-it people said to me, "You have to hear this new record: *Leonard Cohen.*" That was the first time I heard his album. I was as surprised as anyone.

The reaction of friends in the Montreal poetry community was mixed.

NORMAN ALEXANDER: I distinctly remember listening to his first record. His singing was very depressing. I didn't tell him. I just didn't listen to the record again. I remember saying to my wife, "This is ridiculous. He's so depressed."

MAX LAYTON: My whole opinion of him changed when I heard [that album], which was really great stuff. At the same time, the songs merely confirmed that he was not really a great poet. He's a singer-songwriter, and a great one. But poetry is higher on the scale of virtues than singer/songwriter. Same with the novels—some powerful scenes. But this whole idea of being on the low end of things—a beautiful loser, the energy of slaves, this putting himself down, was a bit easy, wringing what he could out of that stance.

By the spring, Cohen was in Los Angeles to explore scoring a movie based on "Suzanne." He checked into the Landmark Motor Hotel in West Hollywood [now the Highland Gardens Hotel], where, three years later, Janis Joplin would accidentally overdose on heroin. Joplin was there at the time, as were folk singers Bobby Neuwirth and Eric Andersen, who was recording an album, *Avalanche.*

ERIC ANDERSEN: Everybody was preparing for dinner, the sun was sinking, and I was sitting alone with my feet in the pool, and this guy walked over, rolled up his pants, and sat down next to me, and introduced himself. It was Leonard Cohen. I knew his poetry, of course. He told me that my song "Violets of Dawn" was the song that got him to write songs, to take the leap from pen and paper to guitar. We must have talked for half an hour. Then he came with Phyllis Major, this lovely girl he knew, to a couple of my sessions. [Major later went out with Andersen too, as well as Neuwirth. She married Jackson Browne, and committed suicide in 1976.] Leonard was always a great, charming, courtly individual. As wandering minstrels, we'd run into each other from time to time.

It was at the Landmark, Cohen later said, that he worked on "Story of Isaac," a song that implicitly assails the sacrifice of children in Vietnam and indeed all modern wars.

JAMES DIAMOND: Cohen's treatment of Abraham . . . is nuanced, tinged with both reverence and revulsion . . . The present child-sacrificers are "schemers," not driven by a "vision." Misguided or not, Abraham sets out sincerely to accomplish something much larger than himself, to pursue a vision that connotes ideals, that teaches, that leaves a sacred legacy. A scheme, on the other hand, conveys a sense of deviousness and of immoral plotting to exploit others for one's own benefit.

Uncertainty, however, continued to dog him. Writing to Ihlen via postcard, Cohen insisted that he had "abandoned the career of singing." Perhaps he only meant that he had abandoned performing because the following month, living with Joni Mitchell, he started recording his second album, *Songs from a Room*, with David Crosby. Crosby had been Mitchell's lover—in fact, she had introduced Cohen to Crosby. At least three songs were recorded, including versions of "Bird on a Wire" and "You Know Who I

Am"; Crosby sang harmony on the latter tune. But their professional relationship quickly sundered, apparently over creative differences. Mitchell would later complain that Crosby was an incompetent producer—he had produced her first album. Cohen may have agreed. Crosby himself later conceded that he didn't know what to do with a voice like Cohen's, and encouraged him to speak the lyrics rather than sing. Cohen balked, and subsequently completed the album in Nashville with Bob Johnston. In L.A., Cohen reconnected with his friend Steve Sanfield.

SANDY STEWART: Steve took me up to his hotel in Beverly Hills to meet him. I didn't know who he was. He had this great guitar—a Ramirez, I think. He handed it to me, and though I played a little flamenco guitar, I had total stage fright. I just froze up and handed it back. He was just very gentle, sweet and nice—that was my main impression, which lasted through the years.

Renting a car, Cohen drove to Santa Barbara to stay with Sanfield and his girlfriend, Jacquie Bellon.

JACQUIE BELLON: It was a very intense two days. Leonard said to me, "Blessed art thou among women and blessed is the fruit of thy womb." No one had ever spoken to me in biblical terms. Well, we were young and gorgeous and foolish and brave and we laughed a lot. Leonard was very charismatic, and I loved him immediately. But there was tension—sexual tension—because of Steve, whose attitude was "she's my woman." It was very subtle, in the background, so there was this charged atmosphere. We all tried to navigate it as best we could. Nothing ever happened, but there was definitely mutual attraction. I think Leonard was attracted to me, as he was to many women. He was so generous and funny and kind—really unusual. He was just immediately at ease. We lived in a not-funky but minimal little house with practically nothing in it. We were very poor, and I don't think he had any money then either. Steve was taking a woodworking course—he and Leonard took a night class together and came back with a piece of wood, literally, they had sanded. One day, Steve had to be somewhere, and while we were waiting, Leonard and I climbed into a tree and ate ice cream. He said, "I've never done this before." There was minimal drug use at the time—maybe marijuana.

In the late 1950s, Cohen had written a short story called "The View from the Tree." And years later, when Wexler cowrote *The Leonard Cohen Show* for the Centaur Theatre in Montreal, he situated the central character—Cohen—in a tree house, observing the action onstage.

BARRIE WEXLER: There is a kind of symbiotic relationship between Leonard's life and his art. In *Beautiful Losers*, the narrator inherits F's childhood tree house, where he later honeymoons with his wife—who F had fucked. All that's missing from that scene in the novel are the ice-cream cones.

JACQUIE BELLON: Of course, he was still with Marianne. He and Steve talked about her. Steve and Marianne had been lovers, while she was with Leonard, so that was part of the uncomfortableness. They both did that to each other. It was awkward, but okay. You have to see it in the context of the times. It was the Summer of Love. When [Cohen] left, he left behind a black Italian designer turtleneck. I still have it. It's very small.

It was as he was leaving California that Cohen—in search of a new producer—bumped into Bob Johnston, then running Columbia Records' Nashville operation. Johnston invited him to record there. He readily agreed—Nashville had been his original destination when he embarked on his music career in 1966. He would arrive there that fall.

By May 1968, Cohen was back on Hydra. Preparing for the trip, he discovered that his passport had expired. In those days, to arrange a fast renewal, he had to go to Ottawa. When Cohen arrived, he was told he needed to have someone he knew guarantee his application. Knowing no one in town, he went through the phone book and called a Jewish lawyer, Hy Soloway.

STEPHEN VICTOR: Hy calls me on the intercom and says, "Beano"—that was my nickname—"there's somebody you have to meet, who you know." I go into Hy's office and Leonard tells me how he called Hy to be his guarantor, but Hy said, "I can't be your guarantor—I have to know you for two years. Do you have any connection to anyone at Ottawa?" Cohen said, "Yes, I was a unit head at Camp B'nai B'rith." Hy said, "Well, the only lawyer I know connected to the camp is Stephen Victor." That's how I became his guarantor. He didn't remember my name, but he remembered Beano. He says, "How much do I owe you?" I said, "I can't charge you anything." Six or seven months later, I get a copy of his book of poetry in the mail. "Thank you for your help when I needed it. Your friend, Leonard." Years later, during a move, we sold it to someone for twenty-five dollars.

A young Montrealer, Marianne Feaver, then living in Athens, came to Hydra for a visit. On her first night, she met Cohen in a bar.

MARIANNE FEAVER: Low ceilings, low lights, an intimate setting, everyone seated around the walls. It was decided that we would all play a game. I remember being chosen to be the focus of one session. When I returned to the room after stepping out, I was told I had to guess what everyone was thinking, but they would only answer either yes or no to the questions. If I asked a question ending in a consonant, they would say yes, and if it ended in a vowel, they would say no. The long and the short of it was that that evening, I bared my soul like I never had before—nor ever would again—in front of people I didn't know. This experience, although wrenching, was profoundly moving. I learned a lot about myself. Who masterminded this game? Leonard. This man didn't make small talk. He was deeply interested in people and would go straight to their innermost selves. It was such a pleasure to spend time with him because he was caring. And yes, handsome and charismatic.

That same summer, Cohen also met twenty-one-year-old Greek actress and weaver Despina Politi, who lived in Athens.

DESPINA POLITI: I'd met him once before, but briefly. And I knew Marianna. We swam together. Then we heard he was coming and I wondered if that would be awkward for her. One night, I was sitting at Douskos Taverna when Leonard turned up. I liked Leonard a lot. We went for walks and, on his terrace, he played his guitar—I was begging him. He played so beautifully. He didn't sing; he just played. I had no idea who he was. They told me he was a famous singer, but I couldn't have cared less. I'd never read his poetry. I wasn't interested. I still haven't. But he was such a nice man. So it was a friendship, not the closest of buddies, and he was a very good friend to me. We walked and talked and swam and spent nights on the rocks off Kamini. I don't think I asked him for anything, but when we were sitting together, he would look at you and try to see what was occupying your mind.

BARRIE WEXLER: Despina was breathtaking, a classic beauty who looked as though she had walked off of an ancient Greek urn. Leonard once visited her at her mother's flat in Athens. Prior to his arrival, Despina put on one of his albums. Her mother had no idea who Cohen was, but, anxious that her daughter find an eligible bachelor, said something like, "For Christ's sake, turn that depressing thing off before your boyfriend gets here, or he's going to run straight out the door."

DESPINA POLITI: That's true. She said, "Take this music off. It's so whiny." I said, "Oh, it's the singer who's coming."

A few years later, Politi was in Athens when Cohen called.

DESPINA POLITI: He was at the Hilton and leaving for Paris that afternoon. "Can I see you? Come down." I lived on Lycabettus Hill, and the night before, I'd had a visitor and my heart was broken. I was crying all night, my nose was red, my eyes were puffy. I said, "I can't come down. Come here." So he said "all right." He arrives and I went to the kitchen to make him coffee, come back with his coffee, and we talked and talked and talked. Then he said, "I have to go, but come with me to the airport." So we take a taxi and we talked and then he pulled out my passport. Because while I was making his coffee, he searched around and found my passport. "Come to Paris with me." And so I did. After Paris, he had to go to London and he said, "Do you want to come?" He booked a hotel room for me next to his, and I went. There, he sent me to see the palmist Mir Bashir.

On another occasion, Politi recalls, they shared a hotel room and Cohen asked her how she liked to be touched. She told him she liked to have her back rubbed.

DESPINA POLITI: He spent the entire night rubbing my back. He did not sleep. He was still rubbing it in the morning when I woke. The whole night. That's the kind of man he was. The next day, we were in a pastry shop in Syntagma Square and he said, "Do you think people are equal? Everyone is equal?" And I said, "Yes." And he said, "No, you're mistaken."

It was during this period that Cohen developed a strong interest in Scientology.

BARRIE WEXLER: It was Big Axel, Marianne's former husband, who first got Leonard interested in Scientology. Big Axel was quite into it, had an E-meter on the island, and did "eye-lock auditing" with Cohen. Marianne said Leonard had actually gone onto L. Ron Hubbard's boat with George Lialios, when the ship was docked in Scandinavia in the early sixties.

JUDY SCOTT: George told me he and Leonard became interested in Scientology shortly after *Dianetics* was published. I know he mentioned being on the ship with L. Ron Hubbard, but I'm not sure when. I'm pretty sure George did mention Copenhagen as the location.

HENRY ZEMEL: It was the sixties. Spiritually inclined people checked out what was going on spiritually, and Scientology was one of the things. It's a kind of brotherhood, so there's that kind of attraction. Zen ultimately got him. Leonard is a self-flagellator. He really liked the regimen.

BARRIE WEXLER: Cohen couldn't wait to get off the ship. He described it at various times in contradictory terms: as a big party, and as a paramilitary operation. He was frustrated because Hubbard was more interested in playing songs for him that he, Hubbard, had composed, than explaining his religious beliefs.

Although Cohen later dismissed his dalliance with Scientology as a mere flirtation, it was intense while it lasted. In one letter to Ihlen, written on Church of Scientology letterhead, he said that he was working to put it all together. "The work. The real work. The hardest work. I have begun it. My whole life has led me here." He stayed with it long enough to earn a certificate that declared him a Grade IV Release. And, as late as 1993, while aware that Scientology had become largely "scorned," he maintained in one interview that "from the view point of their data, information, their actual knowledge, their wisdom writings, it was not bad at all." On Hydra, Cohen talked Scientology with a young American writer, Dan Klein.

DAN KLEIN: I was very skeptical. It gave me the creeps. Anthony Kingsmill would tease Cohen a lot, because he was just starting to become a celebrity. Tease him about all the women who came running after him. Which they did. Oh yeah—it pissed me off. One time, we went to Athens and we sat in a café. We're both skinny, Jewish boys with big noses and lots of black hair. And women would come to the table—not knowing that he was a singer—it was just a magnet. To him and not to me—that's the pissed-off part. I don't know what it was. His eyes were liquid and appealing, but he wasn't flashing or preening. They were just drawn to him. People, particularly women, would come to the island, looking for him and sometimes stay. He was worshipped by many. I wouldn't say Cohen was super warm. But he was nice. He was in a dream. He probably—and for good reason—thought he was special. But he also longed for Buddhist transcendence.

PICO IYER: We're all used to men who can swagger into the room and, by being loud and commanding and articulate and masculine, magnetize attention. The fascination of Leonard was how he could come into the room and captivate by being quiet and invisible. He wasn't saying much, but, partly because he wasn't saying much, when he did speak, it felt like something coming up from the deep, a polished pebble coming from a deep well, the deep well of himself.

BARRIE WEXLER: Leonard was a masterful enchanter. He knew every trick in the book. He could conjure up himself.

Back in Montreal, he described his new spiritual interest to friends.

ANNE COLEMAN: It was at Don Owen's house in Westmount. There were just a few of us—myself, Don, and Judy Gault—they were quite close, though both were married—Robin Spry from the Film Board, and Leonard. Marianne was not there. He told us about his experiments with Scientology. He told us about how you hold two tin cans and are asked questions. [In Scientology, so-called auditors question subjects who hold a pair of cylindrical electrodes connected to the E-meter, or electro-psychometer.] He was taking it at least semiseriously, although I didn't sense he was deeply into it. Leonard was full of himself. That sounds as if he was obnoxious. He wasn't. He was compelling and convincing as someone with a special destiny. That evening, he floated the idea that perhaps he was the forever-awaited Jewish Messiah, come at last. He had to have been kidding, yet it felt almost believable. And maybe he wasn't kidding.

PATRICIA NOLIN: He tried to get us into it. He was in Scientology for about three months. He explained it all to us—how you [hooked up to] a machine and you get clear. Derek nearly fell for it. I didn't.

JULIE FELIX: I got involved with that. That was wicked. They hounded me, waiting outside my house in Denmark like locusts.

RALPH GIBSON: He got me up to Scientology for a week, once. We both walked on it, because it was too exoteric. He was a searching individual and went through many religions. I found it very low-grade material.

ISRAEL CHARNEY: I remember him talking about it at a bar on Crescent Street with Marcia Pacaud. It didn't smell good to me.

AVIVA LAYTON: As soon as the Scientologists felt Leonard might become a celebrity and started using that, he left.

The closer Cohen's star was drawn into the orbit of the music world, however, the further he seemed to move from Ihlen. Degree by painful degree, their relationship was unravelling.

BARRIE WEXLER: I once asked him how you know when a poem is finished. He said it was like the end of a relationship. Then the question became, how do you know when an affair is finished? He answered by paraphrasing da Vinci's famous quote: "These things are never finished, only abandoned." It happened by degrees, but at some point, he abandoned his relationship with Marianne.

MARIANNE IHLEN: We couldn't get anywhere. I didn't understand what he was saying, he didn't understand what I was saying. I could not put into words how I felt. Leonard naturally immersed himself in his writing, and continued with his songs.

ERICA POMERANCE: These things were not easy for him. He was not someone who would just let you go after you'd spent time in some kind of fusion. Leonard was probably feeling restless. He'd get to a point in a relationship where he felt there was something stagnating or blocking. It's a search for intimacy, but, as a lone figure, he must move on. It was a reflex, a persona.

ANN DIAMOND: All he said to me about Marianne was "She used to be willowy, but then she thickened." That's how he summed her up in 1981. She was married by then and had put on weight—and he was a pop star. At least he wrote to her for a few years. And she found a man who was ready to be real with her.

BARBARA LAPCEK: I know he regretted things—I could see that. I think he regretted leaving Marianne. He valued who she was.

Ihlen, meanwhile, remained on Hydra, where, that summer, she had met Jean-Marc Appert, a handsome young Frenchman who had begun his adult life selling candy floss on the streets of Paris.

DON LOWE: I remember the day Marianne and him got together. I was sitting in the port and—don't forget, he was a handsome dude back then. I knew that Jean-Marc had his eye on her and vice versa maybe. I see them come along, looking so happy, so beautiful together, holding hands. As they pass, I say to Marianne—she was just glowing—"What happened to you, Marianne?" And she just looked at me and said, "I got fed up with waiting, darling."

MORGANA PRITCHARD: Jean-Marc had been a model in Paris. He was gorgeous.

BARRIE WEXLER: Jean-Marc was an adventurous sort, dashing and full of vitality. He purchased a complete ruin at the top of the hill, and rebuilt it pretty much by himself, stone by stone.

BRANDON AYRE: Leonard never liked Jean-Marc.

JEAN-MARC APPERT: I'm not going to discuss it. The songs have all been sung. It's over. That's all I'm going to say.

But if Appert was a central factor in ending Cohen's long relationship with Ihlen, he was not the only one.

BARRIE WEXLER: Infidelity played a part, but the main cause of their demise was Cohen's unwillingness to commit. That, and the role Hydra played. The island becomes an integral part of any union it gives birth to. It fools you into thinking you own the attraction you share, but it belongs to that rock in the Aegean. Love seeded on Hydra is, by definition, doomed.

When you leave, the invisible partner in the union is left behind. The love you're sure will last beyond its shores dissolves without the life force Hydra provides. It's a bit like bumping into someone in the city you've had a holiday romance with. It's never the same off the beach.

HENRY ZEMEL: When you change the venue, it's no longer the picture postcard.

BARRIE WEXLER: Leonard said, "Once you've lived on Hydra, you can't live anywhere else, including Hydra." But he stole the line from Kenneth Koch, who, in turn, adapted it from what John Ashbery said, "After you've lived in Paris for a while, you don't want to live anywhere else, including Paris."

Folk singer Julie Felix blamed Cohen for the breakup.

JULIE FELIX: A few years later, I spent time with Marianne on Larkollen and wrote a song about Cohen. She indicated that he finally left because of some affair that she had.

> And now you write of madmen and of sailors on their quest
> And all the lovely ladies whom your poems have left undressed.
> Sadness stains your melting mouth but fire fills your tongue,
> While you pray that the angels
> Will believe the songs you've sung.

BARRIE WEXLER: It had nothing to do with an affair Marianne had. That was just a convenient excuse.

JULIE FELIX: Once, when he was visiting me in London, I sang him the song. We were going down in the elevator and he said, "Oh, that's really good. I like being the bad guy."

At one point, Marianne and Felix became lovers.

JULIE FELIX: It's one of the reasons I didn't get more involved with Leonard, because I'm a gay woman or bisexual. I wasn't really lovers with him. I've been to bed with him a couple of times. There was never a commitment. And that was understood. But I have a very deep connection with Leonard. I always felt that, a kindred spirit, being in a world that wasn't very sympathetic. We didn't talk a lot about music. We talked more about philosophical things and, later, about friends we'd known. We didn't party. We had private moments in London—sometimes he'd stay with me in Chelsea, but he preferred his own space. We'd sit in cafés on King's Road and talk and talk.

Other Cohen friends identified different causes for the final rift.

CAROL ZEMEL: Leonard was funny and charming and probably a great seducer. But I was a very good friend of Marianne's. We were intimate friends, very close. I'm not trying to turn her into some kind of saint. Eventually, she was unfaithful to him too. I guess the kicker for me was when I went to spend a landmark birthday with her in the 1990s. We went to her country house in Larkollen, on a fjord, all done with high good taste, because Marianna's grandmother danced with the king. She let you know that she had a lot of *yichus* [pedigree] in her family. So we were driving there and she mentioned Adam and Lorca [Cohen's children, by Suzanne Elrod]. And I said, "Why didn't you have a child [with him]?" And the answer I got from her was that she wasn't Jewish. That just freaked me out. This followed some rather saintly reference about Leonard's son always [being] welcome in the house on Hydra. Her tone was matter-of-fact. I was appalled.

Ihlen herself later confirmed that narrative on two occasions. She told her biographer that she'd have "loved to have his child, but he didn't want that. He never told me, but I sensed it was because I was not Jewish." And Alison Gold, a Hydra friend, quoted her as saying, "I was part of Leonard's secret life. I knew better than to have babies with him. Why? I couldn't give him Jewish babies."

CAROL ZEMEL: He was a hubristic *Kohen*—that's what he was. He took being a *Kohen* from Westmount very seriously. On some levels, he never *wasn't* being that. He was a highly moralizing man, highly judgemental, and highly seductive and brilliant, without question. I'm not saying there wasn't any humility there, but some of it was just a posture. [Marianne] always talked about Leonard with love—never complained. She was the all-enduring, forgiving muse—not that she stayed home, celibate. Robert Hershorn used to say that Marianne always ate from a smaller plate.

STEPHEN LACK: He was rabbinical—totally. He was a *Kohen*, priest class. He carried that, why wouldn't he? It's a major blessing. People say he was a Buddhist. No. He was Jewish and he was into Buddhism and Hinduism. He was looking for a connection. Religion is an aspect of depression relief. You sing songs to feel better. Where do you do it? In a religious setting.

PATRICIA NOLIN: The reason he said that to Marianne was charity, because it was less hurtful to tell Marianne he couldn't have kids with her because she wasn't Jewish rather than tell her, "You don't turn me on anymore." It's very Leonard-y—remain the good guy. Everyone knows that the period where you go up the stairs with your jeans around your ankles—that lasts two years, three years. Then it goes.

Felix, who first met Ihlen on Hydra in August 1968, also asked her about children.

JULIE FELIX: He made her have abortions. Five sounds about right. She told me. But he has that song ["You Know Who I Am"] where he says, "I need you to carry my children in / And I need you to kill a child."

BRANDON AYRE: I heard there were several abortions. Jean-Marc told me.

BARRIE WEXLER: It's difficult to believe that she wouldn't have said something to me in Larkollen about five abortions. She spoke about Leonard very candidly. It's also hard to imagine that he didn't want her to have a child because she wasn't Jewish. He didn't want anybody's child, period.

AVIVA LAYTON: Marianne was in great pain. I'll say it now, because they're all dead. Marianne was pregnant a few times, but she *knew* Leonard did not want to have kids, and she did not want to *burden* him. Leonard was the Poet. And she didn't have the babies. But if anyone deserved to have Leonard's kids, it was Marianne, because she respected his wishes.

CAROL ZEMEL: I once drove her to a hospital for what must have been an abortion. That was the discreet place you'd go, the [Catherine Booth] Salvation Army Hospital in the west end [of Montreal], with a lot of immigrant doctors. They were living on Aylmer and it was summer—1966, I think. It was hot. They were shocked [at the hospital], because all she had on was a dress and underpants and sandals. I must have left when she checked in. I don't know why I didn't stay. She didn't really explain it. She said, "I suddenly feel terribly sick." Leonard must have been away.

British documentary filmmaker Nick Broomfield met and began a short affair with Ihlen on Hydra in the summer of 1968. In his 2019 documentary, *Words of Love*, he disclosed that Ihlen visited him in Cardiff, Wales. She told him that she was pregnant with Cohen's child, and had him drive her to Bath for an abortion.

PETER KATOUNDAS: The *Songs of Love and Hate* album—there's this thing where he says something about "sterilizing the bitch" ["Diamonds in the Mine"]. And Morgana [Pritchard] told me that Marianne had had an abortion, which left her sterilized.

Screenwriter Norman Snider was also on Hydra in 1968.

NORMAN SNIDER: I rented a house from [Quebec painter] Marcella Maltais for forty bucks a month. The colonels had just taken over and they had these Hitlerian-style speeches coming out of the loudspeakers on the port. Here we were, trying to be as free as we could be, and living in a dictatorship. A lot of the Greeks distrusted us, the foreigners, and were careful of what they said, because of the political climate. Marianne was obviously really missing Leonard. And she was determined that I was a singer-songwriter, and was hiding it. I said no. I was trying to write a psychedelic novel and she insisted I was being too modest. Finally, I had to prove to her that I could not play a fucking lick on the guitar. This conversation occurred in her house—his house. She was a delightful, beautiful, sweet woman. David Solway [the Montreal poet], a Leonard imitator, was there with his guitar.

When Cohen heard about Jean-Marc Appert, the long, tumultuous relationship was finally in its death throes.

BARRIE WEXLER: That was his double standard at work. There was never a big breakup. Their connection just faded. The relationship may have spanned a decade, but the actual time they spent together could be measured in months. It shows you the myth a great song can create.

CAROL ZEMEL: Marianne never talked about a final breakup. She always maintained a lover's adoration for Leonard—and anyone he befriended—satisfied perhaps with her named position in the songs. I don't think she ever could imagine a "final" breakup. I have no take on it, except that Leonard embodied the true womanizer for me: relentless pursuit and courtship—the music went a long way—romance and abandonment. Courtly—affectedly so—but that was an elaborate and well-honed mask.

BARRIE WEXLER: Leonard told me Marianne had a more relaxed view of infidelity than he did—more European, Scandinavian. But keep in mind that with Cohen, the open wound was the real muse. Not "what nourishes me, destroys me," but the reverse: "what destroys me, nourishes me."

The wound, indeed, was transformed into art. As he noted in "So Long, Marianne," "You left when I said I was curious . . . I never said I was brave."

ANN DIAMOND: Everyone assumes it's a love song, but I always felt it was full of unspoken trauma. Life on Hydra in those days was nightmarish—sex, drugs, satanism.

BARRIE WEXLER: His love for her was genuine, but was tangled up with his perception of her beauty, and the distance that he himself perpetuated. He was writing songs of longing and parting out of their lives, while they were living them. But Marianne didn't want to live with him in a song, and he didn't want to live with her in a marriage.

Decades later, Cohen framed the parting as inevitable, saying both had accepted it.

LEONARD COHEN: In a way, it was such a graceful parting that it wasn't really designed by us. The parting was as graceful as the meeting. It had stormy qualities of young love, of course—there were arguments and fights and jealousy and betrayals, along with all the other things of nourishment and friendship.

A few years earlier, Wexler had asked Cohen to name the greatest love poem ever written.

BARRIE WEXLER: Without hesitation, he said John Donne's "Sweetest love, I do not go." At the time, I'd never heard of Donne. He recited the whole poem. If Cohen had been a seventeenth-century love poet, he might have written it for Marianne to explain their demise.

The first and last stanzas read:

> *Sweetest love, I do not go,*
> *For weariness of thee,*
> *Nor in hope the world can show*
> *A fitter love for me;*
> *But since that I*
> *Must die at last, 'tis best*
> *To use myself in jest*
> *Thus by feign'd deaths to die.*

> . . .

> *Let not thy divining heart*
> *Forethink me any ill;*
> *Destiny may take thy part,*
> *And may thy fears fulfil;*
> *But think that we*
> *Are but turn'd aside to sleep;*
> *They who one another keep*
> *Alive, ne'er parted be.*

CHAPTER ELEVEN

Nashville Blues

How long can you wait for the prince that doesn't show up?

—Kasoundra Kasoundra

I always felt that I would address the world in some way. I always felt that.

—Leonard Cohen

He knew he was destined for something that others weren't. He seemed to know that all along.

—Linda Book

Through the fall of 1968, Leonard Cohen shuttled back and forth between magnetic poles—Montreal, Nashville, and New York City. Aspects of all three must have struck him as slightly surreal. In Montreal, he'd often stay with his mother on Belmont Avenue, a house haunted by the ghosts of his late father and his own past. Honky-tonk Nashville was at once less familiar but more exotic—a town seemingly caught in a time warp. In Manhattan, he was parked at the Chelsea Hotel, a no less bizarre menagerie. Cohen had heard the Chelsea—at 222 West Twenty-Third Street—was where he might meet "people of my own kind."

LEONARD COHEN: It was a grand, mad place. I love hotels to which, at 4 a.m., you can bring . . . a midget, a bear, and four ladies . . . to your room and no one cares about it at all.

Cohen spent his thirty-fourth birthday in Manhattan with Thelma Blitz, a twenty-four-year-old ad copywriter and handicrafts artist who sat across from him at a communal table at the Paradox, a macrobiotic restaurant run by Scientologists.

THELMA BLITZ: I told him he looked a lot like Dustin Hoffman. He said, "People often tell me that." I said, "When Hoffman came on the scene, people thought he was ugly. But by force of his personality, he changed their perception. Now they think he's handsome." He said, "That's very nice." We began to talk. He was like someone I already knew, so it was easy to talk, of poetry, of Scientology. There was no exchange of names. It was like we already knew each other.

Around 10 p.m., as the restaurant shut down, Cohen asked her to walk with him. On St. Marks Place, the heart of the East Village, they met a young hippie. A large turtle was sitting on his gloved hand.

THELMA BLITZ: "What do you feed that thing?" he asked. "Hamburger meat, speed, and smack," the hippie answered with pride. We resumed our walk. "What a terrible thing to do to a natural creature," I said. "Take it out of its natural habitat, parade it around, and fill it full of drugs." He countered with a multilevel zinger that stopped all further comment in its tracks. "Well . . . at least it had its head out."

Cohen led her across town to the Chelsea Hotel.

THELMA BLITZ: "What's there?" I asked. "Nico," he said wistfully. "Why don't you write?" he asked me. "I have nothing to say," I said. "That's never stopped me," he said. At the hotel, he asked an attendant for his mail. I heard his name for the first time and I clutched. It made me nervous, because I sensed an inequality between us I wasn't conscious of before. Before I knew he was somebody and I was nobody, I was having a good time. I liked the guy. I took him for an academic—the way we discussed and quoted lines of poetry. I didn't know it was a rock star playing prince and the pauper.

Cohen then took Blitz to El Quijote, the Spanish restaurant next to the Chelsea. Sitting across from her in a leather booth, Cohen ordered a plate of celery and olives.

THELMA BLITZ: Not exactly a feast, but we'd already had dinner. That was another thing wrong with that night. The fare was too Spartan. There was only water, no wine, no smoke. It was stone-cold sober, because Scientologists forbid intoxicants. So we talked. Sometimes he paid attention and sometimes he zoned out, which led me to think, "Am I boring him?" Or was his mind someplace else? After, we went up one flight of stairs to his room. It was a small, indistinct room, lonely, dingy, with dirty socks on the floor, which made me feel less intimidated. He sat in a chair, stared me down, took out his guitar, and played "Bird on a Wire" and the "Partisan" song. Little did I know that he was rehearsing for his next album, *Songs from a Room*.

They spent the night together. About that time, Cohen befriended an East Village avant-garde artist named Kasoundra Kasoundra. Germaine Greer's *The Female Eunuch* was dedicated to her.

KASOUNDRA KASOUNDRA: I went into his room one day. He and Henry Zemel were lying on the bed, clothes on, resting. I was wearing a hand-me-down blouse and jodhpur pants and my boots. I walked in saying, "So you're Leonard Cohen. Well, it's certainly delightful to meet you." He gave me that crooked, almost sheepish smile. I'm a little femme fatale. There was a physical unity, a couple of times, but that was it. He was a very quiet lover, austere and gentle.

RAMBLIN' JACK ELLIOTT: She was just madly in love with Leonard. She was very attractive and unique—loved by everybody. Strong and witty. I can see her having a rapport with Leonard because of her intellect. She left home at thirteen to move to New York.

KASOUNDRA KASOUNDRA: We never hung out or went to parties. As a person, he was quite intelligent, kept a lot of things to himself, didn't talk much. You could ask questions—he'd answer. He very rarely asked questions about you. It depended on his mood. I called him a couple of times and he was in a really ugh mood. He said, "Kasoundra, call off your dogs." He was getting vibes from me that were not correct. I designed an album cover for Leonard and wanted to have him okay it—it's very mystical—but I never showed it to him. The friendship disappears, melts into life, bingo. He melted into life himself. How long can you wait for the prince that doesn't show up? He was an experiment that didn't work out. I didn't get the graduate degree.

Through folk circles, Cohen had already met Canadian singer Buffy Sainte-Marie. Then working on her sixth album, *Illuminations*, she asked Cohen for permission to record his "Magic Is Afoot" passage from *Beautiful Losers* as a track. He agreed and came to the studio the day she recorded it.

BUFFY SAINTE-MARIE: I had the text on a stand and just ad-libbed the guitar. That may have been when we went to see Kateri at St. Patrick's

[Cathedral, in New York, where Cohen hung lilies on a bronze fig-urine of the Mohawk saint]. I know we went to the cathedral in Montreal together.

Sainte-Marie was well aware of Cohen's reputation as a ladies' man.

BUFFY SAINTE-MARIE: Of course he hit on me. He hit on everybody. But I never went for it. We were not friends in that way.

Like many others, however, she was struck by Cohen's wit.

BUFFY SAINTE-MARIE: My God, he was funny. It was so much fun walk-ing around with him, really relaxed, talking about any old thing. He always had that. There was a wisdom about him, even when he was young, that would shine through his humour. He wasn't making jokes in order to be popular. It wasn't Borscht Belt humour. He wasn't looking for punch lines at all. The wisdom he had to share seemed to come out of him wrapped in gentleness and humour, so that he could say something really caustic, but say it in a way that you'd love. He could be irreverent and reverent at the same time. His softness was very strong, very powerful. You could tell that he had a sweet heart about the important things in life, the aches and pains, the kisses and hugs. He had a real kid-glove approach.

For Sainte-Marie, Cohen was "just a genius, a true poet."

BUFFY SAINTE-MARIE: We didn't spend a lot of time together. But the time we did spend was more than memorable—enriching. Leonard and I used to talk about God, about *The Urantia Book* [a spiritual tome of unknown authorship that addresses mankind's history and destiny]. We used to talk about Jesus. We used to talk about Jews. We talked about religion a lot.

Later that year, when Sainte-Marie married Hawaiian surfing instructor Dewain Bugbee, Cohen sent her a blanket as a wedding gift. Some native tribes use blankets as part of the wedding ceremony.

BUFFY SAINTE-MARIE: And he sent my husband a knife—the kind you use for hunting. It was very beautiful.

Some years later, a journalist told Cohen he'd heard Sainte-Marie introduce the song "Suzanne" by claiming she wrote it. Cohen corrected him and said suggestively, "You may have got it wrong. I actually taught it to her mouth-to-mouth."

One evening that fall, Cohen wandered up to the roof of the Chelsea and saw twenty-nine-year-old Ralph Gibson strumming a guitar.

RALPH GIBSON: He came up, smiled, went down, and got his guitar. We shook hands and were friends ever since. We spent three, four hours playing. He told me, "Your playing surrounds my music." I was struggling for recognition [as a photographer], and he'd just hit big, just starting [to make it] but still living at the Chelsea. I just barely knew who he was, but I wasn't a fan. Then we'd go to Max's [Kansas City] together—we went to hear Luther Allison, very wild black guy, blues player, completely over the top. I thought he was too exaggerated. Leonard didn't think he was exaggerated at all. Completely bought his act.

Gibson later swapped books and records with Cohen, visited him in Montreal, and played on Cohen's 1974 album, *New Skin for the Old Ceremony.*

RALPH GIBSON: As Francophiles, we were both struggling to improve our French. I watched how methodically he worked at it. He'd learn a verb and stay with it until he had it. He came from a business family and he loved business, in the abstract. He had no trouble doing business. He was not an artist or a poet who couldn't handle a deal, by a long shot. I remember saying—and he played it very cool—"I've always got about a thousand bucks in my pocket," and he said, "Yeah, me too." He probably had a lot more than that, but it was a very nice way of him equalizing things. That's probably how and why we were such good friends. I don't recall drugs—maybe we smoked a few joints. We were buddies, fast friends.

Years later, when Gibson had vernissages in Paris, Cohen would come.

RALPH GIBSON: He understood my photographs in a deeply profound way. I once put up a picture of [the back of] this doorman's head. He walked up and stood in front of that picture for a while and he says, "You're a real artist, Ralph." He knew it was a hard art photograph. With Leonard, as with all my artist friends, the one conversation you have is about the creative process—how do you do it? He'd tell me how long it took him to finish a song. He once told me nobody writes lyrics like in the old days, and he quoted a line from "I'll Be Seeing You."

Another woman Cohen saw at the Chelsea was seventeen-year-old Ann Biderman, whose mother, Peggy, a photographer, lived at the hotel.

ANN BIDERMAN: I'm working on a memoir, so I'm going to keep those stories, but I'll just say Leonard was seminal in my life. Oh God, I was so young. It was probably illegal.

Just before Halloween, Cohen returned to Montreal. One afternoon, at the Winston Churchill Pub on Crescent Street, he met Barbara Dodge, the tall, stunning, blond, Westmount-raised granddaughter of C. D. Howe, one of Canada's most important political power brokers.

BARBARA DODGE: My soon-to-be husband, William Lanterman—Billy, for short—was head bartender. A draft dodger from Colorado. In hiding. Billy introduced me. Leonard was just sitting there, like an old bum, at the bar.

BARRIE WEXLER: Cohen was sitting at the bar in one of his morose moods. Billy asked him how he liked his drink. He didn't respond. Billy turned to me and quipped, "Poets—they're so sensitive, they can't express themselves." At which point, Leonard cracked up.

BILL LANTERMAN: I could talk to Leonard like a poet. I saw him in lots of different moods. I loved the depths of him. Stuff just emanated. You could feel his personal power. That's what people gravitated to. It was gravitas. He had that. And he knew that about himself. The Winston Churchill [was] a whirlwind of poets, artists, ad guys. I was dating a waitress there—Marie, from Antigua.

BARRIE WEXLER: Her name was Marie Merchant. One night, I tried to lure her girlfriend, a statuesque beauty who slept in the same bed, onto our side of the mattress—without much success. Disturbingly, I later found out that Cohen had met no such resistance.

BILL LANTERMAN: I was sitting at the bar on a day off with Marie, and another guy leaned over and said, "Bill, that's Leonard." I said, "Who's Leonard?" I'd never heard the name. He says, "Leonard Cohen?" I said, "So what?" He says, "Marie is his girlfriend. You've been dating his girlfriend, and he's just back." I didn't really care too much. Leonard introduces himself and he was down, real quiet. We just started talking—the three of us—about birthdays. We were both born in September and this was the fall. He said, "Ah. Secret Virgo, are you?" I didn't know anything about astrology. But he was very confident, and very quiet. I stopped seeing Marie. She never said anything about him.

Merchant was a plaything. The woman he was interested in was Dodge.

BARBARA DODGE: I was maybe seventeen or eighteen, young. I didn't know anything. I was modelling. I think Leonard fell madly in love with me immediately, because he asked Billy if he could take me for dinner—he knew Billy and I had some kind of relationship. I really didn't know who Leonard was.

BILL LANTERMAN: I was kind of put out by it, but why would I stop her from meeting someone like that?

Cohen took her to the Parthenon, in Greektown.

BARBARA DODGE: He was intensely interested in me. Here was the big Leonard come-on. He bought me an evil eye, a ring—to protect my virginity, he said. That came up in the conversation, that Billy was courting me and I was still a virgin. I'd barely been kissed. But I was really charmed by him, an older man, of that intense romantic persuasion. I thought, "Wow." Then he drove me home, to 622 Sydenham. He lived two blocks away.

Soon Dodge became part of Cohen's entourage. She met Derek May, Francine Hershorn, the wife of Robert, and later, Suzanne Elrod. Through Hershorn, Dodge later met folk singer Ramblin' Jack Elliott and, for the better part of fifteen years, was his lover, producer, manager, and agent.

BARBARA DODGE: Ramblin' Jack Elliott, Leonard, Bob Dylan, they were the three Jews who made it, the triumvirate. But I grew up in a super-righteous family. That's why Francine was so exciting to me because she—and later Suzanne—would talk about sex. Unbelievable. I didn't know women *did* things like that.

Dodge also played snooker with Morton Rosengarten.

BARBARA DODGE: I adored Morton. He was then more the mentor of everyone, a real teacher. He knew a little bit about everything and was very exact and studied about everything he did, even in pool. An amazing person. They were so similar, he and Leonard. They both had this advanced superior knowledge and talked so precisely. Or maybe they just pretended, but they got away with it. And I was a neophyte, awkward and shy, completely straight. I didn't know how to behave with these people. Leonard read me completely. And what he was amazed by and attracted to was that I was a virgin. I don't think there was anybody he couldn't conquer.

Soon Cohen mounted a full-court press. One night, in a flat on Crescent Street, he serenaded her on guitar, showing off his flamenco chops. Another night, he took her to meet his mother.

BARBARA DODGE: Supposedly. He was staying with her. We go to Masha's—she was wonderful, this big, bruising, Russian woman, very intimidating. It tells you a lot about Leonard. No wonder he became the guy he became, because Masha was so overwhelming—this Russian dominatrix personality, very authoritarian. But she would just melt with Leonard and be very jealous of any woman. I immediately saw her sizing me up. Leonard just dismissed her. I think he told her to make us something to eat. Then he took me upstairs to "show me the house"—very modest. He had run a bath and there were bubbles in the bathtub. I was still so incredibly shy and still a virgin. I was thinking I was falling in love with him, but I was confused because I thought I'd fallen in love with [Lanterman]. But he is so seductive. He says, "We're going to have a bath." I had on a onesie—I had modelled in them—so I wasn't too shy to wear that. So I stripped down to my onesie and he said, "You have to take your onesie off."

I was feeling manipulated, but didn't have the chutzpah to say no. "Okay, I guess I have to take my onesie off." So I got in the bathtub with him. And then he tried every technique he could to hold me, embrace me, and get me into something, and I was as cold as ice. I did grow up a WASP. I really knew how to pull that off.

Cohen was undeterred.

BARBARA DODGE: He kept trying. He thought he was going to get me. He brought me out, took a towel, wrapped me in a towel, took me into his bedroom, laid me out on the bed, proceeded to try every seductive trick in the book. But I was a virgin, which means I had not been turned on sexually to anyone. I'd been at boarding school. I was a person who wrote poetry and fantasized about great romance but had no idea what that meant. I was flattered, but said, "Look, I'm an idiot. I have no idea what to do here. I don't know what you expect, but I'm just a poet, someone who cares about words." He just loved that about me—that I could not be coerced into his setup. It wasn't a rejection. If anything, I think he felt like he failed. Masha was there, but he just ignored her. I drove myself home, ashamed, because I was supposed to be getting married.

BARRIE WEXLER: He couldn't understand her resistance and, for the longest time, thought I was sleeping with her, which bothered him no end. I wasn't, but didn't go out of my way to disillusion him. He once joined Morton, Barbara, and me at a pool hall on The Main. Things went from bad to worse because she kept snookering him— not only was *she* unavailable, so were his coloured balls.

There were few eighteen-year-old women that Cohen failed to seduce, even virgins. That he failed with Dodge spoke volumes about her core values.

BARBARA DODGE: He so deeply recognized that. He wasn't just stymied. I believe it was the first and maybe the last time he saw the truth. It exposed him, not me. But that's what pure innocence can do to us. He was already a veteran of so many lies.

A few years later, in *The Energy of Slaves*, Cohen wrote a poem about their encounter.

BARBARA DODGE: Suzanne told me later it was about me . . . "I perceived the outline of your breasts through your Halloween costume." I was really flattered. But the table turned. He was the one in the Halloween costume, whose motives were stopped by a simple transcendent moment of truth which "remained with him all night and probably forever."

BILL DODGE: I remember when my sister sat reciting a poem by heart about a woman who had impressed the outline of her breasts upon a poet's "shapeless hunger." Listening to my sister's proud and solemn voice, I knew her breasts had been immortalized. They were big round pumpkins, where before they had only been seeds. That's when I first began to doubt W. H. Auden's line that poetry doesn't make anything happen.

On Halloween, Cohen dropped in on the Pomerance family. Presumably, he came to see his former lover, Erica Pomerance, but she was in New York City. Instead, he spent the evening with her younger sister.

SHELLEY POMERANCE: I was about thirteen. I was there with a friend and Leonard came over and we sat on the floor and ate pomegranates and drank apple juice out of jars. He talked about how the Jews in Europe had been persecuted on Halloween. He was expounding. It was very pleasant and easy.

A few days later, Cohen met African-American political activist Eldridge Cleaver. His friend Henry Zemel had befriended Concordia professor Benson Brown, who was supporting the black activist movement.

CAROL ZEMEL: I get a call from Benson. He says, "Carol, we have somebody who needs to stay in your apartment. I'm not going to tell you his name. Maybe it's good for you to go out of town." Eventually I learn who it was—Eldridge Cleaver. He was smuggled out of the States and was waiting for a Cuban ship, which got delayed. Eventually, Henry and I return and Leonard comes over to meet him. Cleaver was no fool. He was a very smart guy. He had this riff—first, the British came [to America], then the Irish and then the Italians. He turns to Henry and says, "What are you, man? Italian?" "No, man, I'm Jewish." That became an important thing to Henry, to tell Cleaver it was Jews who had smuggled him out of the States and were getting him to Cuba. At one point, the movement got Cleaver a woman—she moved into my house too.

Cleaver knew and liked at least one Cohen song—"The Partisan." A biography of Timothy Leary—*The Most Dangerous Man in America*—describes Cleaver playing the song repeatedly in Algeria in 1970, "quietly murmuring the words while caressing a pistol."

Cohen spent most of the fall of 1968 in Nashville, recording. On his first trip, he took Henry Zemel—he ended up playing Jew's harp on the album. Charlie Daniels picked them up at the airport.

CHARLIE DANIELS: I didn't know who Leonard Cohen was. I didn't know what he did. It was a very pleasant surprise that Leonard Cohen was as down-to-earth and nice as he could be.

Cohen stayed initially at the Noelle Hotel on Fourth Avenue. From there, he wrote to Marianne Ihlen, saying the album was being finished "on acid, amphetamine and prayer," and that he often thought "of a blonde girl-monkey when I masturbate." Not long after, he assumed music producer Bob Johnston's lease on a 1,500-acre ranch in Franklin, Tennessee, about twenty miles south of the city. The house was a simple wooden cabin that stood on a 1,200-acre, heavily treed property. Cohen rented it for seventy-five dollars a month from its owner, songwriter Boudleaux Bryant. Cohen's neighbour was a cowboy, Kid Marley. His son, Cody, later remembered "these folks [as] being very nice and quick to laugh."

CODY MARLEY: He'd literally sing for his supper. We'd eat, then he'd pull out the guitar and do cowboy/country songs. My father would pull out his French harp [harmonica], and they'd play "Red Wing," "Little Brown Jug," or whatever. I remember riding my horse up to his house. He'd come outside or invite me in. Heck, I could just walk in. Leonard gave me candy. I don't know what kind it was, but I can still taste it to this day. It was great. My father was a good judge of people. He liked Leonard. Me too.

CHARLIE DANIELS: If there ever were people who came from opposite ends of the spectrum, it was Leonard Cohen and Kid Marley. But they just hit it off and got to be friends. Leonard was that kind of guy. He spoke a different way than everybody else around. But he had a great sense of communicating with people.

ROBERT FAGGEN: I believe it's in Tennessee where he first owned guns.

FRANCINE HERSHORN: Leonard sent Robert and [me] a Polaroid picture from Nashville. He was shooting a gun and said, "There are some of us they won't take alive."

Cohen later confessed to owning a Walther PPK automatic pistol and, for a brief time, carrying it in New York, until his lawyer, Marty Machat, locked it up. He also owned rifles, which were "locked up in somebody's closet." And he owned pellet guns and, in his Montreal home, set up targets and taught his children how to shoot.

RON CORNELIUS: The first time I met him he greeted me at the door buck naked. We'd sit drinking on the front porch with an old moonshiner named Willie York and Kid Marley. Being out in the woods like that, you could tell that Leonard was completely out of sorts, but loving every minute.

HENRY ZEMEL: I don't remember the studio time. Going out at 1 a.m. to some diner with some blonde is more imprinted on my memory—a diner run by a southern floozy and an ex-con.

That fall, *Look* magazine's Tony Vaccaro flew to Nashville for a Cohen photo shoot.

TONY VACCARO: He wanted to stay in Nashville. He never wanted to come to New York. I put pressure on him—"If you want to go anywhere, you just gotta go to New York." We had a good time together. A nice man.

Cohen was car shopping, so Vaccaro shot him standing in a car lot.

TONY VACCARO: The light was so beautiful. The electricity was all around. The leading picture in the *Look* article is him towering over those cars. Then we stopped to eat and had a little bit of extra juice and were both a little tipsy. We went on the side of this hill and rolled like two little kids, down the hill. Anything I wanted, he posed for it. He was one of the top five people I ever photographed [a list that includes Pablo Picasso, Shirley MacLaine, Marcel Marceau, and Frank Lloyd Wright]. He was a great human being. He had something to say.

For Charlie Daniels, a veteran of honky tonk and rock and roll, Cohen was a novelty. Daniels later compared the imagery of his lyrics to a Georgia O'Keeffe painting.

CHARLIE DANIELS: His casings were so delicate that one out-of-place guitar lick could bend it out of shape . . . You had to get in sync with what he was trying to convey . . . Sometimes it only called for a well-placed note or two, spare but meaningful . . . I did learn from working with Johnston and Cohen that "less is more." With a guy like Cohen, you didn't try to embellish what he was doing. You didn't try to guide what he was doing. You just tried to fit in. And there was a whole mind-set to that . . . Leonard tuned his guitar down a full step—how he played it I could never figure out. That was the thing about his music, though. It was so fragile. It was so "stay out of the way."

* * *

In January 1969, Cohen flew to Los Angeles to attend the wedding of his friends Steve Sanfield and Jacquie Bellon, at the Rinzai-ji Zen Center; Joshu Sasaki Roshi officiated. Cohen witnessed the signing of the marriage certificate, signing his own name in Hebrew. Bellon was three months pregnant at the time.

JACQUIE BELLON: That's when he met the Roshi for the first time. Steve kept urging him to study with this guy. He thought he was exceptional.

RUTH SEYMOUR: Leonard brought *keif*—Moroccan hash—for everybody.

MICHAEL GETZ: I remember standing with Steve and Leonard at the reception. Leonard asked me, "Don't you feel you're a spokesman for your generation?" I said, "No, I don't." And he said, "Well, you're just on a higher rung." Which made me feel great, of course. He was a friendly fellow, Leonard, interesting to talk with, really bright, funny, kind of quiet, curious.

By February 1969, Cohen was back in Paris, visiting Madeleine Lerch.

MADELEINE LERCH: He told me he met this girl at the hotel and was going to take her to the Azores. He said, "She's married." She was with her husband in the hotel! He said, "Yeah, her husband doesn't mind." He had rented this car and said I could have it until the end of the lease.

KENNY FEUERMAN: Her name was Nicole. I met her with him in Morocco. Dark hair. Quite pretty.

Cohen was in Morocco, when, on February 28, it was struck by a powerful earthquake—7.8 on the Richter scale. Eleven Moroccans were killed.

CHARMAINE DUNN: I can't remember if he went to Morocco for genealogical research, because the Cohen family, part of the tribe, had once been there, or if he just wanted to go there. But he was in Essaouira, a little north, and I was in Agadir. I was sleeping on the beach with my head on the ground. I woke up and called, "Earthquake's coming!" I was afraid of a tidal wave. I assume he was with a woman there. It was a terrible earthquake. They felt it in Lisbon.

JENNIFER BIGMAN: I slept through the earthquake . . . my father, Sidney, was a writer. He had a house in Essaouira and used to have these huge parties, 150 people. He told me this guy came up off the beach—Leonard—and had just composed a song, "Bird on a Wire," and could he play it for everyone and get their opinion? My father said no one thought very much of him.

In Essaouira, Cohen hung out with Kenny Feuerman, a young American on holiday from medical studies in Grenoble, France. Their encounter was remarkable in part because there were few American tourists in Morocco in those days, and in part because Feuerman was, even then, a huge Cohen fan.

KENNY FEUERMAN: I had played his album religiously. I had read *The Favourite Game.* Late one morning, I stumble out of our hotel room—I'd been playing "Suzanne" in my room while smoking *kief* and making love—and look down at the reception area. I said, "What? That's Leonard Cohen!" I couldn't believe it. I was twenty-one, a flaming hippie. We'd go out in the morning to a café, just the two of us, never as a foursome. I'd basically listen to his stories. We smoked a bunch of *kief* in *sebsis*, those traditional Moroccan pipes, sometimes on the waterfront, sometimes on the roof of the hotel. I think I played him Dylan's [1967] *Basement Tapes*, a copy of which I had. He played no music and I don't remember him having a guitar. I was a little star struck. I just found him so interesting—politics, philosophy, comparing our Jewish upbringings in Montreal and New York. I remember mostly listening, not doing too much talking.

One day, as they were walking along the waterfront, a man approached with what looked like a bowl of peanuts.

KENNY FEUERMAN: They turned out to be fried grasshoppers. Peanuts with eyes. We each ate a couple. They tasted like fried peanuts, crunchy. Peanuts that look back at you.

Cohen subsequently included a three-line poem called "Morocco" in *The Energy of Slaves.* He reportedly had one other romantic encounter in Morocco.

AVIVA LAYTON: He told me he was with Margaret Trudeau—then Margaret Sinclair—there. They saw each other occasionally after that. Later, Pierre [Elliott Trudeau] told Leonard he was interested in her and asked if it would be okay if he pursued her. Leonard said it was, that she was a lovely girl.

In her 1979 memoir, *Beyond Reason*, Margaret Trudeau chronicles her six months in Morocco, wandering from one sex, *kief*, and hash-filled hippie commune to another. She says she met Cohen and his girlfriend—here called Claire—in Essaouira and travelled with him to Tangiers. She quotes Cohen as describing her as "every guy's great date."

Back in New York, Cohen was still lending financial support to Ihlen, who was on Hydra. He sent her a certified cheque in early May and suggested he might soon join her in Greece. Instead, he had a fateful encounter with the future mother of his children, Suzanne Elrod. There are conflicting accounts of how they met. In one version, it's in the elevator of the Plaza Hotel. In another, it's in a Scientology class, which both were studying. Elrod was then living with an older man at the Plaza.

BARRIE WEXLER: I heard both versions, both from Leonard. His faithfulness is to the story, not to the history. He used to say, "My pen never lies—then again, I write fiction." Suzanne told me they met in a hotel ballroom where they held Scientology seminars, which she and Leonard signed up for independently.

Cohen later told his friend Eric Lerner that he first saw Suzanne standing at a table, leaning over to fill out the registration forms. He told Lerner, "You know how short skirts were in those days. I was completely captivated by the sight of her ass. I didn't even see her face. Just her ass."

VIVIENNE LEEBOSH: She told me she met him in Scientology, and I believe it. She was probably looking for a guy and she snagged him.

BARBARA DODGE: Maybe he gave her an invitation [to Montreal] and she took him up on it. She did have that predator thing going. She was definitely going to get Leonard. But Leonard was not catchable. In those days, he went through women like water. I wouldn't have guessed that he'd have ended up with Suzanne, the way he did. Suzanne was a kept woman her whole life.

PATSY STEWART: I understood he met her at the Rainbow Bar & Grill in Montreal. He said that's where he was when she approached him the first time. It wasn't like "fucking bitch [what nerve]." Not at all. This is what happened. Maybe they met first in New York and she followed him to Montreal. That makes sense to me.

BARRIE WEXLER: Suzanne wasn't stalking Leonard. The first time she came to Montreal, it was with him. If anything, in the beginning, it was he who was all over her.

KELLEY LYNCH: He told me when they met that she was a whore having sex with old men in coffins.

In a poem later included in *The Energy of Slaves*, Cohen wrote that she stayed with him in the Chelsea Hotel and watched *Star Trek* before returning to "a rich man who lived in the Plaza Hotel." The poem was titled "Valentina Gave Me Four Months."

PETER KATOUNDAS: In the poem, there's a reference to a Valentina, and you're not quite sure if she's a kept woman or a hooker. The photograph on the back of the book is credited to Valentina. And on the album cover [*Death of a Ladies' Man*], she's identified as S. V. Elrod.

BARRIE WEXLER: Valentina was her middle name. She occasionally used it as an alias, or wrote it just for fun, as Leonard did [with] "September."

CAROL ZEMEL: Her name was not Suzanne then. It became Suzanne, as if she was the Suzanne of his famous song. She was presenting herself as the spirit of the song. I knew better. She was not impressive to me or especially interested in anybody around Leonard.

MORGANA PRITCHARD: I met her in the fall of 1973 and she was Susan.

BARBARA DODGE: She was Susan when I met her. Leonard called her Susan. She was just in the process of changing her name to Suzanne. She was interested in being the mythological woman of the song, and as she took the name, everyone would identify her as the person she became.

PETER KATOUNDAS: One day, Gary Young, who looked after Leonard's houses, says to me, "You know, Suzanne's really not her name. She had him introduce her as Suzanne so people would think she's the Suzanne of the song."

SHARON KEMP: She told me that Leonard asked her to take the name Suzanne.

BARRIE WEXLER: He introduced her as Suzanne the first time they came to Montreal. He called her a lot of things when he was pissed off, but never Susan.

BRANDON AYRE: As angry as Leonard was towards Suzanne, for him to have used the changing of her name against her would've been beneath him. It would have made him look petty. I think he just let it sit there, as evidence of her self-immolation weakness and immense vanity.

BARRIE WEXLER: People automatically took Leonard's side when it came to Suzanne for reasons that he himself had no particular allegiance to. She eventually became his foil, almost like a plot device. Like any writer, he needed a villain in the piece.

BARBARA DODGE: I'd see them in postfight mode, where he'd be very silent. And silence was not his big thing. When he was silent like that, he didn't want to talk to anyone. But Suzanne was very perky, like a waitress making coffee for everyone.

BARRIE WEXLER: They referred to themselves as the F. Scott Fitzgeralds of Montreal, a comparison Suzanne liked until she learned more about Zelda. And, like the Fitzgeralds' toxic romance, it wasn't long before Cohen began to describe their relationship as "a nightmare of regret and recrimination."

Settling into a rented flat on Avenue de l'Esplanade, opposite Parc Jeanne-Mance, Cohen had invited a young protégé, Lewis Greenblatt [now Lewis Furey], to bring him poems to work on. Out of that invitation emerged something they dubbed the Sonnet Club—exercises in developing poetic skills by writing Shakespearian or Spenserian sonnets. Wexler soon joined the group.

BARRIE WEXLER: The Sonnet Club was something they cooked up as a whenever-Leonard-was-in-town workshop. We weren't exactly the Bloomsbury Group.

LEWIS FUREY: We did it three, four, five times. Leonard liked to exercise his craft. It wasn't just writing on inspiration. That was a great lesson: it was a muscle. He had a great sense of humour—very caustic. It was his way of poking you a bit, and of making light of the most serious things. I always felt he was a teacher of mine. I don't think he ever [was satisfied with] a first draft and he always, always had a pad and a pencil. I'd never see him without it. Sometimes he'd leave his notebooks lying on the table and there'd be thirty or forty pages—the same quatrain but a word changed, writing and rewriting until he felt that it was right. That concentration, that quest for the right word, the perfect word, was breathtaking. He wasn't going to be satisfied with something that expressed it less. He was looking for the essence.

LINDA BOOK: His interest in words was such that it would bother him if he couldn't find the right one. He'd refine words all the time, not just in poetry but in speech. Leonard had a difficult psychology. He was narcissistic and egocentric. To be emotionally committed was an intense experience for him. It was all or nothing and all was never enough, so relationships became very problematic. And when he couldn't say or experience what he wanted, he had sex. Relating physically took the pressure off his need for words.

BARRIE WEXLER: I was pretty lousy, bordering on disinterested. Lewis was much better and took it seriously. Cohen, of course, left us in the dust. The two of them were into esoteric rhyme schemes, Spenserian sonnets. In a way, their later movie, *Night Magic*, came out of those initial get-togethers.

Although Cohen once told Wexler "I hunt alone," they occasionally went to clubs together in search of women.

BARRIE WEXLER: Every occasion was distinguished by our failure to score. We'd get a couple of girls to come over, then they'd ask us to dance. Neither Cohen nor I was a good dancer . . . The girls would eventually dance with each other, or meet someone on the dance floor and not come back. Cohen blamed me and I blamed him—our raillery was more fun than our attempts to get laid. After a while, when we arrived somewhere, he'd say, "You go your way, I'll go mine." The next day, we had to confess we'd both struck out. Leonard eventually worked up a theory. It was, he said, due to the fact that our major literary influences—for him, Lorca; for me, Rimbaud—were *gay* poets. I responded that we should have gone with Lord Byron.

That spring, Cohen won the prestigious Governor General's Award for poetry for his 1968 book, *Leonard Cohen, Selected Poems 1956–1968*. To the astonishment of many, he declined it. There are various accounts of his rationale. In one interview, he cryptically explained, "Art is the verdict you give to writing that is important, but to write for art is wrong." Elsewhere, he said, "The world is a callous place and [he] would take no gift from it." In his official rejection, sent via telegram, he wrote, "May I respectfully request that my name be withdrawn from the list of recipients of the Governor General's Award for 1968 . . . Much in me strives for this honour but the poems themselves forbid it absolutely." He may also have spurned the prize in sympathy with Quebec author Hubert Aquin, a French separatist who had declined the French-language literature award on political grounds. Another winner that year, Fernand Dumont—for nonfiction—donated his prize money to the separatist Parti Québécois.

ARNIE GELBART: The refusal played into the feelings of nationalism in Quebec. It was politically right at the time. He had good friends in the Francophone community.

Cohen might also have been influenced by Jean-Paul Sartre, who refused a more prestigious prize, the Nobel, in 1964, saying, "It isn't the same thing if I sign Jean-Paul Sartre or if I sign Jean-Paul Sartre, Nobel Prize winner. A writer must refuse to let himself be turned into an institution." But Naim Kattan, then the civil servant charged with organizing the Governor General's Awards, offered what he thinks was the real story.

NAIM KATTAN: Cohen called me at my office. He said, "Naim, I'm not coming. Don't take it personally. I am very grateful. You were the first one to write about me in French and my friendship is real. It's not against you but against the government, because they are ill-treating people who smoke marijuana. They're arresting my friends and I can't accept an award from a government that arrests people for something like that." I said, "Leonard, your book is the best. The decision is yours and, for me, nothing changes."

Cohen did, however, turn up in Ottawa for a party to celebrate the honourees. There he was famously confronted by novelist Mordecai Richler in a washroom. Incensed by Cohen's action, Richler demanded to know why he had declined the award. Cohen replied, "I don't know." That seemed to appease Richler, who reportedly told him, "Any other answer and I would have punched you in the nose."

DIANE GIGUÈRE: I went to Ottawa with him. I don't know why he went, because he refused the prize. I went because I knew him. He was a very good friend at the time.

BARRIE WEXLER: The Giguère thing represents a kind of double irony. He took her, a Quebecois writer, to a celebration of the prize he declined partly as an expression of his solidarity with the separatist movement. Yet she herself, at that very moment, was applying for the most prestigious grant in the English-speaking world, the Guggenheim, which she won the next year.

ANN MANDEL: We were in Ottawa for the presentation because Eli [Mandel] had won the award the year before. Leonard showed up at the after party at the Château Laurier. It was a huge crush and I was looking for a place to sit down. Leonard had found a big chair and beckoned me, and as I sat down, he turned his hand up, and I sat down on his hand and he felt me up and said, "Not sagging yet, Annie." I was twenty-seven. That's the last thing I remember. Nobody called me "Annie."

Around that time, Cohen read Wexler a passage from Rilke's *Letters to a Young Poet*, about how the writer must choose solitude and silence.

BARRIE WEXLER: Apropos of the award, there's actually a passage where Rilke says that, when the literary establishment finally honours a writer who has spent his life glued to the page, there are very few who don't look up.

Rilke's Letter 6 also says: "What is necessary, after all, is only this: solitude, vast inner solitude . . . to meet no one for hours—that is what you must be able to attain. To be solitary as you were when you were a child, when the grownups walked around involved with matters that seemed large and important because . . . you didn't understand a thing about what they were doing. And when you realize that their activities are shabby, that their vocations are petrified and no longer connected with life, why not then continue to look upon it all as a child would . . . from the vastness of your own solitude, which is itself work and status and vocation?"

BARRIE WEXLER: Leonard didn't say this passage related to his own rejection of the award, but he read it to me in late '69, and I took it as the reason. Later, he told me the story of a young man who, having mistaken the meditation hall at Mount Baldy for a Shaolin temple, asked Roshi which martial art he should study—jujitsu, aikido, karate. Roshi replied, "Better study the wind." Leonard's rationale for declining the award may have involved a gesture of solidarity towards Quebec nationalism, jailed friends, and artistic self-preservation. But at bottom, the explanation he gave to Richler makes more sense: it was something nebulous like the wind, an element he was very much in tune with.

During his visit to Ottawa, Cohen stopped in at an art gallery on Sussex Drive.

DAVE WILSON: One day, I came up from the basement. From the top of the stairs, I beheld Leonard Cohen on the sidewalk, looking at my painting of Leonard Cohen. He and a lady walked on after a minute and I was so excited that I determined to meet him. With the boss's permission, I went out and looked for him. [When] he exited a photo shop, I said, "Excuse me. Aren't you Leonard Cohen?" His hand extended, he said, "Leonard." Close to stammering with excitement, I said, "I saw you looking at my painting in the window." He asked if it was for sale and I said, "Yes, but it costs fifty dollars." "Can I buy it?" "Sure." The next day, Mr. Cohen came by on his own and wrote a cheque for fifty dollars. My boss gave me thirty-five—he was charging his own employee a 30 percent commission! I asked for two autographs, which Leonard kindly wrote. Mine is lost. To my brother he wrote, "Hello Bruce. All good things. Love, Leonard." My brother still has his. Leonard left with the painting, whose image was derived from a 1969 *Chatelaine* magazine. Later, friends came to visit me, and I pointed out Leonard's wet footprints on the newly cleaned floor. I felt famous for days.

In June, Cohen flew to Rome to discuss working with Leonard Bernstein on a score for a film about Saint Francis of Assisi, *Brother Sun, Sister Moon*, to be directed by Franco Zeffirelli. One night, he attended a party at Zeffirelli's villa in Positano.

BARRIE WEXLER: Zeffirelli told Leonard there would be Italian celebrities, including starlets, and so he planned to stay overnight. As it turned out, the attendees were the director's gay friends, with the odd drag queen. Staying the night seemed a little risky. Around 2 a.m., Cohen snuck out. He said it was an expensive cab ride back to Rome, but worth every lira.

Both Cohen and Bernstein later withdrew from the project. Meanwhile, on the strength of some samples of prose, Cohen arranged a $1,500 first-novel advance for Barrie Wexler, from Jack McClelland.

BARRIE WEXLER: Leonard taught subtly, tilting my prose towards comedy. I began reading Joseph Heller, Philip Roth, P. G. Wodehouse, Dan Greenburg, and later, Gail Parent. When I first brought him stuff to look at, he would occasionally smile. On the next few rounds, he chuckled but would say, "There's no real belly laugh." After a couple of years, I came by with thirty pages of a novel, *The Life and Death of a Canadian Single*. For the first time, he laughed out loud. Then he said, "We're going to Toronto."

BRANDON AYRE: Barrie's work was good. I remember being a little jealous.

BARRIE WEXLER: He asked if I was thinking of someone when drawing the main character—a brilliant lunatic. I said, "Mark Pomerance—and don't get any ideas. You've got Moscovitch." Then he said, "I've been thinking about using Pomerance myself. Tell you what, I'll give you half of Moscovitch." "Sounds like an even swap," I allowed. Remembering that I used to complain he hadn't left me anything to write about, he added, "It's only fair, since I grabbed all of Westmount."

To sign the contract, Cohen took him to Toronto.

BARRIE WEXLER: He stared around the boarding area, then scribbled something in his notebook. I was curious and asked to see. The pages were all blank, except for the line he'd just written: "three weeks passed." At which point he said, "See what you have to look forward to?"

While Wexler thumbed through Cohen's notebook, a girl who'd been glancing at him quizzically finally worked up the courage to ask, "Are you Leonard Cohen?"

BARRIE WEXLER: "Who's Leonard Cohen?" he replies. "A poet and a singer." . . . Cohen asks, "Is he any good?" The girl starts to explain. A couple comes over and requests his autograph. The girl exclaims, "So you *are* Leonard Cohen!" Leonard grins. "Well, people around here seem to think so." Still not entirely certain, she hands him her boarding pass to sign, just in case.

At McClelland & Stewart, they went to Jack McClelland's office.

BARRIE WEXLER: The first thing out of his mouth was "Young man, if you're half as good as your friend Cohen says you are, you'll make me millions." Leonard chimed in: "Jack, just read the first few pages." He flipped through all forty for what felt like an eternity, then called the most junior editor in the building and asked her to arrange a contract. Afterwards, we went to her office to get acquainted. She was far more interested in talking to Cohen than she was to me.

At least until the 1990s, Cohen preferred to blacken his pages in a cheap, small, white, spiral-bound, cardboard notebook made in Greece—Block #5.

BARRIE WEXLER: He bought them by the fistful at a variety store called Serellis on the port. The quality of the printing wasn't that great, which was why he liked them—you could barely make out the lines. His favourite pen was a black felt-tip which he wore clipped to the front placket of his shirt—angled like a gunslinger wears a holster for a quick draw.

On that same June trip, Cohen dropped into the Toronto Pop Festival at Varsity Stadium, a two-day event featuring Blood, Sweat & Tears, Sly and the Family Stone, Dr. John, Steppenwolf, and the Velvet

Underground. An aspiring folk singer, Sandy Crawley, had a gig at a secondary stage.

SANDY CRAWLEY: There were fifteen or twenty people listening and one of them, by God, was Leonard Cohen. It knocked me out. Afterwards, I went to sit at the feet of the master and he was very kind. I boldly asked him what he thought of my extremely experimental songs and he said— probably a line he had ready because he got [asked] this a lot—"some people will think they're the greatest songs they've ever heard, but most people won't understand them." Which made me feel good at the time.

Cohen continued to keep on the move through the last half of 1969. In New York, he met Bob Dylan for the first time, although there are conflicting accounts of precisely where. In one, it's at the Bitter End nightclub—both had gone to hear Tim Buckley—in Greenwich Village. In another, it's at Kettle of Fish, a bar on MacDougal Street, also in the village. In July, Cohen went to dinner in the El Quijote restaurant, attached to the Chelsea Hotel.

DON GUY: I was in New York editing a film and staying at the Chelsea, in the White Room—all white. You had to wear socks. Anyway, Leonard was at the head of the table and above his head was the TV, projecting images of the Apollo 11 landing on the moon.

That night, Guy met his future wife—Cohen's friend Yafa Lerner.

DON GUY: Yafa came in with her good friend Suzanne Brockman. I knew who Leonard was—I had played his first album endlessly. He was very low-key. He speaks softly.

In Toronto, in September, Cohen celebrated his thirty-fifth birthday at the Windsor Arms Hotel.

ERIC ANDERSEN: It was a nice evening. David Blue and Morton Rosengarten were there. Morton is wonderful. It was a quiet little thing, downstairs in the restaurant.

In Nashville, Cohen started work with Bob Johnston on his third album, *Songs of Love and Hate*. Suzanne Elrod had joined him.

LEONARD COHEN: I had a house, a Jeep, a carbine, a pair of cowboy boots, a girlfriend, a typewriter, a guitar. Everything I needed.

While Cohen worked, Elrod made dresses and pottery. She often made Cohen drive her to town for burgers, but after a vegan period, he had adopted a new, macrobiotic regimen. His diet seemed to change as often as his spiritual interests, possibly in tandem. Years later, Elrod told *People* magazine that the couple "admired the wild peacocks, listened to the stream in the morning, watched the sunset in the evening. I was devoted to him. As long as someone like him was in the universe, it was okay for me to be here. I was walking on tiptoe—anything for the poet. Our relationship was like a spider web. Very complicated." It's an apt simile, though it was a web they had conspired to weave together.

In Montreal briefly that fall, looking for an apartment, he gave an interview to aspiring poet Michael Harris. The interview took place at Harris's Bishop Street apartment, above Café Prag, where Cohen is said to have written "Suzanne."

MICHAEL HARRIS: There was a house of ill repute across the road. That amused him. He was very present, quiet, very well behaved, and allowed the thing to go on as long as I wanted. Suzanne sat on the floor at the end of the couch. He sat on the couch, smoking—excellent . . . French-perfumed cigarettes. He had on his blue raincoat. I have never seen him not well dressed. He was smaller than one imagines, like the Queen. I'm entirely immune to flattery, but when Leonard [used to say to me], "Ah, the poet," I'd always feel a little warm glow, thinking Muhammad has come down the mountain to M. Harris.

Years later, Harris and Cohen remained in touch via e-mail.

MICHAEL HARRIS: He fell in love with the jpeg and he'd send little doodles. He doodled [a portrait of] me, having to do with my love of women. I think he connected with that.

It was during that trip to Montreal that Cohen introduced Elrod to his friends. Wexler met her at the Sir Winston Churchill Pub on Crescent Street, a bar started by Hungarian émigré Johnny Vago, a former adviser to Fidel Castro and a friend of Che Guevara's. Winnie's was a gathering spot for writers, journalists, and broadcasters.

BARRIE WEXLER: One day—he had on a long black coat—he waltzed in with Suzanne. Physically, she was slender, almost waif-like. We thought she was just another girl he was hanging out with. After a while we realized she wasn't going anywhere. Suzanne got a bad rap with Leonard's friends. I always thought it unfair because Cohen had a real portion in how people perceived her. She never pretended to be anything she wasn't, though what that was remained something of a mystery.

PATRICIA NOLIN: I remember very clearly Leonard coming back and talking to Derek and [me]. He said that she was a professional hustler in Miami. He said he was in love, and he smiled and he chuckled, because Leonard chuckled a lot. Leonard Chuckle Cohen. What a chuckle. He was tickled pink about that. He was *bragging*. He said, "Suzanne is a hustler in Miami, a professional hustler." A call girl, whatever. She was very beautiful and very sexy. That's the whole point of whores—sex. And Jewish. Was she smart enough? Who cares?

BARBARA LAPCEK: Suzanne was venomous. She was very self-conscious, very conscious of who she was. That's a sort of brittleness all by itself. Very insecure. She just wasn't very interesting. She could not see outside of herself. I've known other women like her. They marry men who are very well known, and part of them wants that spotlight on themselves. It's all "me, me, me." She and Marianne both had a little bit of the need for celebrity. Years later, walking through the house in Hydra, Leonard was lightly critical of her—but lightly. He never tried to tell me that she was a creep, which I could not have resisted, but only because of the truth of it.

STEVE MACHAT: Suzanne was like this little sex kitten. She basically would curl at you and when you turned your back, she'd hit back at you.

VIVIENNE LEEBOSH: She was very manipulative. She knew how to deal with men. She could have been a Japanese geisha girl. She was really good at it. [Cohen] was totally manipulated, because there aren't that many women who would have stood for that kind of life . . .

BARRIE WEXLER: Suzanne was brilliant at recruiting girls. That was one part she played. She would have made a terrific madam. It's one of the things which attracted Leonard. Suzanne sized him up a lot faster than he did her. Every so often I took on the role of their exit strategy, becoming the beneficiary of their various procurements. Not that there were a lot of complaints from me. But the characterization of Suzanne as a whore or as having been one is as wrong as can be. Leonard did sometimes speak of her that way, first out of some romantic notion, and later as an act of recrimination, but he knew it wasn't true. And it wasn't.

PHOEBE WALKER: He talked to me about Suzanne and the wildness of their relationship—they would go out looking for people—the sexuality of their relationship. It was a wild time apparently. They would go out trolling.

BARBARA DODGE: Suzanne was procuring all the time. I thought he was miserable. She made sure he was going to marry her. She made sure she was going to get pregnant. She never talked to me about abortions, but there aren't many women in the sixties who didn't [have them]. We all had them. You know why? Because no one was practicing safe sex. We could barely get birth control. They wanted to use their freedom to experience whatever they could and nobody thought there would be any consequences. Suzanne was no dummy, but it was street smart, street savvy. And heavily manipulative. She probably confessed that to me—how she used sex to manipulate men. Very beautiful, but not impressive.

BARRIE WEXLER: Leonard's fascination with Suzanne had something in common with Alexander Portnoy's attraction to the Monkey in *Portnoy's Complaint*. Like the Monkey, who fulfilled Portnoy's adolescent fantasies, Suzanne more than matched Leonard's voracious appetite for sexual activity, though, unlike the Monkey, Suzanne could spell.

BARBARA DODGE: Montreal was a pyjama party. Everybody was doing everyone else. There were secrets buried under secrets buried under secrets. It was like a big Shakespearian play. The times were so chaotic. The FLQ was coming in. We would later be put under martial law. There were snipers on the roofs.

HENRY ZEMEL: I always thought she was a little twat—a typical Jewish yenta. A princess. I dismissed her. I don't know what her trip was, with him, what he thought of her. I took a look at her—this is a young woman with good-sized teats and she's Jewish. I don't know if Leonard really liked big teats or what his relationship with teats was.

I didn't feel he had a special relationship with teats. My attitude was, why her? Well, she was Jewish, and that was it. The family tradition.

In fact, Elrod's origins were a frequent subject of discussion.

FRANCINE HERSHORN: Leonard always said she was Jewish. Her maiden name is Elrod. That's all I know.

BRANDON AYRE: The rumour was Suzanne was Mafia—Jewish mafia.

BARRIE WEXLER: I was skeptical of Leonard's belief that Suzanne was Jewish, and her own halfhearted claims, but did accept the story of her growing up in a household affiliated with the mob. During Cohen's 1974 interview with Danny Fields, she served them pastries, which she claimed she had loved since she was three, from "the best bakery in Manhattan." Years later, at her New York apartment, she brought out a box of cannoli from a bakery in Little Italy. Relying on this meagre evidence, I developed my own urban legend—Valentina was originally from New York, of Italian-American descent, perhaps orphaned, then adopted by extended members of La Familia.

Cohen's "belief" itself was not deeply grounded. During the interview with Fields, Elrod said at one point, "I'm very happy I'm Jewish." To which Cohen responded, "And you're not even Jewish."

VIVIENNE LEEBOSH: I think she told me that she was Jewish or maybe just her father. But whatever she told me could have been fictional. I never knew what was real or not with Suzanne.

BARBARA DODGE: Suzanne was Jewish and I'm pretty sure full-on. From Lithuania. I think her mum was somewhere in the mix, but her aunt was raising her. I thought the mum and sister were living together and the uncle worked for Meyer Lansky. Her uncle was the head of the Mafia in Miami.

Indeed, it became an urban legend in Montreal that Elrod was the niece of notorious underworld mobster Meyer Lansky. Like many such legends, it was false.

MEYER LANSKY II: Meyer has two nieces. Neither is named Suzanne.

BARRIE WEXLER: I wouldn't put it past Cohen to have started the rumour himself. He understood the value of myths. That's what he did with Marianne. But he didn't have to do that with Suzanne. She'd already done it for herself. Had she been a hooker? Was her family in the Mafia? No one really knew. One thing was for sure. She was intuitively smart and could be brilliantly devious. If she was in a "sit-down" with the American crime bosses, they'd all be taking notes.

BARBARA DODGE: He said I was the only person in Montreal he trusted to be with Suzanne—because he was probably certain all the men would come on to her. Hydra had been a real cesspool. Marianne was sleeping with all his friends and he was angry about that. So he asked me to take Suzanne under my wing. I did, though she likely took me under *her* wing. She was way out there. At the beginning, I was probably Suzanne's best friend. We did everything together. Shopped—she shopped till she dropped. Suzanne came on to me so many times. She wanted to have a gay relationship with me first and then hookups with other people. And I was absolutely not interested. She was constantly hinting. I'm not sure it ever stopped. She and Leonard would like to sleep with me. I said to her, "You've got to be kidding. You do not know who you're talking to. I'm sorry. That's not who I am. It's not what I do. I'm not interested." The whole idea was so repulsive to me. It's disrespectful to love. I don't see how you mix love up with that kind of game playing. No wonder Leonard is such a mournful dove. Where could he ever find satisfaction? His theology sucked. That's probably why he spent so long in the Zen monastery. He was trying to find God and all he did was find Roshi. But then I'd say, "Tell me what kind of sex you're having," because I wanted to know all about it. She told me everything, in intimate detail—how he'd force her into a washroom at parties and demand she give him a blow job. I was losing respect for Leonard every day. I was being wiped out by it. I could not believe what he was getting into.

Years later, Dodge told Cohen she was shocked by his intense attraction to Elrod.

BARBARA DODGE: In so much of the poetry, you see he's resentful. He didn't want her, but he was stuck with her. In the way that sick people get attached to each other, he became pathologically attached to her. I don't know if it was one of her tricks, because she really had a bag of tricks, continually reinventing everything. It was all sexual. She was pretty blunt with me about that. Leonard liked that—he liked that she was the whore. He loved it and he hated it, because then he was up against all those men. He always seemed to be making himself into some kind of a cuckold, right? That was his whole thing with Marianne. Marianne set him up and she took him down.

BARRIE WEXLER: It was the other way around. Suzanne knew how to get under Leonard's skin. She understood the game better than he did, even figured out that he fed off it. In 1973, on Hydra, he was writing a really nasty manuscript-length tome about their relationship—a litany of complaint—and she helped him *organize* it. I saw her doing that in the basement they had recently redone. He'd set up a little worktable there because it was cooler. Leonard always wanted to leave things as they were, but she had gotten him to whitewash the walls and polish the stone floor.

In Montreal, Elrod had befriended Francine Hershorn. She had a key to their L'Esplanade flat and was having an affair with Wexler.

BARRIE WEXLER: When Leonard and Suzanne were away, Francine and I used their apartment. Cohen would call looking for Robert, Robert would call looking for Cohen. I didn't know if the phone was bugged, but I kept quiet because Hershorn had hired private detectives to follow Francine.

One night, Cohen visited his old girlfriend, Erica Pomerance, at her parents' home on Upper Trafalgar Place. She had been in New York recording an album, *You Used to Think*.

ERICA POMERANCE: I had been in Paris before that. I'd had an abortion there [not Cohen's child]. The doctor had done a poor job of the curettage and I ended up in the hospital. I wrote this song for him— "To Leonard from the Hospital"—a woman's lament about pain and destiny. I remember sitting in my parents' den. I played him the album. Leonard listened and said, "it's the kind of record that will have a small but a cult following." He thought it was a bit wild. I sensed he wasn't sure it would ever be appreciated or understood. And he was right. It never sold a lot, but it was reprinted many times in Europe. Leonard was like a family figure—he was also friendly with my brother, Mark. One of his poems was written for Mark, because he'd already made several attempts at suicide. And he eventually jumped off a roof. A lot of people got lost in those days, with drugs and Eastern religions.

However, it was schizophrenia that, in 1976, propelled Mark Pomerance off the rooftop sundeck of an apartment building at the corner of de Maisonneuve Blvd. and Green Avenue. Then, in the fall of 1969, everyone fled.

CAROL ZEMEL: Marianne and Axel were staying at my house and Marianne said to him, "You better call your friends to say goodbye." So he did, and I heard him say, "Hi, this is Axel. Goodbye forever. I'm going to New York." Then I went too, to study art history. Henry ran off with some woman to the desert. Leonard was everywhere—New York, Nashville, Montreal.

If there was solace for Cohen, it was in his music. Soon he would begin work on what would become his third album, *Songs of Love and Hate*—a thin offering of eight songs. He would later call it "an experiment that failed." Still, several tracks about suicide—"Last Year's Man," "Avalanche," "Dress Rehearsal"—would brilliantly capture the desperate, psychic mess in which the once golden boy of Canadian letters found himself. It would not get better anytime soon.

CHAPTER TWELVE

A Flake of Your Life

Irving always said to him, "Leonard, make sure you're doing the wrong thing." And you know what? He obeyed.

—Aviva Layton

Leonard's a spider. He draws the audience in and eats them one at a time.

—Stephen Lack

In New York that fall of 1969, Ihlen, Axel, and Zemel shared an apartment at 179 Stanton Street on the Lower East Side.

CAROL ZEMEL: Being in New York was [Marianne's] way of staying close to Leonard.

But if she entertained hopes of rekindling the relationship, it was soon clear that was a nonstarter.

BARRIE WEXLER: Leonard wasn't interested in building a life together in New York. And Marianne wasn't interested in the music and underground scene he was trying to crack. She needed to make a life for Axel. They had tried separations, but distances made it worse, gradually eroding their connection. The relationship didn't actually break up because it never really came together.

The Stanton Street apartment was sublet from a painter. It had two bedrooms, a kitchen, one bathroom, and a large living room.

CAROL ZEMEL: You went through a door on Stanton Street to a back house. There was a loft there, a lovely apartment. Axel had one room and Marianne and I had twin beds in the other, with a television at the foot of the bed. Marianne had many suitors, who were probably as interested in Leonard as they were in her. Men were buzzing around her. She was very beautiful, very wise, and men just loved her. They'd crowd into the loft. Marianna had her boyfriends because Leonard was not to be depended on, though Leonard paid half the rent. I paid the other. He was in and out.

Both women were living a kind of fantasy.

CAROL ZEMEL: Her fantasy was that she was an Ibsenesque, aristocratic heroine because, as she frequently mentioned, her mother or grandmother had danced with the king of Norway. My fantasy was that I was an intellectual immigrant girl from the Lower East Side, missing the babushka. We both made long skirts. Marianne's went to the floor. Mine went to the knee or midcalf. Marianne rolled *perfect* joints, but always pushed the dope and papers over to whatever suitor was visiting.

Prominent among Ihlen's lovers was Jean-Marc Appert, the French photographer she had met on Hydra.

CAROL ZEMEL: He was very young and something of a photographer *manqué*. He owned a Hasselblad. He lived in the loft with her after I left. Until then, I was sort of in the way. Axel was always quite jealous. One night, we're watching TV and he says, "She's out with so-and-so." I say, "Yeah." He says, "She's probably going to sleep with him." He knew. He says, "I don't want her to do that." I said, "Well, I understand that you don't want her to do that, but that's up to her." He says, "I want to be the one to sleep with her." I said, "Right, but you can't." "Well, why not?" I said, "I don't know, Axel, but it's against the rules. It can't happen." Later, I thought, "I can't explain it—why should a kid understand it?" He said, "Okay."

Cohen did occasionally see Ihlen. He took her to the Chelsea Hotel and introduced her to Andy Warhol, Buffy Sainte-Marie, and Joni Mitchell. On December 19, he took her to a Janis Joplin concert at Madison Square Garden. But they were leading separate lives. Cohen told her, "This isn't your scene." He was then working on "Famous Blue Raincoat," which would also be included on *Songs of Love and Hate*. The raincoat itself had recently been stolen from the New York apartment. Cohen thought Appert might have been the culprit, but had no proof. Earlier in Montreal he had played the new melody for his mother in her kitchen.

LEONARD COHEN: I remember her perking up her ears while she was doing something else, and saying, "That's a nice tune."

The lyric, among the most forensically examined in the Cohen canon, came later. Part of it was written in the Stanton Street flat. The song describes an apparent love triangle involving a woman, Jane, and two men—the writer/narrator and his friend/brother, the recipient of a letter the narrator is writing. If the writer/narrator is Cohen, who is the other man, who stands accused of stealing Cohen's woman Jane? It was a question that apparently haunted Cohen's old friend Steve Sanfield, who had, years earlier, slept with Marianne. Was he the "brother" referred to in the lyric, the one who "treated my woman to a flake of your life / And when she came back she was nobody's wife"?

JACQUIE BELLON: Steve always thought it was about him, and once asked Cohen outright, at our house. Cohen answered elliptically, cryptically, but not directly. I was there and the atmosphere was very dense.

JOHN BRANDI: Well, Steve would [say that]. In my correspondence with him, there were some really intense periods with women that he shared with me in great detail. But Cohen was never mentioned and he never talked about love matters of Hydra or the past. I would have thought that if he shared that Marianne [story] with anybody, it would have been with me, but he never did.

JACQUIE BELLON: Or it could be Dennis Hopper, who was also into "going clear," although I think that's a stretch. It also could be that when the song mentions building a house deep in the desert, Cohen is thinking that Nevada County or Nevada City [where they were living] was in the Nevada desert. My own take is that he pulled in a lot of bits of pieces of his life and stitched it together into an embroidered quilt.

Carol Zemel, however, adds another intriguing piece of the puzzle.

CAROL ZEMEL: It's December 1969, winter vacation, and Marianne has gone. Leonard comes by, and stays in the loft for a few days, just me and him, separate bedrooms. He was then into Scientology, which I thought was the goofiest bullshit in the world. My ex-husband, Henry, is living in Arizona. Henry wasn't building a house, but he was in the desert. In the song, "Jane" is asleep, somewhere. I was asleep on the couch while Leonard was writing. I'd been reading a book and must have rolled over. He looked up from where he was writing, a pile of cocaine beside the table. And he said, "Oh, I'm writing to Henry." And I said, "Give him my regards." And the line in the song is, "She sends her regards." That's how I make that connection. The lock of her hair? That's someone else.

BRANDON AYRE: My sense always was that it was a revenge fuck that Marianne had with a friend, and he tried to be big about it—what's the word?—gentlemanly. Open. I've always thought there was some Jean-Marc [Appert] in it. He built his own house with his own hands on Hydra. Could that be what Leonard is alluding to when he refers to "building your [little] house deep in the desert"?

BARRIE WEXLER: It's a pointless guessing game because when a confessional poet uses the second-person singular, they're almost always talking about themselves. Setting up an alter ego is a device Leonard often employed. I got this from the best of authorities. In many songs and poems, the pronouns "I" and "you" are virtually interchangeable. Here, he just coloured in the "you" a bit more.

LEON WIESELTIER: Leonard cherished the rules because he recognized his inclination to break them. He was bored by innocence, by the calm before the storm, by stormlessness. But the calm after the storm—that was his ideal. His poise was his triumph, his method of self-mastery, the profoundly moving evidence of his sovereignty over his rioting appetites. But the appetites accounted for as much of Leonard's flavour as the poise.

CHRISTOPHE LEBOLD: This is a man who has lost a woman, a lover, who has lost everything, who has lost the centre. And they are each looking for the other lover who has lost something, until this little rise in the harmonics, and they're all saved by the lock of your hair, this little gift. A flake of your life. What a wonderful image. Life has the texture of snow. You cannot hold it in your hand. Yet a flake is enough to break something between two people. It is so strong that the other relationship is broken forever. It means we are very fragile. The little things—a lock of hair, a flake of your life—can change the course of [everything].

BRANDON AYRE: "Raincoat" is a classic Leonard song. The changes—A minor to F major—are classic Cohen. Songs are never just one story. Part of it probably was about Sanfield. But we were listening to that song on Hydra—I was with a woman named Denise—and she said, "Why does he sign it at the end El Cohen?" And I said, because that's his name—"L. Cohen." And she said, "Oh, I thought it was El Cohen, like El Cid." I told Leonard that, and he changed the lyric. He changed it to "Sincerely, a Friend." Even on his live album, he sings that. He constantly said his works were always in progress.

GUY SPRUNG: I always assumed it was about [folk singer] David Blue. It's as if they had shared a woman or something. Just a feeling, nothing concrete. That Leonard was out of town and he had a quick fling with his lady. That would not have been the end of the world to Leonard—to share. And it is called famous *blue* raincoat.

Blue did have a brief relationship with Ihlen. It's captured in his 1971 song "Marianne," which describes Leonard Cohen, "her favourite lover," arriving the morning after Blue spent the night. Cohen's friend, dancer Margie Gillies, later choreographed a dance to "Famous Blue Raincoat."

MARGIE GILLIES: What I'm really keen about is the song's attempt at forgiveness—that it's an honest struggle. When the song ends, you feel a resolve—the person will have to revisit it. Who the players are or aren't—that is utterly and completely private. The characters for me are constantly changing, sometimes all women, or all men, or two men and one woman. It really doesn't matter. I dance it solo, in a conversational manner, leaving things dangling. I dance it with an empty chair.

Cohen himself often voiced reservations about the lyric, without clarifying its central mystery. He even claimed to have forgotten the original love triangle—although his friends would insist that he invoked the amnesia alibi to avoid naming names. "I always felt that there was an invisible male seducing the woman I was with," he told the BBC in 1994.

LEONARD COHEN: Whether this one was incarnate or merely imaginary, I don't remember . . . But I did have this feeling that there was always a third party, sometimes me, sometimes another man, sometimes another woman. It was a song I've never been satisfied with . . . I've never felt that . . . I really nailed the lyric.

BARRIE WEXLER: Leonard even envisioned his alter ego as the other man in connection with his own relationships. If it took too long for a woman he was involved with to betray him, it was almost as though he'd take on the job of cuckolding himself.

Cohen returned to Montreal in November to attend a press conference with media guru Marshall McLuhan and Quebec writer Gratien Gélinas. They were jurors for a public competition to name a new Canadian communications satellite. The name chosen was Anik—"little brother" in the Inuit language of Inuktitut. The winning name, from a group of two hundred, was submitted by a young woman living in the Montreal suburb of Saint-Leonard.

That same month, book contract in hand, Barrie Wexler left Montreal for Hydra. He didn't know it at the time, but by the spring of 1970, he and Marianne Ihlen would be living together in Cohen's house.

BARRIE WEXLER: Leonard completely set this up. One can speculate what his motives were—maybe one last nail in the coffin. He knew what he was doing. What twenty-year-old would say no to a beautiful older woman? At Jewish funerals, mourners take turns dropping soil onto the coffin. One reason given is that the *sound* of earth thrown forces them to confront the reality of what has happened. In other words, my time with Marianne was more of a burial rite for their relationship which Leonard arranged. I was the dirt.

FRANCINE ZELSMAN: Leonard's blessing was again a power trip for Leonard. This guy, if nothing else—power trip. If I give you my blessing, it makes me the almighty.

BRANDON AYRE: Leonard did sanction that [relationship]. He played chess there. He did. It was a little weird, the whole thing. He was trying to get it to be over [with Marianne]. I got to know her a little better afterwards, in the seventies. She was a little lost, before she went back to Norway. She talked to me about Orgone boxes, which are said to increase your sexual energy. She was into that. We never did anything together. I think she wanted to. I didn't want to, because she was Leonard's girlfriend, or ex.

One warm night, sleeping on Cohen's terrace, Wexler was bitten by a centipede.

BARRIE WEXLER: My arm was killing me. It looked like Popeye's, swollen from the elbow down. Marianne clobbered the centipede with her sandal, then rushed me to the pharmacist. He injected me with something. The pain went away almost immediately. When we got back, she made tea, then went to bed. I sat up for a long time scanning the floor, walls, and ceiling for anything that moved. Wondering what was taking so long, she came back, took one look at me, and said, "God, you Jewish boys are all the same."

In the spring, Cohen embarked reluctantly on his first tour, a few cities in North America and then Europe.

BUNNY FREIDUS: He was indeed reluctant to tour. His producer, Bob Johnston, was really good at giving Leonard confidence, which he needed very much. It was amazing—the humility you hear in his music, see when he performs—that's him. He was always self-effacing and insecure about people wanting to hear him. This is after he'd sold a ton of records.

Cohen and CBS promotion executive Freidus were clearly sympatico. Years later, Freidus stumbled on an old *Billboard* interview with Cohen in which, asked about his record company, he said he didn't have any contacts there except for her.

BUNNY FREIDUS: He used to come up and hang around my office, just the two of us. We didn't socialize, which is strange, but we'd meet in my office and have lunch there and talk about life. I really felt he had something to tell me. He seemed very wise. He did that for years and years. If I hadn't been a straitlaced kid from the Midwest . . . I was married—he was attractive. But he did not hit on me. My marriage was in trouble at that point, and I was speaking to him about it and he said, "Well, marriage is the only place where you can be your true self." The line has always stuck with me because it's true—it's the relationship in which you were freest to be you. He didn't take the advice and nor did I. But in the music business, people remembered you as long as you were doing something for them. I never had that feeling about Leonard. He was unlike any other artist I worked with, a world apart. I liked him because he was real. And I found him absolutely hysterical. I looked forward to these stop-bys. He would never do what most of the other artists or their representatives would do—"you gotta do this for me."

After a couple of warm-up gigs in Hartford and Washington, D.C. in April 1970, the band flew to Europe in early May, performing nine concerts in Germany, Austria, England, France, and Holland.

AILEEN MUSMANNO FOWLER: It was a crazy, crazy time—the Kent State killings happened when we were in Germany. Leonard addressed it with some kind of beautifully obscure poetic reference. When we got to Munich, we were met with police and German police dogs, and things got pretty strange. He gave the Nazi salute, and a hiss went up from the crowd. But he wooed them and won them with his hypnotic charm.

Fowler later described Cohen as "enigmatic, seductive, gentle. A mysterious and benign presence. Warm, yet distant. Inscrutable. Charming. There is something so deeply endearing about him. I loved him then, and always will."

CHARLIE DANIELS: I was amazed at [his] popularity in Europe. He sold out the Royal Albert Hall in London and the Olympia Theatre in Paris, and caused a near riot in Hamburg when he raised his arm in a misunderstood *sieg heil* salute.

LIONEL TIGER: That was his response to the Nazis. He wanted to rectify an incredible wrong, and the only thing he could do was abuse people from the stage. Which was not much.

In his memoir, *The Guitar Behind Dylan and Cohen*, Ron Cornelius recalled that when Cohen made the gesture, he explained that it had once stood for evil, "but here tonight, for just one moment in time, let it stand for peace and love." Cohen then threw out his right hand and clicked his heels. The audience, one member of which was carrying a gun, had to be forcibly restrained from mounting the stage. Cohen, Cornelius writes, was often capable of such pranks. On other occasions, he performed an encore while standing on his head and issued invitations to engage in red wine enemas.

A future Cohen collaborator, Jean-Michel Reusser, recalled the impact that Cohen's music, even then, had on the Paris audience.

JEAN-MICHEL REUSSER: I remember going to a party at high school and two girls were coming back from the Olympia concert with Leonard, and they were completely illuminated inside. Leonard was a universe in himself.

The day after his Olympia concert, May 13, Cohen was interviewed by music journalist Jacques Vassal—possibly his first European interview—at the Prince de Galles hotel.

JACQUES VASSAL: The question for the audience was would the performer match the man of the records. And he did. Very quickly, there was magic in the air. At the interview, Cohen sat cross-legged on the floor, was very courteous, very much a gentleman, which was not the case with all the artists I met. Asked his response to being seen as a prophet, he said, "I don't know if I have anything to teach, but I made a promise to say everything I know. Sometimes I just see myself as a bad example. If education exists in this sense, yes, perhaps."

He also claimed that he no longer lived in Greece, implying a protest against the military regime that had seized power in 1967. Not exactly true, as he returned there the next summer and almost every year thereafter with the colonels still in charge. In fact, he went to Hydra immediately after the tour. An awkward situation presented itself—sleeping arrangements.

BARRIE WEXLER: Leonard and Marianne slept in the upstairs bedroom, and I slept downstairs with Axel. It was an uncomfortable arrangement, and it wasn't long before Marianne and I left for Norway.

Indeed, retracing virtually the same path Cohen and Ihlen had taken a decade earlier, Wexler and Ihlen set off for Norway in the same cream-coloured Karmann Ghia VW—with well-worn, mud-brown leather seats and whitewall tires—that she kept parked in Athens.

BARRIE WEXLER: When we left for Athens, Leonard saw us off. We watched him leaning against a lamppost on the port. He looked terribly solemn and sad. I'd never seen him like that. It was one of those moments that stay with you. Even though Leonard had a portion in it, there was regret. Perhaps it was because we were setting out on the same journey he and Marianne had taken. Perhaps because it was *her* who was leaving *him* this time. Marianne stood motionless, almost paralyzed. This sounds trite, but as the boat pulled away, it was as if an invisible cord between them had stretched and snapped.

Cohen, of course, had frequently handed off other women to male friends, but this was of a different order of magnitude.

BARRIE WEXLER: It was the first flush of our romance, or so it seemed. Axel was fine—he'd seen it all before. But it was *her* leaving that gave rise to the mixed emotions I read on [Cohen's] face. It didn't have a lot to do with me. There, I happily allowed myself to be his tool.

Wexler and Ihlen spent the next several months at her family's farmhouse in Larkollen, about two hours south of Oslo. "We didn't formally split up," he says. "I don't think Marianne officially broke up with anyone."

In July 1970, Cohen performed in Washington, D.C., and New York. Sitting in box seats for his July 25 performance at the tenth annual Forest Hills Music Festival was Bob Dylan. According to writer Howard Sounes, Dylan went backstage afterwards to see both Cohen and Bob Johnston, who had earlier produced two Dylan albums. In his book, *Down the Highway: The Life of Bob Dylan*, Sounes quotes Cornelius as saying the conversation between the two men was stilted.

RON CORNELIUS: It was like two cats with their hair up. It was like "What's going on?" The answer would be, like, "Everybody's gotta be somewhere." . . . "Oh yeah, well, where are you?"

Cornelius felt Dylan wanted the band to abandon Cohen and work with him. Apparently, Johnston and Charlie Daniels discussed the idea, but decided to stick with Cohen. A few days later, they all returned to Europe to appear at the three-day Aix-en-Provence Festival, a mini Woodstock with a rambunctious crowd of young hippies. Cohen famously rode onto the stage on a white stallion, courtesy of a ramp erected for the occasion. He later thought he might have been shot at.

LEONARD COHEN: The Maoists resented the fact that they actually had to buy a ticket. A lot of them broke down the fence and came into the concert and I did notice one of the lights on the stage go out, after a kind of crack that sounded like a gunshot . . . They're tough critics, the Maoists.

BARRIE WEXLER: He made a joke about trying to assassinate Canadians, but later conceded the sound was probably a popped lightbulb. He was uneasy with his own reaction to the audience's hostility, feeling that he, then thirty-seven, may have been out of step with the younger generation. He said what took the edge off of it was that he'd never seen so many scantily clad girls.

Cohen might have been reflexively sympathetic to the crowd's revolutionary instincts—at one point, he invited the police to "leave their armour, internal and external, and . . . join us." But he was also wary of the antiliberal impulse that could seize an angry proletariat. Indeed, at Aix, he took them on, saying, "If you believe that freedom is being able to shout anything at any time, then you know nothing of freedom. But if you want to attack us, then come up on the stage. We will defend ourselves." It was after the Aix concert that Cohen's band dubbed themselves the Army. Cohen himself became known as Captain Mandrax, referencing his serious appetite for speed.

BARRIE WEXLER: Jacques Mallet du Pan's well-known quote—"Like Saturn, the Revolution devours its children"—summed up his view of revolutionary fever at the time. Later, he was conflicted; not philosophically, but emotionally. It was his own combative reaction that bothered him—that he'd come across as too confrontational. There was also an issue in some reviews about money.

In fact, Cohen and other musicians were accused of betraying the revolution by accepting fees for performing.

BARRIE WEXLER: He found that amusing, but it disturbed him. A few years later, in England, he told [an] audience that he'd lost the rights to a few of his songs, but that the theft had been justified—that it would have been "wrong to write this song and get rich from it too." That may sound like an inherent contradiction, but Leonard was never quite sure which side of the "revolution" he was on.

From France, Cohen's Army decamped for England. On August 28, the band arrived at the Henderson Hospital in Surrey—it treated personality disorders—and played a three-hour concert for about fifty staff and patients. As Ian Milne, a male nurse, set up his recording equipment, Cohen asked on whose behalf he was recording.

IAN MILNE: I said, "Just for myself." He asked that I didn't sell it. I have respected that to this day.

The program began with "Hey, That's No Way to Say Goodbye," and "Bird on the Wire." Before the second song, Cohen said, "Now if you don't like the way we are doing this . . . just tell us what was wrong as you see it." Later, introducing "You Know Who I Am," he said, "I don't know why, but this song seems to have something to do with some three hundred acid trips I took." When a patient left the room, Cohen quipped: "Don't let anyone else out." About "One of Us Cannot Be Wrong," Cohen appeared to confirm its connection to Nico, the German singer, saying it was written "coming off amphetamine. I was also pursuing an incredibly beautiful singer in a small café in the Village and I was completely taken." When the concert concluded—with the still-unrecorded "Famous Blue Raincoat"—Cohen said, "This is the audience we have been looking for and I never felt so good before playing before people."

According to Bob Johnston, the reason Cohen wanted to play mental institutions was because "he was in a bin one time." It's a provocative, but so far unverified allegation. Among medical interns at McGill in the early 1970s, it was rumoured that Cohen had been committed for a mental disorder, possibly for six months. But there has been no independent verification that he was ever hospitalized.

AVIVA LAYTON: I'd say unequivocally not. The only institutionalization [he experienced] was at Mount Baldy.

CHARLIE GURD: Brandy Ayre and I were at the Bistro one night and Graham McKeen, the outrageous drunk, told us Leonard had been locked up in an east-end Montreal insane asylum. We called his mother, who freaked out. She thought he was fine, but drove to the place to try and find him. A real McKeen prank we fell for.

MAX LAYTON: I once was reading a book about a mental hospital—I wish I could remember it—and [it said] one of the patients—no names are used—wrote a song, "Ring out the bells that still can ring. Forget your perfect offering. There is a crack in everything." They quoted this anonymously in a book. So I thought, "Leonard at some point was in an institution."

ANN DIAMOND: [The poet] Ken Hertz also claimed he saw Leonard at the Allan [Memorial Hospital] "often," before 1960. Ken was one of Irving Layton's protégés, along with Henry Moscovitch and Seymour Mayne.

BOB JOHNSTON: We played four, five, six asylums. Goddamn, there was one place, the wheelchair [patients] had made a pact: At a certain time they would all piss their pants! While Leonard's singing, they all piss their pants. The nurse and interns were wheeling them out—screaming and crying. We played in a place called the Purple Dome room. They had maybe twenty or thirty crazies in there. First song we played was "Marianne," and [it] will never be played like that again, and we all knew it. The rest of eternity, it would never be played that good. We finish, and one guy was scraping his chair up and down. Leonard said, "Look at that! Look at how they love us!" We went into the second song. About the tenth song, it was a symphony! BANG! BANG! All of them making different sounds while we were playing. When we got ready to leave, they wouldn't let us, so the interns had to straitjacket a couple people.

The Henderson gig was merely a warm-up for the huge open-air concert on England's Isle of Wight on August 31, 1970. The eclectic lineup also featured Miles Davis, Kris Kristofferson, Joni Mitchell, the Who, the Doors, the Moody Blues, and Jimi Hendrix. By some accounts, the alcohol-hazed, drug-addled crowd—as many as six hundred thousand—was anarchic, throwing chairs, lighting small fires, and hurling invective at the performers. Cohen, weary, unshaven, also on drugs, took the stage after Hendrix, sometime between 2 and 4 a.m., and somehow seduced the crowd with his subdued, genuine patter.

RICHARD WICKISON: I've never been in such a large crowd before or since—three or four packed football stadiums at least. The majority were very well behaved. Acid and pot saw to that.

AILEEN MUSMANNO FOWLER: We went on at about 3 a.m. after Hendrix—it turned out to be his last concert. It was beginning to feel like people were dropping all around us. Charlie Daniels . . . threatened to quit, saying, "I didn't come over here to fight no war—I'm just a guitar player!"

PETER DALE SCOTT: This furious crowd was nearly out of control and setting fire to the stage and he pacified them. The big names tried to calm them and it didn't work. Leonard was understated. He came in from underneath.

BARRIE WEXLER: What was extraordinary was that he had the same effect on thousands as he had on someone across the table from him. It wasn't the melodies. And it certainly wasn't his voice. It was a vibe you sensed intuitively.

RICHARD WICKISON: The corrugated walls were beaten down. It was quite intimidating at times. Kris Kristofferson and Joni Mitchell were booed very unfairly.

STEPHEN LACK: Leonard's a spider. He draws the audience in and eats them one at a time.

BOB JOHNSTON: His guitar always sounded like a black widow spider. Nobody ever played like that. Nobody ever.

RICHARD WICKISON: I'd been stoned or tripping for four days and had not slept for more than two hours at a time [but] my recollections are of a man with an audience in the palm of his hand, which he achieved by talking slowly and quietly. Getting us all to light up the night sky and in my case burn my fingers—twice. With matches and lighters. His voice hung in the air. I fell asleep almost the moment he left the stage, sated with songs and poems.

EDWARD TRAPUNSKI: It was one big party, lots of drugs, mostly pot. There was a wall and people were yelling, "Tear down the wall, tear down the wall." They did eventually take it down—that's when Leonard came on. There'd been a long lull before he came on and that's when it became rowdy. The stories are true, but it's a matter of perception—it was rowdy and there were fires, but they were bonfires, not arson. I can't say it was six hundred thousand, but it was big.

MURRAY LERNER: He told the audience how his father would take him to the circus as a child. He didn't like circuses, but he liked when a man would stand up and ask everyone to light a match so they could see each other in the darkness. "Can I ask of you to light a match so I can see where you all are?" When he sang, he had 'em in the palm of his hand . . . It was remarkable. The banter was very much in tune with the spirit of the festival. And, more particularly, what he said, "We're still a weak nation and we need land. It will be our land one day." It was almost biblical. When he did "Suzanne," he said, "Maybe this is good music to make love to." He's very smart.

He's very shrewd. The audience . . . felt he was echoing something they felt. It was incredible and captivating. That night, Leonard was on some sort of mission.

Another Canadian in the crowd that night was a young Torontonian, Jody Simmons, now deceased. His sister, Tara Danon, recalls the story.

TARA DANON: Jody, of course, hustled his way backstage, where he got to speak to Leonard. I guess he gave Jody his phone number in London, so when Jody was up to some shenanigans—trying to cash bogus Amex travellers' cheques—he got busted. The only number he had was Cohen's, so he called him and Leonard bailed him out, so the story goes. I just wonder if he stuck Leonard with a bill.

In mid-September, Cohen flew to Nashville to complete *Songs of Love and Hate* with Johnston, then embarked on a series of new concert dates, including appearances at Queen's University in Kingston, Ontario.

PETER RAYMONT: I arranged that concert—October 15, 1970. It was too expensive to just bring him to Queen's, so I arranged concerts at the University of Toronto and Waterloo as well. I remember driving back to the Holiday Inn after the show—in the Jock Harty Arena, not Grant Hall. He's in the front seat and the band is in the back and we see this group of very attractive women on the sidewalk. He says, "Stop the car." And he gets out and heads in their direction. That's the last I saw of him.

Raymont did, however, manage to spend the night with one of Leonard's backup singers. The previous night—October 14, 1970—aspiring Toronto filmmaker Paul Saltzman had approached Cohen's manager, Marty Machat, about making a documentary film.

PAUL SALTZMAN: "Is he coming to Toronto?" "No, do you want to bring him?" I said, "Sure." Which is how I ended up coproducing four Leonard Cohen concerts later that year—Massey Hall in Toronto, a free concert at Carleton University in Ottawa, Place des Arts in Montreal, and a free concert at the Douglas Hospital, near Montreal. I never made the film. In fact, I forgot all about it. They were my concerts! I could have filmed them! How stupid. I pick him up in Toronto and we're driving into town and one of the band members says, "How long have you lived here?" And I say, "Since the beginning." I got a good laugh from everyone, including Leonard. Leonard was a beautiful soul. I could feel the depth of it. The fineness of his mind. Not an academic mind, but the fineness of the thinking of a sage. He was dear and warm and kind and friendly. We didn't become friends, but we were buddies during the tour.

During intermission of the Ottawa show, someone passed around in the dressing room a vial of what turned out to be angel dust, the popular name for phencyclidine (PCP).

PAUL SALTZMAN: People are wetting their finger and putting it on their tongue. It was a reddish colour. The person next to me said, "Just take a little," so I did. I've never gone into outer space as fast. Everyone does it, even Leonard. Suddenly I'm conscious of someone banging on the door—the second half of the concert was overdue. I go onstage and sit at the back, cross-legged, on the floor against the wall. And I had an experience I had not had before or since. I could not see the audience—but they're screaming for an encore and won't stop. I felt the rapaciousness of the people, the hunger—for good reason, because Leonard was great. But it's a demand. Later, I can't sleep. It's 3 a.m. and I say to my roommate, "I have to ask Leonard a question." "Now?" he asks. Yes, now. I'm confused about that weird energy of the audience. How does Leonard deal with it? So we bang on the door until a tired Leonard voice says, "Who is it?" And I say, "It's Paul, I have to ask you a question." "Oh, man," he says. "Can it wait until morning?" "No, it can't." So a few minutes later, Leonard comes out, a towel wrapped around him and sits down. We're both cross-legged. A few minutes later, a young woman appears, with a towel around her bosom, just a woman of that night. We talked for about an hour and I say, "Leonard, what was that? That energy vortex. So intense, so demanding." He agreed and said, then—and again in Nashville a couple years later—that touring was like an Italian wedding—too much of everything—and you have to stay focused and centred and grounded. At one point, he held up two palms towards me and said, "Paul, slow down. I don't know what your passions are. You know, when the Japanese meet, they greet each other by bowing from a distance. Then they come closer and bow again. And then closer and bow again. It's important how you enter the space. Slow down." That's a life lesson I'm still learning. He was a gift.

At the end of the month, Cohen arrived in Madison, Wisconsin. There, only weeks earlier, a homemade bomb had exploded, blowing up a building and killing a young researcher—part of the continuing Vietnam War protests. Cohen's October 30 appearance was sponsored by a student antiwar association. Later that fall, Cohen performed at Massey Hall in Toronto. His publisher, Jack McClelland, came backstage afterwards with Anna Porter, his deputy.

ANNA PORTER: [Jack] had barely introduced me before he launched into a speech about why Leonard was wasting his talent singing. His voice was shit, but he was a great poet. Leonard mainly nodded and smiled.

During the concert, Cohen had seemed to occupy the entire stage, so commanding was his presence. Backstage, Porter was struck by "how fragile he seemed."

*   *   *

Earlier that year, Cohen changed managers. When he first signed with Mary Martin, in 1966, they had created Stranger Music, with each of them owning equity shares. The name not only referenced one of Cohen's earliest works, "The Stranger Song"; it also alluded to the difficulty of categorizing exactly what kind of musician Cohen was. On another level, perhaps, it hinted at Cohen's Judaic sensibility—the Jew as the eternal stranger. Perhaps hoping to get Cohen's songs to the next level musically, Martin had put him in touch with Jeff Chase, a young music publisher and arranger, to help create some demos. But in a deal he would come to regret, Cohen agreed to "temporarily" assign to Chase publishing rights to three songs: "Suzanne," "Dress Rehearsal Rag," and "Master Song."

KELLEY LYNCH: Mary thought Chase could enhance the songs. He worked with Cohen to put together a demo tape for publishing. Cohen signed the documents, giving Chase the rights to the songs. They were not stolen. In exchange, Chase would represent Cohen. Cohen was contractually bound. When Cohen pulled out of the deal, Chase retained the publishing rights.

Martin's lawyer, E. Judith Berger, knew nothing of the agreement.

JUDITH BERGER: I was not a party to whatever took place. I never saw a copy of the agreement. In fact, I was shocked when I did.

BARRIE WEXLER: Initially, Cohen viewed Martin as a go-getter who had his back and understood the value of the songs. She was the one who got Columbia's John Hammond interested.

And Martin could be tough. At one point, she fired off a cease-and-desist letter to Joan Baez, who, in performance, had changed some lyrics to

"Suzanne" without consent, saying, "I don't think you would take another brush to Andrew Wyeth and his paintings. Therefore, do not alter Leonard Cohen's poetry."

BARRIE WEXLER: Leonard said Mary advised him to relinquish the copyrights because Chase was starting his own publishing company and could help. He held her responsible for the ensuing fiasco.

KELLEY LYNCH: Mary and Judith [had] got him the [Columbia] deal. They knew people, but he wanted to be backed by more powerful managers. Bob Johnston brought Leonard [to] Marty Machat. Bob understood Marty was legendary, had an extraordinary client base, etc. Marty was obviously a lot higher up the totem pole than Mary. Marty negotiated a deal to close down the management agreement with Mary and Judith. They were bought out. I don't think the breaking up was that awkward except that Cohen bad-mouthed her afterward.

BARRIE WEXLER: What precipitated Johnston's introduction was Bob's disbelief at Mary having advised Cohen to sign away his publishing rights. Leonard came to realize his mistake and that Mary was just too inexperienced to manage him.

SYLVIA SPRING: I bumped into him at the Chelsea around this time. We were in the elevator with Buffy Sainte-Marie and he was really angry about people stealing his music. He talked about carrying a gun—I don't know if he did. But he was very angry about that.

STEVE MACHAT: Leonard was desperate to get rid of his two managers, Judy Berger and Mary Martin, who he believed had stolen the rights to his songs and records. Even back then, Cohen was convinced that women were ripping him off. My father [Marty Machat] duly got rid of Berger and Martin, and agreed to manage Leonard for 15 percent, as well as 15 percent of Stranger Music. The idea of the company was twofold: maintain ownership of the copyrights duly created, and minimize Leonard's exposure to American taxes.

In the end, Machat and Johnston each owned 15 percent of Stranger Music Inc. Cohen owned 70 percent. Johnston's share may have been on hold for Cohen, pending his later ability to buy out Johnston's interest.

JUDITH BERGER: The split [with Mary] was amicable. Leonard was always a gentleman.

KELLEY LYNCH: I don't understand Bob Johnston's compensation. I wrote him about it prior to his death, but heard nothing back. Something's wrong with the situation.

STEVE MACHAT: Why did Bob Johnston get 15 percent? That's what Leonard offered him. Let's get rid of all the moronic nonsense that goes on with he said, she said. What is Stranger Music? Stranger Music was Leonard Cohen, my dad, and Bob Johnston in 1970. So, "okay, Bob, I'll give you 15 percent to help me do x, y, and z." But Stranger Music isn't Leonard Cohen. Stranger Music is a facilitated scam so you don't have to pay individual taxes. What is a corporation? A corporation is a device created by the few in power so they can hide behind a corporate veil. It's a tax scam. Did Bob Johnston steal from Leonard? No. Did Leonard steal from Bob? No. Did these two figure out a way to get money? Maybe. Johnston said he would comanage Leonard Cohen with my dad. My dad would be the agent. But Bob Johnston wasn't capable of managing anyone, so Bob Johnston went bye-bye. They didn't buy him out. He left.

BARRIE WEXLER: Leonard wouldn't have paid cash for his shares—they'd have been granted to him for the contribution of his intellectual property as the core asset of the enterprise. Marty and Bob combined got a 30 percent ownership interest, for which they paid $130,000, for 49 percent of the stock. Leonard's noncash contribution of intellectual property gave him 51 percent of the outstanding shares—controlling interest in terms of voting rights. But the value of his intellectual property, and therefore ownership interest of 70 percent, was deemed higher than the cash contribution made by Marty and Bob.

Almost two decades later, in 1984, Cohen met again with Chase, hoping to recover rights to the three songs.

KELLEY LYNCH: Chase had contacted Barrie Wexler and told him that Cohen should have the rights to these songs and he was open to an offer.

BARRIE WEXLER: Leonard was peeved, as well as a bit apprehensive, when I told him about the overture, and wanted me to feel Jeff out before deciding whether to get together. There was a lot of back-and-forth—I kept having to mask Leonard's sarcasm—and there was almost no meeting. I finally set one up, I think at the Royalton, which I didn't attend.

Chase reportedly asked Cohen what he was willing to pay to recover the rights. "One dollar, motherfucker," Cohen said. The meeting ended right there.

ROBERT FAGGEN: I don't know if it's true, but Leonard later told me that he said to Chase, "You give me those songs back or I'll fucking kill you."

It was not until 1987 that they reached agreement.

KELLEY LYNCH: With Cohen's lawyer, Peter Shukat, I negotiated the buyback. He bought the songs back for $75,000, which was a deal.

["Suzanne"] wasn't making money for years. No mention in the negotiations, including with Cohen's input, that Chase stole it or any evidence of anything undue happening. I think Leonard Cohen [still] had part of it. He didn't lose all of his rights. I think Jeff owned a third of it.

Marty Machat himself garnered mixed reviews from Cohen's friends and musical colleagues.

JOHN LISSAUER: Marty was territorial beyond belief and Leonard was his only class act, the only person he felt ennobled by. No one stayed with him very long. Marty was terrifying. He whispered—a creepy, wispy voice. He answered the phone . . . *"hellooo."* You'd hear the slithering all around. Leonard told me he was Jewish Mafia and he'd send him out to settle scores and threaten people. But around Leonard, Marty was around *Art.*

BUNNY FREIDUS: I thought that was a funny alliance. Martin was a little mysterious. There was an elegance to Marty, but he was a record industry guy, and a business guy, and that's all he was interested in. But I have to say—he loved Leonard. He absolutely loved Leonard. That was unusual for Marty because he was a cold guy, very cold, distant. Leonard melted through all that. He had a special place in his heart.

STEVE MEADOR: What did I make of Marty Machat? He was a crook. A grade-A, number-one heavy.

TONY BRAMWELL: Marty was a good friend. After I left Apple Records, he became my lawyer in a film company. I loved him. He was fantastic—a friendly godfather. He always reminded me of George Burns. He was very funny. There was always that inkling that there was some sort of Mafia shit in the background, but he trusted me to do things for him. We were friends till he died.

RICK ROWE: I had a lot of respect for the late Marty Machat. Very impressive as an attorney. Nothing bad was going to happen as long as Marty was pulling the strings. He would frighten the bejesus out of anybody challenging anything. He was the heavy.

KELLEY LYNCH: Marty was very sophisticated, an elegant, classy guy. His whole gig was, he really loved Leonard Cohen. He thought he was an extraordinary artist. He isn't generating gazillions of dollars in royalty income, so go and get a big advance for him, because it takes six, seven, eight years for it all to dribble-drab in. Mainly, that's what he did. Marty had a lot of great connections, knew a lot of promoters, and put Leonard Cohen in the right hands. He was a little lax. He liked to leave the office at 2 p.m. and go play gin. He was a gin master.

HENRY ZEMEL: Machat? A typical shyster lawyer. Not loud or in your face, but he was the guy who takes care of things.

SOFIA HIDALGO: The most unattractive creature I've ever seen in my life. Unfortunately, God makes some that are really attractive, genetically and some [were] just unlucky. Maybe he was brilliant. He was like Danny DeVito, a little taller version, a comical character. There was a movie by this Japanese graphic artist and there was a character that was half monster, half human. I could only think of Marty Machat.

ERIN DICKINS: Managers and businesspeople are an odd couple with any musicians. It's the nature of the beast. Marty had a certain—dare I say—elegance. He would fly in on a cloud from London, because his girlfriend, Avril Giacobbi, was there, beautiful and charming, looking so well heeled, and charm the pants off everyone. But he was a suit and we weren't.

BARRIE WEXLER: Considering that he knew I'd had a brief affair with Avril, Marty was good to me. Years later, he represented a show of mine in New York, and also connected me with one of his rock-star clients for a project that didn't work out. I thought that was big of him.

Later that fall, Cohen led the band to Austin, Texas, to perform at the Municipal Auditorium, now the Long Center. Among the attendees was Steve Herrigan, a rabid fan who had read *Beautiful Losers* and owned the first album.

STEVE HERRIGAN: I grew up a very sheltered Catholic in Texas, didn't know what Jews were, and always assumed Leonard was Catholic too, because there were all these references to saints and Christian ecstasy. The image of that woman being burned alive on the back of the album—that was catnip to a Catholic boy. If you grew up where martyrdom is the highest value, it had a visceral impact on me. The songs weren't recognizable to me as songs, but they were recognizable as hymns—coming from that Catholic liturgical background. There's never been a singer-songwriter who's meant as much to me as Leonard. To me, he's a long distance ahead of everyone else as a lyricist, as a composer.

At the concert, Cohen took off his shirt, reached down, and pulled a young girl from the front row onto the stage.

STEVE HERRIGAN: I remember him starting to take off his clothes. He was kind of taunting the audience about getting naked, but he stopped.

BOBBY ZIRKEL: Then, twenty or thirty people come running down and he pulls them all up onstage, while he's singing. And all of a sudden the lights go out, the music stops, and Leonard says, "They've turned off the power till everyone leaves the stage. So everyone, go back to your seats and we'll finish the concert. But I see you have a nice park across the street"—what we call Auditorium Shores—"so after the concert, bring whatever you have to drink and we'll have a party." So the concert resumes, but when it finishes, we go across the street. The band was there, not playing, just milling around. Charlie Daniels said, "Got anything to smoke? Our lead guitar player is the fastest joint roller in the world." I got something from my car and he calls over [Ron Cornelius] and he sprinkles the pot in the paper and, with one twist, rolls the most perfectly rolled joint I've ever seen. Before long, there were thirty or forty people standing around, with this haze above us. Leonard was not part of this.

STEVEN HERRIGAN: I ended up with Cohen, Charlie Daniels, another friend of ours, only twelve or thirteen people. Cohen was listening to my friend E. B. Baker play guitar. Somebody tried to interrupt E.B.'s playing and Leonard said, "No, let's let him play. He's really good." Leonard Cohen onstage was the tortured poet, a role he was playing. Here, he just felt like a normal guy, very welcoming and inviting. He hung around for a couple hours.

In November, Cohen played two dates in California, on the fourteenth at UCLA's Royce Hall, and the next night at the Berkeley Community Theater. The two dates are particularly notable to Cohen trivia buffs because Michelle Phillips, one of the Mamas and the Papas, filled in for Corlynn Hanney as a backup singer.

AILEEN MUSMANNO FOWLER: It fell to me to teach her the parts, and, at least at that time in her life, she could not sing. At all. It was sad. I don't know what particular cocktail of drugs she was using, but it didn't help.

Phillips had just married actor Dennis Hopper, a fellow traveller in the world of Scientology. At UCLA, Hopper reportedly started yelling incoherently and eventually jumped up onstage, where Cohen patiently talked him down. Then Cohen invited the audience to join him onstage; it was soon filled with people.

AILEEN MUSMANNO FOWLER: Dennis Hopper charged in, protesting something, and before security could remove him, Leonard graciously let him have his say. Leonard's grace and charm were astonishing, and moving.

What Hopper may have been protesting was Cohen himself.

BARBARA DODGE: What I heard was that Cohen stole Michelle Phillips from Hopper. We know there was an abrupt dissolution of her marriage.

PETER DALE SCOTT: I went to the stage door after the concert and was not admitted. When I told him about it later, Leonard said, "That's because you weren't eighteen and you weren't female."

In an interview later with *Rolling Stone*, Cohen was asked about his second album, *Songs from a Room*, and assumed a now familiar role, combining self-criticism with social prophecy.

LEONARD COHEN: It was very bleak and wiped out. The voice in it has much despair and pain. I think it's an accurate reflection of where the singer was . . . at the time. I mean very, very accurate. Too accurate for most people's taste. But as I believe that a general wipeout is imminent and that many people will be undergoing the same kind of breakdown . . . the record will become more meaningful as more people crack up.

Later that month, Cohen and Suzanne Elrod managed a quick trip to London. He bought her a gift, a book titled *The Language of Flowers*, originally created by a husband for his wife on their golden wedding anniversary in August 1913, and published in 1968. Notably, Cohen's inscription reads, "This book commemorates a visit to London in November 1970 by the travellers Valentina and September."

In early December, Cohen performed at SUNY Stony Brook on Long Island. Tired and stoned, he came onstage and immediately issued a mock Nazi salute. A bottle of wine had been placed on a nearby stool; Cohen poured from it and made a toast: "For those who cannot be with us tonight," possibly in memory of Janis Joplin and Jimi Hendrix. At the after party, students gathered around, speechless. One participant later said, "I felt like everyone was waiting for him to levitate."

In the audience that night was nineteen-year-old English literature student Ken Norris. He had read Cohen's *Selected Poems* and had heard Judy Collins's *Wildflowers* album, with its three Cohen songs.

KEN NORRIS: Derek and the Dominos [with Eric Clapton] were at Suffolk Community College [the same night]. I chose Leonard. The concert was weird. His background singers carried him onstage, physically, arms linked beneath him. He was high on something. He did some kind of ritual spilling of wine at the lip of the stage. The thing I remember most is "Please Don't Pass Me By," which seemed to go forever and was trying to be more than entertaining. He kept on chanting over and over and over again—"Give up your tiny vision of pain." It was like he was exorcising demons or something. His shows were always weird as entertainment. "We're doing something else here tonight." That set him apart from pretty much everyone else. But Leonard was for me as Lorca was for Leonard. In our dorm, we smoked pot, dropped LSD, and listened constantly to Cohen's first album or Bob Dylan's *Blonde on Blonde*.

On December 10, Cohen made his debut at Place des Arts, perhaps Montreal's most prestigious cultural venue. It might have been a gala reception, welcoming a local hero. But Cohen himself later acknowledged that the concert was "an abomination," in part because he was nervous performing for so many relatives and friends. At one point, a drunk managed to crawl onstage and disrupt the proceedings, before passing out.

CHARLIE GURD: That was Graham McKeen, a regular at the Bistro. He was screaming, "I taught you everything you know." It was a horror show.

LEONARD COHEN: It got off to a terrible start. The timing was off and nothing seemed to go right.

MARIANNE FEAVER: At intermission, I went backstage. He invited me to follow him as he started the next set—took a chair and put it in the wings, just behind the curtain. There I sat, enjoying what seemed to be my own private concert. After the show, he certainly was the instigator, and led perhaps five of us into a car. We went for steamers [hot dogs] on the Main. This was what he loved to do, just [a] way of winding down from a show that suited him, hanging out in these somewhat seedy places.

The Montreal critics were not kind.

JUAN RODRÍGUEZ: He had developed an intense cult following, fans hugging the stage, hanging on every precious word. The mood was sickeningly reverent—along the stage they'd put candles. It was like going into St. Joseph's Oratory, except it was a show. I thought he just droned and droned. He bored me stiff. My review was something like "It made me pine for Roy Rogers and Dale Evans to add some pep to this country music."

A few days later, Rodríguez got word that Cohen wanted to meet him at a coffee shop on Crescent Street.

JUAN RODRÍGUEZ: He was absolutely furious. "That wasn't a review, it was gutter talk." I said, "Come on, Leonard, I thought it was kind of funny." He says, "You know, my band would like to beat you to a pulp." [He was] visibly angry. He was trying to keep cool, but he was talking very loudly. Years later, he told me that he was so pissed off because his mother asked him, "Leonard, how come you're getting so many bad reviews in Montreal?"

AVIVA LAYTON: He said he couldn't get arrested in Montreal or be more reviled if he'd "left shit on their doorstep or raped one of their daughters." He said that.

STEPHEN LACK: I remember Juan backing up a little during the meal. I leaned over and said, "Leonard, I'm Stephen Lack, one of your cousins." And you know Leonard—ever gracious. "Oh yes, very pleased to meet you, of course. Oh, you're a Glickman, very nice. A Glickman Cohen." The next day, it was in Juan's column. "I was with Leonard Cohen and one of his 150 cousins said hello." That was the first time I'd met Leonard.

Lack's subsequent relationship with Cohen was always friendly, but somewhat distant.

STEPHEN LACK: Celebrity is a very difficult thing to wear. It engenders fear, envy, sexual attraction, idolization. It's a real burden. Here was a guy who deserves respect, but who's family. So to erase all of that, I concentrated on his lizard aspects. I would know that this was another human being, full of flaws. In fact, he's somebody researching his flaws to correct himself.

The day after his Place des Arts performance, Cohen and the band gave a free concert at the Douglas Hospital in Verdun to an audience of more than two hundred patients and staff.

TERRY SULLIVAN: He took the initiative. He said he was interested in coming to play for the patients, and we arranged it. He played in Douglas Hall, with the Army and his Sisters of Mercy, the backup singers. He played from 6:30 to about 9, then we had a little reception.

PAUL SALTZMAN: I said, "Why do you want to do that gig?" He said, "Because they're the most honest audiences. If you can't hold them, they get up and walk out."

TERRY SULLIVAN: He flirted with my girlfriend. But he was extremely humble and charming. He opened it by saying the "people in our hospitals might be the real political prisoners of our time." He gave little preambles before each song. He said, "Maybe I'll fall in love tonight," and this very large woman who'd been in the hospital for a long time said, "Would you fall in love with me?" It was an audience of patients in long-term care units who were pretty crazy, so there was always some kind of fracas going on, but it went extremely well, a unique and special experience.

MARIANNE FEAVER: I attended the Douglas concert at his invitation. It was an out-of-this-world experience for me, being the only nonpatient [or nonstaff] in the crowd.

When the concert ended, there were thirty centimetres of snow on the ground, and the temperature was minus 15 degrees Celsius. The tour was finally over. It was almost 80 degrees Fahrenheit in Miami. Cohen and Elrod booked a flight.

Epilogue

Leonard Cohen was never given much to self-congratulation. But on that Floridian sojourn, perhaps gazing out on an Atlantic sunrise, he might have been forgiven for surrendering to a quiet moment of pride. At thirty-six, he had published five books of poetry and two novels, largely acclaimed. Of course, one could not live on literary reviews, however glowing, and so, in his early thirties—late in the day for musicians—he had effected a transition many people said would be impossible, from respected but obscure poet-novelist to popular singer-songwriter.

His timbre was mediocre at best. His vocal range was limited. His guitar skills were marginal. Yet there was clearly something in his voice and lyrics that resonated, that penetrated to the very heart of his audiences. The boy magician, the entertaining camp counsellor, the star debater, the mesmerizing seducer—these had all been rehearsals for the role he now would play, the charismatic troubadour, transparently unpolished, but deeply authentic. It was like the fulfillment of the prophecy he had made long ago to his childhood friend Krantz in Murray Hill Park. "I can make things happen."

During the next two decades, a period explored in the second volume of *Untold Stories*, Cohen's star would rise. He would acquire an international reputation and legions of disciples, principally in Europe. His personal life, however, would often be an exercise in controlled chaos, as he sought to balance the competing demands of family—a de facto wife and two children—and scores of lovers with his craft and art. A Faustian bargain had been struck with the gods of stardom. He would have to tour, which he hated, and answer the same questions from journalists a thousand times. How would he continue to honour the essential truths if he had to sing "Suzanne" and other songs in his repertoire thirty consecutive nights in thirty different cities? As Cohen famously sang, "A singer must die for the lie in his voice." Money, women, adulation—all of this was wonderful, no question. But Cohen had read his Bible and he took it seriously. "For what shall it profit a man, if he shall gain the whole world, and lose his own soul?"

Acknowledgements

It would surely have been possible to compile an oral biography of Leonard Cohen before the arrival of Facebook, Google, WhatsApp, et al., but it would have been more difficult. The Internet made it possible to locate people once part of Leonard Cohen's life, but long since disappeared. And finding them was critical because, as the title suggests, I was especially interested in those whose Leonard Cohen Experience, as I call it, had not been previously recorded. So thank you, Mark Zuckerberg, Larry Page and Sergey Brin, and Tim Berners-Lee (creator of the World Wide Web).

Of course, I owe the single largest debt of gratitude to my five-hundred-plus interview subjects. They not only gave freely of their time, stories, and observations but, in many cases, referred me to other essential voices, and even facilitated introductions. I can't possibly list them all in the space available here, but I do want to offer a deep collective bow to the backup singers, poets, band members, record producers, friends, family members, journalists, professors, filmmakers, rabbis, Buddhist monks, and, certainly not least, lovers—satellites in diverse orbits around Planet Leonard Cohen.

Still, I would be seriously remiss if I did not single out the extraordinary aid and assistance accorded me by Cohen's dharma brothers and sisters from the zendos of Zen Buddhism. I am beholden particularly to the tough-minded Eric Lerner, the delightful Ginny

Matthews, the welcoming David and Marcia Radin, the incisive Susan Ray, and the brilliant Harold Roth.

For material dealing with Cohen's formative years in Montreal, I was fortunate to be guided by the helpful Mark Bercuvitz, the waggish Robert Cohen, the plein d'esprit Patricia Nolin, the lawyerly Joe Nuss, the reflective Hersh Segal, the redoubtable Peter Dale Scott, the questing Alfie Wade, the truth-telling Carol Zemel, the contrarian Henry Zemel, and, my friend, matchmaker par excellence Berl Schiff (may his memory be a blessing).

The Mousai, the mythic goddesses of music, chose to dispatch a number of beneficent emissaries, among them the magical Perla Bettala, the constructive Paul Burger, the hospitable Chris Darrow (may his memory be a blessing), the irrepressible Ramblin' Jack Elliot, the serene Lewis Furey, the effervescent Rob Hallett, the divine Sarah Kramer, the unforgettable John Lissauer, the alluring Teresa Tudury, the resonant Cantor Gideon Zelermyer, and the engaging Steve Zirkel.

Serendipity led me to many other interviewees who proved indispensable: the astute Sandra Anderson, the compassionate Brandon Ayre, the indelible Jacquie Bellon, the supportive Irwin Block, the generous Dominique Boyle (he of the vast Cohenian press archive), the candid Linda Clark, the kind-hearted Soheyl Dahi, the conspiratorial Ann Diamond, the regal Barbara Dodge, the charming Charmaine Dunn, the erudite Rabbi Mordecai Finley, the gifted Charlie Gurd, the soulful Sofia Hidalgo, the doppel-ganging Albert Insinger, the incomparable Pico Iyer, the catalyzing Peter Katoundas, the convivial Stephen Katz, the memorable Harvey Kubernik, the droll Stephen Lack, the empathetic Celine La Freniere, the resourceful Dianne Lawrence, the vivacious Aviva Layton (a life force that should be cloned), the combative Kelley Lynch; the thoughtful Alan Mendelsohn, the wise Despina Politi (may her memory be a blessing), the elegant Madeleine Poulin, the spirited Violet Rosengarten, the obliging Patsy Stewart, and the indefatigable Maria Cohen Viana. Because *Untold*

Stories will be a chronologically structured trilogy, many of the people will not actually appear until the second and third volumes.

However, there would be no books at all without the support, encouragement, and counsel of writer and producer Barrie Wexler. Another product of Jewish Westmount, sixteen years younger than Leonard, Wexler befriended him in the mid-1960s and was soon accorded a ringside seat on Cohen's life—his wit and wisdom, romantic pursuits, marital struggles, battles with depression and, more largely, his entire sui generis way of being. Cohen's confidante and co-conspirator in pursuit of female companionship, Wexler functions in this and the later books as a kind of trenchant Greek chorus of one, a modern-day Boswell to Cohen's Samuel Johnson.

Three years can sometimes feel like a marathon in book writing terms. Rooting me on, thankfully, were loyal cheering sections, sympathetic sounding boards, and receptive audiences for my accumulating Leonard Cohen stories. Among these, my astonishing and cherished children, Lauren, Susan, and Sam (the last, an intellectual property lawyer, doubly useful); my always supportive siblings, Gerry Posner and Linda Segal; and good and patient friends, Vafa Akhavan, Lori Calman, Stanley Cohen, Bill Gladstone, Henry Gold, David Groskind, Paul Michaels, Liz Preiss, Dave Pyette, Rob Smithen, and Judy Steed. And I was blessed throughout with the constant encouragement of my partner in crime, Netflix, and speed-walking, Denise Levinter, from whom I guiltily stole many precious evenings and weekends.

If you've read this far, you will know that a number of people interviewed over the four years of the book's development have passed away. Alas, that list includes my own literary agent, Arnold Gosewich, an extraordinary man who dearly loved this project and never gave up on it, but sadly did not live to see its publication. May his memory, too, be a blessing.

When Arnold passed, an old friend—my first and best journalistic mentor, John Macfarlane—put me in touch with publisher Al

Cummings. Al himself, it turned out, not only had a good Leonard Cohen story in his pocket, but was able to connect me to Kevin Hanson, president and publisher of Simon & Schuster Canada. By then, another old friend, writer David Hayes, had kindly introduced me to Hilary McMahon, the Westwood Agency's executive vice president. It was Hilary who promptly stepped up and so ably represented the book in the home stretch. Under Simon & Schuster's classy umbrella, the book was conveyed to the steady hands of a crackerjack editorial team, led by the unflappable Justin Stoller.

Unless otherwise indicated, the Leonard Cohen quotes used throughout were drawn from his various newspaper, magazine, radio, and television interviews. The Irving Layton quotes are from a *Chatelaine* magazine profile by Sylvia Fraser, who kindly granted permission for use.

For whatever errors and omissions may be found within these pages, I hereby absolve everyone—but myself.

Finally, inevitably and appropriately, I humbly offer thanks to Leonard Norman Cohen for the enormous, unmatchable blessing of his life and work.

Dramatis Personae

NORMAN ALEXANDER: friend during childhood and adolescence

PATRICIA AMLIN: American painter, Hydra friend

ERIC ANDERSEN: American folk singer, friend after the late 1960s

SANDRA ANDERSON: psychologist, friend after the late 1970s

JEAN-MARC APPERT: Hydra acquaintance

NIEMA ASH: Montreal friend during the 1960s and 1970s

HAROLD ASHENMIL: lawyer, college fraternity friend

TONY ASPLER: fraternity brother

HOWARD ASTER: publisher of the poetry of Cohen's friend Henry Moscovitch

FRAN AVNI: singer, friend during the 1960s and 1970s

BRANDON AYRE: doctor, singer, friend after 1971

STEPHANIE AZRIELI: sister of Cohen's childhood friend, Malcolm Lefcort

TONY BABINSKI: Montreal filmmaker, acquaintance

NANCY BACAL: writer, filmmaker, close friend from childhood

JACQUIE BELLON: friend after the late 1960s, first wife of Steve Sanfield, mother of Cohen's godson

MARK BERCUVITZ: childhood friend and fraternity brother

JUDITH BERGER: American lawyer, friend during the late 1960s

PERLA BETTALA: American singer, close friend, sang back-up on Cohen albums and tours

ANN BIDERMAN: TV writer, producer, New York friend, late 1960s

JACK BIDNIK: acquaintance

THELMA BLITZ: New York acquaintance

IRWIN BLOCK: Canadian journalist, acquaintance

HERB BLUMER: college fraternity friend

MARILYN BLUMER: college friend

ALEXIS BOLENS: businessman, raconteur, Hydra friend

LINDA BOOK: art gallery manager, friend

TONY BRAMWELL: friend, British music producer and promoter

JOHN BRANDI: American poet, friend

SHIRLEY PRIPSTEIN BRAVERMAN: camp friend, 1958

LESTER BROWN: fan

ARMELLE BRUSQ: French documentary filmmaker, friend after the mid-1990s

HOWARD BUCKMAN: summer camper, 1958

FRED CATERO: American sound engineer on first album

ISRAEL CHARNEY: Montreal artist, friend during the 1960s and early 1970s

LINDA CLARK: friend from the late 1980s and early 1990s

ADRIENNE CLARKSON: Canadian writer, editor, Governor General, friend for fifty years

CHARMIAN CLIFT: Australian journalist, Hydra friend

ANDREW COHEN: Canadian journalist, cousin, son of Edgar Cohen

AVRUM COHEN: lawyer, no relation, McGill debating partner

DOUG COHEN: Montreal businessman, no relation, friend after 1951

ESTHER COHEN: sister

GORDON COHEN: first cousin, friend

HORACE COHEN: uncle

LAWRENCE COHEN: uncle

LAZARUS COHEN: paternal great-grandfather

LYON COHEN: paternal grandfather

MASHA COHEN: mother

MICHELE HENDLISZ COHEN: no relation, girlfriend in 1964

ROBERT COHEN: psychotherapist, first cousin, friend, adolescent singing partner

RUTH COHEN: wife of Edgar, friend

SOREL COHEN: Canadian artist, wife of Gordon Cohen, friend

ZVI HIRSCH COHEN: rabbi, paternal great-great uncle

ANNE COLEMAN: Canadian writer, college friend

JUDY COLLINS: American singer, friend, catalyst of Cohen's music career

JULIE COPELAND: friend and Australian broadcaster

RON CORNELIUS: American musician, producer, played on three Cohen albums, toured with him

PIERRE COUPEY: Canadian artist, poet, acquaintance

MARQUITA CREVIER: Montreal poet, briefly Cohen's lover in the 1960s

CHARLIE DANIELS: American musician, member of Cohen touring band, 1970

CHRIS DARROW: American musician, band member, Kaleidoscope, played on first album

ANN DIAMOND: Canadian writer, friend

JAMES DIAMOND: Canadian scholar, acquaintance

ERIN DICKINS: Cohen's friend and backup singer

SANDRA DJWA: Canadian literary critic, acquaintance

BARBARA DODGE: artist, friend after 1968

BILL DODGE: friend, brother of Barbara

MICHAEL DORSEY: Canadian musician, acquaintance

CHARMAINE DUNN: friend after 1971

GEORGE ELLENBOGEN: poet, college friend

RAMBLIN' JACK ELLIOTT: folk singer, friend after the late 1960s

SUZANNE ELROD: girlfriend from 1969–78, mother of Adam and Lorca Cohen

ROBERT FAGGEN: American professor, writer, friend of Cohen's from 1995

MARIANNE FEAVER: Canadian filmmaker, acquaintance

ABE FEINSTEIN: summer camper

JULIE FELIX: British/American folk singer, occasional girlfriend, from 1969

JOHN FENWICK: childhood friend

GEORGE FERENCZI: Montreal writer, acquaintance

KENNY FEUERMAN: American film producer, acquaintance

MORRIS FISH: Canadian judge, debating union partner, friend

JIM FJELD: Montreal acquaintance

ALISON FLEMINGER: daughter of American artist Irwin Fleminger, Cohen's friend in summer of 1953

ANNE FOUGERE: wife of Dave Fougere

DAVID FOUGERE: Stormy Clover musician, friend during the late 1960s

AILEEN MUSMANNO FOWLER: American backup singer, 1970, friend

HARRIET PASCAL FREEDMAN: wife of Cohen's friend, Harold Pascal

ALICE FREEMAN: acquaintance

BUNNY FREIDUS: Columbia music executive, friend

VERA FRENKEL: Canadian artist, friend

PATRICIA HUGHES-FULLER: acquaintance

BILL FUREY: Montreal poet, writer, friend from the early 1970s

LEWIS FUREY: Canadian singer-songwriter, collaborator on *Night Magic*, friend after 1966

LINDA GABORIAU: Canadian dramaturge, translator, friend

MICHEL GARNEAU: Quebecois writer, friend, neighbour, translator of Cohen's work

DEMETRI GASSOUMIS: artist, Hydra friend

JUDY GAULT: Canadian actress, friend after the late 1950s

ARNIE GELBART: Canadian film director and producer, friend

NAHUM NOOKIE GELBER: lawyer, friend from the 1950s

MICHAEL GETZ: American film exhibitor, acquaintance

DOUG GIBSON: Canadian publisher, acquaintance

RALPH GIBSON: American photographer, friend after late 1960s

DIANE GIGUÈRE: Canadian novelist, girlfriend during the 1960s

MARGIE GILLIES: Canadian choreographer, dancer, friend

ALLEN GINSBERG: American poet, friend after the late 1950s

MICHAEL GNAROWSKI: Canadian poet, editor and critic, college friend

PATRICIA GODBOUT: Canadian professor, Montreal friend

ALAN GOLDEN: Montreal lawyer, cousin, friend

MARVIN GOLDSMITH: college friend

PHILIP GOSEWICH: summer camper

ROGER GREEN: British writer, Hydra friend

EVELYN GREENBERG: co-counsellor summer camp

CHARLIE GURD: Canadian artist, friend after 1971

FREDA GUTTMAN: Canadian artist, Cohen's girlfriend in the mid-1950s

DON GUY: American filmmaker, husband of Yafa Bunny Lerner, friend

JOHN HAMMOND: legendary American record producer, producer on Cohen's first album

MICHAEL HARRIS: Canadian poet, friend, sometime neighbour

STEVEN HERRIGAN: American journalist, fan, acquaintance

FRANCINE HERSHORN: friend, wife of Robert Hershorn

ROBERT HERSHORN: businessman, close friend through the 1950s and '60s

SELMA HERSHORN: sister of Robert Hershorn

SOPHIA HIDALGO: friend

JACK HIRSCHMAN: American poet, friend after 1965

PETER HODGSON: singer, ex-husband of Susan Jains

ROBERT LANDORI-HOFFMAN: McGill debating partner, friend

NAOMI BERNEY HORODETZSKY: fan

CHUCK HULSE: Hydra friend

MARIANNE IHLEN: girlfriend from 1960–1968, friend for life

PICO IYER: writer, friend from after 1995

SUSAN JAINS (NÉE GEMMELL): lead singer of the Stormy Clovers, friend

BOB JOHNSTON: American record executive, produced two Cohen albums, friend

DON JOHNSTON: Canadian politician, diplomat, friend after 1958

GEORGE JOHNSTON: Australian writer, Hydra friend

KASOUNDRA KASOUNDRA: artist, New York friend, late 1960s

PETER KATOUNDAS: Montreal friend after 1977

NAIM KATTAN: Canadian novelist, critic, friend after 1955

SARAH AVERY KELLY: college friend

SHARON KEMP: talent agent, Los Angeles friend

CHERYL KENMEY: Canadian sculptor, friend from the early 1970s

JUDIT KENYERES: Montreal acquaintance

WENDY PATTEN KEYS: girlfriend, 1963–64

ANTHONY KINGSMILL: British painter, conversational foil, close Hydra friend

DAN KLEIN: American writer, Hydra acquaintance

SOLOMON KLONITZKY-KLINE: American Rabbi and scholar, maternal grandfather

KATHERINE KOCH: Hydra friend, daughter of Ken Koch

KEN KOCH: American poet, Hydra and New York friend

DANIEL KRASLAVSKY: college fraternity friend

RUSSELL KRONICK: summer camper

HARVEY KUBERNIK: American music journalist, friend

STEPHEN LACK: Canadian/American painter, cousin

PENNY LANG: Montreal folk singer, acquaintance

BILL LANTERMAN: former bartender, friend during the late 1960s

BARBARA LAPCEK: American artist, Hydra friend

AVIVA LAYTON: writer, friend for fifty years, wife of Irving

IRVING LAYTON: pugnacious Canadian poet, friend after 1954

MAX LAYTON: Canadian poet-songwriter, friend, son of Irving

HARRIET LAZARE: college friend, wife of Jack Lazare

JACK LAZARE: Canadian music executive, friend after the late 1950s

CHRISTOPHE LEBOLD: French professor, Cohen biographer, friend

DENNIS LEE: Canadian poet, editor, friend

VIVIENNE LEEBOSH: friend from the 1960s and '70s

FRANCES LEFCORT: childhood friend, sister of Malcolm Lefcort

MALCOLM LEFCORT: friend through childhood and adolescence

MADELEINE LERCH: Canadian/French model, friend during the 1960s and '70s

ERIC LERNER: American screenwriter, friend for forty years

MURRAY LERNER: American filmmaker, director of 1970 Isle of Wight concert film

YAFA BUNNY LERNER: friend from the 1950s on

ELLIE LEVINE: camp friend, 1958

GEORGE LIALIOS: Greek student of classical music, friend from Hydra

DAVID LIEBER: Montreal writer, acquaintance

JOHN LISSAUER: American composer/producer, friend from 1973

HELAINE LIVINGSTONE: sister of Lenore Schwartzman

DON LOWE: writer, Hydra friend

PAUL LOWENSTEIN: Canadian businessman, college fraternity friend

KELLEY LYNCH: friend, Cohen's business manager from 1988

MARTY MACHAT: American lawyer, Cohen's business manager from 1970–1988

STEVE MACHAT: American lawyer and music producer, Marty's son

ROY MACSKIMMING: Canadian writer, acquaintance

ALFIE MAGERMAN: Canadian lawyer, Cohen's friend during the 1950s

BARBARA MAGERMAN: camp friend, wife of Alfie

MENDL MALKIN: Canadian doctor, acquaintance

ANN MANDEL: Canadian literature professor, wife of the late poet Eli Mandel, friend

CODY MARLEY: son of Kid Marley

KID MARLEY: Tennessee cowboy, neighbour of Cohen's 1969–71

MARY MARTIN: Cohen's manager from 1966–1970

DEREK MAY: filmmaker, close friend through the 1960s and '70s

DAVID MAYEROVITCH: summer camper, 1958

ROBERT MAYEROVITCH: summer camper, 1958

SEYMOUR MAYNE: Canadian poet, editor, and translator, and friend after 1961

BARRY MCKINNON: Canadian poet, acquaintance

STEVE MEADOR: American drummer, performed on albums and on tours, friend

ALAN MENDELSOHN: fan

CHARLOTTE MENSFORTH: visual artist, Hydra

GORDON MERRICK: American novelist, Hydra friend

BRUCE MEYER: Canadian poet, acquaintance

DORIAN MILLER: Montreal poet, acquaintance

MICHAEL MORGULIS: fan

HENRY MOSCOVITCH: Canadian poet, friend after the early 1960s

FRANCIS MUS: Belgian professor, biographer of Cohen

LYNN MYERS: New York acquaintance

TONI MYERS: Canadian filmmaker, friend of Mary Martin's

MICHAEL NERENBERG: Montreal acquaintance

PATRICIA NOLIN: Canadian actress, friend, wife of Derek May

KEN NORRIS: Canadian poet, friend

JACK NOVICK: American psychoanalyst, camp friend, 1958 and after

JOE NUSS: Canadian lawyer, fraternity brother

CHRIS NUTTER: Canadian film editor, acquaintance

ALANIS OBOMSAWIN: Canadian filmmaker, friend during the 1960s

MAUREEN O'DONNELL: Canadian public relation executive, acquaintance

ANNIE SHERMAN ORSINI: American writer, Cohen's girlfriend during the late 1950s

JULIANNA OVENS: Canadian federal civil servant, friend during the 1960s

DON OWEN: Canadian filmmaker, friend from the 1960s

MARCIA PACAUD: Canadian seeker, friend during the 1960s

HAROLD PASCAL: Canadian advertising executive, friend during the 1950s and 1960s

IVAN PHILLIPS: American businessman, cousin, childhood friend

DESPINA POLITI: Greek weaver, friend

ERICA POMERANCE: Canadian filmmaker, girlfriend mid-1960s

SHELLEY POMERANCE: Canadian broadcaster, friend, sister of Erica

JACOB POTASHNIK: Montreal writer, friend

ANNA PORTER: publisher and writer

ANNA POTTIER: friend, fifth wife of Irving Layton

MADELEINE POULIN: Canadian broadcaster, girlfriend in 1959

BILL POWNALL: British painter, Hydra friend

NANCY PRIDDY: American singer, sang backup on Cohen's first album

MOISHE PRIPSTEIN: camp friend, 1958

MORGANA PRITCHARD: Montreal friend, in the 1970s

ANTON RAFF: Canadian/American doctor, summer camp friend, 1940s

MARK RANGER: roadie for the Stormy Clovers

LOUIS RASTELLI: Montreal archivist

PETER RAYMONT: Canadian film director/producer, acquaintance

JEAN-MICHEL REUSSER: French music producer, friend from the mid-1980s

JOSHUA RIFKIN: American arranger

CHANTAL RINGUET: Canadian writer, editor, Cohen scholar

CARMEN ROBINSON: Canadian psychotherapist, college friend

JUAN RODRÍGUEZ: Montreal music journalist, acquaintance

MORTON ROSENGARTEN: Canadian artist, Cohen's friend from childhood

VIOLET ROSENGARTEN: artist, former wife of Morton Rosengarten, friend

PAUL ROSMAN: American doctor, fraternity brother, friend

GAVIN ROSS: childhood friend

BERNIE ROTHMAN: Canadian/American TV writer/producer, friend for sixty years

RICK ROWE: American sound engineer, friend

BUFFY SAINTE-MARIE: Canadian folk singer, friend for fifty years

PAUL SALTZMAN: Canadian filmmaker, acquaintance

HERBERT SAMUELS: summer camp friend, late 1940s

NORMAN SAMUELS: summer camper, 1958

ELLEN SANDER: American music journalist, friend

STEVE SANFIELD: American writer, friend from 1961

PANDIAS SCARAMANGA: Greek amateur philosopher, Hydra friend

RONA FELDMAN SCHEFLER: childhood friend

BERL SCHIFF: Canadian sociologist, camper under Cohen in 1956

ISAAC SCHIFF: American doctor, summer camper, 1958

MARILYN REGENSTRIEF SCHIFF: friend from summer camps

MORTY SCHIFF: Canadian/American mathematician and poet, college friend

MUSIA SCHWARTZ: Canadian cultural figure, friend after the 1950s

LENORE SCHWARTZMAN: friend, co-owner with Cohen of the Four Penny Gallery, 1958

PETER DALE SCOTT: Canadian poet, friend for more than fifty years

JUDY SCOTT: American writer, Hydra friend

HERSH SEGAL: Canadian businessman, friend for fifty years

RUTH SEYMOUR: American PBS executive, wife of Jack Hirschman

LILI SHATZKY: friend from 1950 summer camp

MORRIS SHOHET: Canadian businessman, college friend

WILFRED SHUCHAT: Rabbi at Montreal's Shaar Hashomayim Synagogue

BRIAN SIDAWAY: boat captain, Hydra friend

ROBERT SILVERMAN: Canadian bookstore owner, casual friend from the late 1950s to the 1970s

RENEE ROTHMAN SIMMONS: friend, sister of Cohen's friend, Bernie Rothman

ANDREW SIMON: CBC TV producer, acquaintance

JOHN SIMON: American music producer, worked on Cohen's first album

CHARLIE SISE: Canadian writer, acquaintance

CAROL TALBOT-SMITH: Canadian educator, Montreal friend

MARVIN SMITH: fraternity brother, early 1950s

STEVE SMITH: Canadian poet, friend in the early 1960s, died 1964

NORMAN SNIDER: Canadian screenwriter, acquaintance

KIM SOLEZ: Canadian doctor, friend

MEL SOLMAN: Canadian journalist, friend

DAVID SOLWAY: Canadian poet, friend from the 1960s on

CHERYL SOURKES: Canadian artist, friend from the mid-1960s

SARAH SPARKS: friend, second wife of Steve Sanfield

SYLVIA SPRING: Canadian journalist, distant cousin

GUY SPRUNG: Canadian theatre director, acquaintance

PATSY STEWART: friend from the early 1970s

SANDY STEWART: Zen monk, friend

MEGAN STUART-STUBBS: daughter of friend of Cohen's sister, Esther

TERRY SULLIVAN: fan, acquaintance

SHELDON TAYLOR: summer camper, 1958

LIONEL TIGER: Canadian/American sociologist, friend after the mid-1950s

EDWARD TRAPUNSKI: fan

MARGARET TRUDEAU: former wife of Canadian Prime Minister Pierre Trudeau, mother of current Canadian Prime Minister Justin Trudeau, friend

TERESA TUDURY: American singer, friend met on Hydra 1973

DAN USHER: Canadian economist, childhood and college friend

TONY VACCARO: American photographer

MANNY VAINISH: accountant, casual friend from the 1960s

PETER VAN TOORN: Canadian poet, friend

JACQUES VASSAL: French music journalist, friend from 1970

MARIA COHEN VIANA: fan, Cohen researcher

STEPHEN VICTOR: Canadian lawyer, summer camper, 1958

FRANK VITALE: Canadian/American filmmaker, acquaintance

STEPHEN VIZINCZEY: Canadian writer, friend during the 1960s

ALFIE WADE: Canadian musician, DJ, friend of Cohen's from high school

MIRIAM WAGSCHAL: Canadian artist, acquaintance

PHOEBE WALKER: girlfriend during the early 1980s

SHEILA WALKER: acquaintance, sister of Steve Smith

BIM WALLIS: New Zealand writer, Hydra friend

PHYLLIS WEBB: Canadian poet, friend during the 1950s and '60s

BARRIE WEXLER: Canadian writer and producer, friend for fifty years

RICHARD WICKISON: fan

LEON WIESELTIER: writer and friend

DONALD WINKLER: Canadian translator, husband of Sheila Fishman, acquaintance

RUTH ROSKIES WISSE: Canadian/American scholar, college friend

BYRON WOODMAN: childhood friend

DIANNE WOODMAN: Canadian publishing executive, friend during the 1960s and 1970s

HARVEY YAROSKY: Canadian lawyer, fraternity brother
SANDRA YUCK: Montreal friend during the 1960s
ROZ VAN ZAIG: stepsister, 1949–56
GIDEON ZELERMYER: cantor, friend, sang on *You Want It Darker*
FRANCINE ZELSMAN: friend
CAROL ZEMEL: Canadian professor of art, friend during the 1960s
HENRY ZEMEL: Canadian filmmaker/physicist, friend from the 1960s on
ZVI ZEMEL: summer camper, 1958
BOBBY ZIRKEL: fan